CLASSIC FOREIGN FILMS

From 1960 to Today

ALSO BY JAMES REID PARIS

The Great French Films,
introduction by François Truffaut
(Citadel Press)

Overleaf
Don Fabrizio, Prince of Salina (Burt Lancaster), waltzes with
Angelica (Claudia Cardinale) *(The Leopard).*

Gaspard Manesse *(left)* and Raphaël Fejtö in *Au Revoir les Enfants*.

Max von Sydow in *Pelle the Conqueror*.

(left to right) Akira Terao, Jinpachi Nezu, Daisuke Ryu, Kazuo Kato, and Masayuki Yui in *Ran*.

Garry Cadenat in *Sugar Cane Alley*.

Günter Lamprecht in *Berlin Alexanderplatz.*

CLASSIC FOREIGN FILMS

From 1960 to Today

James Reid Paris

A CITADEL PRESS BOOK

Published by Carol Publishing Group

ACKNOWLEDGMENTS

I am most grateful to the persons cited herein, without whose valued assistance this book would not have been possible.

For their unstinting loan of many beautiful and rare stills used in the book, I wish to thank Bill Kenly, Jonathan Turell of Janus Films, and my dear friend Hans von Specht—my *Bruder in Kino*—of the Deutsches Schauspieler-Archiv in Fulda, and his charming wife, Helga.

Among the others who have kindly lent me stills, I must mention Bavaria Film for their remarkable stills from *Berlin Alexanderplatz*, Louis Malle and Mme. Marie-Christine Breton at the Nouvelles Editions de Film, Miramax Films, Joanna Ney of The Film Society of Lincoln Center, John Poole of Corinth Films, Helma Sanders-Brahms, Mme. Catherine Verret at Unifrance, and Aries Films for *Lovers*.

For their bountiful gift of stills, I am indebted to John Hadity at Orion Classics, especially for the handsome stills from *Ran*; Edgar Reitz, who sent along as well his wonderful film book of *Heimat*; and Susan Fedak from IFEX. Special homage to the *Berliner Filmantiquariat* who, upon learning that the requested stills were meant for a book, contributed a bunch without charge. May his store flourish!

Additional stills were purchased from the Museum of Modern Art Film Stills Archive—with the friendly assistance of Mary Corliss—Jerry Ohlinger's Movie Material Store, Consolidated Poster Service, Inc, and the Royal Film Archive in Brussels, with a *merci* to M. Jean-Paul Dorchain. The remainder of the stills came from my private collection.

I am deeply appreciative to John Montague of New Yorker Films for lending me titles to reevaluate along with stills, the New York Public Library for the Performing Arts at Lincoln Center and the Donnell Media Center—both with a most helpful staff—the French Institute/Alliance Française, and Charles Silver at the Museum of Modern Art Film Study Center for arranging screenings.

At Seton Hall University I am much obliged to the provost, Dr. Bernhard Scholz, and to Dean Jerry Hirsch, for a sabbatical to work on this book; to Dr. Robert C. Hallissey for his generous research grant; to Ron Myzie at the Educational Media Center; to the Seton Hall Library and the aid from Jean Ellmer; and to my colleagues, Al Butrym, John Sweeney, Sr. Anna Zippilli, Anna Kuchta, Ihor Zielyk, and Carlos Rodriguez.

I must express my gratitude to my brother, William, for his encouragement; to my friend Ditmar Boysen for his advice and ungrudging efforts to help me in this project; to Frank Schramm for translating my letters into impeccable German; to the knowledgeable Frau Scheib-Rothbart at the Goethe House in New York, whom I have besieged with questions; and to Jiri Menzel for answering my query.

Grouped together, I wish to express my thanks to the following for a variety of reasons: Alan's Alley for their videos and useful information, Facets Video, Rose Gallo, the Japanese consulate, Steve Kasyanenko, Hermann Knall, Al Marill, Monika Prautzch, Ron Schwartz, Jaroslav Suchman, the Spanish consulate, the Danish consulate, the Vasata Restaurant, and Jerry Vermilye.

To my editor, Allan J. Wilson, who initiated this work, I am much indebted for his patience and consideration, and I am grateful to A. Christopher Simon for his wonderful design.

And, above all, my thanks to Angela for her much-needed support—and love.

A Citadel Press Book
Published by Carol Publishing Group
Citadel Press is a registered trademark of Carol Communications, Inc.
Editorial Offices: 600 Madison Avenue, New York, N.Y. 10022
Sales and Distribution Offices: 120 Enterprise Avenue, Secaucus, N.J. 07094
In Canada: Canadian Manda Group, P.O. Box 920, Station U, Toronto, Ontario M8Z 5P9
Queries regarding rights and permissions should be addressed to Carol Publishing Group, 600 Madison Avenue, New York, N.Y. 10022

Carol Publishing Group books are available at special discounts for bulk purchases, for sales promotion, fund-raising, or educational purposes. Special editions can be created to specifications. For details, contact: Special Sales Department, Carol Publishing Group, 120 Enterprise Avenue, Secaucus, N.J. 07094

Designed by A. Christopher Simon

Manufactured in the United States of America

10 9 8 7 6 5 4 3 2 1

LIBRARY OF CONGRESS CATALOGING-IN-PUBLICATION DATA

Paris, James Reid.
    Classic foreign films : from 1960 to today / by James Reid Paris.
        p.   cm.
    "A Citadel Press book."
    ISBN 0-8065-1442-6 (pbk.)
    1. Foreign films—United States—Reviews. I. Title.
PN1995.9.F67P37   1993
791.43'75—dc20
                                 93-11662
                                     CIP

François Truffaut directing *Day for Night*.

This book is dedicated to
FRANÇOIS TRUFFAUT

The film of tomorrow appears to me as even more personal than an individual and autobiographical novel, like a confession, or a diary. The young filmmakers will express themselves in the first person and will relate what has happened to them: it may be the story of their first love or their most recent; of their political awakening; the story of a trip, a sickness, their military service, their marriage, their last vacation . . . and it will be enjoyable because it will be true and new. . . . The film of tomorrow will be an act of love.

—François Truffaut (1957)

A film is something intimate like a letter.
　　　　　　　　—François Truffaut (1971)

François Truffaut relaxing with Jeanne Moreau during the shooting of *Jules and Jim.*

CONTENTS

AUTHOR'S NOTE

Unless otherwise specified, all dates indicate the year a film was released, a book was published, or a play presented. That is why I can regard Jiri Menzel's *Larks on a String* as a "new film" brought out in 1990, although it was made—and censored—back in 1969.

Of necessity, I had to include four major titles discussed previously in my book on French cinema. Nonetheless, for *Classic Foreign Films* I have prepared fresh essays and used different stills to illustrate them.

I've tried to present my selections chronologically, films from Europe (alphabetized by country) first, then those from elsewhere. When two films from a nation were issued in the same year, I mention the one that arrived in the United States first.

Limitations of space have forced me to mention only movie honors awarded at the film festivals of Cannes, Berlin, and Venice; selected prizes; recognition by the Academy of Motion Picture Arts and Sciences in Hollywood; and the top London citations. It was not my intention to slight the others.

Stéphane Audran in *Babette's Feast*.

INTRODUCTION

Filmmaking is a marvelous craft, and the proof is in the fact that, of all those who have the chance to work at it, no one wants to do anything else.

—François Truffaut, from a press kit for *Day for Night*

Jean-Paul Belmondo and Jean Seberg in *Breathless*.

In *Classic Foreign Films* I have limited my choices to the thirty-odd years from 1960 to the early 1990s. I have restricted the meaning of that absolutely relative term *foreign* to be simply "other than in the English language"—thus excluding the outstanding works that have appeared during the last three decades in Great Britain and Australia, many of whose directors, such as Stephen Frears, Peter Weir, and Bruce Beresford, subsequently became absorbed in the mainstream of American filmmaking.

Only a tiny portion of each country's cinematic output has managed to find distribution in the United States—and once opened, each film has been at the mercy of critics, who could either encourage viewing or dismiss into oblivion. Considering this as well as the impossibility of re-screening certain movies, first viewed decades ago, to determine if they retain their power, and the unavailability of representative stills from several worthy pictures, it would be ludicrous indeed to promote this book as a "definitive study." It can be no more than a selection of some prominent, distinguished foreign films from a vast—and to a large extent unexplored—host. Certain objective criteria have helped in the decision making: awards garnered for the movie at the major film festivals at Cannes, Venice, and Berlin as well as the bestowal of American and British Academy Awards and sundry prizes; the critical reputation of a film; and the picture's significant and lasting influence. Pressed to the wall to cite my subjective criteria, I can only say that I'm more sympathetic to traditional, "impressionistic" criticism than aligned with any particular school, and I point to Anatole France's notable definition: "The good critic is he who narrates the adventures of his soul among masterpieces."

This book is for the reader who *loves* movies and may perhaps be willing to try something unusual or little known. I wish to share my passion for a fascinating, incredible art form and try to take a middle ground between mindless, gushing journalists and dry, cerebral academicians, realizing that the cinematic experience is primarily emotional, not abstract. As Ingmar Bergman writes in *The Magic Lantern*, "No form of art goes beyond ordinary consciousness as film does, straight to our emotions, deep into the twilight room of the soul."

15

Sabine Haudepin and Jeanne Moreau in *Jules and Jim*.

Claudia Cardinale in *The Leopard*.

Sophia Loren in *Two Women*.

Marcello Mastroianni and Edra Gale in *8½*.

Alain Delon and Monica Vitti in *Eclipse*.

I hope that I have provided a variegated group for your enjoyment, pictures that are beyond sheer escapist fare, that are moving—even disturbing—reflective, intimate, deeply personal, provocative, poetic, and above all, richly entertaining. One may expand to film Robert Frost's dictum that a test of a good poem is that the reader feels "he has taken an immortal wound."

Because of the restrictions of space, I have considered feature films exclusively, thereby omitting significant developments in documentary, short, and animated film. Glancing through the contents, the reader will perceive that, in general, my tastes run to the nongenre as well as adaptations from the theater, novels, and short stories. The 1960s found France in the excitement of the New Wave, and appropriately, the book opens with Jean-Luc Godard's landmark *Breathless*. François Truffaut's unforgettable *Jules and Jim*—talk about

17

an immortal wound!—is here from that heightened period, as well as subsequent work from his career. The more recent *Story of Women* of Claude Chabrol completes the cluster of films of directors classified together as the New Wave. Brilliant films of Alain Resnais and Louis Malle, a historical drama by the Polish Andrzej Wajda, and a late entry by veteran director Robert Bresson complete the French selections. In Italy, Vittorio De Sica developed intermittently his studies of neorealism, to be continued by Mario Monicelli and afterward adopted by the younger Ermanno Olmi. Michelangelo Antonioni in *Eclipse* concluded his trilogy analyzing his contemporary world.

For Italy, 1963 was a cinematic *annus mirabilis*, for it saw the release of the work of two masters at the peak of their talent: Federico Fellini in *8½* and Luchino Visconti in *The Leopard*. That nation's cinema was reinvigorated with the arrival of such directors as Pier Paolo Pasolini, Gillo Pontecorvo, Bernardo Bertolucci, Ettore Scola, and Lina Wertmuller. In what was then the USSR, there are adaptations from veteran directors Josef Heifitz and Grigori Kozintsev, along with the work of a later generation whose members include Grigori Chukhrai and Andrei Konchalovsky and the two nonconformists, Sergei Paradjanov and Andrei Tarkovsky. Sweden's Ingmar Bergman is unquestionably the world's greatest *auteur* and has the most titles discussed herein.

In Spain, the veteran Luis Buñuel returned to give the Franco regime a jolt with *Viridiana*. Vicente Aranda, Carlos Saura, and Victor Erice represent important voices from the younger generation. In Denmark, veteran director Carl Theodor Dreyer made his last film, *Gertrud*. In recent years

Eiji Okada in *Woman in the Dunes.*

Enrique Irazoqui *(left)* in *The Gospel According to St. Matthew.*

that country has made an impressive showing with pictures by Bille August and Gabriel Axel. From Eastern Europe there is Roman Polanski in Poland and Pal Gabor and Istvan Szabo in Hungary. Special attention is paid to Czechoslovakia, which experienced a remarkable outburst of cinematic enterprise when that nation relaxed its oppressive hand. Jan Kadar, Elmar Klos, Milos Forman, Ivan Passer, and Jiri Menzel made memorable contributions to world cinema.

In what was formerly West Germany, there suddenly emerged, after a long, moribund period, splendid artists who, with the assistance of government and television, made their names internationally known: Werner Herzog, Wim Wenders,

Stefania Sandrelli *(left)* and Dominique Sanda in *The Conformist.*

Ida Kaminska in *The Shop on Main Street.*

Kika Markham *(left)* and Stacey Tendeter in *Two English Girls.*

Early film commentators had the luxury of evaluating movies at a time when art houses were still flourishing along with revival theaters; when more foreign films were imported than currently; and although television helped to shrink movie attendance then—and the ubiquitous VCR had yet to make its appearance—the chances of a quality foreign film succeeding here were greater than at present. Statistics indicate that today, out of the millions of dollars that films generate annually in

and Rainer Werner Fassbinder. Among the more recent directors are Percy Aldon, Helma Sanders-Brahms, Edgar Reitz, and Wolfgang Petersen. And from Japan there is work from veterans Yasujiro Ozu and Akira Kurosawa, plus films from Hiroshi Teshigahara and Nagisa Oshima from a succeeding generation. Completing our overview is the Martinique-born Euzhan Palcy.

Looking over my inclusions, I became curiously cognizant of the prevalence of World War II and the Holocaust as subject matter in approximately one-quarter of my seventy titles. Whether re-creating the reality of Fascist Italy *(Two Women, Seven Beauties, A Special Day)*, life in Occupied France *(Lacombe, Lucien; Au Revoir les Enfants)*, Czechoslovakia *(Closely Watched Trains)*, Hungary *(Confidence)*, the world of Nazi Germany *(Germany Pale Mother, Mephisto, Das Boot)*, or the brave defense of the Soviet Union *(Ballad of a Soldier)*, the film medium was enriched by treating the most momentous war of the century. Would Joseph Goebbels find consolation in the fact that while most of the movies made under his supervision were artistically negligible—for example, Veit Harlan's elephantine *Kolberg* (1945), made to immortalize the Third Reich on film when the Minister of Propaganda realized that it would not last its vaunted thousand years—the Nazi regime that he helped engender would provide the stimulus for an extraordinary array of first-rate films?

the United States, the profits derived from the foreign-film portion constitute a mere five percent of the total. (The same proportion is true of classical music here, alas.) Soaring production costs abroad, the gradual erosion of national identities as more and more "international" films are being made, the dearth of art theaters and the near-demise of the cherished repertory houses in this country, and the prohibitive cost of importing and promoting a foreign film are but several ominous trends that qualify the foreign film as an "endangered species."

It is to be hoped that, in spite of the mounting cost of producing a film, there will constantly arise artists worldwide with visions who endeavor to make their personal statement on film in spite of great difficulty—rather than revamping whatever genre is commercial at the moment—and that there will be an audience (who miraculously survive the onslaught of rock music videos with their

Lino Capolicchio and Dominique Sanda in *The Garden of the Finzi-Continis.*

21

Irina Miroschnichenko in *Uncle Vanya.*

Jacqueline Bisset and François Truffaut in *Day for Night.*

sensibilities intact) ready and eager to support them. That quality may somehow triumph—or at least manage to persist—against the mordantly cynical view of filmmaking as depicted in Robert Altman's *The Player* (1992). That we keep in mind the plea of the great Spanish poet, Federico García Lorca, made back in 1934, which we may easily apply to movie theaters also: "From the smallest theatre to the most eminent, the word 'Art' should be written in auditoriums and dressing rooms, for if not we shall have to write the word 'Commerce' or some other that I dare not say. And distinction,

discipline, and sacrifice and love." That future commentators have a plethora to choose from in the continuing, glorious history of the foreign film.

When I began this work in 1989, the continent of Europe was pretty much as it had been since the Cold War started after World War II. However, since then, we have witnessed the breakup of the USSR, the reunification of Germany, and the liberation of Eastern Europe. It is fitting, indeed, then for my penultimate film to stress a note of hope with Jiri Menzel's *Larks on a String*, finally ex-

humed after twenty-one years—a testament to man's hopes for a better world. Although Czechoslovakia split into two nations in 1993, the Czech Republic and Slovakia, may the cheerful optimism evinced in that endearing film be a harbinger for a less muddled century than the one that is soon ending!

Barbara Sukowa in *Berlin Alexanderplatz.*

Isabel Telleria *(left)* and Ana Torrent in *The Spirit of the Beehive.*

Percy Adlon at the time of *Céleste*.

A GALLERY OF DIRECTORS

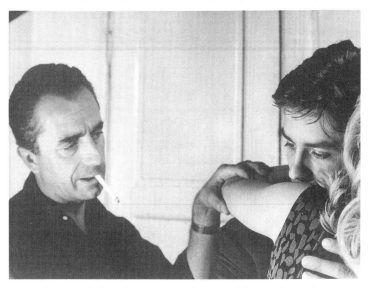

Michelangelo Antonioni directing Alain Delon and Monica Vitti in *Eclipse*.

Vittorio De Sica directing Sophia Loren in "The Raffle" episode from *Boccaccio '70* (1962).

Ingmar Bergman at the time of *Persona*.

Rainer Werner Fassbinder *(right)* directing Günter Lamprecht in
Berlin Alexanderplatz.

Portrait of Carl Theodor Dreyer.

25

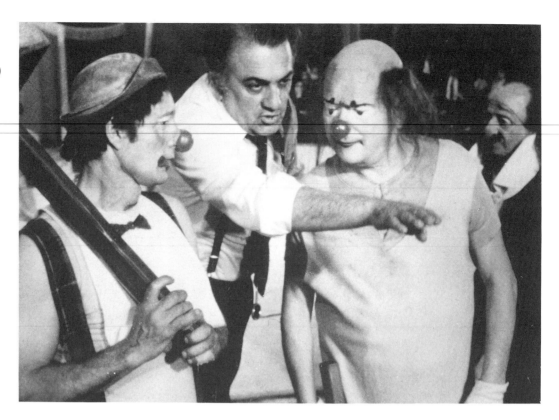

Federico Fellini *(center)* directing *The Clowns* (1970).

Werner Herzog *(left)* directing *Aguirre, the Wrath of God.* Del Negro is in the center and Klaus Kinski is on the right.

Akira Kurosawa directing *Ran.*

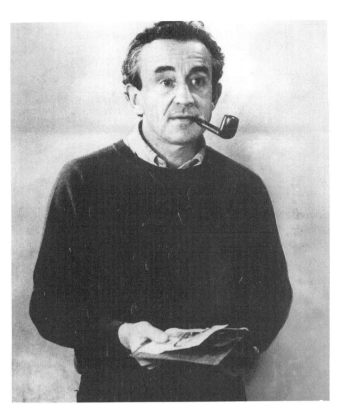

Louis Malle at the time of *Au Revoir les Enfants*.

Wolfgang Petersen directing *Das Boot*.

Gillo Pontecorvo directing *The Battle of Algiers*.

Pier Paolo Pasolini directing *Accattone* (1961).

Edgar Reitz directing Marita Breuer in *Heimat*.

Helma Sanders-Brahms *(left)* with daughter and Eva Mattes during the shooting of *Germany Pale Mother.*

François Truffaut directing Catherine Deneuve in *The Last Metro* (1980).

Wim Wenders directing Solveig Dommartin in *Wings of Desire.*

Andrei Tarkovsky *(right)* consulting with famed cinematographer Sven Nykvist during the shooting of *The Sacrifice* (1986).

THE FILMS

Patricia (Jean Seberg) stops hawking the *New York Herald Tribune* momentarily on the Champs-Elysées to kiss Michel (Jean-Paul Belmondo).

1
BREATHLESS

A Bout de Souffle

FRANCE / 1960

Société Nouvelle de Cinéma

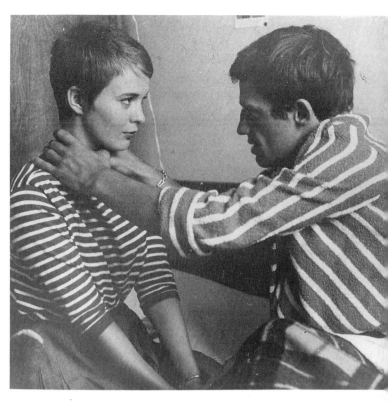

If Patricia doesn't smile when Michel counts to eight, he threatens playfully to strangle her. Much underlying tension in their relationship is suggested in this extended hotel-room sequence, which shifts between the serious and the comic.

CREDITS

Director and screenwriter: Jean-Luc Godard (based on an original treatment by François Truffaut); *Assistant director:* Pierre Rissient; *Producer:* Georges de Beauregard; *Cinematographer:* Raoul Coutard (black and white); *Music:* Martial Solal, Mozart's Clarinet Concerto (K. 622); *Editor:* Cécile Decugis; *Running time:* 89 minutes; *16mm rental source:* New Yorker; *Videocassette:* Connoisseur.

CAST

Michael Poiccard, aka *Laszlo Kovacs:* Jean-Paul Belmondo; *Patricia Franchini:* Jean Seberg; *Inspector Vital:* Daniel Boulanger; *Antonio Berrutti:* Henri-Jacques Huet; *Carl Zombach:* Roger Hanin; *Van Doude:* Van Doude; *Michel's Friend:* Liliane Robin; *Plainclothesman:* Michel Favre; *Parvulesco:* Jean-Pierre Melville; *Used Car Dealer:* Claude Mansard; *Informer:* Jean-Luc Godard.

Amazingly, more than three decades have passed since *Breathless* opened successfully and began to exert an influence that can truly be said to be extraordinary. In 1959, its French director, Jean-Luc Godard (1930–), a former passionate film critic, was provided the opportunity to direct his first feature film, which he completed on a very limited budget and in one month's time. While ostensibly working within the conventions of the American-style gangster film, the young director made an innovative, provocative, and arresting film that, above all, was a personal statement. *Breathless* became a touchstone for the French New Wave, a model for fledgling directors rejecting the staid, conformist tendencies of the existing cinema. Godard showed the liberating way for a *cinéma des auteurs,* a cinema created by filmmakers who, to use François Truffaut's famous phrase, write "in the first person"—making films that are intimate, individual, and vital. The seminal *Breathless* still retains its power and has achieved the status of a classic.

The plot is simple: A young thug, Michel Poiccard (Jean-Paul Belmondo), speeding to Paris from Marseilles in a stolen automobile, kills an interfering policeman. In the capital he spends time with his girlfriend Patricia (Jean Seberg), an American student whom he hopes to take with him in an escape to Italy. Meanwhile he tries to find a friend whose signature on a check (given for some presumably illicit activity) he desperately needs to obtain the necessary money. A dragnet for the cop-killer tightens. Patricia, vacillating and indecisive, telephones the police, revealing Michel's whereabouts, and he is soon shot down in the streets. The entire action is crammed into three intense days.

Although we see Michel deliberately shoot a cop, he nonetheless emerges as an attractive *mauvais garçon*, a bad boy. Godard's attitude is not judgmental. With the criminal's genuine capacity for love, he is much more sympathetic than the shallow Patricia. Michel is a nihilist, an anarchist, loyal to the tenets of the underworld. His final words as he lies dying in the gutter, "That's really disgusting" *("C'est vraiment dégueulasse")*, can be interpreted either as a commentary on life or a reference to the "bitch" who turned him in. The literal translation of the French title is "out of breath," indicating the fast-paced, danger-laden life of the outlaw who is obsessed with death. The use of jazz appropriately underlines Michel's moods and actions. The callow Patricia is drawn to

Patricia calls the police and informs on her lover.

Later, an affectionate moment between Michel and Patricia.

Michel and even experiments briefly in his illegal activities by helping him rob a car. Yet she is confused about her feelings, both wanting him to love her and not to love her anymore. To add to her perplexity, she is pregnant with his child. Afraid of commitment, she longs to be independent and has ambitions of being a journalist. Her betrayal of Michel, she rationalizes, was a test to see if she had really loved him. From the moment of Jean-Paul Belmondo's initial appearance, wearing a fedora and jacket, smoking the ever-present cigarette and making a gesture of rubbing his thumb back and forth across his lips, he exerts a magnetic presence that launched him into stardom. At times the hard-boiled tough guy, on other occasions he is sportive, boyish, and most appealing. Although Jean Seberg has the betrayal role, this is the best-remembered performance of this lovely actress, who died in 1979.

Godard's idiosyncratic style dominates the film. Not wishing to make the typical fare of doomed lovers, which arouses strong audience identification—as, for example, Nicholas Ray's *They Live by Night* (1949)—Godard opts rather for a distancing effect to involve our mind so that we do not get lost in an emotional torrent. Early in the film Michel addresses the camera directly while driving an appropriated vehicle, thus violating the realistic demands of the cinema. We are forced to reflect on the behavior of a felon who will live up to his private code to the inevitable finish, emphasized when he passes a theater playing Robert Aldrich's *Ten Seconds to Hell* (1959) with the advertisement "To live dangerously until the end." The lively character of *Breathless* is that of an exuberant, original director finally being allowed to make his own movie. Godard said that he wished to give the feeling that film devices had just been discovered.

This cinema of "reinvention" used, for example, the venerable iris-in and iris-out transitions from silent movies, as well the current techniques of cinema in a fresh and startling manner. Thus we find long takes with a tracking camera, the use of a speeding hand-held camera, unusual angles, and circular shots with a 360-degree movement. Most astonishing of all is the jump cut—a jump in the continuity of time within a shot. This came about when Godard realized that an hour of the footage needed to be cut. He said, "I discovered that when a discussion between two people became tedious and boring, you may as well cut between the dialogue. I tried it once and found it went fine, then I did the same thing right through the film. But it was done in the style of the movie." The jump cut was much imitated.

Breathless abounds with cinematic references. Michel pays homage to a poster of Humphrey Bogart outside a Champs-Elysées theater; Patricia gets to interview the writer Parvulesco, who turns out to be Jean-Pierre Melville, the maverick, independent director of French thrillers. There is a density of references to film, painting, literature, philosophy, music, etc., to add resonance to the imagery and dialogue. Jim McBride transplanted the story to L.A. in his 1983 American remake with Richard Gere and Valerie Kaprisky, but this was a hollow film with scant impact. Godard's version captured the alienation, sense of revolt, and existentialist atmosphere of the period, which could hardly be duplicated more than twenty years later in a foreign country. While Godard dominated the 1960s with his prolific and influential work, his movies grew increasingly didactic, and film eventually became not a basic narrative but a form of essay in which he could address his audience via images and ideas. *Breathless* remains the director's most accessible and popular film.

HONORS

Prix Vigo (1960)
Prix Méliès (1960)
Silver Bear for Best Director, Berlin Film Festival (1960)
L'Etoile de Cristal (Crystal Star) to Jean-Paul Belmondo for Best Actor, L'Académie de Cinéma (1961)*

2
TWO WOMEN

La Ciociara

ITALY/FRANCE / 1960

COMPANIA CINEMATOGRAFICA CHAMPION (ROME)/LES FILMS MARCEAU/COCINOR/SOCIÉTÉ GÉNÉRALE DE CINÉMATOGRAPHIE (PARIS)

CREDITS

Director: Vittorio De Sica; *Producer:* Carlo Ponti; *Screenwriters:* Cesare Zavattini, Vittorio De Sica, based on the novel by Alberto Moravia (1958); *Cinematographer:* Gabor Pogany (black and white, CinemaScope); *Music:* Armando Trovajoli; *Editor:* Adriana Novelli; *Art direction:* Gastone Medin; *Running time:* 105 minutes; *16mm rental source:* Films Inc.; *Videocassette:* Orion.

CAST

Cesira: Sophia Loren; *Michele:* Jean-Paul Belmondo; *Rosetta:* Eleonora Brown; *Giovanni:* Raf Vallone; *Florindo:* Renato Salvatori; *Michele's Father:* Carlo Ninchi; *Fascist:* Andrea Checchi.

Two Women is one of the most popular films of Italian director Vittorio De Sica (1901–74) and is another of his brilliant collaborations with noted screenwriter Cesare Zavattini (1902–89), with whom he created such neorealistic masterpieces as *Shoeshine* (1946), *The Bicycle Thief* (1948), and *Umberto D* (1952). Alberto Moravia's forceful, realistic novel of the hardships endured by a strong

*Henceforth referred to simply as L'Etoile de Cristal.

Cesira (Sophia Loren) visits Giovanni (Raf Vallone) to ask him to look after her store and house while she's away.

Cesira grips her daughter, Rosetta (Eleonora Brown), after narrowly avoiding a strafing attack by an Allied plane.

Roman widow who flees the capital with her sheltered daughter to escape Allied bombardment only to confront unexpected and harrowing adversity in the countryside was transposed to the screen in a generally faithful manner. The screenwriters, of necessity, condensed much of the action; omitted episodes; dropped the first-person narration of Cesira, who is the central character in the book; lowered her daughter's age from eighteen to approximately twelve; and added a love interest, Michele, for Cesira. The great Anna Magnani was originally considered for the part of the mother, but it eventually went to a young Sophia Loren, who was tired of the fluff she had been making in Hollywood exploiting her rare beauty and sex appeal and was determined to prove that she could be a mature, serious actress. The Italian title, *La Ciociara*, refers to a peasant woman from the Roman country. The English title, however, is plural, implying that the daughter, after her devastating violation, has to be regarded now as a woman, too. An enormous hit, *Two Women* was a coup for the talented Miss Loren, who was widely honored for her riveting performance. Sensitively directed, superbly written and acted with unflinching honesty, *Two Women* has justly earned its critical and commercial success; its impact has not diminished.

The year is 1943. Cesira (Sophia Loren), a comely widow, is fearful for her overprotected, childlike daughter, Rosetta (Eleonora Brown), during the constant air raids on Rome and wishes to get away to the less troubled region where she grew up. She asks a friend, Giovanni (Raf Vallone), to watch her grocery shop and home. He agrees, then makes love with her. In spite of various obstacles, mother and child manage to get to Sant'Eufemia, a mountainous area filled with refugees. There Michele (Jean-Paul Belmondo), a young intellectual, is attracted to Cesira. All wait for the dreadful war to end, coping with hunger and deprivation. The retreating Germans impress Michele as a guide, while soon all welcome the advancing American troops. The widow resolves to return to Rome and leaves, but she and Rosetta are brutally raped in a church in a deserted village by Moroccan soldiers. The convent-bred child is traumatized; Cesira is filled with anguish and guilt. A young worker, Florindo (Renato Salvatori), gives them a lift in his truck and eyes Rosetta. The mother awakes from a rest at his home and sees her daughter is missing. Later, when Rosetta enters with nylons, Cesira gets hysterical and slaps the sullen, embittered girl. Only when Cesira informs her that Michele has been killed is Rosetta able to cry and find release for her pent-up emotions. Mother and daughter embrace, restored now in peace, love, and hope.

Cesira is a typical bourgeois shopkeeper—practical, shrewd, a survivor. We can understand her passion for security from her impoverished background, which propelled her into a loveless marriage to an older man who brought her to Rome and prosperity. Politically naive, she is indifferent to Mussolini and concerned chiefly with making money. Cesira's most praiseworthy characteristic is her unselfish, vigorous maternal love for her frightened daughter. Even while she's being sexually molested, her anxious stare is on the helpless Rosetta. For the pubescent girl to be ravaged so is to mar her self-image and impel her to be abused again by such as Florindo. *Two Women* was a triumph for the twenty-six-year-old Sophia Loren, who, without makeup and dressed shabbily, showed she could move us deeply with her remarkable talent. Jean-Paul Belmondo is interestingly cast against type as a shy, bookish youth. Eleonora Brown as Rosetta is effective as the gentle innocent who becomes a victim of war.

De Sica depicted this neorealistic film with masterly control and assurance. *Two Women* goes beyond an apt documentary re-creation of the World War II period to explore man's feelings and potential. "Neorealism was born of the war," the director said in 1962, "and we artists were touched by the misery of humanity after the war. . . . But our *verismo* is not the realism of Zola; it is interpretive and poetical. Lyrical. Life is crude, but there is also the poetical, lyrical side of life. There is always the great hope of the marvelous thing which is man." Several scenes linger in the memory: While calling on his friend in Fondi, Michele and Cesira quickly fall to the ground during a sudden air assault. They raise their heads and notice a ladybug moving along a blade of grass, oblivious of the lethal human battle. Later, an exhausted Cesira and Rosetta retire to an empty church in what they believe to be an abandoned hamlet. Each lies down to rest. While the camera observes them from the entrance, abruptly and ominously we see first the shadow of one soldier appear, then a second. In a chilling long shot we

Retreating Nazis select Michele (Jean-Paul Belmondo) to lead them to the next valley as his mother reacts and Rosetta and Cesira look on.

watch hordes enter to chase their unfortunate prey. While the horrified mother is pinned to the floor, the camera zooms in on the petrified daughter's face screaming *"Mamma!"* And there is the haunting final sequence: Cesira, up all night and deeply distressed about the absent Rosetta, confronts her hardened, damaged child when she gets in tardily. Angrily, Cesira hits her, but there is no response. However, when Rosetta learns of Michele's death, she dissolves in tears. Cesira weeps, too, begs for her daughter's forgiveness, and while Rosetta lies cuddled in her mother's arms crying—each providing solace for the other—the camera discreetly backs away to a long shot while the scene contracts, bordered in black.

Earlier in the films, in the mountains, Michele had tried in vain to read to his restless exiles the story from the Bible of Lazarus, which becomes a significant theme in the movie since both mother and daughter "died" in the church and were "resurrected" in the tender conclusion. Both were battered indeed by the war, but not destroyed, and were restored to their humanity with hope for the difficult days ahead. *Two Women* is a powerful, unforgettable film, a classic.

The aftermath of the barbarous rape scene in the church: Cesira with daughter Rosetta in a state of shock.

HONORS

Best Actress to Sophia Loren, Cannes Film Festival (1961)
Best Actress, New York Film Critics Award (1961)
Best Foreign Actress, British Academy of Film and Television Arts (1961)*
Best Actress, Academy of Motion Picture Arts and Sciences (1961)**

3

BALLAD OF A SOLDIER

Ballada O Soldate

USSR / 1960

MOSFILM

CREDITS

Director: Grigori Chukhrai; *Screenwriters:* Valentin Yoshov, Grigori Chukhrai; *Cinematographers:* Vladi-

*Henceforth referred to as the British Academy Award.
**Henceforth referred to as Oscar.

mir Nikolayev, Era Saveleva (black and white); *Music:* Mikhail Siv; *Editor:* M. Timofeiva; *Running time:* 89 minutes; *16mm rental source:* Corinth; *Videocassette:* Hollywood.

CAST

Alyosha Skvortsov: Vladimir Ivashov; *Shura:* Shanna Prokhorenko; *Alyosha's Mother:* Antonia Maximova; *General:* Nikolai Kruchkov; *Crippled Soldier:* Eugeni Urbanski; *His Wife:* Elsa Lezhdey; *Driver of Truck:* Valentina Telegrina.

Less than fifteen years after the end of World War II, Ukrainian born Grigori Chukhrai (1921–   ), one of the leading Soviet directors of the 1950s, felt compelled to pay cinematic tribute to the nation's brave soldiers who met the Nazi onslaught with outstanding courage and tenacity. Like a ballad, the work would be a simple, poetic narrative of an unassuming youth from the country who distinguishes himself by his boldness in combat, one who has the makings of a folk hero.

Chukhrai had first-hand knowledge of the war since his studies at the State Institute of Cinematography were interrupted after the German invasion of June 1941. Mobilized, he served with the airborne forces, then the infantry, fought in the Battle of Stalingrad, was wounded five times, and decorated for valor. "I have lost some of my dearest friends," he said later concerning the war, "and I wanted my film to be a memory of them." The director continued, "I knew a young soldier who had destroyed two tanks, and when I asked him how he did it, he said he did not know—all he could remember was that he had a great fear. That remark stayed with me and became the point of departure for the film." With its unaffected, direct narrative line and rich, appealing characterizations, *Ballad of a Soldier* went on to achieve worldwide success and remains the director's best-known work.

The film begins with a battle at the time of the German push toward Stalingrad in 1942. As a tank threatens the life of Alyosha (Vladimir Ivashov), a nineteen-year-old signalman, he manages heroically to disable it and then another. In lieu of a medal, he requests from the general (Nikolai Kruchkov) a brief pass so that he could see his faraway mother and repair the roof. The compassionate officer grants him a six-day leave. In the course of his odyssey, he promises to deliver soap (a present from a serviceman to his wife); misses trains while he tends to a wounded soldier (Eugeni Urbanski) who had one leg amputated and is reluctant to see his wife again; bribes a ride on a freight train with a tin of beef; and meets a pretty, young stowaway, Shura (Shanna Prokhorenko), who is initially terrified of him though they quickly became friends. After several mishaps and further delays, they find the soldier's wife who is to receive the soap and are disheartened to notice her living with another man. Alyosha and Shura catch a troop train; soon they have a tender parting and the soldier shouts out the name of his town amidst the din. The train is attacked by planes and Alyosha helps the passengers evacuate. Time running out, he fords a river on a raft since the bridge has been destroyed and hitches a ride on a truck to his home. The mother (Antonia Maximova) is summoned from the fields and clasps her son tearfully in their hasty reunion. He then dashes back off to the front. A narrator informs us that he never returned: "We remembered him as a hero . . . a soldier."

Alyosha is a shy, innocent, and thoroughly decent young man. When he wreaks havoc upon the two tanks, his bravery is commingled with fear, thus making him seem totally believable without false heroics. Selfless and generous, he surrenders his precious time on a pass to help others. "I wanted to describe him without any big words," Chukhrai said, "quietly, with no obvious 'arty' style. Since this film was devoted to my dear friends, I wanted it to be as they were—simple, dutiful, and humble. Nobody shouts at a friend's grave."

The casting was excellent. Vladimir Ivashov makes a most attractive and convincing Alyosha, performing with naturalness and sincerity. Shanna Prokhorenko is lovely as Shura, her expressive face projecting a range of emotions from fright to sadness. *Ballad of a Soldier* was the initial screen appearance for both. A virile Eugenie Urbanski is particularly impressive in his few scenes as the brooding soldier full of misgivings about how his wife will react to him as a cripple. (She turns out to be loving and supportive.)

Chukhrai directs this, his third feature with a documentary realism. Train stations crowded with refugees, city streets with bombed-out buildings, trains assaulted by planes at night—the look and feel of wartime Russia is effectively captured. The stress is on characterization, however, and the director makes his hero and all whom he comes across vividly and unforgettably alive. He involves us in Alyosha's fate and keeps the pace swift and exciting. Mikhail Siv's score is stirring and appropriate. Certain scenes stay with us, such as the

The general (Nikolai Kruchkov) *(left)* gives permission to the valiant young soldier, Alyosha Skvortsov (Vladimir Ivashov) *(seated)*, to take a short leave.

The soldier Alyosha readily gives assistance to the crippled serviceman (Eugeni Urbanski).

After their curtailed relationship has blossomed into love, the young couple, Alyosha and Shura (Shanna Prokhorenko), are forced to separate.

Finally, Alyosha has a hurried but touching meeting with his mother (Antonia Maximova).

opening warfare sequence. Chukhrai directs from a low angle so that the ominous tank pursuing Alyosha looks even more menacing. At one point it completely covers the camera. Then a high-angle shot shows the young soldier narrowly avoiding it. When he is able to fire on the tank and we see smoke billowing from it, the same with a second one, we have vicariously lived his courageous behavior in just a few quick scenes.

A richly evocative moment on the train after Shura leaves is beautifully photographed by Vladimir Nikolayev and Era Saveleva. Alyosha stares out the window and recollects in montage fashion memories of the radiant girl—all of which are superimposed on shots of birch trees caught from the speeding train. In the course of this exquisite sequence he realizes the depth of his feeling for her. Finally, there is the poignant climax, the all-too-brief encounter between mother and son. She rushes through the fields when she learns that her beloved Alyosha is here. A long shot shows that the truck with her boy has passed her. She screams. The vehicle stops and the young soldier races back to hug his mother. Then in a close shot he tells her he must go in a moment. "Let's talk"—but they cannot bring themselves to speak. At last the mother asks if he has begun to shave. The truck honks. After their final embrace, he shouts, "I'll come back, Mother." There's a shot of her in the road, then the narrator ponders what this fine youth might have become and reveals his tragic end.

We realize that young Alyosha represents the Russian Everyman, a microcosm for the millions killed during the devastating war. We sense the lost potential, the overwhelming waste of war. Chukhrai said, "We looked for a way to condemn war that was simple and total." *Ballad of a Soldier*, after thirty years, still stands as a deeply human and moving experience. This powerful film is universal and one of the great antiwar movies of all time.

HONORS

Special Prize "for lofty humanism and artistic excellence," Cannes Film Festival (1960)

Shared British Academy Award for Best Film, Any Source (1961)

Nominated for an Oscar for Best Story and Screenplay, Written Directly for the Screen (1961)

4

THE LADY WITH THE DOG

Dama s Sobachkoy

USSR / 1960

LENFILM

CREDITS

Director, producer, and screenwriter: Josef Heifitz,* based on the story by Anton Chekhov (1899); *Cinematographers:* Andrei Moskvin, Dmitri Meskhiyev (black and white); *Music:* Nadezhda Simonian; *Editor:* Y. Bazhenova; *Art directors:* Bella Manevich, Iosif Kaplan; *Running time:* 86 minutes; *16mm rental source:* Corinth; *Videocasette:* White Star.

CAST

Anna Sergeyevna: Iya Savvina; *Dmitri Gurov:* Alexei Batalov; *Madame Gurov:* Nina Alisova; *von Diederitz:* Peter Krimov; *Frolov:* Dmitri Zebrov; *Natasha:* Maria Safonova.

The year 1960 was the one hundredth anniversary of the birth of Russia's great playwright and short story writer Anton Chekhov, and to mark the occasion veteran Soviet director Josef Heifitz (1905–) prepared a film version of one of the master's best stories, "The Lady With the Dog," which treats a romance between two unhappily married people with the greatest delicacy. Heifitz engaged the widely respected actor and director Alexei Batalov—known in the United States for his role in *The Cranes Are Flying* (1958)—for the role of Gurov and, discovering Iya Savvina performing in a play at Moscow University, cast her as Anna, in which role she made her screen debut. The result of perfect casting, careful direction, brilliant photography, and affecting music made *The Lady With the Dog* a model of a faithful film adaptation as well as a cinematic gem.

The movie opens at the fashionable resort of Yalta at the turn of the century. Gurov (Alexei Batalov) is a banker approaching middle age whose

*Known in Russia as Iosif Kheifits.

At Yalta on a holiday Dmitri Gurov (Alexei Batalov) meets the desirable Anna (Iya Savvina), who is irresistibly drawn to him.

While Frolov (Dmitri Zebrov) *(right)* finds solace in alcohol at their Moscow club, Gurov is obsessed with his love affair of last summer in Yalta.

joyless marriage has produced three children. Vacationing by himself, his philandering proclivities are stimulated when he sights an attractive young

Reunion in a Moscow hotel: Gurov tells his beloved Anna to continue wearing his favorite gray dress—even in ten years' time.

With her lover Dmitri next to her, Anna compares their relationship to that of a pair of trapped birds of passage.

woman strolling alone with her Pomeranian. She is Anna (Iya Savvina) who, too, has a loveless marriage. She gradually falls in love with him although she has religious scruples and is ridden with guilt. When her ailing husband, von Dieder-

itz (Peter Krimov), summons her home to Saratov, she submits to her fate, bids farewell to her lover, and departs. Back in wintry Moscow, Gurov discovers that what he mistook for a casual liaison was genuine love. He longs for Anna and recoils from the meaninglessness of his friends' lives. Impulsively he heads to Saratov and surprises Anna in a theater. Overcome, she tells him she couldn't forget him and promises to visit him. In a Moscow hotel the couple meet for another of their brief reunions. Although their ardor is strong, she is tired of all the deception involved; he convinces himself there must be a solution to their problem. Soon Gurov is forced to leave while Anna gazes wistfully through the window.

Gurov is a sensitive man, a scholar whose youthful dreams of being a singer lie buried in an unrewarding banking career. His wife is cold and pretentious. When he discovers a powerful love for the first time, it is all the more painful for him to partake of the endless cards, drinking, and small talk of his society. Once, drunk, he realizes his life is like living behind bars. Anna had wedded at twenty to escape to what she had hoped would be a better existence. Instead she is tied to a man she considers a lackey and is engulfed in a stifling, provincial town. The theme of incarceration extends to her also, for Gurov walks past the imposing wooden fence that confines her house in Saratov like a prison. The two lovers are trapped in the suffocating inertia of their epoch and crave fulfillment. With his penetrating eyes, Alexei Batalov is commanding as the unfortunate Gurov. The beautiful Iya Savvina, with sorrowful eyes and a heartbreaking voice, conveys the fragility of the gentle, lovely Anna. There is that necessary chemistry between the two that moves us deeply.

Heifitz's direction is most assured. He re-creates the distant period meticulously with significant detail so that we see a hat blow off a stroller's head at Yalta in addition to the dozing ticket-taker in a horse-drawn trolley in the snow-laden capital. He displays absolute fidelity to the original story down to the shabby inkpot "surmounted by a headless rider, holding his hat in his raised hand," which Gurov finds in his Saratov hotel. Besides involving us intensely with the pair of lovers, the director manages to sustain an ambience of elegiac sadness and suggest Chekhov's criticism of his stagnant world. An added touch is the opening shot of the Black Sea, then a pan to a liquor bottle floating in the water evoking a sense of decadence. The cinematography of Andrei Moskvin and Dmitri Meskhiyev is praiseworthy, particularly in capturing the sea and sky at Yalta. Nadezhda Simonian's score is romantic and eloquently evokes the absent Anna when Gurov yearns for her in Moscow.

The closing sequence is especially memorable. While the lovers embrace in the hotel, there is a cut to the courtyard where an old street musician playing a soulful oboe in the falling snow sets a poignant mood. Each of the lovers inquires how the other has been faring. After turning on a lamp, Anna tells Gurov that "we are like a pair of birds of passage. They've been caught and forced into separate cages. And they will pine to death." A clock strikes tellingly. She hates all the lies, these unbreakable bonds that prevent them from living together in honesty and dignity. Gurov insists, "We'll think of something." There's a quick top-to-bottom wipe, and now the camera is outside the closed window out of earshot. The music soars to a climax as we see first Anna, then Gurov speak, implying they have reached an impasse, that there really is no ready answer (recalling Chekhov's concluding line "that the end was still far, far away, and that the hardest, the most complicated part was only just beginning.") Gurov kisses Anna passionately. The camera cuts to the corridor as he slowly walks away from his weeping lover, then to the window again, and we see her watching below. A crying Anna nods forlornly to Gurov in the courtyard. The next cut reveals a melancholy lover stopping, looking up, and removing his hat. Lastly, an extreme long shot of the hotel appears with its sole lit window and solitary figure.

This lack of resolution to the characters' complex situation is typical of Chekhov, for he felt the artist's job was not unriddling complications, but simply "stating a problem correctly." Chekhov also abstains from pronouncing judgment on Gurov and Anna. "The artist should be not the judge of his characters," he wrote, "but only an unbiased witness." Unbiased, yes, but one such as he with deep understanding and profound compassion. In the story and in the superb movie, both Gurov and Anna are most sympathetic and real. Heifitz declared, "I learned from Chekhov the humanity of art." Nikita Mikhalkov retold this tale along with three other Chekhov stories in *Dark Eyes* (1987). Although it was in color and featured Marcello Mastroianni, it did nothing to eclipse the memory of Heifitz's classic film. Undoubtedly the most successful of the film adaptations of Chekhov's fiction, *The Lady With the Dog* remains a haunting and endearing movie, one deserving to be remembered and cherished.

Special Prize "for lofty humanism and artistic excellence," Cannes Film Festival (1960)

5

LATE AUTUMN

Akibiyori

JAPAN / 1960

SHOCHIKU

CREDITS

Director: Yasujiro Ozu; *Screenwriters:* Kogo Noda, Yasujiro Ozu, based on the novel by Ton Satomi; *Cinematographer:* Yuharu Atsuta (Agfacolor); *Music:* Kojun Saito; *Editor:* Yoshiyasu Hamamura; *Art director:* Tatsuo Hamada; *Running time:* 127 minutes; *16mm rental source and videocassette:* New Yorker.

CAST

Akiko Miwa: Setsuko Hara; *Ayako:* Yoko Tsukasa; *The Uncle:* Chishu Ryu; *Yuriko:* Mariko Okada; *Goto:* Keiji Sada; *Mamiya:* Shin Saburi; *Taguchi:* Nobuo Nakamura; *His Wife:* Kuniko Miyake; *Hirayama:* Ryuji Kita.

On a superficial level, the films of the Japanese director Yasujiro Ozu (1903–63) might appear to have limited interest to a Western audience. The plots of his films are slight; they are neither teeming with violence nor pulsating with throbbing melodrama. While no puritan, Ozu's treatment of sex is tasteful, not exploitative. There is scant evil to dwell on, much less neurotic behavior in his characters. The focus of his mature work is domestic drama of the middle class, whom he handles sympathetically and apolitically. Hardly a firebrand, Ozu is essentially a conservative with respect for traditional values. Even his style eschews dazzling camera movement or dynamic editing; instead the camera lingers to record without moving in what might be considered a static manner by those weaned on rock music videos. In brief, Ozu is an acquired taste, like Robert Bresson and Carl

Dreyer. It would certainly be our loss to ignore such a brilliant—and rewarding—figure, one hailed as a genius whose work Wim Wenders calls "a sacred treasure of the cinema."

The chief emphasis in Ozu's oeuvre is on characterization. Hence the avoidance of a distracting plot or pyrotechnical camera movement to enable the viewer to concentrate on his marvelous people and in doing so gain insights and much pleasure at a contemplation of the human condition. In his late work Ozu occasionally remade an earlier film, as *Floating Weeds* (1959), or simply revamped one. In the latter case, *Late Autumn* became a variation of *Late Spring*, his masterpiece of 1949. In *Late Autumn*, set in contemporary Japan, a widowed mother fears that her caring daughter in her solicitude for her is passing up an opportunity to have a fulfilling marriage. The plot is a reversal of *Late Spring* in which the father, Chishu Ryu, pretends to consider wedding again in order to nudge his attentive daughter, Setsuko Hara (the mother in *Late Autumn*), into matrimony. The director was most fortunate to be able to use his wonderful actors, such as these two, repeatedly. *Late Autumn* is charmingly written with Ozu's longtime collaborator, Kogo Noda, beautifully directed, flawlessly acted, and deserves to be better known in this country.

The film opens at an anniversary service in a temple for the husband of Akiko Miwa (Setsuko Hara), who has been dead seven years. Three middle-aged friends of the deceased, Mamiya (Shin Saburi), Taguchi (Nobuo Nakamura), and Hirayama (Ryuji Kita), notice that Akiko's attractive daughter, Ayako (Yoko Tsukasa), is of marriageable age and, subsequently, attempt to introduce her to prospective mates. Ayako, however, is not eager to rush into marriage; she is happy as she is and feels protective toward her mother, whom she doesn't want to subject to a lonely fate. The selfless Akiko, nevertheless, only wants her twenty-four-year-old daughter to be happily wedded, not to sacrifice her youth on her. The men propose that the widower Hirayama marry Akiko, thus freeing Ayako to marry. After some maladroit maneuvers on the part of the trio and misunderstanding leading to tensions—the daughter falsely believes her mother wishes to remarry, which Ayako finds repugnant—the young woman is drawn to the personable Goto (Keiji Sada). Yuriko (Mariko Okada), her girlfriend, adds to the imbroglio by calling Ayako narrow-minded and siding with what she construes to be Akiko's wishes; she approves of her widowed father's desire to take a second wife. On a trip to Nikko to visit her husband's brother (Chishu Ryu), the mother tells Ayako she really has no thoughts of wedlock, but will live with her fond memories. Ayako and Goto marry, and Akiko returns, resignedly, to her now-empty apartment.

In considering her child's welfare before her own needs, the mother acts in a wise, noble manner. One recalls C. Day-Lewis's poem "Walking Away": "And love is proved in the letting go." It is late autumn in Akiko's life, a time for nostalgia, a time to prepare for winter. Setsuko Hara is superb as the mother. Kind, graceful, delicately feminine, she is unforgettable as a woman who recognizes the trap her daughter is falling into and encourages her to find joy in a marriage of her own. Her radiance will linger with the spectator. Yoko Tsukasa and Mariko Okada are impressive as the young ladies.

Ozu's direction is remarkable for its simplicity, its restraint, his subtle control of his actors, and his ability to commingle in a compassionate way humor and sadness. "Life, which seems complex, suddenly reveals itself as very simple," he said, "and I wanted to show that in this film." He makes extensive use of the so-called tatami shot, a low-angled shot about three feet from the floor, approximating the eye level of a person sitting Japanese fashion on a tatami. Ideally suited for a close examination of his characters, the tatami shot is as associated with Ozu as the tracking shot is with Max Ophüls. He does not employ this shot exclusively—a misconception one frequently encounters.

The conclusion is a poignant scene. The evening of her daughter's wedding, Akiko comes back to her vacant rooms. Yuriko pays a brief call and tells her that Ayako was lucky to have such a nice mother. Alone, Akiko goes to the bedroom. In a profile shot, she stares, reflecting, sorrowful. Then in a quick close-up we see her smile with a serene and luminous expression that is overwhelming. This is a cinematic manifestation of the richly connotative Japanese phrase *mono no aware*, which may be understood as to accept humbly and tearfully the vicissitudes of life. It is a swift, yet priceless moment. Setsuko Hara is exquisite.

Late Autumn is mainly a light comedy with serious overtones of pathos. We share the amusing meddling of the professional men and enjoy the irony and gentle teasing. The theme, prevalent in much of Ozu's work, is the breaking up of the family. While the parents criticize the behavior and values of the younger generation—a gibe is made about Elvis Presley!—the director remains impartial and reveals an understanding of both points of view. For two hours we live the lives of the various characters and come to know them well. It is a quotidian world, but one that Ozu makes absorbing and enlightening.

Late Autumn arrived in America thirteen years after its initial release. Critic Stanley Kauffmann wrote of Ozu's films: "Each work is like a psalm in a book of psalms to sad, lovable, sacred life." More than a craftsman—and my personal favorite Japanese director—Ozu is truly a master whose films are to be savored. *Late Autumn* ought to serve well as an introduction to his work, an appealing, delightful, and profound film.

Portrait of the three women who dominate the film: the mother *(center)*, her daughter, Ayako *(right)*, and her companion, Yuri (Mariko Okada). These first three stills illustrate Ozu's idiosyncratic, low-angled tatami shot.

At a Buddhist commemoration service for her late husband *(left to right)*: the widowed mother (Setsuko Hara), her daughter, Ayako (Yoko Tsukasa), family friend Taguchi (Nobuo Nakamura), and her brother-in-law (Chishu Ryu).

The theme of generational conflict affects Taguchi and his wife (Kuniko Miyake) as well.

The wedding photograph of Ayako and Goto, her husband (Keiji Sada).

6

LAST YEAR AT MARIENBAD

L'Année Derniére à Marienbad

FRANCE/ITALY / 1961

Terra Film/Société Nouvelle des Films Cormoran/Precitel/Como Films/Argos Films/Les Films Tamara Cinétel/Silver Films (Paris) Cineriz (Rome)

CREDITS

Director: Alain Resnais; *Assistant directors:* Jean-Pierre Léon, Volker Schlöndorff; *Producers:* Pierre Courau, Raymond Froment; *Screenwriter:* Alain Robbe-Grillet; *Cinematographer:* Sacha Vierny (black and white, Dyaliscope); *Music:* Francis Seyrig, performed by organist Marie-Louise Girod; *Editors:* Henri Colpi, Jasmine Chasney; *Art director:* Jacques Saulnier; *Running time:* 94 minutes; *16mm rental source:* New Yorker; *Videocassette:* Connoisseur.

CAST

The Stranger (X): Giorgio Albertazzi; *The Woman (A):* Delphine Seyrig; *The Husband or Escort (M):* Sacha Pitoëff; with Françoise Bertin, Luce Garcia-Ville, Héléna Kornel, Françoise Spira, Karin Toeche-Mittler, Pierre Barbaud, Wilhelm von Deek, Jean Lanier, and Gérard Lorin.

The first feature of French director Alain Resnais (1922–   ), *Hiroshima, Mon Amour* (1959), proved an international hit. Innovative and unusual, the film led the director to search for more experimental projects. Resnais was impatient with the conventions of the popular film, which, he said, restricted one to "straight-line plots in which nothing was left unclear, unsettling, or unexplained, with every shot justified by a link to strictest cause and effect." His meeting with Alain Robbe-Grillet was indeed fortuitous, for the chief male exponent of the French *nouveau roman* ("new novel"), which had emerged in the 1950s, agreed to prepare a scenario for him, which became *Last Year at Marienbad*. Among the tenets of the practitioners of the "new novel" are a skepticism of our knowledge of "reality"; an emphasis on description rather than exposition; a disdain for psychological analysis of character; an employment of the most tenuous of "plots" since causality is difficult to ascertain; and a replacement of chronology with a truer depiction of the ways the mind works in regulating past, present, future, or conditional. Robbe-Grillet complained that people "feel the work of art is made to explain the world to them, to provide them with reassurance . . . . If the world is so complex, then we must re-create its complexity."

For once the aims of the director complemented perfectly those of the screenwriter. Resnais declared he wished "to construct a film on a foundation other than the 'story,' to invent forms that will imperceptibly but effectively stir the spectator, apart from any external meaning, through the sheer impact of these forms." The characters would be presented without psychological clarification, and the work, he said, would be "nonchronological." The director stressed his major point of departure: "The camera is placed not in reality but in the minds of the characters." After the film's coup at the Venice Film Festival, Resnais would have further worldwide acclaim along with endless critical controversy and analyses. One of the purest cinematic films ever made, *Last Year at Marienbad* continues to intrigue subsequent generations with its fluid direction and distinguished screenplay and has justly received classic status.

Since our understanding of what "happens" in the film is debatable and "open" to every viewer, the following synopsis is, of necessity, tentative. I have employed the scenarist's practice of referring to his unnamed characters by letters. The movie begins with arresting tracking shots of some rich, baroque château while the voice of X (Giorgio Albertazzi) describes this singular and enigmatic place, with frequent repetitions, then subsides as we cut to a performance for the guests of a play, *Rosmer*, whose story line foreshadows the film's plot. We soon perceive X, who notices the lovely, elegantly coutured A (Delphine Seyrig) seen with the older, somber M (Sacha Pitoëff) to whom she may or may not be married. Through much of the film X tries to convince A that they had met a year ago at Frederiksbad (or Marienbad perhaps), had become lovers, and that he had respected A's plea

X imagines A in her bedroom at a critical point in her life. The ever-changing ornamentation in the chamber undermines his credibility, according to Alain Robbe-Grillet: "When the room has an extraordinarily complicated decor, we are probably watching a rather unreliable image."

One of the many shots of X (Giorgio Albertazzi) unceasingly attempting to lead A (Delphine Seyrig) to believe that they had been lovers last year and planned to run away together at this time.

to postpone their elopement until now. A finds his claims droll, completely denies the many scenes he "recollects" (which we see), but gradually yields to his powerful inducement. This results in a state of crisis: Should she remain in her safe and ordered world with M or set forth with the passionate X for an unknown fate? An imagined scene has

One of the frequent scenes at Frederiksbad of A, X, and the mysterious, portentous statue.

A hypothetical scene in which the forbidding M (Sacha Pitoëff) shoots A to prevent her from leaving him. But whose fantasy is this? A's? Or X's?

M shoot A, who is deserting him. Recurringly, M subdues X in a strange game played with cards, matchsticks, dominoes. A implores M to keep her from going, but he feels it's too late. Finally A departs with X into the labyrinthine gardens. In a long shot of the darkened mansion the voice of X states that although "it seemed, at first glance, impossible to get lost here," they, in truth, were now disappearing into the night. . . .

Thanks to Robbe-Grillet's clever, yet elusive, writing, we are nonplussed when it comes to the matter of characterization. The author wrote: "We know absolutely nothing about them, nothing about their lives." Only when the viewer decides on how to interpret the film would he then define who these figures are. The late Delphine Seyrig, with her delicate beauty, was most effective as the ambiguous heroine A in this, her first, feature film. Were she not so ethereal, she simply wouldn't be believable in the role. Giorgio Albertazzi, from the Italian stage, plays X with a fervent intensity; Sacha Pitoëff, from the Parisian theater, captures a melancholy, perhaps vampirish M. Resnais suc-

cessfully brought off a daring and brilliantly imaginative film. His beautiful tracking shots seen on a wide screen are truly hypnotic. The director confessed that he aimed to evoke the fascinating allure of the silent cinema. Enhanced with the haunting music of Francis Seyrig (Delphine's brother), the exquisite photography of Sacha Vierny, the outstanding sets of Jacques Saulnier, and the impeccable editing of the Colpis, *Last Year at Marienbad* is a challenging and unforgettable visual experience whose impact has not diminished over the years.

From its baffling, nonlinear narration; its mannequinlike characters who walk, talk, even dance in a highly stylized manner (on occasion "freezing" in midframe); its confusing treatment of time; its circular structure—does it end at the point where it began? (X's commencing recitation starts with "Once again—I walk on, once again, down these corridors"); its surrealistic tendencies summoning our intuitive rather than our rational faculties; we may deduce that we are watching a dream, perhaps a recurring dream—but through whose mind? X's? A's? M's? Is the garden a cul-de-sac, as much of a labyrinth as the hotel? There have been countless interpretations of the film— one even wonders what a Marxist reading would produce. Resnais admitted that it "is open to all the myths" and invites us to "complete the meaning." Curiously, the director feels that the lovers did meet the year before, while the screenwriter regards X as a liar. No wonder that critic Dwight MacDonald described the work as "the *Finnegans Wake* of the movies." Although dismissed by some as pretentious and empty, this film, which its director said "looks like a statue and sounds like an opera," is not an aesthetic tease, but a stunning and provocative experiment that Resnais considered "a protestation against the uncertainties and confusion of life." Those seeing *Last Year at Marienbad* for the first time might echo Robbe-Grillet's initial response: "I found it far more beautiful than I had imagined. I recognized it as my film, but it had become marvelous."

HONORS

Golden Lion for Best Film, Venice Film Festival (1961)
Prix Méliès (1961)
Nominated for an Oscar for Best Story and Screenplay, Written Directly for the Screen (1962)

7

THE SOUND
OF TRUMPETS

Il Posto

ITALY / 1961

Twenty-Four Horses Production

CREDITS

Director and screenwriter: Ermanno Olmi; *Producer:*
Alberto Soffientini; *Cinematographer:* Lamberto Caimi
(black and white); *Music:* Pier Emilio Bassi; *Editor:*
Carla Colombo; *Art director:* Ettore Lombardi; *Running
time:* 90 minutes; *16mm rental source:* Films Inc.

CAST

Domenico Cantoni: Sandro Panzeri; *Antonietta:* Loredana Detto; *Psychologist:* Tullio Kezich; *Old Woman:*
Mara Revel.

Every now and then a low-budget, unheralded
foreign film opens, receives critical applause but
no audience—and is soon forgotten. But it has
power and stays alive in the memory. And when
reseen many years later, it retains its impact and
deserves to be remembered and, for many, discovered. Such a film is the second feature of the Italian
director Ermanno Olmi (1931–   ), *The Sound of
Trumpets,* an awkward title (which only has significance in an ironic sense) for the prosaic Italian
one, *Il Posto* or *The Job.* This type of film critics
like to describe as a gem, which it certainly is.
Olmi made a series of short documentaries for the
Edisonvolta Company before completing his first
feature, *Time Stood Still* (1959). In *The Sound of
Trumpets,* as in his other films, he demonstrated
that neorealism was still a vital cinematic style
and not restricted solely to the early postwar masterpieces of Rossellini and De Sica. The economy
of Italy was booming in the 1960s; the northern
part was becoming increasingly industrialized.
Olmi would target a contemporary young man and
his relation to forces that will dominate his life.
The camera would observe carefully, and in true
neorealistic fashion the director would use non-

Domenico (Sandro Panzeri) *(center)* in the midst of taking
his examinations to get a job. His expressive eyes convey
the fear and bewilderment he's feeling.

The shy Domenico *(right)* is drawn to fellow applicant
Antonietta (Loredana Detto).

Domenico at the cheerless New Year's Eve party for the
workers. The empty chairs underscore his sense of isolation.

professional actors, employ a documentary method in staging and photography, and provide a "slice of life" in lieu of a complicated or melodramatic plot. The goal, as before, was to be honest, to reveal the truth—not the sociologist's impersonal facts but the poet's human and compassionate insight. The film was shot in Milan and realistically captures its streets, shops, dance halls, buses, and apartments. It is also, Olmi confessed, autobiographical. And in a current age of outlandish multimillion-dollar productions it is somewhat astonishing to learn that the movie cost a mere $55,000 to make.

The film consists of a series of episodes rather than a tight plot. This may make it seem banal, but Olmi renders it engrossing, even riveting. Domenico (Sandro Panzeri), fresh out of high school, lives with his family in Meda, a suburb of Milan. The film opens in the early morning on the day the youth is applying for a job in a huge but, significantly, nameless firm. His security-minded mother tells him, "Once you get there you're set for life. You'll have no more worries or responsibilities." Domenico, competing with others, takes a battery of tests and notices an attractive aspirant, Antonietta (Loredana Detto), whom he befriends. He is hired, but the only billet is for that of an errand boy. Thus, in uniform, he goes to the various offices, looks for Antonietta, and waits for a clerk position to open up. Domenico attends the office party on New Year's Eve eager to see the young lady, who'd promised to come. The celebra-

tion is a dreary disappointment, for Antonietta doesn't appear. Later a worker dies and Domenico is finally in an office, but as the film ends, we sense that the appointment will be suffocating.

Domenico is an average, typical young man. There has been such an emphasis on "security" (resulting undoubtedly from his parents' lifelong economic struggle) that he is grateful to be hired and will undeniably remain there. Though timid, he can be charming with Antonietta, who will quickly be preferring another youth. Domenico has the potential for a rich, human life—but will it be destroyed at his soul-killing post? Olmi offers some hope for him: "When the boy reaches the position at the desk before the end of the film, we realize that he has become a cog in a wheel, but if he wants to, he can still remain a free man. Freedom is not the ability to wander in the mountains or to live outside society; it is internal." With his soulful eyes, Sandro Panzeri is perfectly cast and outstanding. Olmi, like De Sica earlier, has a talent for discovering remarkable types, nonactors who project a genuineness and with whom the audience can readily identify. Loredana Detto is natural in her small role as Antonietta; she was soon to become the wife of the director.

In the noble tradition of neorealism Olmi skillfully engages us to pay attention to the comic and sorrowful aspects of our daily lives. The legions who have had to cope with inane examinations when they applied for a job can relish the director's satirical treatment of the solemn aptitude tests and the inevitable psychological exam, which the hapless Domenico struggles through. And then later when a worker dies whose situation the lad shall inherit, bundles of an unfinished novel are found in the man's desk, startling us with a glimpse at a life of frustration and sadness. Olmi scores with the telling detail: the stingy clerk who cuts his cigarettes in half to make them last longer; the thrifty wife who clips her husband's hair and hides the pile when a neighbor knocks on the door; the elderly woman reprimanded by a glum petty official for being late for the third time that month; and the "festive" New Year's Eve affair—a brilliant depiction of people straining to amuse themselves amidst a feeling of inexorable loneliness. All the touches seem right; there are no false notes or sentimentality. The most powerful scene is the climax. Relegated to an inferior desk with a bothersome lamp, Domenico at long last has his much-sought position. While the camera lingers on him in a close shot, we hear the rumbling mimeograph machine ominously getting

An opening in the office for Domenico at last! But his superior makes him give up the contested desk when another with seniority claims it.

louder and louder and perceive that he will be trapped in this heartless, menacing treadmill. We realize his vulnerability; the impact is shattering.

Olmi said that the workers, formerly farmers, no doubt regarded "the city as a place where one achieves a tranquil station in life. But this station they look toward is also the renunciation of responsibility. . . . When a person renounces responsibility, he dies." Implicit in the underside of the Italian economic "miracle" is the director's criticism of the unconscionable leaders of the technological society who are robbing their employees of their very spirit.

The Sound of Trumpets led to a distinguished career for Olmi. Faithful to the enduring spirit of neorealism, the director could say almost thirty years after this achievement, "If I lived in Rome, I'd be forced to talk about film as though it was the most important thing in the world. Life is what's important. My films don't derive from cinema (which is a very dangerous thing), but from reality, life." The fate of poor Domenico lingers with us in this rich, human film; he is unquestionably an Italian Everyman. *The Sound of Trumpets* has a universal application, and it is hoped that a new generation may be alerted to this haunting, unforgettable film.

HONORS

British Film Institute Award (1961)

8
VIRIDIANA

SPAIN/MEXICO / 1961

UNINCI FILMS 59 (SPAIN)/GUSTAVO ALATRISTE (MEXICO)

CREDITS

Director: Luis Buñuel; *Assistant directors:* Juan-Luis Buñuel, José Puyol; *Producers:* Pedro Portabella, Ricardo Muñoz Suay; *Screenwriters:* Luis Buñuel, Julio Alejandro; *Cinematographer:* José A. Aguayo (black and white); *Music:* Handel's *Messiah*, Mozart's *Requiem*, and the song "Shimmy Doll"; *Editor:* Pedro del Rey; *Art director:* Francisco Canet; *Running time:* 90 minutes; *16mm rental source:* Corinth; *Videocassette:* Hen's Tooth.

CAST

Viridiana: Silvia Pinal; *Jorge:* Francisco Rabal; *Don Jaime:* Fernando Rey; *Ramona:* Margarita Lozano; *Lucia:* Victoria Zinny; *Rita:* Teresita Rabal.

In 1960, possibly to lend a touch of legitimacy to Franco's regime or perhaps create an illusion of toleration, the Spanish government invited the maverick surrealistic director, Luis Buñuel (1900–83), the greatest Spanish filmmaker in the world, to return from his exile in Mexico (where he was surviving by making chiefly potboilers) and film again in his native country, which he had not visited since the Civil War. He desired to see his homeland once more, and the offer of a large budget, carte blanche regarding subject matter, and total freedom in the work proved irresistible despite protests from Republican émigrés, who saw his acceptance as a betrayal.

As Buñuel recalls in his autobiography, *My Last Sigh* (1982), "I decided to write my own screenplay about a woman I called Viridiana, in memory of a little-known saint I'd heard about when I was a schoolboy. As I worked, I remembered my old erotic fantasy about making love to the queen of Spain when she was drugged, and decided somehow to combine the stories." The censors approved the innocuous-seeming screenplay, and the film was shot in Madrid over two months, a luxury compared to his Mexican "quickies." For the sake of realism, the clothes of the beggars were genuine, bartered from the city's impoverished for fresh attire and then disinfected, but not cleaned. Shrewdly, Buñuel flew each day's rushes to Paris, where he later went to help edit it.

Viridiana, with the censors' sanction, amazingly represented Spain at Cannes where it caused a sensation by winning the Golden Palm. The Spanish censors were promptly fired and the film banned in Spain. Alberto Isaac's cartoon ("*Vini, Vidi, Vinci*") perfectly captures the "scandal": In the first panel Generalissimo Franco is laying the welcome mat for the arriving director. The next panel shows a smiling dictator with a ribboned box marked "Viridiana" that is ticking away as Buñuel departs. The last panel shows a humiliated El Caudillo in tatters after the "bomb" went off. *Viridiana* won Buñuel an international audience, spurring the director (whom Henry Miller called the dynamite-flinging miner of Asturias) into a late period of remarkable creativity. Its power has

The lovely Sister Viridiana (Silvia Pinal) starts to undress in her bedroom at her uncle's home.

Don Jaime (Fernando Rey) has the narcotized Viridiana in his arms. (She had catered to his whim and worn the wedding dress his wife had died in.) He plans to ravish her, but cannot bring himself to do it.

not diminished and *Viridiana* deservedly belongs among the world's classic films.

In a convent the young Sister Viridiana (Silvia Pinal) is preparing to take her final vows and to renounce the world forever. The Mother Superior insists that she pay a visit to her generous uncle, Don Jaime (Fernando Rey), who paid for her education. Dutifully she travels to his untended estate. The older man is struck by her resemblance to his late wife, who had died on her wedding night, and finds himself becoming fixated on her. Viridiana dismisses his offer of marriage, but to please him agrees to put on the aunt's wedding dress. Don Jaime has the servant Ramona (Margarita Lozano) drug her coffee. Alone with the sleeping novice, he changes his mind about violating her. The next day he lies to Viridiana that he had her the night before and therefore she must stay with him. The horrified woman packs quickly even though her uncle admits he was prevaricating. He realizes she now hates him.

At the bus station Viridiana is brought back by the police to see Don Jaime hanging from a tree. Feeling responsible for his suicide, she resolves to stay on and do the Lord's work in her own way. Jorge (Francisco Rabal), the owner's illegitimate son, is co-heir and turns up with his mistress Lucia (Victoria Zinny), who, bored, soon leaves. Viridiana collects a loathsome group of mendicants whom she believes she'll redeem. The dynamic and practical Jorge modernizes the estate, takes up with Ramona, and has nothing but contempt for what he views as Viridiana's outdated Christian charity. When the masters are away, the vagrants break into the mansion, stuff themselves with food and drink, and wreak havoc. The owners return unexpectedly. As the "leper" knocks Jorge unconscious and a tramp rapes Viridiana (the one who, earlier, wished to paint her as the Virgin!), Ramona comes back with the police. The film ends as Jorge seductively invited Viridiana to join Ramona and him in a game of cards.

The proud Viridiana is a sincere but completely naïve young woman. Frightened by life, she is prevented by circumstances from hiding away in a convent and forced to come to terms with the world, which includes accepting her sexuality. (At the farm she's loath to touch the cow's phalluslike teats). Don Jaime is a fascinating, complicated character, a cultivated man obsessed with his late bride and living in lonely isolation. Jorge is a virile,

Jorge (Francisco Rabal) admires his late father's knife while his mistress, Lucia (Victoria Zinny) looks on. Besides symbolizing his sexual power, the knife also suggests his eventual domination over the estate.

The vagabonds gather together for a photo in the manor house. A freeze-frame parody of da Vinci's *Last Supper*, this scene continues to jolt audiences.

sensible man—Viridiana's antithesis. Silvia Pinal is beautiful and persuasive as the idealistic postulant in whom hibernates a sensuous woman. Fernando Rey brings a strong screen presence and a sense of mystery to the role of Don Jaime. Francisco Rabal, with his rugged masculinity, makes Jorge a forceful character.

Buñuel's direction is masterly, both precise and economical. In just one impressive shot, for example, we see in the background the approaching official car with Viridiana inside, then the camera pans slightly to the right to reveal in the foreground the dangling body of Don Jaime. A haunting, dreamlike scene discloses the uncle trying on his wife's slippers and corset to Mozart's *Requiem*. Then to his astonishment a sleepwalking Viridiana appears, picks up ashes from the fireplace, and dumps them onto his bed. Memorable is the montage sequence in which brief shots of workers busily sawing wood, plastering a wall, etc., are intercut with those of Viridiana leading her wastrels in the Angelus. Solid, rewarding labor is pitted against seemingly ineffectual prayer. The most unforgettable and shocking scene—approximating that of Luis Buñuel's calmly slitting his mistress's eyeball in *Un Chien Andalou* (1928)—is the group photograph of the derelicts that turns out to be a travesty of da Vinci's *Last Supper*, accompanied by Handel's "Hallelujah Chorus" on a phonograph. Where, in this bestial lot, the director implies, is the "Christ in Everyman"?

The censors refused the original ending, which, Buñuel writes, "showed [Viridiana] knocking at her cousin's door, entering, and the door closing slowly behind her. . . . I had to invent a new one, which . . . was far more suggestive . . . because of its implication of a ménage à trois." One recognizes that Don Jaime's neglected estate is a microcosm for Spain itself locked like Viridiana into a medieval religion, with decadent leaders holding on to their privileges. Change and hope for the future are seen through Jorge, who, like a modern Candide, "cultivates his garden." Buñuel said, "In *Viridiana* I hold a mirror up to life," and, elsewhere, "I think that it has in it most of the themes which are closest to me." *Viridiana* is Buñuel's masterpiece, "pure" cinema with a striking impact that clearly demonstrates the director's assertion that "The cinema is a marvelous and dangerous weapon if it is in the hands of a free spirit."

HONORS

Shared Best Film, Cannes Film Festival (1961)
L'Étoile de Cristal for Prix International (1962)

9
THROUGH A GLASS DARKLY

Sasom i en Spegel

SWEDEN / 1961

SVENSK FILMINDUSTRI

CREDITS

Director and screenwriter: Ingmar Bergman; *Assistant director:* Lenn Hjortzberg; *Producer:* Allan Ekelund; *Cinematographer:* Sven Nykvist (black and white); *Music:* J. S. Bach, Suite No. 2 in D Minor for violoncello; *Editor:* Ulla Ryghe; *Art director:* P. A. Lundgren; *Running time:* 91 minutes; *16mm rental source:* Janus; *Videocassette:* Orion.

CAST

Karin: Harriet Andersson; *David:* Gunnar Bjornstrand; *Martin:* Max von Sydow; *Minus:* Lars Passgard.

Through such films as *The Seventh Seal* (1957) and *Wild Strawberries* (1957), Swedish director Ingmar Bergman (1918–) gained an international reputation, becoming even a cult figure. "I can't help thinking," he said in 1956, "that I am working with an instrument so refined that with it, it would be possible for us to illuminate the human soul with an infinitely more vivid light, to unmask it even more brutally and to annex to our field of knowledge new domains of reality." This statement anticipated Bergman's deep involvement with psychological exploration, for which the motion picture, with its use of probing close-ups in the dreamlike atmosphere of a darkened theater, is ideally suited, and which resulted in a brilliant trilogy, the first film of which is *Through a Glass Darkly*. He had not set out to create a trilogy; only after *The Silence* (1963) following *Winter Light* (1962) did he realize that the three films were thematically linked with the question of God's existence.

Through a Glass Darkly had a long gestation. In

The Devil's Wanton (1948), an episode in which the heroine sees patterns on the wallpaper transformed into various shapeless faces was cut. "By and by," the director said, "I thought I'd make a film about someone who floated quite naturally in and out of some wallpaper, and I must have seen Harriet Andersson before me as just that person." That was the starting point around which he concretized the drama, as he said, of a "human being who really was in process of slipping away." Bergman described *Through a Glass Darkly*, originally called *The Wallpaper*, along with the two other films of the trilogy and *Persona* (1966) as "chamber works" patterned after the experimental, psychologically astute chamber plays by the great Swedish playwright August Strindberg for the Intimate Theatre in Stockholm. "They are chamber music," Bergman declared, "music in which, with an extremely limited number of voices and figures, one explores the essence of a number of motifs." Traditional character conflict is emphasized less than the dominant leitmotiv; time is condensed—the action in *Through a Glass Darkly* covers a period of twenty-four hours. Harriet Andersson, Gunnar Bjornstrand, and Max von Sydow, long associated with the director's films, were recruited for the movie, which was shot between July and September 1960 in Stockholm and Faro, a small island in the Baltic Sea. Beautifully written, acted, directed, and photographed, *Through a Glass Darkly* is one of Bergman's most rewarding films.

David (Gunnar Bjornstrand), a middle-aged widower who's a writer longing for fame, has returned to his island vacation home for a brief while to join his daughter, Karin (Harriet Andersson), recently released from a mental hospital; Martin (Max von Sydow), her concerned physician husband; and Minus (Lars Passgard), David's fifteen-year-old son suffering from his father's indifference. After dinner David absents himself and breaks down sobbing in his room. Minus stages a morality play he wrote with some pointed, satirical references to his father's thirst for acclaim. That night Karin wakes up early and heads to an unused room upstairs, drawn to the wallpaper, which "whispers" to her. She visits her insomniac father and, when he leaves, discovers his diary. She reads that her condition is hopeless and that, in spite of himself, he's fascinated with her deterioration, which he can use as a writer. Upset, she wakes up Martin, who tries to console her.

Later that morning while David and Martin set sail for supplies, Karin teases Minus, then takes him to her special chamber and confides that she's

Martin (Max von Sydow) tries to comfort his troubled wife, Karin (Harriet Andersson).

A sexually tense Minus (Lars Passgard) apologizes to his sister, Karin, for his sudden display of anger after she playfully grabbed his girlie magazine.

expecting God to appear through a door there. Torn between her delusional world and reality, she informs her frightened brother that she has chosen the former. In the boat, Martin confronts David with his insensitivity regarding the diary; the author then reveals that he had attempted suicide

In the abandoned vessel David (Gunnar Bjornstrand) confesses his shortcomings as a father to his distraught daughter, Karin.

with life. A genetic reason is provided for Karin's mental illness since she apparently inherited it from her mother. Her incest with her brother is shocking but not gratuitous for it demonstrates her destructive capabilities. Significantly, when she calms down, she requests to be institutionalized. Gunnar Bjornstrand plays David, a man who sought to escape his domestic responsibilities through his craft, with assuredness. As Karin, the young woman slipping into the vortex of schizophrenia, Harriet Andersson gives a shattering performance.

Bergman's direction is intense, economical—every shot necessary as he builds to a devastating climax. Sven Nykvist's crisp photography enhances the vivid drama. The title comes from the First Epistle of Paul the Apostle to the Corinthians (13:12): "For now we see through a glass, darkly; but then face to face." With God after death all barriers shall be removed. The director was later to refer to his trilogy as a "reduction," not in the sense of "diminishing" but rather as a "restora-

in Switzerland, but out of the void was born a reawakened love for his family. In the rain, Karin takes refuge in the wreck of a fishing boat. Minus finds her and she seduces the sexually perturbed boy. The two men return. Minus tells them her condition worsened; Martin telephones for an ambulance. Alone together, Karin tells her father what happened with her brother when she was out of control; David asks her forgiveness for neglecting his family for his "art." Later Martin finds his wife in the wallpapered room, kneeling expectantly. As the medical helicopter descends, the door opens from the vibrations and Karin shrieks with horror. Subdued with an injection, she relates that the god who emerged from the doorway was an ugly spider with cold eyes who tried to penetrate her. Martin departs with her. David attempts to solace his confused son by stating his newfound belief in the divine power of love. Minus is ecstatic that his father has finally spoken to him.

The character of David—the cold, self-absorbed artist tormented by his inability to love those who depend upon him—is a recurrent figure in Bergman's films. Nonetheless, in his speech about love to his son he indicates that he's coming to terms

tion" from illusion to a formerly held truth; and to *Through a Glass Darkly*, specifically, as "certainly achieved." The "certainty achieved" is the concept that "God is love," which David tries to convince his skeptical son to accept at the film's end. This tenuous belief seems to be undercut, however, by the disturbing parallel revelation of Karin's perverted vision. Although Bergman was to reject his theological position—feeling more comfortable in raising questions than in presenting solutions—the fact remains that *Through a Glass Darkly* depicts the state of contemporary man—his isolation (geographical, psychological, and spiritual), his inability to love or to communicate—with honesty, outstanding artistry, and an impact that makes the film alive and still provocative after thirty years.

HONORS

Oscar for Best Foreign Language Film (1961); nominated in addition for Best Story and Screenplay, Written Directly for the Screen (1962)

10
JULES AND JIM

Jules et Jim

FRANCE / 1962

LES FILMS DU CARROSSE/S.E.D.I.F. (SOCIÉTÉ D'EXPLOITATION ET DE DISTRIBUTION DE FILMS)

CREDITS

Director: François Truffaut; *Assistant directors:* Georges Pellegrin, Robert Bobert; *Producer:* Marcel Berbert; *Screenwriters:* François Truffaut, Jean Gruault, based on the novel by Henri-Pierre Roché (1953); *Cinematographer:* Raoul Coutard (black and white, Franscope); *Music:* Georges Delerue; *Song:* "Le Tourbillon," words and music by Boris Bassiak (Serge Rezvani); *Editor:* Claudine Bouché; *Art director:* Fred Capel; *Running time*: 110 minutes; *16mm rental source:* Films Inc.; *Videocassette:* CBS/Fox.

CAST

Catherine: Jeanne Moreau; *Jules:* Oskar Werner; *Jim:* Henri Serre; *Thérèse:* Marie Dubois; *Gilberte:* Vanna Urbino; *Albert:* Boris Bassiak; *His Friend:* Dannielle Bassiak; *Sabine:* Sabine Haudepin; *Narrator:* Michel Subor.

Jules and Jim, his third feature, is without question the most treasured film of the brilliant and immensely popular French director François Truffaut (1932–84). While a young man he discovered the novel by Roché from which the movie is derived and vowed to film it one day if he ever managed to become a filmmaker. By 1960 he felt confident enough with his film experience to tackle a conceivably difficult project that dealt with the close friendship of two writers, both of whom love a remarkable woman in the early decades of the century.

Dilettante and art dealer Henri-Pierre Roché (1879–1959), in his seventies, drew on his diary, which he began in 1905, to fashion a novel based to an extent on his life. The director said, "Starting

Karin reacts hysterically after the "visitation from God," while her husband, Martin, watches helplessly.

The first morning at their vacation home: Catherine (Jeanne Moreau) greets Jules (Oskar Werner) *(right)* while perched above them is Jim (Henri Serre). A visualization of the emerging triangle.

Portrait of the bewitching Catherine at the beach.

out with the most scandalous situation there can be—two men and a woman living together through a whole lifetime—one had to bring off a film about love that would be as 'pure' as possible, and to do that through the innocence of the three

characters, their moral integrity, their tenderness, and above all their sense of decency." In spite of the myriad alterations in transposing an unwieldy book spanning twenty years into a workable script, screenwriters Truffaut and Jean Gruault succeeded in remaining faithful to its spirit and evoking a genuine feeling for youth and love, which the novel captures strikingly. They avoided making a static, literary film and instead produced an exceptionally cinematic one. Truffaut and Gruault retained the writer's perceptive omniscient narrator, who distances the viewer from the potentially volatile material and provides a provocative commentary on the characters. The extraordinarily gifted Jeanne Moreau was inspiredly cast as the heroine Catherine. Oskar Werner, the distinguished actor from the Austrian and German stage, played Jules, while Henri Serre, found in a left-bank theater, was recruited to portray his devoted companion Jim. The movie was a huge triumph and won awards at many festivals. Created at the zenith of Truffaut's talent in his youthful period, exquisitely written, acted, directed, photographed, and scored, the classic *Jules and Jim* has not dated and continues to exert its radiant spell on each new generation of film lovers.

The year is 1912. In Paris two young bohemian writers form an intimate bond: Jules, (Oskar Werner), a German, and Jim, (Henri Serre), a Frenchman. When the former's friend Albert (Boris Bassiak) presents spellbinding slides of a woman's head sculpted in stone, the pair head to see it on a Greek island and are entranced by her smile. Back in Paris they encounter Catherine (Jeanne Moreau), a Frenchwoman whose smile bears an uncanny resemblance to the statue's. The trio vacation in the south of France and Jules asks her to marry him. Later at home Catherine defends the progressive heroine of a Swedish play they've just seen, and when Jules spouts a facile tirade against women, she abruptly plunges into the Seine. En route home, her smile is victorious. Soon the two telephone Jim to announce their plans to wed in Germany. The start of World War I divides the men. After the devastating conflict, Jim visits the couple, who now have a chalet near the Rhine and a little girl, Sabine (Sabine Haudepin). Jim is informed by his compliant friend that Catherine has been unfaithful and has even left once for six months.

Despite obvious misgivings, Jim is drawn to the mercurial woman. Afraid of losing her altogether, Jules encourages Jim to marry his wife. The pair become lovers but are forced to separate when Jim's Paris publishers want him. There he dallies with his long-term mistress, Gilberte (Vanna Urbino). Catherine, feeling rejected, has an escapade with Albert, who desires marriage. In Germany Catherine and Jim patch things up, but disturbed over her inability to bear a child—which she thinks would validate her union with Jim—she insists they part for three months. He thinks their affair is over but learns by letter that Catherine's pregnant. However, Jules soon writes that she suffered a miscarriage and doesn't want to see Jim anymore. Jules and Catherine move to France and come upon Jim. Alone with her, he presents an honest critique of their shortcomings and reveals his decision to espouse Gilberte; Catherine threatens him with her revolver. The trio unexpectedly run into each other in 1933 at a theater showing a newsreel of Nazis burning books. In a café Catherine cautions a seated Jules to observe attentively and then, smiling perversely, steers her car with an unsuspecting Jim alongside across a destroyed bridge into a river, killing them both. The film ends as a disburdened Jules attends their cremation and interment.

Setting letters that she calls "lies" ablaze, packing vitriol for a pleasure trip—Catherine is most certainly a puzzling woman. There is scant exposition about her save that her father was an aristocrat while her mother was English and poor. As a result she becomes an intriguing enigma. She has a passionate craving for independence, identifying herself with the character in the Swedish play: "She wants to be free. She invents her life every moment." Catherine is for Jules a symbol of Woman, a visionary goddess who must be worshipped and treated as if she were a queen. She consents to marry him knowing that she will be treated royally. This need for dominance, for an absolute commitment from her lover, fuels her tyrannical tendencies and helps explain in part her tragic gesture when Jim decides to withdraw from her tenacious grasp. Truffaut regarded her as probably the most powerful personage he had created for the screen. It was Jules's "generosity, his innocence, his vulnerability," as Catherine states, that led her to accept him in marriage; nevertheless, he lacks, she adds, "natural authority." He sadly comes to realize that he's not the man she needs and resigns himself to being a cuckold. Jim is more sophisticated, more assured with women than his friend. Not content to find satisfaction solely with the quiet, docile Gilberte, he tells Catherine, "I

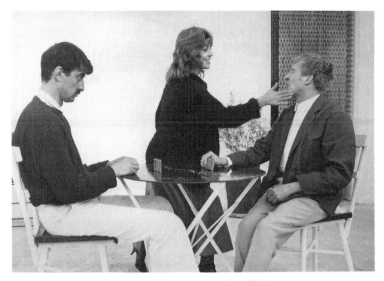

Peeved that she's being ignored by the men absorbed in their game of dominoes, Catherine playfully but maliciously slaps Jules soundly while Jim looks on.

Jim tenderly strokes the face of Catherine, a prelude to their tempestuous affair.

After the cinema, while Jules arranges his wife's scarf, Catherine stares at Jim (off-camera), possibly contemplating their fateful ride that afternoon.

feel the need for adventure, for risks"; after their first night together, the narrator reports that he was "enslaved." It is thanks to the controlled direction and splendid performances that regardless of these characters' weaknesses—the men's self-serving deportment and Catherine's monstrous cruelty—we find them fascinating, attractive, even lovable. By turns willful, sweet, impulsive, and ardent, Jeanne Moreau perfectly embraces all the facets of the richly textured Catherine and persuades us that these two men would certainly devote their lives to her. Oskar Werner and Henri Serre memorably incarnate their characters; *Jules and Jim* is the best-known work of this adept trio.

Tracking, pan, tilt, zoom shots, superimpositions, spectacular long shots taken from a helicopter, the use of a hand-held camera and the freeze-frame—Truffaut revels in his medium, achieving a visually arresting film dense with allusions to cinema, literature, and painting. After the initial frenzied and effervescent scenes of his unconventional heroes, his skillful, riotous direction shifts; an "allegro" style is replaced with an "andante" one as the characters' youthful spirits soon confront an inevitable, slow attrition. Since Truffaut disdained the use of makeup to show his personages aging, we glimpse the passage of time through the use of newsreels and Picasso prints from the various stages of his career. Raoul Coutard contributed outstanding photography, especially in evoking a fog-steeped landscape, while Georges Delerue composed unforgettable music alternately sprightly and poignant.

There are no models for the lifestyle of Catherine, Jules, and Jim, and we are free to judge them brave explorers or unthinking hedonists. Is it possible to live in total freedom? What, then, about responsibilities, the demands of being a mature adult? These three are no mere triflers in their quest, but dedicate their lives to their goal and live at such a fever-pitch intensity that we cannot but respect and admire them, acting out a myth of living free that strikes deep chords in many viewers. Attempting to live without restrictions, they wind up inflicting pain on each other; ultimately two are destroyed. Jim reflects, "It is a noble thing to want to rediscover the laws of humanity; but how convenient it must be to conform to existing rules. We played with the very sources of life, and we failed." There is as much an avoidance of oversimplification of the issues involved as there is of sentimentality or sensationalism. As with all great poetry there is an evocation of mystery, awe—even terror. A rare blend of comedy and tragedy, *Jules and Jim* endures as an astonishing, beloved, and influential masterpiece. In 1979, Truffaut said, "In all my twenty years of cinema, the filming of *Jules and Jim*, thanks to Jeanne Moreau, remains a luminous memory, the most luminous." It is luminous for us as well—and indelible.

HONORS

L'Etoile de Cristal for Grand Prix and to Jeanne Moreau for Best Actress (1962)

11
ECLIPSE

L'Eclisse

ITALY/FRANCE / 1962

INTEROPA FILM/CINERIZ (ROME) PARIS FILM PRODUCTION (PARIS)

CREDITS

Director: Michelangelo Antonioni; *Assistant directors:* Franco Indovina, Gianni Arduini; *Producers:* Raymond and Robert Hakim; *Screenwriters:* Michelangelo Antonioni, Tonino Guerra, Elio Bartolini, Ottiero Ottieri; *Cinematographer:* Gianni Di Venanzo (black and white); *Music:* Giovanni Fusco; *Editor:* Eraldo Da Roma; *Art director:* Piero Polletto; *Running time:* 130 minutes; *16 mm rental source:* Museum of Modern Art; *Videocassette:* Connoisseur.

CAST

Vittoria: Monica Vitti; *Piero:* Alain Delon; *Riccardo:* Francisco Rabal; *Vittoria's Mother:* Lilla Brignone; *Stock Agent Ercoli:* Louis Seigner; *Anita:* Rossana Rory; *Marta:* Mirella Ricciardi; *Drunk:* Cyrus Elias.

Eclipse is the completion of a thematically related trilogy by Italian director Michelangelo Antonioni (1912–), the first two films of which, *L'Avventura* (1960)—which established his international reputation—and *La Notte* (1961), began his penetrating analysis of modern Italian society. The focus in the finale of his triptych would be on an educated, upper-middle-class woman (portrayed by Monica Vitti) and her emotional relationships. "I choose intellectual types," Antonioni said, "mainly because they have a greater awareness of what is happening to them, and also because they have a more refined sensibility, a more subtle sense of intuition through which I can filter the kind of reality I am interested in expressing." This time the setting would be Rome and the director could once more dramatize his recurring themes of contemporary alienation, lack of communication, and emotional desolation as well as criticize savagely the crazed pursuit of wealth represented by the stock exchange.

Antonioni is a cerebral director whose "distancing" techniques—almost plotless films, scant motivation provided for his characters, a bleak analytical tone—undercut an emotional response and instead stimulate the critical faculties of the audience. The main emphasis is on characterization—"I put cameras inside my characters to express their emotion," Antonioni said—and an incisive evocation of mood. The influence of his "minimalist" style has been enormous. An innovative director who originated a personal style, Antonioni was impelled by what he has referred to as "a compulsion to look pitilessly right to the bottom" of human frailty, and he created with *Eclipse* a revelatory and unusual work of art.

The plot is little more than a situation. The film opens as Vittoria, (Monica Vitti), a young Roman woman, terminates her affair with Riccardo (Francisco Rabal). Later she visits her mother (Lilla Brignone), who plays the stock market avidly, and meets Piero (Alain Delon), a young stockbroker who revels in his hectic work. Soon a financial crisis produces panic; Vittoria's mother suffers losses. While Piero calls on Vittoria, a drunk (Cyrus Elias) steals his car and plunges it into a river. Vittoria is uncertain about Piero, who pursues her aggressively. They become lovers and agree to see each other later on a Sunday evening. In a series of shots that conclude the film we do not see either of them at their place of rendezvous.

Vittoria, adrift in a world without meaning, detached from the feverish speculations of her mother, who's frightened of poverty, needing love but fearful of getting hurt again, is a most engaging character. Ironically, although she is a translator by profession, she has difficulty communicating her feelings. After their breakup, she bears no rancor toward Riccardo and even requests that a mutual friend help him in this difficult period. While she's attracted to Piero, he displays such

Vittoria is doubtful about her association with Piero.

Piero (Alain Delon) *(center, in profile)* in the midst of the frantic activity of the Rome stock market, which he thrives on.

A pause at the stock exchange to pay respect to a deceased broker. The shot is framed as if to imply that beyond the pillars the multitude is worshiping at the Temple of Mammon. Vittoria (Monica Vitti) *(left foreground)* is next to her mother (Lilla Brignone).

After the empty rhetoric of promising to "see each other tomorrow—and the day after tomorrow," Piero and Vittoria make a date for that evening, which, apparently, neither keeps.

callousness, being concerned about his dented, sopping automobile with no thought for the poor drowned driver, that she is cautious about their involvement. Musing on escape, she says, "Here everything is so complicated. Even love." Self-absorbed, thirsty for power and money, Piero is the ultimate yuppie. Antonioni said that the youth "might be the one love of her life, but this man is locked up in his world of investments, speculations. He is lost in the convulsive activity of the market." That first Piero, then near the end, Vittoria, are succinctly shot behind the same fence suggests similar entrapment.

Attractive, sensitive, intelligent, Monica Vitti is fascinating to watch, especially when she shifts moods within the same shot or conveys an abyss of ennui. Her director was most accurate when he said that she "has an extremely expressive face." Monica Vitti adds depth and nuance to the character of Vittoria; she became the quintessential Antonioni heroine whose countenance mirrors the anxieties of our times. The handsome Alain Delon is convincing as the cool and shallow Piero; Francisco Rabal is impressive as Riccardo. Veteran French actor Louis Seigner lends strong support in his role as a stock agent.

Antonioni's direction is beautifully controlled and individualistic. An idiosyncratic shot is his tracking his characters walking. "I felt," he said, "the best way to capture their thoughts, their state of mind, was to follow them around physically with the camera. Thus the long shots, the continuous panning, etc." Since so little exposition is provided, the viewer must work with the film to flesh out backgrounds—to determine for example why Vittoria left Riccardo—interpret glances, gestures, paintings on a wall, books displayed—any pertinent clue to contribute to an understanding of the personages. What could have proved a tedious movie is engrossing and compelling.

Eclipse is replete with memorable scenes, such as the opening sequence in which Vittoria decides to sever her liaison with Riccardo. A typical director would stress dialogue in a heated confrontation, but Antonioni, instead, relies on images with limited conversation to achieve his effects. Thus we see the woman pacing back and forth in a state of crisis as a loud fan drones in the early morning and the male glowers from his seat. At times there's a faraway look in Vittoria's eyes; she is bored, restless, and enervated. A vast amount of tension builds even in the silences. Remarkable, too, is the scene in the stock market when the frenzy halts to honor a broker who recently died with a few "moments of silence"—during which we hear phones ringing incessantly and an impervious Piero whisper to Vittoria, "One minute here costs billions"—only to resume minutes later at its normal furor, which the director catches with a documentary realism and scathing reproof.

"The world today is ruled by money," Antonioni said, "greed for money, fear of money. This leads to a dangerous passitivity towards problems of the spirit." And, lastly, the striking montage of the area where the couple were to meet that closes the film, to the eerie accompaniment of Fusco's music. A passenger exiting from a bus reads a newspaper with "The Atomic Age" in headlines and a lead article titled "Peace Is Weak." The sense of anxiety mounts with recurring shots of the deserted trysting place of the lovers, the approaching darkness, an extreme close-up of a person's troubled face, and as the music crescendos, the concluding apparition of the glare of a streetlamp. A daring and poetic tour de force. "I was trying for a sort of decomposition of things," the director said of this acclaimed coda.

Besides the astronomical explanations of the term *eclipse* (which would indicate a temporary condition), the secondary definitions, cited in various dictionaries as "a falling into obscurity, decline" or "any obscuration of light," add connotative richness to the title. Ermanno Olmi has said of Antonioni, "He is our most lucid director, the first one to see the weakness and emptiness of our world." *Eclipse*, this "story of imprisoned sentiments," as its director said, is like a cinematic *Waste Land* and remains powerful and disturbing.

HONORS

Special Jury Prize, Cannes Film Festival (1962)

12
KNIFE IN THE WATER

Noz w Wodzie

POLAND / 1962

Film Polski

CREDITS

Director: Roman Polanski; *Assistant directors:* Andrzej Kostenko, Kuba Goldberg; *Producer:* Stanislaw Zylewicz; *Screenwriters:* Roman Polanski, Jerzy Skolimowski, Jakub Goldberg; *Cinematographer:* Jerzy Lipman (black and white); *Music:* Krzystof T. Komeda; *Editor:* Halina Prugar; *Running time:* 94 minutes; *16mm rental source:* Janus; *Videocassette:* CBS/Fox.

CAST

Andrzej: Leon Niemczyk; *Christine:* Jolanta Umecka; *The Young Man:* Zygmunt Malanowicz.

Knife in the Water marked a brilliant feature debut by the young Polish director Roman Polanski (1933–   ) that would assist him in earning an international reputation and a successful, if troubled, film career in England, Hollywood, and France. In his autobiography, *Roman* (1984), the director presents a lively, often amusing, account of the difficulties encountered both in the producing and then in the anxiety-ridden shooting of this, his sole Polish full-length film. An earlier screenplay was rejected by the Ministry of Culture since "it lacked social commitment." Subsequently, after plans to shoot it in France fell through, the Communist-controlled Polish film industry finally gave him approval.

Filming took place in the summer of 1961. Leon Niemczyk was recruited from the stage to play the comfortable journalist husband; Zygmunt Malanowicz was a Method-trained young actor engaged to portray the nameless hitchhiker (Polanski wanted to take this role but was discouraged from doing so). The director claims to have sighted Jolanta Umecka at a municipal swimming pool in Warsaw; she would appear as the fleshly wife. After the movie was shot it was discovered that the original sound could not be used. Niemczyk did his own postsynchronization; an actress dubbed Miss Umecka, while Polanski himself supplied the voice of the young man.

"The members of Poland's *nomenklatura*," Polanski wrote, "were starting to get rich quickly at this period, and *Knife* was, among other things, an attack on privilege." The film was criticized in Poland—*Youth Flag*, the official young-Communist magazine, wrote that "the director has nothing of interest to say about contemporary man"—and spottily distributed. The individualistic, nonconforming Polanski seemed unemployable. Fortunately, the film won foreign awards and the director was able to leave and continue his distinguished work elsewhere. *Knife in the Water* is a subtle, psychological film, a remarkable achievement whose impact has not diminished.

The plot is deceptively simple: On a Sunday morning Andrzej (Leon Niemczyk), an affluent, middle-aged sports reporter, and his bored, younger wife, Christine (Jolanta Umecka), are driving to their yacht when a young hitchhiker (Zygmunt Malanowicz) appears in the center of the road defying them to stop. Angrily, Andrzej shoves the youth into the rear seat and later invites him to join them for a day's sail. The driver's tone is not friendly, but gruff and authoritative. In spite of the insults thus far, the unidentified young man consents.

Throughout the day tension mounts as Andrzej continues to humiliate the stranger in various ways, asserting all the while his superiority, with only an occasional riposte from the harried youth unfamiliar with the mechanics of yachting. The contest for masculine supremacy persists, and the browbeaten young man expresses his anger by jabbing the deck with his sharp knife. Rains send them below where the contention is renewed with a game of pick-up-sticks. Christine and the hiker are slowly being attracted to each other. All prepare for sleep. Andrzej wakes up, sees the empty cabin, pockets the knife, and joins the sleepless duo on the deck. He orders the youth to start

A rare, genial moment for Andrzej (Leon Niemczyk) and his wife, Christine (Jolanta Umecka), as their young guest amuses them by holding on to the boom while dangling over the water.

Christine and the young man (Zygmunt Malanowicz) try to straighten the sloop listing in the shallow water. He holds the knife that becomes an important object in the film.

After a heated exchange, Andrzej hits the youth.

Losing his balance after the scuffle, the hiker slides apprehensively into the water. He revealed earlier that he did not know how to swim.

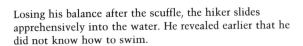

wiping up. The angry hiker demands his knife. The journalist switches the blade out, then flings the knife as the young man lurches for it; it plunges into the water. Andrzej strikes the youth, who falls in as well. The wife dives in to save him since he remarked before that he couldn't swim. The concerned husband joins in the rescue attempt. The hiker hides behind a buoy, then overhears Christine back on the boat accusing Andrzej of murder and ordering him to swim to shore to get the police. After he departs, the young man heads to the sloop. Christine does not resist his sexual advances. Later she coolly drops him off, then sails into the harbor where her husband has been waiting for her. Sadistically, she withholds the news about the lad's safety. When at last she says that he did not drown, Andrzej thinks she's lying to protect him. Irked, she reveals that she was unfaithful to him. They near the police station and stop. He wants to believe the lad's alive but cannot accept her infidelity. In a long shot we see the halted car in a freeze-frame, leading the audience to resolve the ambiguous ending.

Leon Niemczyk plays the overbearing journalist to perfection. Zygmunt Malanowicz had "the right kind of look," Polanski wrote, and is persuasive as the hiker. Jolanta Umecka is effective as the sexual bait who has no illusions left about her marriage. Polanski's direction is skillful with a display of technical virtuosity. Employing extensive medium shots and close-ups, with an infrequent long shot as a needed relief, he creates a sense of confinement and exacerbates the growing struggle between the men. His work is spare, unmelodramatic, concise, and unsentimental. Jerzy Lipman's depth-of-field photography is impressive; Krzystof T. Komeda's jazz score sharpens the mood.

A multileveled conflict is tightened dramatically by the unities of time, place, and action. There is first of all the generational hostility between the aging man and the healthy youth. When Andrzej announces that there will be a storm, the hiker sallies, "How do you know? Rheumatism?" Then there is the enmity in this allegedly "classless" society: the poor youth could well envy the older man's luxury car and yacht. There's even tension from a possible unacknowledged homosexual attraction between the pair. And apparently political bickering here as well—Andrzej, stressing the importance of discipline and defending the rigors of his helmsman's training, could easily regard askance the hiker's bohemian deportment and laxity. Perhaps each instinctively recognizes

in the other his own failings that he despises. From their initial meeting the journalist engages the far-from-innocent young man in an unrelenting power struggle. While agreeing to join them in their boat, the hiker says knowingly, "You want to carry on the game." The constant antagonism is heightened when Andrzej's jealousy is aroused as he senses the the mutual sexual interest between the youth and Christine. So shattering to his ego would be the realization of her infidelity that the wife quickly dissembles, "No more jokes like that," at the end. It is Christine who sees through the male wrangling. She accuses Andrzej of showing off before the youth and calls him a humbug whom she hates. Alone with the hiker, she says he's just like Andrzej, "only half his age, weaker, and more stupid." You're not better than him, she adds, "He was just like you and you'd like to be like him. You will be if you have the cheek." We are privy to some cruel, vicious behavior by three unsympathetic but arresting characters. *Knife in the Water* is a triangle of exceptional force and ranks with Roman Polanski's later critically praised and popular *Rosemary's Baby* (1968), *Chinatown* (1974), and *Tess* (1980).

HONORS

International Film Critics Award, Venice Film Festival (1962)
Nominated for an Oscar for Best Foreign Film (1963)

13
WINTER LIGHT

Nattvardsgasterna

SWEDEN / 1962

SVENSK FILMINDUSTRI

CREDITS

Director and screenwriter: Ingmar Bergman; *Assistant director:* Lenn Hjortzberg; *Producer:* Allan Ekelund; *Cinematographer:* Sven Nykvist (black and white); *Music:* Several traditional Swedish religious hymns; *Editor:* Ulla Ryghe; *Art director:* P. A. Lundgren; *Running time:* 80 minutes; *16mm rental source:* Janus; *Videocassette:* Orion.

After listening to an account from Mrs. Persson (Gunnel Lindblom) of the state of anxiety that her husband, Jonas (Max von Sydow) *(center)*, is in, the Reverend Tomas Ericsson (Gunnar Bjornstrand) replies that life "becomes too much for us and God is so far away."

Hearing Stravinsky's *A Psalm Symphony* on the radio during Easter helped Ingmar Bergman formulate the basic situation of what would evolve into *Winter Light.* "I'd like to make a film about a solitary church on the plains of Uppland," he had said. "Someone goes into the church, locks himself in, goes up to the altar, and says, 'God, I'm staying here until in one way or another You've proved to me You exist. This is going to be the end either of You or me!' " One morning the director awoke with a key to tightening the work-in-progress: "I felt the minister's waiting needn't continue as long as I had first thought. Just as much can happen in one or one and a half hours." The original Swedish title signifies "Guests at the

To his compassionate mistress, Marta (Ingrid Thulin), Tomas speaks of "God's silence."

CAST

Rev. Tomas Ericsson: Gunnar Bjornstrand; *Marta Lundberg:* Ingrid Thulin; *Jonas Persson:* Max von Sydow; *Karin Persson:* Gunnel Lindblom; *Algot Frovik:* Allan Edwall; *Frederik Blom:* Olof Thunberg; *Knut Aronsson:* Kolbjorn Knudsen; *Old Woman in Church:* Elsa Ebbesen; *Schoolboy:* Eddie Axberg; *Police Inspector:* Lars-Owe Carlberg.

Marta consoles the feverish Tomas near the altar in Mittsunda. Sven Nykvist achieved a striking effect of light in this studio re-created church.

Last Supper," which the English approximated with *The Communicants.*

Winter Light forms the center of the director's famous trilogy, an introspective "chamber work" set in isolated northern Sweden. While the prior *Through a Glass Darkly* had only four characters, in *Winter Light* there are just two chief figures, a minister undergoing a crisis of faith and the plain woman who loves him unreservedly. The action in the former film took place in an interval of twenty-four hours; here Bergman condenses the time to three hours, which links the Reverend Tomas Ericsson's suffering to Christ's three-hour agony on the cross. Theme and characterization are once more emphasized in this almost plotless film. Gunner Bjornstrand, Ingrid Thulin, and Max von Sydow, distinguished performers in Bergman's "stock company," are the leads in the movie,

which was shot in Dalarna and Stockholm between October 1961 and mid-January 1962. Although somewhat limited in its appeal due to its religious focus, *Winter Light* proved to be another strong, penetrating film by the world's most acclaimed auteur.

The film opens in a medieval church in Mittsunda on a November Sunday at a noon service officiated by the Rev. Tomas Ericsson (Gunnar Bjornstrand), a middle-aged widower suffering from influenza and—much graver—a loss of faith. Among the handful of worshipers are Marta (Ingrid Thulin), a frumpy, unbelieving schoolteacher who loves him resolutely; Jonas Persson (Max von Sydow), a fisherman in a state of depression; his pregnant wife (Gunnel Lindblom); and the hunchbacked sacristan Frovik (Allan Edwall). Tomas conducts the Lutheran rite without conviction. After the ceremony the Perssons stay to seek Tomas's help. For months Jonas has had a sense of foreboding ever since he learned that the Chinese might soon be acquiring nuclear weaponry; at the pastor's insistence the suicidal man promises to return shortly. With Marta, Tomas reveals his spiritual doubts. She would like him to marry her but knows he doesn't care for her. Leaving, she tells the unresponsive man that he must learn to love. Alone, a sick Tomas reads a long letter that she has given him in which she discloses her difficulty in communicating and the depth of her devotion to him, then closes his tired eyes to rest.

The following scene, the sudden appearance of Jonas, may be real or a dream. Instead of comforting him, the vicar attests to an awareness of his ineffectuality and the tatters of his belief, which finds a temporary resolution in atheism. Awake, with no one around, Tomas cries out the final words of Christ, "God, why hast thou forsaken me?" Marta comes back. They embrace, but an old woman (Elsa Ebbesen) enters to inform the clergyman that Jonas has shot himself through the head. They visit his body and then stop at Marta's home in the schoolhouse for cough medicine. There, an angry Tomas pours forth his disgust with her, then asks her to accompany him for the three P.M. vespers at Frostnas. He breaks the horrible news to Mrs. Persson. In the empty church at Frostnas, Frovik reflects to Tomas that the worst suffering of Christ on the cross was a feeling of abandonment by His Father, "God's silence." In spite of the fact that there are only the disabled verger, the bored organist Blom (Olof Thunberg), and the steadfast Marta, Tomas insists on a service and begins it with an apparently renewed affirmation.

Tomas and Marta arrive for vespers at the church in Frostnas.

In his emotional remoteness and icy demeanor, Tomas is a typical character found throughout Bergman's films who is severely criticized for an inability to love. Moreover, the doubt-ridden pastor is experiencing "the dark night of the soul." It doesn't ultimately matter whether Jonas's visit was actual or not, for in either instance Tomas would be woefully inadequate to inspirit him while he himself was in despair. Clumsy, clinging, yet loving unconditionally, the hapless Marta has been viewed by several critics as a Christ figure. While Bergman rejects this interpretation, he said, "I believe Marta constitutes the clergyman's only hope of any sort of life." Gunnar Bjornstrand is flawless as the tormented cleric; the beautiful Ingrid Thulin makes the role of the homely, subservient Marta entirely credible. Bergman directs this compelling drama with mastery. Through an extensive use of close-ups, he achieves an intimate, confessional effect. The extended shot of Marta speaking her long letter was a bold stroke, a

device he would employ again. There is an unforgettable moment when Tomas and Marta stop the car as a locomotive approaches. The noise starts to drown out his admission that he became a reverend to please his parents. A cut to the passing train shows a cargo of ore wagons shaped like coffins. A chilling touch! Sven Nykvist's superb cinematography contributes much to the aching perception of desolation.

Winter Light, which Bergman was later to describe as "certainty unmasked," was meant to be a corrective to David's concluding speech about God to his son in *Through a Glass Darkly*. When he wrote that film, the director said, "I thought I had found a real proof of God's existence: God is love." Blom mocks such outpourings as David's at the end of *Winter Light*. "I destroy that proof of God in this new film," Bergman said. "I do away with God the Papa, the God of autosuggestion, the security God." In the skillfully crafted unburdening scene with Jonas, Tomas lays to rest the image of a God who carefully shielded him from reality. "In *Winter Light* I swept my house clean," the director said. In keeping with Bergman's inclination to present problems rather than solutions, the ending is deliberately ambiguous. Is the pastor a total failure, symbolized by the deserted church, or is there optimism in his persistence to hold the service and possibly the beginnings of a more substantial belief? Bergman said of Tomas, "There stands a newly scoured vessel that can be filled by mercy. By a new image of God." Because it honestly and most artistically treats of timeless themes, *Winter Light* has not dated and remains, in every sense, a classic.

14

"8½"

Otto e Mezzo

ITALY / FRANCE / 1963

Cineriz (Rome)/Francinex (Paris)

CREDITS

Director: Federico Fellini; *Assistant director:* Guidarino Guidi; *Producer:* Angelo Rizzoli; *Screenwriters:* Federico Fellini, Ennio Flaiano, Tullio Pinelli, Brunello Rondi; *Cinematographer:* Gianni Di Venanzo (black and white); *Music:* Nino Rota; *Editor:* Leo Catozzo; *Art director:* Piero Gherardi; *Running time:* 135 minutes; *16mm rental source:* Corinth; *Videocassette:* MPI.

CAST

Guido: Marcello Mastroianni; *Luisa:* Anouk Aimée; *Claudia:* Claudia Cardinale; *Carla:* Sandra Milo; *Rossella:* Rossella Falk; *French Actress:* Madeleine Lebeau; *Gloria:* Barbara Steele; *Mario:* Mario Pisu; *Pace:* Guido Alberti; *Daumier:* Jean Rougeul; *Saraghina:* Edra Gale; *The Beautiful Unknown Woman:* Catarina Boratto; *Guido's Father:* Annibale Ninchi; *Guido's Mother:* Giuditta Rissone.

After the sensational, international critical and commercial success of *La Dolce Vita* (1960), famed Italian director Federico Fellini (1920–93) brought

In her hotel room Carla (Sandra Milo) permits her lover, Guido (Marcello Mastroianni), to alter her makeup so that she resembles a streetwalker prior to their lovemaking. The exaggerated eyebrows recall Saraghina from his youth.

off another coup with *8½*, which won even more praise for its brilliance, daring, and innovation. Its title, like an opus number in music composition, specifies which position this film represents in his oeuvre—counting *Variety Lights* (1950), which he had codirected with Alberto Lattuada, as a half plus six features and two contributions to sketch films as each a half.

After visiting the mud baths at Ischia and taking a rest cure at Chianciano, Fellini conceived the idea of making a movie about an artist in a state of crisis at a wealthy spa. Eventually the screenplay evolved into the specific dilemma of a troubled film director prior to the start of the shooting of an expensive production. As Fellini explained, Guido, the hero, "lives on two levels—reality and fantasy." On the realistic plane he is faced with personal emotional problems, bombarded with questions from his bewildered actors and staff, and full of self-doubts and uncertainty concerning a project not in clear focus that he even abandons at one point. "On the subconscious level," Fellini continues, "he recedes into the past and fantasy."

8½ has a complex narrative movement, both chronological—Guido assembles his notions gradually while fending off an importuning staff, ac-

In the lobby of the spa hotel Guido kneels and bows at the arrival of his producer, Pace (Guido Alberti) *(center, in white)*. Among the onlookers is the French actress (Madeleine Lebeau) *(left, in furs)*.

The appearance of his mistress, Carla, at their café exacerbates the tension between Guido and his neglected wife, Luisa (Anouk Aimée).

tors, and producer—and associational—aspects of his present life evoke childhood memories or prompt disturbing dreams and vivid chimeras. "8½ is the story of a man," Fellini said, "who frees himself from the ideological monsters of his past that try to devour him." The director admitted the film was "autobiographical, but only superficially." Besides the well-known Marcello Mastroianni (playing Guido), Anouk Aimée, and Claudia Cardinale, Fellini cast many nonprofessionals with great effect; the unforgettable Saraghina, for example, was an American studying opera in Italy. The shooting, shrouded in mystery, was between May and October 1962. Managing to avoid the pitfalls of self-indulgence as well as self-pity, Fellini achieved a fresh triumph in 8½. Beautifully written, directed, acted, photographed, and scored, this pivotal film has the justly deserved status of a classic.

The film opens with Guido, (Marcello Mastroianni), trapped in his car in an underpass. Smoke starts pouring in; suffocating, he endeavors to climb out a window and fly away, only to soon find himself, like a kite, held by a press agent below. Untying the cord, he plunges to the ground. . . . Waking up after this harrowing dream, which reveals his anxieties and desires to escape, the forty-three-year-old director is attended to by a doctor at a spa where he is following a regimen and struggling to forge his scenario, impeded by writer's block and the acerbic criticism of his cowriter Daumier (Jean Rougeul). A recurring vision of his lovely screen heroine as a nurse (Claudia Cardinale) seems tenuous. Halfheartedly, Guido meets his mistress, Carla (Sandra Milo), whom he installs in a hotel near the train station. He dreams of his mother (Giuditta Rissone) and his late father (Annibale Ninchi). Guido is besieged by agents, an insecure actress (Madeleine Lebeau), pesty journalists, the formidable producer Pace (Guido Alberti), etc. Later, he recalls a scene from childhood in which he was pampered by adoring nannies. When Guido requests a cardinal to verify some aspects of his script, the strong Catholic presence and an approaching thickset woman raising her skirt climbing down a hill trigger a recollection of his parochial-school days when he was a boy sneaking off to see the buxom Saraghina (Edra Gale) dance, only to be caught and chastised by the repressive priests.

A disaffected Luisa (Anouk Aimée), married to Guido, shows up and recognizing Carla, confronts her husband with his adultery and habitual lying. He muses that he's master of a harem where his obedient wife and a cluster of women from his past and current life wait on him submissively. When they rebel, he cracks his whip like an animal trainer. In a theater Guido daydreams that he gives an order for the hanging of the hypercritical Daumier. Luisa subsequently walks out during this running of screen tests, telling him that their marriage has reached an impasse. During a splashy cocktail party on the spaceship set to launch the film, a depressed and exhausted Guido, acknowledging artistic impotence, envisions suicide and then calls a halt to the intractable undertaking. While Daumier concurs with this despairing step, Guido, however, suddenly finds himself inspired again, and finally accepting himself for what he is (as opposed to what he *should* be) and his confusion as a normal part of his existence, he implores Luisa to be tolerant with him and recommences the film zestfully. With a lively band, the director, friends, and crew dance jubilantly around a ring on the set.

In his seraglio fantasy Guido, the hubristic overlord, luxuriates in his bath.

The emphasis in *8½* is on characterization, not plot. We glean a multifaceted portrait of Guido, an artist stalled in his creative flow, contending with such irresolvable conflicts as the demands of marriage versus unrestrained sexual freedom and the legacy of a guilt-producing Catholicism from which he revolts but is still drawn to. It is understandable when he, as an intuitive artist, imagines the "execution" of the interfering, intellectual Daumier, who persistently rejects what the director brings forth from his bountiful subconscious. After his epiphany near the end during which, as Fellini said, "the film's hero recognizes that complexes and anguish are also part of his wealth," he succeeds in coming to terms with himself and can vivaciously begin work once more.

With his great screen presence and distinctive voice, Marcello Mastroianni is simply wonderful as Guido, the unquestioned alter ego of Fellini. Commanding and totally convincing, he inhabits the difficult role perfectly. Anouk Aimée is effective as Guido's unhappy wife, Luisa, while the lovely Claudia Cardinale is believable as an appa-

A projection in Guido's thoughts of the beautiful young woman (Claudia Cardinale) at the springs who could be the salvation of his distressed hero in the director's forthcoming film.

rition of the director's inspirational anima figure. Oscillating between reality and fantasy, the inimitable Fellini directs in a masterly fashion. One long remembers the magical sequence of dapper sophisticates queued up for their mineral water while a live orchestra renders Wagner's "Ride of the Valkyries," then switches to Rossini's overture to *The Barber of Seville*. Such heightened realism! Then the powerful Saraghina episode in which a young Guido and his companions pay, who seems to their eyes, an alluring giantess with flashing eyes to dance a seductive rhumba for them. In spite of the ensuing punishment from the disapproving priests—"But don't you know that Saraghina is the devil?" he hears in confession— the boy returns to this irresistible woman. Significantly, she reappears in his harem fantasy. The climax on the spaceship set with rapid camera movement after Guido becomes revivified is spectacular: A band dressed as clowns and a caped Guido as a schoolboy parade past; the director paces back and forth, talking to himself and guiding the players. The exciting music reaches a crescendo as an enormous curtain falls and hordes of friends, staff, actors, etc., descend a huge staircase. A stunning sequence. They form a line and dance around a circle; Guido takes Luisa's hand and joins the group. We cut to evening and see in long shot the musicians now performing diminuendo; a spotlight shines on a solitary young Guido playing his fife and then is shut off. Di Venanzo's photography is remarkable; particularly striking are his light and shadow effects from a swinging lamp throughout the insurrection of Guido's concubinage. Rota's vigorous circus music is outstanding and haunting.

8½ affords us insights into the fascinating world of a director attempting to free himself from constraints that inhibit him as a man and as an artist and, also, into the mysterious creative process where one trusts in one's subconscious and intuition and tries to keep at bay the destructive, faultfinding pressure of a cerebral Daumier. On a psychological level—Fellini had been strongly influenced by Jung—the film can be viewed as an effort to integrate the warring conflicts within Guido to affect a condition of harmony, which endeavor the great Swiss psychiatrist would call a "psychosynthesis." In his midlife crisis the director must come to terms with his inner self, his spiritual nature, which is represented by the visionary Claudia, whom Guido perceives intuitively. The happy ending is not deus ex machina but a visualization indicating that all the clashing elements inside Guido—wife, lover, prelate, etc.— unite to form a circle that symbolizes wholeness. Realizing the imperative to love, Guido resumes his work and continues on his journey to his self. "This film is more than a confession," Fellini said. "It is my testament."

8½ is an extraordinarily influential film—one thinks of Bob Fosse's *All That Jazz* (1979) for instance—and has served as the basis for a Broadway musical, *Nine* (1982). Now thirty years old, *8½* has not lost its capacity to astonish and thrill and may very well be ultimately considered Fellini's masterpiece.

HONORS

Best Foreign Film, New York Film Critics Award (1963)

Oscars for Best Foreign Language Film and to Piero Gherardi for Costume Design (Black and White); nominated in addition for Direction, Original Story and Screenplay, and Art Direction (1963)

15
THE LEOPARD

Il Gattopardo

ITALY/FRANCE / 1963

Titanus (Rome)/Société Nouvelle Pathé Cinéma/S.G.C. (Société Générale de Cinématographie) (Paris)

CREDITS

Director: Luchino Visconti; *Assistant directors:* Rinaldo Ricci, Albino Cocco; *Producer:* Goffredo Lombardo; *Screenwriters:* Suso Cecchi D'Amico, Pasquale Festa Campanile, Enrico Medioli, Massimo Franciosa, Luchino Visconti, based on the novel by Giuseppe di Lampedusa (1958); *Cinematographer:* Giuseppe Rotunno (Technicolor, in Technirama); *Music:* Nino Rota and an unpublished waltz by Giuseppe Verdi; *Editor:* Mario Serandrei; *Art director:* Mario Garbuglia; *Running time:* 205 minutes; *16mm rental source:* Films Inc.

CAST

Don Fabrizio Corbera, Prince of Salina: Burt Lancaster; *Tancredi Falconeri:* Alain Delon; *Angelica Sedara:* Claudia Cardinale; *Don Calogero Sedara:* Paolo Stoppa; *Maria Stella, Princess Salina:* Rina Morelli; *Padre Pirrone:* Romolo Valli; *Colonel Pallavicino:* Ivo Garrani; *Chevalley:* Leslie French; *Don Ciccio Tumeo:* Serge Reggiani; *Concetta:* Lucilla Morlacchi; *Carolina:* Ida Galli; *Francesco Paolo:* Pierre Clementi; *Paolo:* Carlo Valenzano; *Count Cavriaghi:* Mario Girotti; *Donna Margherita:* Lola Braccini; *Don Diego:* Howard Nelson Rubien.

In 1958 the celebrated novel *The Leopard* was published in Rome. Set in the time of the Risorgimento, as the period of the unification of Italy in the 1860s came to be known, its author, Giuseppe Tomasi di Lampedusa, Duke of Palma, magnificently re-created the world and the personage of his great-grandfather. After several firms rejected his manuscript, the cultured writer died without learning that his book would eventually be critically hailed and an international best-seller. Italian director Luchino Visconti (1906–76) found its theme of the imminent death of the ruling class in Sicily intriguing and wanted to film it. A notable

With Father Pirrone (Romolo Valli) *(left)* the Prince of Salina (Burt Lancaster) participates in a daily rosary. His safe universe is about to be threatened.

When they arrive for their summer residence at Donnafugata, Don Fabrizio (Burt Lancaster) and his wife (Rina Morelli), sequestered in the choir stall of the town's church, hear a traditional Te Deum in their honor.

aristocrat himself (Count Don Luchino Visconti di Modrone was his title), Visconti was *the* director to impart to the film a sense of authenticity and had already demonstrated in *Senso* (1954) his ability to bring this historical epoch to cinematic life.

Twentieth Century-Fox was willing to help finance *The Leopard*, Visconti's most ambitious

Exploring an abandoned section of the Donnafugata Palace, Angelica (Claudia Cardinale) offers herself to her betrothed, Tancredi (Alain Delon).

The Prince of Salina at the ball with the engaged couple, Tancredi and Angelica, whose elegant dress indicates the opulence of the movie. For his noteworthy artistry Piero Tosi was nominated for an Oscar for Best Costume Design for a film in color (1963).

project until then. Nikolai Cherkassov (of Eisenstein fame), Laurence Olivier, and others were considered for the dominant role of The Leopard, as the captivating Prince of Salina was called, but the part went to Burt Lancaster—a superb choice. Shooting took place between March and October 1962 in Sicily and Rome. Visconti and his screenwriters were faithful to the novel save for ending the movie after the ball, while Lampedusa depicts the Prince's death sixteen years later. Although *The Leopard* was an enormous success in Europe, when presented in America, dubbed into English, with forty-five minutes cut and employing an inferior color stock that the director disowned, it proved a failure. Twenty years afterward, the definitive, uncut Italian version was released in the United States, permitting us a belated look at a splendorous work of art.

The year is 1860, a point when the Bourbon realm of Naples and Sicily (The Kingdom of the Two Sicilies) would be invaded by the popular leader Giuseppe Garibaldi in his effort to make the Italian peninsula of wrangling feudal states one unified nation. The tranquil, secure universe of Don Fabrizio, the middle-aged Prince of Salina, (Burt Lancaster), is imperiled when a dead Bourbon soldier is found on his estate in Palermo. His cherished, orphaned nephew Tancredi (Alain Delon) leaves to join the revolutionary forces of Garibaldi. The youth's insistence that "If we want things to stay as they are, things will have to change" lingers with the Prince, who is prescient enough to realize that the aristocracy will lose power and that the "jackals" or greedy bourgeois will soon replace the "leopards." Garibaldi's troops, the Redshirts, attack Palermo and Tancredi is wounded. Don Fabrizio and family travel to Donnafugata where they summer. While Concetta (Lucilla Morlacchi), his rather passive daughter, is in love with Tancredi, the shrewd patriarch realizes that the future for his penniless but ambitious nephew would be more assured with the enchanting Angelica (Claudia Cardinale), whose father is the opportunistic, wealthy parvenu Mayor Don Calogero (Paolo Stoppa). A plebiscite for unification is unanimous (with a few negative votes suppressed); the adaptable Tancredi is soon wearing a royalist uniform and is now a conservative. He and Angelica fall in love. When Secretary Chevalley (Leslie French) urges the Prince to accept a seat in the Senate, Don Fabrizio rejects the offer; he is too old to start a new life. At the concluding ball in the Palazzo Ponteleone, which will officially introduce Tancredi and Angelica to society, the Prince has intimations of his own pending death and that of his class.

Intelligent, imperial, maintaining no illusions, Don Fabrizio is well aware of what fate lies ahead for him and the aristocracy, yet he cannot bring himself to avert the impending end. Perceptive, though detached, he escapes from the world symbolically through his avid interest in astronomy, which provides solace. "The Prince of Salina knew he belonged to a class doomed to die," Visconti said. "Finally he sensed Death all around him; it was the only thing that held any meaning for him. I can understand his nostalgia, but his world *had* to go, and that is what I want to show in the film." With his powerful physique, his distinct and expressive face, Burt Lancaster flawlessly incarnates the complex role of The Leopard. Visconti spoke of his "mysterious" quality that added dimensions to a part that is one of the highlights of the actor's distinguished career. The lovely Claudia Cardinale as Angelica is an embodiment of Lampedusa's marvelous phrase "the bugle call of feminine beauty"; the handsome Alain Delon is her ideal lover, Tancredi.

The Leopard is brilliantly directed by Visconti, emphasizing the fascinating character of the Prince and evoking an autumnal, melancholy mood at the passing of his world. The pacing is deliberately leisurely to enable the audience to comprehend and feel what Don Fabrizio is experiencing. Much has been written about the meticulous details of the production, such as the director's orders for twenty dyeings of the shirts of the "Garibaldini" to achieve the correct shade of red. Homage, too, for Giuseppe Rotunno's remarkable cinematography and for Nino Rota's rich, romantic score. The closing ball sequence, constituting about a quarter of the movie, filmed in an actual palace—the Palazzo Gangi in Palermo—is the film's pièce de résistance, one of the richest and most lavish scenes ever captured by the camera. This sequence is shot chiefly in a subjective manner through the tired eyes of the Prince. Through exquisite high-angle and long shots of the dancers; shots of the excited young ladies jumping on the divans; Tancredi and Angelica executing a mazurka; then the Prince waltzing with a radiant Angelica to Verdi's charming music—even the realistic touches of guests perspiring and visible chamber pots in the men's rest room—we share this memorable fete vicariously. Before long, Don Fabrizio sends his family home in a carriage and

starts walking. A priest hurrying to give someone the last rites—another memento mori—passes the sad and exhausted Prince. We see the pensive Leopard ambling along on the streets with his cane seemingly contemplating, perhaps welcoming, his approaching death. *The Leopard* is visually stunning and breathtaking and may well be Visconti's masterpiece, an unforgettable classic to savor.

AWARDS

Best Film, Cannes Film Festival (1963)
L'Etoile de Cristal to Burt Lancaster for Foreign Actor Award (1964)

16
THE ORGANIZER

I Compagni

ITALY/FRANCE / 1963

Lux Film/Vides (Rome)/Méditerranée Cinéma Productions (Paris) with the collaboration of Avala Film (Belgrade)

CREDITS

Director: Mario Monicelli; *Producer:* Franco Cristaldi; *Screenwriters:* Agenore Incrocci and Furio Scarpelli, Mario Monicelli; *Cinematographer:* Giuseppe Rotunno (black and white, VistaVision); *Music:* Carlo Rustichelli; *Editor:* Ruggero Mastroianni; *Art director:* Mario Garbuglia; *Running time:* 126 minutes; *16mm rental source:* Images.

CAST

Professor Sinigaglia: Marcello Mastroianni; *Raul Bertini:* Renato Salvatori; *Niobe:* Annie Girardot; *Martinetti:* Bernard Blier; *Adèle:* Gabriella Giorgelli; *Maestro Di Meo:* François Périer; *Pautasso:* Folco Lulli; *Baudet:* Vittorio Sanipoli; *Cenerone:* Giuseppe Cadeo; *Cesarina:* Elvira Tonelli; *Cerioni:* Pippo Mosca; *Omero:* Franco Ciolli.

The Italian director Mario Monicelli (1915–   ) is best known in this country for *The Big Deal on Madonna Street* (1958), his amusing comedy of a

Sinigaglia (Marcello Mastroianni) *(in dark coat, facing camera)* beseeches the scab workers brought in from Saluzzo to return home, but a melee breaks out.

Rififi-type of robbery with Marcello Mastroianni and Vittorio Gassman playing hopelessly incompetent burglars. More impressive is *The Organizer*, which treats of the plight of the oppressed laborers in Turin at the end of the nineteenth century and their painful efforts to ameliorate their harsh working conditions through unionism. The versatile Marcello Mastroianni has the title role of the leader who tries to guide and inspirit them in the face of overwhelming odds.

The film was shot in Turin with a superb cast and crew. "The reconstruction of the period was very difficult," Monicelli observed. *The Organizer* captured the era perfectly. Its theme is timeless. "Like those of today," the director said, "the workers' struggles of that period had the basic motivations," which amount to the fundamental needs to find respect at work and not be treated inhumanly. After establishing the locale, the film's introduction goes on to mention, "But the same forces that had made a nation of the Italian peninsula were leading the common man toward an awareness of wider horizons. He had just begun to see himself as an individual with his own dignity, his own rights. This story is of the very beginning of that struggle to conquer a new world of dignity and social justice." *The Organizer* is a powerful and universal film that much to our loss is little known here.

The film opens as a documentation of a typical workday: Hordes of workers head to the textile plant to start their day at six A.M. After a thirty-minute lunch break all are back to their arduous tasks. At eight P.M. they're still laboring, some nearly falling asleep. When an old man crushes his hand in a machine, Martinetti (Bernard Blier) and his coworkers decide to complain about the exploitative fourteen-hour workday, but the manager ignores them. They then decide to blow the stop siren at seven, but this job action fails. A mild, bespectacled stranger appears who is a labor agitator: Professor Sinigaglia (Marcello Mastroianni). While the police are looking for him in Genoa, he soon convinces the workers to organize and fight management with a strike. The professor is boarded with an angry bachelor, Raul (Renato Salvatori), who now has no place to bring his girlfriends. The plant's wealthy owner refuses to comply with the strikers' demand for accident insurance among other things and solicits scab workers from Saluzzo. The scabs are hungry, too, and ignore Sinigaglia's rational pleas to return home. Soon a fight breaks out and a leader, Pautasso (Folco Lulli), is killed by an express train. At

Reading the good news that the "scabs" were sent back, Sinigaglia *(center wearing glasses)* says "We've got them licked" to the striking workers *(left to right)* Martinetti (Bernard Blier), unidentified player, Cesarina (Elvira Tonelli), Raul (Renato Salvatori), and a beaming Di Meo (François Périer).

A hungry Sinigaglia, wanted by the police, notices Niobe (Annie Girardot), who will offer him refuge in her apartment.

Exhorting the striking workers not to give in but to hold out for just a little bit longer, Sinigaglia sways Martinetti *(left)* and Raul along with his audience.

his wake the professor reads an encouraging news account that the scabs were sent home. Losing orders to competitors, the owner calls on the police to arrest the instigating Sinigaglia, who evades them and hides out with Niobe (Annie Girardot), a local woman who turned to prostitution to avoid the drudgery of the factory. At a meeting, a demoralized Martinetti calls for a return to work; a now-politicized Raul disagrees. The professor enters and urges them to continue the strike in spite of evident hardships. Stirred up, renewed with hope, the workers march to a demonstration in the square only to be met with police fire. Sinigaglia is led off by soldiers. Now wanted by the police, Raul takes up the professor's gauntlet and escapes to help others elsewhere. The film ends with the employees glumly returning to the plant. Yet we hear the rousing workmen's song. . . .

Meek, gentle, scholarly, with an abstract look about him, Sinigaglia is an atypical hero, yet for all his muddled activities his impassioned words are effective in getting the workers to unite and act. A loner, estranged from his wife and family, he is quite aware of what lies in store for him at the hands of vengeful plutocrats and is prepared to sacrifice everything for the labor movement. Marcello Mastroianni is superlative as the slovenly, self-effacing, but actually quite courageous professor. Here is another outstanding performance by the greatest Italian film actor of his generation. Renato Salvatori as Raul is persuasive as he moves from despising the organizer to replacing him

when he's arrested. Strong support is lent by Annie Girardot as Niobe, Bernard Blier as Martinetti, and François Périer as Di Meo. Monicelli's direction is assured. The opening scenes make their point about the unjust conditions in a subtle manner. Monicelli resists any inclination to harangue us or to "ennoble" his poor workers by treating them sentimentally. We see their faults as well as their virtues; above all, they are *real* people whom we can recognize and identify with. The director has a fast-moving pace, a flair for documentary realism, and an eye for the telling detail. So cold is it in the early wintry morning that Omero (Franco Ciolli), a boy working at the mill, uses the end of a broom to break up the ice in the pitcher; the impoverished Sinigaglia has holes in his gloves. Giuseppe Rotunno's photography stunningly and masterfully recreates the past. We feel as if we are watching old newsreels or perhaps daguerreotypes. Carlo Rustichelli contributed a vigorous workmen's song. One scene lingers in memory: The young Omero, forced to go to work and thus never able to learn to read, hears that his kid brother is not applying himself at school. Omero encounters him after classes and pushes him against a wall angrily. "You gotta study. You understand?" Omero shouts, then slaps him. "If you grow up like me, I'll kill you." Then quietly the older brother picks up the lad's scattered books, tenderly puts the kid's cap on, and wipes away the boy's tears. He takes his hand and they walk home together. A beautiful moment. It is shocking later, first, to discover that Omero has been killed in the confrontation with the police, then to see this little child join the crowd of workers returning to the mill.

Monicelli viewed the capital-versus-labor contention with optimism: "Defeat is never total, it serves to strengthen, to make comprehensive what one needs to say to struggle together." No facile, happy ending here but a realization of how slow progress is—and what remains to be done. *The Organizer* is a rich, deeply affecting film of the human spirit. It has that rare quality of compassion and sense of authenticity so prevalent in the best of Italian films. Unfortunately, this movie can only be seen rarely in America in a poorly dubbed print on television. It deserves to be rescued and discovered again.

HONORS

Nominated for an Oscar for Best Story and
  Screenplay—Written Directly for the Screen (1964)

17
THE SILENCE

Tystnaden

SWEDEN / 1963

SVENSK FILMINDUSTRI

CREDITS

Director and screenwriter: Ingmar Bergman; *Assistant directors:* Lenn Hjortzberg, Lars-Erik Liedholm; *Producer:* Allan Ekelund; *Cinematographer:* Sven Nykvist (black and white); *Music:* Excerpts from J. S. Bach's *Goldberg Variations* and R. Mersey's "Mayfair Waltz"; *Editor:* Ulla Ryghe; *Art director:* P. A. Lundgren; *Running time:* 96 minutes; *16mm rental source:* Janus; *Videocassette:* Orion.

CAST

Ester: Ingrid Thulin; *Anna:* Gunnel Lindblom; *Johan:* Jorgen Lindstrom; *The Old Waiter:* Hakan Jahnberg; *Waiter in Café:* Birger Malmsten; *Dwarf Troupe:* The Eduardini; *Their Manager:* Eduardo Gutierrez.

The Silence, originally called *God's Silence,* brings to a conclusion the trilogy Ingmar Bergman began with *Through a Glass Darkly* and *Winter Light.* Another "chamber work," the film's action is restricted to approximately one and a half days; the personages are just two sisters and a child; and in this instance, mood and theme take precedence over characterization and story. In his autobiography, *The Magic Lantern,* as well as in several interviews, Bergman mentioned the various threads that his creative process would weave into *The Silence.* Hearing the fierce dissonance of Béla Bartók's Concerto for Orchestra would stimulate in him a cinematic expression. "My original idea," the director said, "was to make a film that should obey musical laws, instead of dramaturgical ones. A film acting by association—rhythmically, with themes and counterthemes." In addition, there was an urge to evoke a strange city, similar to an eerie Berlin that had haunted him in many dreams. A basic situation evolved: "Originally I'd imagined two men, one older and one younger, traveling together," Bergman said. "One of them couldn't go on any longer, fell sick, and ended up in

In their stifling compartment Anna (Gunnel Lindblom) *(left),* her son, Johan (Jorgen Lindstrom), and her sister, Ester (Ingrid Thulin), travel through an unnamed country with an unfamiliar language.

While his ill aunt, Ester, rests, young Johan peers out the window, noticing a menacing tank approach. A striking effect of contrasting light by Sven Nykvist.

a hospital." Then it struck him that it would work better with two *women* and cast Ingrid Thulin and Gunnel Lindblom for the parts. While the director initially desired to make *The Silence* in some Central European city, he finally decided to create his own mysterious metropolis via sets and shot the movie in Stockholm from July to September 1962.

Although *The Silence* was an enormous success in Sweden, going on to receive a Swedish Academy Award in 1963 for Best Film of the Year, it proved to be his most controversial film when shown abroad. Argentina ruled it obscene and banned it

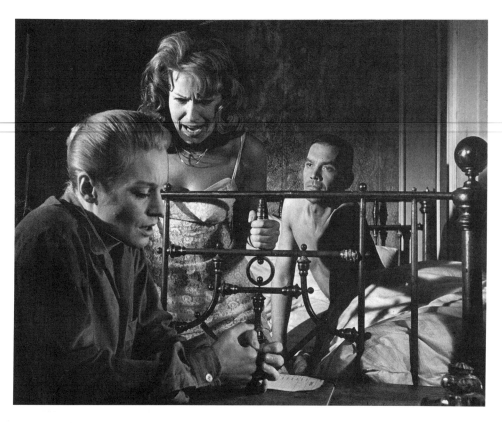

The puzzled waiter (Birger Malmsten) watches while Anna, the woman he brought to the hotel room, lashes out at her interfering sister, Ester.

and so did Israel; in West Germany it became a test case for the Censorship Board. Far from being pornography, *The Silence*, with its bare and direct style, its minimal exposition and ambiguities, was a brilliant experiment in which Bergman dared to eliminate character development—also much dialogue—to focus on the dark side of the human psyche and to produce a visual, remarkable masterpiece.

The plot is stark: Ester (Ingrid Thulin), her younger sister, Anna (Gunnel Lindblom), with her ten-year-old son, Johan (Jorgen Lindstrom), are returning home after a vacation. The women are in their thirties and it is entirely possible that they are having or have had a lesbian relationship together. Ester is an intellectual, a translator by profession, used to dominating the earthy, sensual Anna. Traveling by train through an unspecified country at dawn, Ester is convulsed by coughing. They decide to stop and rest for a day or two. Johan observes a strong military presence; the country is at war or preparing for combat. The sisters rent a double room at an old, baroque hotel. As Anna and her son take a nap, Ester tries in vain to converse with the kindly old floor waiter (Hakan Jahnberg) who knows only the local tongue. She drinks, masturbates, and falls asleep. Johan wakes up and explores the labyrinthine corridors. His adven-

tures include meeting a group of performing dwarfs (The Eduardini). Anna dresses and leaves while Ester is beset again by agonizing cramps and vomiting. The aged waiter is most attentive to her needs. At a nearby café Anna encounters a waiter (Birger Malmsten) who's attracted to her. Later, an anguished Ester questions a sullen Anna about her day and attempts to dissuade her from keeping her tryst with the waiter. Johan sees his mother embrace the man and enter a room with him. Anna tells the stranger she wishes her sister were dead. Johan mentions his mother's whereabouts to a concerned Ester. Anna senses her sister is outside crying and unlocks the door. The sick woman comes in and finds Anna spitefully embracing the foreigner. The younger woman vents her spleen at Ester. The next day a hostile Anna informs Ester she's taking a train at two for home. The ill sister, who may be near death, manages to write a note for Johan, as promised, "a few words of the foreign language." Coldly, Anna departs. On the train with his mother the boy reads Ester's letter and concentrates on the perplexing words.

The sisters are opposites. The cerebral Ester looks with disdain upon the carnal Anna. She is struggling against her dreadful sickness, which humiliates her and fills her with disgust at her body. That their relationship may be physical can

78

be gathered by Ester's jealous behavior. Anna is striving to free herself from her sister's subjugation. Johan is aware of the animosity between them. He acts withdrawn and morose and uses his puppet show to voice his fears. With her beautiful, expressive face Ingrid Thulin conveys both the physical and psychological torment Ester's suffering; her performance is outstanding and gripping. Gunnel Lindblom effectively gives Anna a sultry presence. The direction of Bergman is extraordinarily controlled, especially the low-angle shots by which we delve into the secrets of the hotel through the eyes of Johan. There are many shocks throughout the film: The boy is with a sleeping Ester. All is quiet. Suddenly a glass rattles against a carafe. Johan goes over to the window. We see below a threatening tank come into view. . . . And, near the end, the image of Ester screaming, racked by excruciating spasms, while afterward a loud, mournful siren wails is one of the most indelible and wrenching moments in Bergman's films. Sven Nykvist's impressive photography assists in creating a dreamlike, at times surrealistic, world.

Bergman referred to *The Silence* as "God's silence—the negative impression." He said, "At the film's bottommost layer lay the collapse of an ideology and a way of life." Elsewhere the director noted that *The Silence* "is about the complete breakdown of illusions. . . . it is a sort of personal purgation: a rendering of hell on earth—my hell." Fittingly the name of this soulless city is Timoka, an Estonian word he came upon by chance in a book of poetry. His intuition was certainly on target, for Kabi Laretei, his Estonian wife at the time, told him its meaning: "appertaining to the executioner." Ester's message to Johan is significant, "the one essential positive thing" in the film, as Bergman said. In a concluding close-up we watch the boy mouthing *Hadjek*, which we learn from the screenplay means "spirit." Ester's vital spark will continue with Johan. With the absence of God, there is a terrifying void, a moral degeneration, physical disintegration, pain—it is easy to see Ester's bouts of suffocation as spiritually symbolic—and war. In evoking a compelling mood—the oppressive atmosphere of a nightmare—Bergman triumphed once more with a disturbing, provocative, and richly poetic film.

HONORS

L'Étoile de Cristal to Ingrid Thulin for Foreign Actress Award (1964)

Portrait of Gertrud (Nina Pens Rode) at the outset of the film, ready to jettison her moribund marriage in her quest for romantic love.

18
GERTRUD

DENMARK / 1964

PALLADIUM FILM

CREDITS

Director and screenwriter: Carl Theodor Dreyer, based on the play by Hjalmar Soderberg; *Assistant directors:* Solveig Ersgaard, Jens Ravn; *Producer:* Jorgen Nielsen; *Cinematographer:* Henning Bendtsen (black and white); *Music:* Jorgen Jersild; *Editor:* Edith Schlussel; *Art director:* Kai Rasch; *Running time:* 119 minutes; *16mm rental source:* Corinth; *Videocassette:* N.Y. Film Annex.

CAST

Gertrud: Nina Pens Rode; *Gustav Kanning:* Bendt Rothe; *Gabriel Lidman:* Ebbe Rode; *Erland Jansson:* Baard Owe; *Axel Nygren:* Axel Strobye; *Kanning's Mother:* Anna Malberg; *Vice-Chancellor:* Eduard Mielche; *Kanning's Maid:* Vera Gebuhr.

It was in 1962 that esteemed Danish director Carl Theodor Dreyer (1889–1968), whose previous film was *Ordet* (1955), made the discovery of a recently

Gertrud has a pleasant reunion with her friend Axel (Axel Strobye). The tapestry of a nude woman overtaken by dogs relates to a recent dream the heroine had that she interpreted, "I realized that we are alone in the world."

published thesis that affirmed that Hjalmar Soderberg's play *Gertrud*, written in 1906, was in large measure autobiographical and that the heroine's name in actuality was Maria von Platen, who had been the Swedish author's mistress, although he was then married. When he was free after finally divorcing his wife, he was furious to learn that Maria was having an affair with a young writer, who openly bragged of their relationship, and left for Denmark where he quickly wrote *Gertrud*. This revelation awakened interest in Dreyer in Soderberg's work; in the 1920s he tried unsuccessfully to film one of his novels as well as *Gertrud*, which proved too verbose for the silent medium. Now stimulated with the news that the protagonist had really lived, Dreyer secured the film rights and wrote several versions of the scenario before finding a producer. Dissatisfied with the play's climax, he shortened the third act and added an epilogue to round out the principal's later years. "The conflict in the drama is as real today as it was sixty years ago," Dreyer said. When the shooting was delayed in the summer of 1964 because the Hellerup Studio in Copenhagen was booked, the

perfectionist director took advantage of the wait to supervise such details as the costumes, hairstyles, and furniture. "*Gertrud* is a film that I made with my heart," Dreyer said. Unfortunately, at its premiere in Paris the movie met with a disastrous critical response. However, after the great director's death in 1968 there was a reevaluation of this, his last work, and in the succeeding decades *Gertrud* came to be regarded as one of Dreyer's finest achievements. "It is a modern subject," he said, "that I have tried to stretch towards tragedy." A beautiful, probing psychological study of a woman's pursuit of absolute love, which leads to a withdrawal into a life of solitude, *Gertrud* is like intimate chamber music and reveals the touch of a master.

The film opens in the year 1907. After lawyer Gustav Kanning (Bendt Rothe) discloses to his wife, Gertrud (Nina Pens Rode), who was previously a singer, his intention of running for the post of cabinet minister, she unsettles him by stating that she no longer desires to be his wife. She declares that his work is paramount and she feels neglected: "The man I choose to live with must belong to me completely." Gertrud's fallen in love and rushes off to meet her beloved Erland Jansson (Baard Owe), a young, undisciplined composer. She consents to go to his apartment. Celebrated erotic poet Gabriel Lidman (Ebbe Rode), still in love with Gertrud, who left him several years before, is honored at the university on the occasion of his fiftieth birthday. Feeling unwell, Gertrud retreats to a reception room where she comes across her cordial friend Axel Nygren (Axel Strobye), who invites her to study psychiatry with him in Paris. Alone with the disillusioned poet, Gertrud learns that Gabriel witnessed Erland's tasteless boasting of his latest conquest at a rowdy party. She is deeply hurt. Shortly after, performing for the vice-chancellor (Eduard Mielche) with Erland accompanying her on the piano, the perturbed woman collapses. At a tryst in the park the next day Gertrud invites the shallow Erland to go away with her. He declines, protesting that he couldn't live off her, but the truth emerges: he has impregnated a benefactress; besides, the callous youth had thought Gertrud simply wanted an affair. Visiting the Kannings, a heartsick Lidman pleads with his former inamorata to run off with him, but Gertrud, dressed in black, says, "There is only loneliness left for me"—it is impossible to revive what is dead. In a postmortem on their liaison she points out that he rejected her, gradually preferring, like Gustav, his vocation to loving her. She telephones Axel and informs him that she's coming to Paris. Gustav fails in his entreaty to make her stay. In the epilogue, Axel calls on an isolated Gertrud on her birthday in her modest home. Both are white-haired; he recalls that it must have been thirty or forty years since they attended lectures together at the Sorbonne. They confirm their long, platonic friendship, and she reads an indicative poem written when she was sixteen with the refrain "But I have loved." On her tombstone she simply requests two words: *Amor Omnia.* "Love is all," Axel renders. He departs; Gertrud returns to her cherished reclusive life.

Although one may regard Gertrud's demands for total devotion as too exacting and unrealistic—and agree, perhaps, with Gustav's observation, "Love alone is not enough in a man's life"—Dreyer's tone toward her is nevertheless sympathetic and admiring. In his epilogue the director evokes much dignity and strength of character in his heroine, who comes to embody a line from Lidman's poem, "I believe in the pleasures of the flesh and in the irremediable loneliness of the soul." With her sensitive, expressive face Nina Pens Rode most effectively incarnates Soderberg's unhappy lady. Taking a cue from the playwright's recurring pointer, "They spoke past each other," Dreyer fashioned a deliberate style of mise-en-scène in which there is an almost absolute avoidance of direct confrontation in the scenes between Gertrud and her three lovers and Axel. Instead of the traditional shot of a character talking followed by a reaction shot of the partner, both players are

constantly kept within the frame, either the pair staring ahead seated on a sofa or Gertrud facing forward with a man behind her speaking in profile, permitting us to see in medium shot the fascinating interplay of the actors, whether dealing with a current crisis or recollecting some pertinent exposition from the past. From such deliberate distancing an idea of the aloneness of the individual, of the difficulty in communication, is implied. The scenes are long, the rhythm slow, but accordingly, we are privy to the unmasking of a soul. "What I want to obtain," Dreyer said, "is a penetration to my actors' profound thoughts by means of their most subtle expressions." In addition the director wished his actors to appear statuesque in order to elicit a sense of tragedy. As the old Axel leaves, Gertrud shuts the door; the camera lingers on it, bells toll, and Dreyer completes his final study of yet another oppressed woman. *Gertrud* is a demanding film, hardly one with mass appeal. Yet to the discriminating, this austere masterpiece is quietly overwhelming, affecting, and compassionate. *Gertrud* is a rich, intense, and exquisite film, the brilliant finale to an extraordinary career.

19
THE GOSPEL ACCORDING TO ST. MATTHEW

Il Vangelo Secondo Matteo

ITALY / FRANCE / 1964

Arco Film (Rome)/Lux (Paris)

CREDITS

Director and screenwriter: Pier Paolo Pasolini, based on the Gospel According to St. Matthew; *Assistant director:* Maurizio Lucidi; *Producer:* Alfredo Bini; *Cinematographer:* Tonino Delli Colli (black and white); *Music:* Luis E. Bacalov with selections from Bach, Mozart, Prokofiev, Webern, the Congolese *Missa Luba,* and Negro spirituals; *Editor:* Nino Baragli; *Art director:* Luigi Scaccianoce; *Running time:* 142 minutes; *16mm rental source:* Corinth; *Videocassette:* Video Yesteryear.

While singing an art song for the vice-chancellor, Gertrud suddenly feels ill, upset at the duplicity of her lover, Erland (Baard Owe), who's at the piano.

The Gospel According to St. Matthew, his third feature, launched the international reputation of the Italian poet and novelist Pier Paolo Pasolini (1922–75). Confined to his hospital room in Assisi in 1962 because the unexpected arrival of Pope John XXIII engendered a massive traffic jam, the director picked up the New Testament, the only reading material available, and became inspired to do a film on St. Matthew's Gospel, which he found particularly striking. "I liked the Christ of Matthew," Pasolini said. "He was rigorous, demanding, absolute. This is the Christ who says, 'I came not to send peace, but a sword.' " Unlike previous versions, his treatment would be plain and unadorned. Although a nonbeliever and a professed Marxist, Pasolini would make the film from the point of view of a true devotee.

With the exception of two appropriate interpolations from Isaiah, all the dialogue in the film and the events dramatized come from Matthew. To be sure, the director could only deal with a portion of what Christ taught and did. Many passages were condensed, rearranged, or simply omitted (as the Lord's Transfiguration). A trip to Israel, which Pasolini found too industrialized to be a suitable location, convinced him that he was wise to proceed, as he said, by "analogy," to use the impoverished southern Italians in arid Calabria as "an equivalent of the simple people among whom Christ lived."

Pasolini refused to make an accurate, historical movie. "With authentic costumes and scenery it would have had a facile commercial aspect I was trying to avoid," he said. Similarly, for the sake of realism, he insisted on utilizing nonprofessional actors, finding his Christ in Enrique Irazoqui, a young student from Barcelona who was visiting Italy and whose thin face reminded the director of El Greco's painting. For the part of Mary as an older woman, he chose his own mother. The costumes for the Sanhedrin tribunal were based on the medieval frescoes of Piero della Francesca, which Pasolini thought were consonant with Italian physiognomy; in keeping with the director's wish to scale everything down to the humble dimensions of the Gospel, Christ, the apostles, along with the villagers, all wear poor, nondescript clothing. Color photography, which would have worked against the severity of the film's style, was avoided. *The Gospel According to St. Matthew—* the *Saint* was added over the director's objections when it was released in America and England— was dedicated "To the Dear, Familiar Memory of Pope John XXIII," who had died the year before the film appeared. A model example of the critical dictum "Less is more," Pasolini's modest, very cinematic adaptation—forceful yet respectful— was a triumph and, after almost thirty years, still remains unsurpassed.

The film opens with a perplexed Joseph (Marcello Morante) discovering Mary (Margherita Caruso), his betrothed, pregnant. In a dream an angel (Rossana Di Rocco) informs him that Mary's Son is conceived of the Holy Ghost and is to be called Jesus. The celestial messenger later warns Joseph to flee with his family to Egypt, for a jealous King Herod, fearing a prophecy concerning a future Jewish ruler, plans to slaughter all the infants in Bethlehem. After the sovereign's death, the same angel tells Joseph to return to Galilee. . . . An adult Jesus (Enrique Irazoqui) approaches John the Baptist (Mario Socrate) for the rite of baptism. Christ spends time alone in the desert where He is tempted by Satan and then recruits Peter (Settimio Di Porto) and eleven other apostles. He begins His ministry: healing the insane and lepers, preaching, performing miracles and preparing the disciples to carry on His work. Christ enters Jerusalem and is hailed by the populace. His enemies wait to destroy Him. At the Last Supper, Jesus effects the sacrament of Holy Communion. Soon after, His apostle Judas (Otello Sestili) betrays Him. Christ is brought before Caiaphas, the high priest, where He is charged with blasphemy. Judas, in despair of his perfidy, runs off and hangs himself. Pontius Pilate, the governor, senses Jesus' innocence but accedes to the demands of the crowds that He be crucified. Christ is led to Golgotha and nailed to a cross; witnessing His excruciating death is His agonized mother (Susanna Pasolini). The third day after His burial, she and some followers head to the tomb. Suddenly the slab falls back and the angel announces, "He has risen." The film ends, as does the Gospel account, with the resurrected Lord in Galilee exhorting His disciples to teach all nations, "Behold, I am with you all days, even unto the consummation of the world."

While some critics have objected to Pasolini's emphasis on an angry, denunciatory Christ in-

Portrait of Jesus Christ (Enrique Irazoqui) praying prior to the intercession by the apostles regarding the needs of the multitude that results in the miracle of the loaves and fishes.

A happy Christ with children in Nazareth: "Let the little children be, and do not hinder them from coming to me, for of such is the kingdom of heaven."

stead of a loving, merciful Savior, no one doubted his achievement in creating a compelling Jesus who projects both a human and a divine nature. With his sharp, penetrating eyes, Enrique Irazoqui successfully captures a fervent Christ. After a false start in attempting to direct his *Gospel* in, as he said, "a reverential style," which proved mere "rhetoric," Pasolini abandoned traditional methods and decided to employ such techniques as the hand-held camera, which follows Jesus as He turns to instruct the disciples, and a cinema-verité style for Christ's two trials, which create a documentary effect and enhance realism. Very short scenes propel the narrative onward; frequent close-ups of Jesus produce a feeling of intimacy. The director's skill at selecting marvelous, rough-hewn faces add a mark of authenticity in addition to the decisive details: a fly on a sleeping apostle, another buzzing around the shrouded corpse of the Lord. Tonino Delli Colli's photography is impressive, particularly the shot of lightning illuminating a close-up of Christ in darkness before He imparts the Our Father. An eclectic choice of music is notable; thus when the Magi visit the infant Jesus, we hear Odetta sing the Negro spiritual "Sometimes I Feel Like a Motherless Child." If Cecil B. DeMille's *King of Kings* (1927) stressed the divinity of the Lord at the expense of His humanity—the reverse being true of Martin Scorsese's *The Last Temptation of Christ* (1988)—while other interpretations

The Lord pouring wine at the Last Supper: "All of you drink of this; for this is my blood of the new covenant, which is being shed for many unto the forgiveness of sins." To the left is Peter (Settimio Di Porto); to the right is John (Giacomo Morante). The casual, informal grouping is a fresh departure from traditional pictorial representation.

83

In the garden of Gethsemane, Judas (Otello Sestili) *(left)* betrays Christ with a kiss.

blurred the focus on Christ with ornate spectacle, distracting cameo appearances of stars, or stereotypical pieties, Pasolini's *The Gospel According to St. Matthew* is an extraordinary accomplishment, universally considered to be the best film on Christ ever made. Far from having the audience a passive spectator at some idealized Passion Play, Pasolini shocks and disturbs, making his film extremely relevant, potent, and beautiful as he aims it at our contemporary world.

HONORS

Special Jury Prize, Venice Film Festival (1964)

20
HAMLET

Gamlet

USSR / 1964

LENFILM PRODUCTION

CREDITS

Director and screenwriter: Grigori Kozintsev, based on the translation of Shakespeare's play by Boris Pasternak; *Cinematographer:* Ionas Gritsyus (black and white, Sovscope); *Music:* Dmitri Shostakovich; *Editor:* E. Ma-

khankova; *Art directors:* Yevgeny Enei, G. Kropachev; *Running time:* 148 minutes; *16mm rental source:* Corinth.

CAST

Hamlet: Innokenti Smoktunovsky; *Claudius:* Mikhail Nazvanov; *Gertrude:* Elsa Radzin; *Ophelia:* Anastasia Vertinskaya; *Polonius:* Yuri Tolubeyev; *Horatio:* V. Erenberg; *Laertes:* C. Olesenko; *Rosencrantz:* I. Dmitriev; *Guildenstern:* V. Medvedev; *Fortinbras:* A. Krevalid; *Gravediggers:* V. Chekoerski, V. Kolpakor.

It was not until the 1950s that seasoned Soviet director Grigori Kozintsev (1905–73) had an opportunity and the resources to film Shakespeare. He had earlier staged *King Lear, Hamlet,* and *Othello* with success and was indeed a respected scholar on the great Elizabethan playwright (his tome, *Shakespeare: Time and Conscience,* was published in the United States in 1966). According to the director, his film of *Hamlet* took six years of preparation and one and a half more to shoot. "I shall try to show the general feeling," he said, "the general philosophy of the poetry, but I shall not use the medium of traditional theater staging. I want to go the way of the cinema." Kozintsev stressed, "In my view Shakespeare on the screen must become more a tragic poem than a play, more of a relationship between characters and landscape, a historical and geographical representation. . . . It's necessary to create a pictorial imagery, a visual poetry with the same quality as that of the Shakespearean verse." With the brilliant Innokenti Smoktunovsky heading a superb cast and famed composer Dmitri Shostakovich creating a memorable score for this lavish production, Kozintsev's *Hamlet* is a stirring and remarkable picture, although relatively little known in this country.

We seem to be more willing to accept a foreign treatment of Shakespeare if it's totally transformed and does not rely upon a translation of the text for its screenplay (Kurosawa's 1957 rendition of *Macbeth, Throne of Blood,* for example) than on one, such as Kozintsev's, that does. If we can overcome our natural reluctance to hear the glorious words of Shakespeare in a language besides English, we might concur that Kozintsev's adaptation is pure cinema and worthy of our consideration. In this dynamic Russian film, his virile hero is not tortured with vacillation, but is resolved to avenge his father and bides his time for the right moment. As with the other versions of *Hamlet,*

Seated before Ophelia (Anastasia Vertinskaya), a cunning Hamlet (Innokenti Smoktunovsky) waits for the performance by the players to enable him to "catch the conscience of the King."

evening the prince encounters the ghost, who discloses his murder by Claudius and demands vengeance. Hamlet is devastated by this revelation and at the odious mission thrust upon him. To facilitate his objective, he utilizes the ploy of assuming a suddenly deranged disposition and distances himself from a bewildered Ophelia, whom he loves. His two schoolmates, Rosencrantz (I. Dmitriev) and Guildenstern (V. Medvedev), are sent for by Claudius to spy on him. A troupe of actors approaches; the crafty Hamlet requests they stage a play that resembles the regicide of his father. Alone, the anguished prince broods, "To be, or not to be. . . ." Witnessing the disconcerting reenactment of his crime in pantomime, Claudius abruptly storms off. Hamlet is

Hamlet confronts his grief-stricken mother, Queen Gertrude (Elsa Radzin), in her room.

the Soviet director abbreviated the play by making many cuts in the speeches and scenes and rearranging the narrative. Unlike Laurence Olivier's 1948 film—the apogee of sonorous Shakespearean diction—Kozintsev does not omit Rosencrantz, Guildenstern, and Fortinbras and avoids both a tendentious Oedipal interpretation of the protagonist and occasional distracting, vertiginous camera movements. Unlike Tony Richardson's disappointing 1969 movie, the Soviet director's film is never static, unengaging, or claustrophobic. And unlike Franco Zeffirelli's uneven 1990 film, Kozintsev's *Hamlet* never allows the pace to slacken and has a great actor in the lead who can project nobility with ease. Visually arresting in its wide-screen sweep, Kozintsev's excitingly directed and powerfully acted *Hamlet* is a major achievement that awaits rediscovery.

The film opens with Prince Hamlet (Innokenti Smoktunovsky) having learned of the death of his father, the king, returning swiftly to the court in medieval Denmark. He is disillusioned at the hasty, ill-timed marriage of his widowed mother, Queen Gertrude (Elsa Radzin), to his father's brother, Claudius (Mikhail Nazvanov). Horatio (V. Erenberg) informs the prince that he saw the youth's late sire the night before. Laertes (C. Olesenko), son of the counselor Polonius (Yuri Tolubeyev), departs to resume his studies in Paris. The garrulous advisor cautions his other child, a daughter, Ophelia (Anastasia Vertinskaya), to be wary concerning Hamlet's interest in her. That

summoned to his mother's chamber where Polonius has hidden behind a tapestry to eavesdrop. When her son enters, Gertrude, frightened, calls for help; hearing a cry behind the arras, Hamlet runs his knife through it, killing Polonius. He upbraids his tormented mother, who thinks he's mad. Accompanied by Rosencrantz and Guildenstern, the prince is dispatched to England. Aboard ship he unseals the regal orders and reads he's ordered to be executed immediately upon landing. Rewriting the command and substituting his classmates' names, he escapes. Laertes, vowing to avenge his father's death, comes back accusing the king and is pained to behold the demented state of his sister, Ophelia. Claudius divulges the mur-

With a gravedigger (V. Kolpakor) watching, Hamlet reflects on the skull of the jester Yorick, who entertained him when he was a child.

Alarmed horses neigh and dash off at night; in a low-angle shot we see the eerie phantom moving in slow motion, followed by Hamlet. Then near the edge of a cliff where below tumultuous waves crash on the rocks, the wraith shocks his son with his terrifying message. Using short scenes, Kozintsev builds to a forceful climax. Shostakovich's atmospheric music perfectly complements the compelling imagery. Intense and vigorous, amazingly tangible and authentic-looking, Kozintsev's *Hamlet* is the most cinematic thus far of the several renderings on film of Shakespeare's most popular play and merits our reevaluation and esteem.

HONORS

Special Jury Prize, Venice Film Festival (1964)
British Film Institute Award (1964)

derer. Later at a cemetery where the now drowned, hapless Ophelia is to be buried, Hamlet and Laertes quarrel. The prince consents to a duel with his late beloved's brother masterminded by the king to insure his nephew's death. In the ensuing conflict Gertrude drinks deadly envenomed wine intended for the prince; Laertes wounds Hamlet with a poisoned rapier and, after a scuffle in which they exchange swords, is himself injured. Dying, he blurts out the king's perfidy and the enraged prince stabs Claudius. Fortinbras (A. Krevalid), Prince of Norway, arrives and decrees an honorable tribute for the distinguished slain hero.

In Kozintsev's film Hamlet does not fear that the vision of his father was diabolical or berate himself constantly for his procrastination in obeying the deceased king's injunction to rectify his homicide. It is significant that the director omits the ghost's second visit to spur his negligent son to action when the prince is alone with his mother. Hamlet here is steadfast in his determination but lacks a chance to punish Claudius. Supported by an impeccable ensemble, Innokenti Smoktunosvky with his strong screen presence makes a towering and unforgettable Hamlet. Kozintsev's direction is beautifully controlled and gracefully fluid. After a mounted Hamlet enters the gloomy castle at the film's start, the drawbridge rises and the portcullis descends ominously as if sealing the fate of our tragic prince. Only after his death does the grating ascend and the bridge lower as if to designate release. The apparition of the specter, on the grounds—not on the ramparts—is striking.

21

SHADOWS OF FORGOTTEN ANCESTORS*

Teni Zabytykh Predkov

USSR / 1964

DOVZHENKO FILM STUDIOS (KIEV)

CREDITS

Director: Sergei Paradjanov; *Screenwriters:* Sergei Paradjanov, Ivan Chendey, based on the novelette *Wild Horses of Fire* by Mikhail Kotsiubinsky and western-Ukrainian folklore; *Cinematographer:* Yuri Ilyenko (Magicolor); *Music:* M. Skorik; *Editor:* M. Ponomarenko; *Art directors:* M. Rakovsky, G. Yakutovich; *Running time:* 99 minutes; *16mm rental source:* Janus; *Videocassette:* Connoisseur.

CAST

Ivanko Paliichuk: Ivan Nikolaichuk; *Marichka Gutenyuk:* Larissa Kadochnikova; *Palagna:* Tatiana Be-

*aka *Shadows of Our Forgotten Ancestors* and *Wild Horses of Fire*

stayeva; *Yura the Sorcerer:* Spartak Bagashvili; *Vatag:* N. Grinko; *Miko:* L. Yengibarov.

The life of the Armenian director Sergei Paradjanov (1924–90)—the name has been transliterated variously and sometimes appears as Paradzhanov—had enough conflict and drama to make a fascinating film. His talents were multifarious (besides being a film director, he was a painter, sculptor, and musician), but his unorthodox ways appeared threatening to the Communist authorities: a visionary confronting the stodgy and moribund official line of socialist realism; a religious person in an atheistic society; a man pursuing an openly gay lifestyle in a nation where the penalty for a homosexual act was five years; and a filmmaker whose celebratory depiction of the cultures of Ukraine and Armenia seemed suspiciously "nationalistic" to the monolithic Soviet Union. Tried for "anti-Soviet agitation" in 1974, Paradjanov, after being told, "This ought to be enough to exterminate you!" was sentenced to five years imprisonment in a Siberian gulag. A petition by such luminaries as Truffaut, Malle, Fellini, Visconti, etc., helped to effect his release by 1978. The pariah's films were banned; he was forbidden to work in or to leave the country and was reduced to begging on the streets of Tiflis in Georgia.

conti, etc., helped to effect his release by 1978. The pariah's films were banned; he was forbidden to work in or to leave the country and was reduced to begging on the streets of Tiflis in Georgia.

Shadows of Forgotten Ancestors, Paradjanov's sixth feature, is regarded as this persecuted artist's masterpiece. It was filmed to commemorate the centenary of the author Mikhail Kotsiubinsky's birth in 1864. The director said that as soon as he read the novelette, he wished to film it: "I fell in love with this crystally clear feel for beauty, harmony, and infinity. A feel for that line where nature passes into art and art into nature." This tragic myth of a Romeo and Juliet archetype of love that transcends death was set and shot in northern Bukovina, a remote alpine region in the Carpathian Mountains in western Ukraine. "We wanted to make a film about passions understandable to every person," Paradjanov said, "and tried to convey these passions in a word, a melody, in every tangible thing. And of course in color. And here I really relied on painting. . . . Love, despair, solitude, death—these are the frescoes from the legend of a man that we were trying to create." The result was one of the strangest, most personal and original, most visually astonishing films ever made, albeit one little known here.

The action evolves over a number of years; the time is not specified, more likely the legendary past. In the isolated Carpathian Mountains live the Hutsuls, primitive, violent peasants whose Christianity is intertwined with a vigorous paganism. We meet Ivanko Paliichuk as a small boy bringing lunch to Olexa, an older brother cutting trees in a snowy forest. He pushes the child away

An exotic marriage practice: a yoke for oxen is placed over the blindfolded Ivanko (Ivan Nikolaichuk) and his bride, Palagna (Tatiana Bestayeva).

During a Christmas procession, Ivanko, significantly holding a scythe, removes his skeleton mask and broods on his late beloved, Marichka. We perceive how preoccupied he is with death.

87

from a falling tree; it crushes Olexa instead. In church the lad's father censures the religiously hypocritical Gutenyuk for fleecing the poor and mockingly laughs at him. Outside, the outraged wealthy man strikes and kills Paliichuk with his ax. The impoverished widow has only Ivanko now. In spite of the hostility between the families, he and Gutenyuk's daughter Marichka become inseparable. Time flows by and Ivanko (Ivan Nikolaichuk) is a young man, forced to go to work as a hired hand for a faraway shepherd. Before departing he asks his betrothed, Marichka (Larissa Kadochnikova), now pregnant with his baby, to wait for him. Each promises to stare at the North Star every evening to keep their love alive. Later, one foggy night Marichka, yearning for her lover, follows the star in his direction. Attempting to rescue a lamb on a rocky pass, she falls into a river and drowns. Sensing something's amiss, Ivanko searches until he comes upon her body. After a period of depression and drifting, he meets and marries the sensual Palagna (Tatiana Bestayeva). Obsessed with the dead Marichka, Ivanko can only make his unhappy wife feel rejected. Thinking that having children would save her marriage, Palagna conducts a pagan rite for childbearing

when spring arrives. She is soon impressed, however, with the powers and sexual magnetism of the sorcerer Yura (Spartak Bagashvili) and in a tavern starts to flirt with him. When her angry husband comes over to them, Yura hits him over the head with his hatchet. Staggering through the woods, Ivanko has an apparition of his loved one before expiring. The film ends with his wake, which moves in spirit from the mournful to the festive.

The Hutsuls are portrayed as simple people, impelled by the universal basic drives. Handsome Ivan Nikolaichuk and graceful Larissa Kadochnikova incarnate the folkloric lovers perfectly. Above all, *Shadows of Forgotten Ancestors* is a director's film. From the opening sequence during which the point of view becomes that of a huge tree plummeting to the ground, through frequent hand-held camera shots, zoom shots, tracking shots, and unusual angles, to the dizzying, tarantellalike, 360-degree whirling at Ivanko's obsequies, Paradjanov's mobile camera is rarely still, but pounding and dynamic as he successfully captures the pulsing, throbbing soul of this race. Enriching his daring camera work is what the director referred to as "the dramaturgy of color"; certain portions of the narrative are dominated by

While he is dying, Ivanko has a vision of his adored Marichka (Larissa Kadochnikova).

On the first day of spring, having left her home naked to perform a witchcraft ceremony to beget children, Palagna looks back to see if Yura the Sorcerer is following her.

Marichka, then he rushes back to rejoin the cortege of mourners, who in a striking long shot appear like dark specks in the niveous field. With this remarkable film exalting the indomitable spirit of man, Paradjanov proves himself to be one of the great romantic poets of the cinema and bequeaths an exhilarating and unforgettable classic to be savored.

a major hue to enhance the mood. Thus there is white throughout the lovers' childhood when they are surrounded by snow; there is green when they abandon themselves as youths in the woodland and subsequently part there as adults; there is gray to underscore Ivanko's disconsolate state after the death of Marichka; and there is red after Yura cleaves our hero's head with an ax and he falters in slow motion through the now rubescent inn.

In addition to Paradjanov's painterly skills, the almost continuous and diversified music plays a vital role. Included are long hunters' horns, eerie organ music, flutes, Jew's harps, bagpipes, church bells, folk songs, chants and choirs, lyrical themes and leitmotivs. To augment the arresting visual and auditory splendors, there is dance and ritual. One could say that this film truly has an "operatic" quality. Yuri Ilyenko contributed beautiful cinematography. A single scene can serve to illustrate the vivid pictorial values of the movie: the funeral procession of the slain father, Paliichuk. A low-angle shot reveals a bank of snow. Gradually a long, slow column appears; some men with bright red jackets holding black banners; horses drawing the coffin reposing on a sled; the wailing wife. Little Ivanko runs down the hill to chat with

22
WOMAN IN THE DUNES

Suna no Onna

JAPAN / 1964

TESHIGAHARA PRODUCTIONS

CREDITS

Director: Hiroshi Teshigahara; *Producers:* Kiichi Ichikawa, Tadashi Ohono; *Screenwriter:* Kobo Abé, based on his novel (1962); *Cinematographer:* Hiroshi Segawa (black and white); *Music:* Toru Takemitsu; *Editor:* Fusako Shuzui; *Art directors:* Totetsu Hirakawa, Masao Yamazaki; *Running time:* 127 minutes; *16mm rental source:* Images; *Videocassette:* Connoisseur.

CAST

Jumpei Niki: Eiji Okada; *Widow:* Kyoko Kishida; *Villagers:* Koji Mitsui, Sen Yano, and Hiroko Ito.

The successful adaptation by Japanese director Hiroshi Teshigahara (1927–) of Kobo Abé's novel *The Woman in the Dunes* launched into international prominence not only the filmmaker, whose second feature this was, but the author as well, for interest in his work led to various translations. To date, it is still the greatest achievement for both artists. The plight of a man kept prisoner in a remote sea hamlet and compelled to spend each day excavating cascading sand from high dunes that threaten to bury him and the simple widow who lives there found ready resonance in Western audiences immersed in the existential and absurdist tradition of Franz Kafka, Samuel Beckett, and Harold Pinter. "I was trying to explore the limits and mystery of life," Teshigahara said, "which is a paradox. In the film a man always escaping from life by taking field trips to collect insects becomes trapped in a sand pit. He is forced to face life itself. In the beginning, he is not aware of it. He tries to escape. But by the end, he finally accepts the situation as it exists." To create Abé's totally imagined world, mountainous cliffs of sand were constructed in Hamamatsu, near Mt. Fuji. The director had organized his own production company a few years before; the reported cost of the film was a mere $100,000. Hailed in Japan, acclaimed in Europe and here, *Woman in the Dunes* has lost none of its power after nearly thirty years.

The film opens as Jumpei Niki (Eiji Okada), a teacher-entomologist in his early thirties, goes on a field trip for rare beetles in a secluded sea village. A townsman approaches, informs him that he missed the last bus, and offers to find him accommodation. They arrive at a huge hole beneath a towering mountain of sand, at the base of which is embedded a rickety wooden house. Niki descends a rope ladder. The sole occupant is a recent widow (Kyoko Kishida), around thirty. The dwelling is primitive and he is startled to see that sand is constantly falling from the roof. Niki retires while the woman readies to spend the night collecting sand in the courtyard. In the morning the entomologist is disconcerted when he notices the ladder missing. In vain he tries to mount the enclosure of sand. Niki perceives with fear that the steps were hung from above and learns from the embarrassed widow that he's being kept captive to assist her in the arduous but necessary task of the daily sand removal. While Niki is outraged at his illegal detention, she is humbly submissive, recognizing that if her house were to be submerged, the one behind would be endangered. He soon rebels by tying her up and using her as a hostage to obtain his release. The ladder drops but the men only lift it partially and Niki falls. He unties her and soon they give vent to their mutual sexual attraction. The water supply exhausted, the revolt is short-lived. Only if they resume shoveling sand regularly into baskets that are hauled up will food and water be brought to them. Niki furtively binds cloths together and one night clambers up. He is detected; the villagers' flashlights maneuver him into a quicksand area where he is caught.

It is now winter. Niki devises a trap for crows in the yard, hoping to tie a message to a bird's leg. Before long, however, he's intrigued to discover water at the bottom of the wooden snare and deduces some capillary action is occurring in the sand. The pregnant widow is in pain and the men take her away for medical attention. Alone, Niki discerns that they left the ladder. Slowly he climbs it and strolls to the sea. The next scene shows him back in the courtyard studying the water found in the container. He tells himself there's no need to run away just yet; he's more interested in telling the people about the water. The film closes on a report on Niki: he's been gone for seven years and is now officially declared missing. . . .

Niki's character undergoes major changes. At the outset he is an arrogant intellectual, hankering after fame, uncommitted to anyone, and dissatisfied with his regimented, bureaucratic Tokyo world. Detained, he is obsessed with freeing himself. He finds the widow's labors meaningless drudgery and questions her, "Are you clearing sand to live, or living to clear sand?" Yet by the end of the film he ignores an opportunity to flee and seems to be realizing his identity: sharing an intimate relationship, acting selflessly by finding water that would benefit his neighbors, and recognizing a sense of spiritual freedom. The unassuming widow whose husband and child were swallowed up during a sandstorm the previous year has no rebellious thoughts, loving her commune along with her fragile home. Poignantly she tells Niki her fears when she goes to bed: "I'm afraid I'll wake up alone again." Eiji Okada and Kyoko Kishida play their roles with forceful conviction. Teshigahara's adroit direction is exemplary; gritty realism

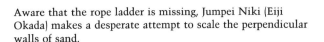

Aware that the rope ladder is missing, Jumpei Niki (Eiji Okada) makes a desperate attempt to scale the perpendicular walls of sand.

Unleashed passion finally erupts between the lonely widow and her imprisoned guest.

Later Niki binds up the woman (Kyoko Kishida) as a bargaining tool for his freedom.

and tension prevent the film from becoming abstract and lifeless. He evokes a claustrophobic mood, generates suspense via Niki's efforts to break away and eroticism as the fingers of the love-starved couple dig into each's flesh, and provokes stimulating thought. The employment of a hand-held camera, use of extreme close-ups, and economical depth-of-field shots are marks of his remarkable technique. Credit to Segawa's exceptional photography, particularly scenes of sand looming as a hypnotic vista or falling in a mesmerizing avalanche, and to Takemitsu's ominous score.

The film is open to many, varying interpretations. Some have viewed it as a bleak reading of the human condition with Niki as a contemporary Sisyphus who, instead of eternally pushing a rock uphill in Hades only to have it roll down repeatedly, now has to monotonously and futilely scoop out sand in a menacing environment. Yet the film is capable of an affirmative construction. Critic Dennis Giles understands it as an expression of the venerable Chinese philosophy of Taoism: "Tao is the path, the process, the way that a man follows, that all things follow. . . . To be in harmony with, not in rebellion against, the fundamental laws of the universe is the first step on the road to Tao. . . . Only by remaining passive, receptive, and yielding can the Tao assert itself in the mind." Thus Niki at the conclusion is not simply resigned, but rather enlightened as he makes his difficult journey to his self and to life. Both as an intense realistic drama and as a provocative allegory of modern man, *Woman in the Dunes* remains a brilliant and engaging film.

HONORS

Special Jury Prize, Cannes Film Festival (1964)
Nominated for two Oscars: Best Foreign Language Film (1964) and Best Director (1965)

91

23

THE SHOP ON MAIN STREET

Obchod na Korze

CZECHOSLOVAKIA / 1965

BARRANDOV FILM STUDIO FOR CESKOSLOVENSKY FILM

CREDITS

Directors: Jan Kadar, Elmar Klos; *Producer:* Ladislav Hanus; *Screenwriters:* Ladislav Grosman, Jan Kadar, Elmar Klos, based on Grosman's novella; *Cinematographer:* Vladimir Novotny (black and white); *Music:* Zdenek Liska; *Editors:* Jaromir Janacek, Diana Heringova; *Art director:* Karel Skvor; *Running time:* 128 minutes; *16mm rental source:* Janus; *Videocassette:* RCA/Columbia.

CAST

Tono Brtko: Josef Kroner; *Rosalie Lautmann:* Ida Kaminska; *Evelina:* Hana Slivkova; *Marcus Kolkotsky:* Frantisek Zvarik; *Rose:* Elena Zvarikova; *Imro Kuchar:* Martin Holly; *Katz the Barber:* Martin Gregor.

One of the results of the gradual easing of Stalinist repression that occurred in Communist-controlled Czechoslovakia in the 1960s was a sudden burst of extraordinary cinematic achievement. Directors were permitted to tackle subjects long held taboo. One such topic was Slovakia's complicity in the Holocaust, which Ladislav Grosman treated in a novella. When Czechoslovak director Jan Kadar (1918–79) came upon it, he and his long-term collaborator Elmar Klos (1910–) (unlike Kadar, a native-born Czechoslovak) instinctively knew that they must film it. It would be called *The Shop on Main Street** and would be their eighth feature together. "For the first time, I wanted to do a picture about the truth of our past," Kadar said, "because nobody wanted to touch it. We always spoke just about the Germans—that was all right. Nobody wanted to speak about our own weak points." Actually, Slovakia had become a German

*Initially known here as *The Shop on High Street*

protectorate in March 1939. An indigenous form of fascism was in power; Slovakia was the first non-German country to endorse Hitler's notorious anti-Semitic Nuremberg laws. Kadar asserts that the "Slovak government paid six hundred crowns for each Jew who was transported to Auschwitz."

Grosman confined his story to a small town and an old Jewish widow's relationship with her "Aryan Controller"; like other stores, hers was placed under jurisdiction of a non-Jewish proprietor—here a carpenter. "All the big tragedy was in one drop of water," Kadar said. "This one drop explicitly and precisely expressed the substance of fascism." The director, a Jew, had suffered terribly in World War II. Both of his parents and a sister were killed in Auschwitz; he spent the war in a Nazi labor camp. Both directors thought Josef Kroner ideal for the part of the carpenter who lets himself be drawn into the destructive vortex of fascism. For the difficult role of the widow Lautmann no suitable Czechoslovak actress came to mind. Kadar and Klos saw Ida Kaminska perform in her theater in Warsaw and knew she'd be perfect for the part. In her autobiography, *My Life, My Theater* (1973), Miss Kaminska recalls initially rejecting the role, which would focus on the comic side of the personage. "In essence her character is a tragic one," she affirmed, and the directors wisely complied with her stipulations. The subsequent film, made in 1964, is stronger than the book (published here in 1970), with a richer characterization and a more powerful tragic dimension. Exteriors were shot in Sabinov, a small Slovak town. The extras were the townspeople, which provided an added realism to the film. The picture was a resounding triumph. *The Shop on Main Street* was the first Czechoslovak feature to win an Oscar for Best Foreign Language Film. The film paved the way for other outstanding movies from that nation to meet with critical and commercial success here. Superbly written and directed, memorably acted, it has attained the status of a classic.

The year is 1942; the setting, an unnamed Slovakian town. Tono (Josef Kroner) is a carpenter nagged by his wife, Evelina (Hana Slivkova), for having no money. Her sister's fatuous husband, Marcus (Frantisek Zvarik), is the residing fascist leader, whom Tono despises. Marcus and his wife, Rose (Elena Zvarikova), visit, shower the couple with food and gifts, and present an official letter naming Tono "Aryan Controller" of the elderly widow Lautmann's button shop. Evelina is ecstatic with the promise of untold luxury. Tono cannot make clear his new position to the charming but hard-of-hearing proprietress (Ida Kaminska). Kuchar (Martin Holly) stops by, reads the letter, and apprises Tono of the situation: the woman is poor, sustained through the generosity of her friends. Kuchar tells the indignant carpenter that perhaps it's better for her to have him than someone else. The Jews will simply contribute more for his "cut." Kuchar makes him see that he's a fool whom the authorities have swindled. An embarrassed Tono goes to work as her "assistant." She is very dear and acts maternal with him; he repairs her furniture and becomes protective of her. "Do her no harm," he is exhorted while Katz the barber (Martin Gregor) pays Tono his comfortable weekly salary, which pleases his greedy spouse. Soon the carpenter learns that a roundup of the Jews is set for the next day. He is shocked to see a beaten-up Kuchar, forced to wear the sign "I Am a White Jew" (ardent Jewish sympathizer), in po-

lice custody. Drunk, Tono wakes the widow later to warn her, but she merely puts him up for the night in the shop. He awakens to a roll call of the Jews outside while Mrs. Lautmann brings in breakfast, oblivious of what's happening. When he overhears, "Woe to him who harbors a Jew!," a frightened Tono starts packing her suitcase and tries to drag her to the street. At last she realizes what is going on and screams, "Pogrom!" Seeing Marcus approaching, he yells at her to hide and shoves her into a room. Tono soon discovers he inadvertently killed her—there's her dead body stretched over the wicker luggage. In despair he hangs himself. The film ends on a note of wish-fulfillment fantasy: in high-key lighting Tono dances with a beaming Mrs. Lautmann in the town square while a band plays zestfully.

Tono is essentially decent but politically naive, weak, and indifferent to the cruelty around him.

Tono (Josef Kroner) lashes out at his brother-in-law, Marcus (Frantisek Zvarik) (right), the local fascist leader (notice the insignia of the Hlinka Guards), for appropriating his wife's inheritance. Evelina (Hana Slivkova), his spouse (left), and Rose (Elena Zvarikova), married to the gauleiter, listen.

The continuation of the reverie that the beleaguered carpenter had earlier. In slow motion Tono escorts a happy Mrs. Lautmann—now both deceased—to a dance through the peaceful streets that concludes the film.

Yielding to his fear of being punished for shielding a Jew, Tono attempts to drag the distraught Widow Lautmann (Ida Kaminska) outside to be transported with the rest of the Jews.

He slowly becomes conscious of the evil he is part of and experiences shame and guilt. Mrs. Lautmann is a dignified old lady cut off from the world by her deafness, who finds solace in her deep religious faith. Evelina is obnoxiously rapacious and completely insensitive to the Jews' plight. To balance the picture, we have the self-sacrificing Kuchar. The directors neither sentimentalize the victims as noble martyrs nor depict the guards as stereotypical villains; all are recognizably real and human. With her enormous screen presence, Ida Kaminska is unforgettably brilliant in the greatest of her few screen appearances. Projecting sweetness and innocence, she affected audiences universally. With his expressive face Josef Kroner makes a vigorous partner. His crisis scene is striking as he veers from panic-stricken anxiety for his own safety to a solicitous concern for the old woman he's come to love. The sequence is almost unbearable in the tension it evokes. The direction is tight and builds toward a devastating climax. Kadar commented, "I had intentionally attempted to erect a monument to all victims of persecution." This forceful, deeply moving, and timeless film proved to be the directors' masterpiece.

HONORS

Oscar for Best Foreign Language Film (1965); in addition, Ida Kaminska nominated for Best Actress (1966)

Best Foreign Film, New York Film Critics Award (1966)

24
LOVES OF A BLONDE

Lasky Jedne Plavovlasky

CZECHOSLOVAKIA / 1965

BARRANDOV FILM STUDIO (PRAGUE)

CREDITS

Director: Milos Forman; *Assistant director:* Ivan Passer; *Producer:* Rudolph Hajek; *Screenwriters:* Jaroslav Papousek, Milos Forman, Ivan Passer; *Cinematography:* Miroslav Ondricek (black and white); *Music:* Evzen Illin; *Editor:* Miroslav Hajek; *Art director:* Karel Cerny; *Running time:* 88 minutes; *16mm rental source:* Janus; *Videocassette:* RCA/Columbia.

CAST

Andula: Hana Brejchova; *Mila:* Vladimir Pucholt; *Vacovsky:* Vladimir Mensik; *Manas:* Ivan Kheil; *Burda:* Jiri Hruby; *Mila's mother:* Milada Jezkova; *Mila's father:* Josef Sebanek; *Tonda:* Antonin Blazejovsky; *Marie:* Marie Salacova; *Jana:* Jana Novakova; *Factory Supervisor:* Josef Kolb; *The Major:* Jan Vostrcil.

Among the gifted directors to appear during the Czechoslovak "New Wave" in the 1960s was Milos Forman (1932–   ) whose first feature, *Black Peter* (1964), revealed a talent for a humorous, authentic look at small-town life. He would continue in this light vein for his next two films until the Soviet invasion of August 1968 necessitated his departure for America. The idea for *Loves of a Blonde*, his second feature, came from a personal experience. Driving home in Prague in the early morning, Forman came upon a young lady walking alone with her suitcase. He stopped the car and went over to her. She confessed that she had traveled to the capital to see a young man she had met in her village. She had made love to him there and he invited her to come to Prague to see him. The address had been false. . . . That incident triggered an exceptional movie with a compelling mixture of comedy and pathos. "My primary aim in *Loves of a Blonde*," the director said, "was to show young people in real situations that I know from life." The film launched Forman's international reputation and is as fresh and entertaining today as it was when it was released more than twenty-five years ago.

Andula (Hana Brejchova) is a pretty young blonde who lives in Zruc and works in the local shoe factory. The film opens in the dormitory as Andula whispers to her friend about the ring her boyfriend Tonda (Antonin Blazejovsky) gave her and her subsequent dating of a forest ranger who turned out to be married. A humane factory supervisor (Josef Kolb) is concerned that there are far too few available men in town for the two thousand young women under his care and demands from the major (Jan Vostrcil) that he station his troops closer. A train pulls in and a dreary group of flabby, older men emerge to the disappointment of the hopeful female spectators. At a dance three chubby and unengaging soldiers try in vain to charm Andula and her friends, but our heroine is

While a bewildered forest ranger watches, Andula (Hana Brejchova) removes a tie from a tree that she had put there when she was going with Tonda.

Late at night the three soldiers, *(left to right)* Vacovsky (Vladimir Mensik), Manas (Ivan Kheil), and Burda (Jiri Hruby), are quite confident about their imminent "conquest" of the young ladies, *(left to right)* Marie (Marie Salacova), Jana (Jana Novakova), and Andula (Hana Brejchova).

more interested in the band's youthful pianist, Mila (Vladimir Pucholt). When they meet, after much persuasion she agrees to go upstairs to his room where he seduces her. Mila regards this as just a flirtation. After a housemother admonishes against promiscuous behavior and speaks of the ideal, loving marriage, Andula sets out at night with her luggage to hitch to Prague. She drops in at Mila's apartment and is subjected to relentless interrogation from his mother (Milada Jezkova), while father (Josef Sebanek) is much more considerate. The son arrives home later after being foiled in an attempt at philandering and is puzzled to find Andula sleeping in his bed. She wakes up and Mila dissembles that he's glad to see her again. The outraged mother separates the couple and drags Mila into the parents' bedroom where there's a long, hilarious scene as they shower recriminations upon their randy son. In the dormitory Andula whispers that she guesses she'll be going to Prague all the time now. A closing scene shows our moody heroine working, as before, on the shoes.

An ordinary person severely isolated in her provincial town, Andula is innocent of the ways of the world. She is gullible, believing what each of her boyfriends tells her, but is decidedly sympathetic because she is searching for love but totally unaware how to find it. Forman's tone is gently ironic

95

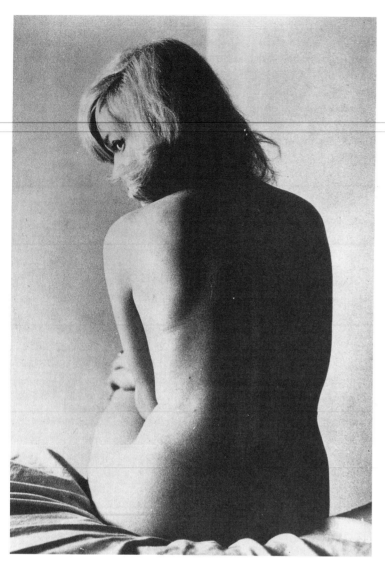

Andula is shy and apprehensive—as well she should be—before giving herself to the lothario Mila.

and compassionate, not mocking. Regarding the younger generation, the director said, "I like them, understand them . . . I am biased in their favor." We can ask, has Andula really learned anything from her experiences since the film both starts and ends with her weaving romantic fantasies about her boyfriend of the moment? In spite of his callousness, Mila is a likable but typically muddled young man. Whether professional or nonprofessional, all the actors in the film seen genuine and natural. The attractive Hana Brejchova is convincing and appealing as the unlucky Andula; Vladimir Pucholt is fine as the bungling playboy. With a concentration on close-ups and medium shots, Forman directs in an intimate, simple style. He admits to being strongly influenced by cinema verité in his close observation of reality to arrive at the truth. Avoiding sentimentality and exaggeration, paying attention to the revealing detail (in Andula's suitcase Mila's mother discovers the very cravat that Andula had earlier fastened to a tree when she was dating Tonda), the director displays a sense of comic realism that is delightfully honest and original. French screenwriter Jean-Claude Carrière praised Forman's work by stating as absolutes, "You can't direct anything artificial, anything which doesn't sound and look real and true."

The dance is one of two priceless scenes in the film. Three soldiers at a table notice Andula and her companions and aggressively plot their maneuvers. They send over a bottle of expensive wine, but a waiter delivers it to a nearby table to a trio of grateful women. The reservist Vacovsky (Vladimir Mensik) hurries over to him, and just as a lady is all set to pour from the unexpected gift, the waiter snatches it without comment and puts it on the correct table. Andula and her friends feel obliged to put up with their boring hosts. A wed-

The uproarious result when Andula turns up unexpectedly at Mila's apartment and occupies his bed. Mila (Vladimir Pucholt) *(center)* is forced to sleep with his parents and gets barrels of abuse from his mother (Milada Jezkova) and his father (Josef Sebanek).

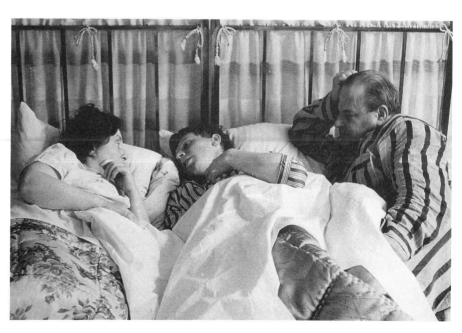

ding ring falls out of another soldier's pocket, whirls across the dance floor, and lands beneath the table of the bottle-deprived ladies. The reservist Burda (Jiri Hruby) bends to retrieve it, rises too soon, and tips a drink, which spills on his back . . . . The later scene in which the puritanical mother insists that Mila sleep with her and her husband is a gem. In a medium shot the camera is focused dead center on the bed and doesn't move while the angry mother and father lash out at poor Mila and each other. Just when there's a moment's silence and you think they're going off to sleep, the mother starts in again. Mila changes places with his dad, who never gets enough of the blanket. After some stillness, another outburst from the mother, this one full of self-pity and recognizable, guilt-inflicting lines—"You'll be the death of me yet"—which will move any audience to helpless laughter. While we are guffawing, Forman skillfully cuts to Andula listening in tears to the heartless manner in which she's being discussed. What a stroke of conflicting emotional responses! With *Loves of a Blonde* Forman makes magic out of the commonplace. Although he would go on to phenomenal success with *One Flew Over the Cuckoo's Nest* (1975) and *Amadeus* (1984), his prior Czechoslovak classic deserves to be remembered and cherished.

HONORS

L'Étoile de Cristal for Prix International (1966)
Nominated for an Oscar for Best Foreign Language Film (1966)

25
INTIMATE LIGHTING

Intimni Osvetleni

CZECHOSLOVAKIA / 1965

BARRANDOV FILM STUDIO (PRAGUE)

CREDITS

Director: Ivan Passer; *Assistant director:* Jiri Ruzicka; *Producer:* Frantisek Sandr; *Screenwriters:* Vaclav Sasek, Jaroslav Papousek, Ivan Passer, based on a story by Sasek; *Cinematographers:* Miroslav Ondricek, Jan Strecha (black and white); *Music:* Oldrich Korte, Josef Hart; *Editor:* Jirina Lukesova; *Art director:* Karel Cerny; *Running time:* 72 minutes; *16mm rental source:* Films Inc.

CAST

Shtiepa: Vera Kresadlova; *Peter:* Zdenek Bezusek; *Kaya ("Bombas"):* Karel Blazek; *Grandfather:* Jan Vostrcil; *Grandmother:* Vlastimila Vlkova; *Marie:* Jaroslava Stedra; *Pharmacist:* Karel Uhlik; *Kaya:* Miroslav Cvrk; *Marie:* Dagmar Redinova.

Another distinguished Czechoslovak "New Wave" director to emerge during the "thaw" in the Novotny regime was Ivan Passer (1933–). Like Milos Forman, with whom he collaborated as a screenwriter on three films (including *Loves of a Blonde*) before defecting with him to America, he chose to do a light comedy when at last he was able to direct his first (and, as it turned out, sole) Czechoslovak feature, *Intimate Lighting.* "We had to do comedy," Passer said, "because we knew we would have an easier time with censorship." He became engrossed in a short story entitled "Something Else" by Vaclav Sasek, which was the basis for the film. Two musicians with contrasting lifestyles—one from Prague and one from the country—have a bittersweet, rural reunion that lasts a weekend. "We were attracted," Passer said, "by the confrontation of the lives of two men of the same age, of the same profession, who were at one

Kaya (Karel Blazek), aka Bombas, has a guest in his garage. Director Ivan Passer amusingly delineates the chaos of rustic life.

Playing their trumpets at a funeral are Kaya and Grandfather (Jan Vostrcil).

felt that I could really examine deeply what I wanted to express. So, in general a film is a question of affinity." The result was an altogether sprightly "slice of life." Although it is little known here, *Intimate Lighting* is a wonderful comedy worthy of our discovery and reevaluation.

Any plot summary can only give the barest indication of the rich visual experience that is the pleasure of the viewer exclusively. The action is set in the present. Peter (Zdenek Bezusek), a cellist in Prague, arrives with his mistress Shtiepa (Vera Kresadlova) at a provincial town where he is to perform at a concert with the local orchestra. They stay at the home of Kaya (Karel Blazek), an old schoolmate who is a violinist and head of the town's music school. Kaya, whom his friend teasingly calls "Bombas" (a nickname whose literal meaning "bombast" can hardly be endearing to a musician), is married to Marie (Jaroslava Stedra), has two children, and lives with his lively parents, Grandfather (Jan Vostrcil) and Grandmother (Vlastimila Vlkova). During the course of the day Kaya and his father play at a burial, drink at an inn, and afterward at home with the visiting pharmacist (Karel Uhlik) and Peter make an unforgettable quartet as they perform "Eine Kleine Nachtmusik." (The rendition is horrid.) At night Peter abandons Shtiepa to have a long talk with Bombas. Over drinks, Kaya reveals the frustrations he has to endure, and when both are drunk, Bombas blurts out his wish to escape. The musicians set out late at night with their instruments. They do not make much progress for a morning scene discloses Kaya sleeping in the car in his garage. The film ends while all are taking their breakfast alfresco.

Each of the charming people we encounter in *Intimate Lighting* is fresh, real, and comes alive as

time motivated by the same ambitions, who at one time had the same perspectives on life, but no longer do." The emphasis in the movie would be neither on the plot, such as it is, nor on characterization per se. "It was even more important for us to try," the director continued, "and give a picture of everyday life, the life which men live from day to day, without pathos, without sensational happenings, but interesting in its own way—in its simplicity." The tone would not be critical or judgmental, but compassionate and gentle. Passer spoke of the vital need to have what he called an "affinity with the subject. If this didn't exist, it would have been impossible for me to work. . . . I

A diverting moment as a cluster of mourners sneak away from the burial ceremony to answer a call of nature and surprise a woman who was sunbathing.

an individual. Life in the country is depicted as unhurried, with a "lento" pace. Kaya, for example, has been building his house for the last seven years. However, he may feel trapped, particularly when he compares himself to Peter, who seems to be living the good life in Prague without being buried with responsibilities. "Have you a house, auto, wife?" he asks his companion. "Then you're not finished." Kaya's situation is nevertheless treated humorously. If Peter is condescending toward Bombas and his neighbors vegetating in the provinces, Passer most certainly is not. Grandfather is a randy old man—even boasting of his sexual conquests during the interment scene; Grandmother is equally vivacious, demonstrating to Peter's girlfriend her agile athletic ability. Shtiepa is most appealing as she discovers the simple country pleasures and thinks nothing of interrupting the string quartet by displaying the black kitten she's found. Passer loves these people and doesn't wish us to feel superior to them but to recognize their humanity and ours as well. "It is necessary to get next to them," the director said, "to understand their problems. It is a film about ordinary people, whose problems are obvious, a film about the current of life, a life we all live, whether we want to or not." The laughter engendered is not bitingly satirical but droll and cordial. All the actors are impeccably cast, notably Vera Kresadlova, Zdenek Bezusek, Karel Blazek, Jan Vostrcil, and Vlastimila Vlkova. Passer had the good sense to avoid sentimentality and not to strain for laughs with exaggerated farce, relying simply on what is natural, which he successfully captured. "I am not interested in the story," he subsequently affirmed, "but in the state of being." With his skillful direction, perceptive eye, and sensitivity for the telling detail, *Intimate Lighting* becomes a sheer delight. Credit Miroslav Ondricek and Jan Strecha for their fine photography.

The many entertaining moments in the film include the invasion of the garage by poultry. In the consequent man versus fowl conflict, a chicken is killed and an egg rolls from beneath the car. The tortured recital of Mozart's music provides a hilarious sequence. When Kaya suggests that his father play it as written, the older man says, "What can you expect with such joints?" Later when the inebriated Peter and Kaya peer inside Grandfather's room, Peter "conducts" while the old man snores. In the closing scene Grandmother has done something to the eggnog for the entire group is holding the glasses to their mouths while she announces, "This needs pa-

tience" before they can relish a delicacy. In a long shot we see them all with upturned glasses and expectant mouths waiting steadfastly for the treat. Whenever it does come, it could not match the fun the audience has been having all along. Passer superbly evoked a sense of life and created a believable, authentic world—a joyful one that enchants the viewer with its high spirits and verve. The director's ensuing career, unfortunately, was not as successful, critically or commercially, as Forman's. Nonetheless, *Intimate Lighting* remains an offbeat treasure and deserves to be remembered.

26
CLOSELY WATCHED TRAINS

Ostre Sledovane Vlaky

CZECHOSLOVAKIA / 1966

BARRANDOV FILM STUDIO (PRAGUE)

CREDITS

Director: Jiri Menzel; *Assistant director:* Bohumil Kouba; *Producer:* Zdenek Oves; *Screenwriters:* Jiri Menzel, Bohumil Hrabal, based on his novel (1965); *Cinematographer:* Jaromir Sofr (black and white); *Music:* Jiri Sust; *Editor:* Jirina Lukesova; *Art director:* Oldrich Bosak; *Running time:* 92 minutes; *16mm rental source:* Janus; *Videocassette:* Fox/Lorber.

CAST

Milos Hrma: Vaclav Neckar; *Masha:* Jitka Bendova; *Stationmaster:* Vladimir Valenta; *His Wife:* Libuse Havelkova; *Hubicka:* Josef Somr; *Novak:* Alois Vachek; *Zdenicka Svata:* Jitka Zelenohorska; *Councillor Zednicek:* Vlastimil Brodsky; *Uncle Noneman:* Ferdinand Kruta; *Victoria Freie:* Nada Urbankova; *The Countess:* Kveta Fialova; *Dr. Brabec:* Jiri Menzel.

An additional Czechoslovak director to gain prominence during the New Wave period was Jiri Menzel (1938–) whose stunning first feature, *Closely Watched Trains*, invited comparisons to Orson Welles's *Citizen Kane* (1941). In each instance a director in his twenties proved his unmistakable

Portrait of the new apprentice Milos Hrma (Vaclav Neckar) at the Kostomlaty Station.

talent in an inaugural effort. Menzel was drawn to a novel by the popular writer Bohumil Hrabal that depicted a small railroad station in Czechoslovakia at the close of World War II. The screenwriters converted a story told through monologues into a simple, tight, visual narration with the time sequence arranged linearly, building to a powerful climax. Hrabal persuaded the director to retain the book's unhappy ending, which gives the film a tragic dimension. With the exception of Vlastimil Brodsky, the superb cast were nonprofessionals; Vaclav Neckar, a pop singer, portrayed the timid hero. The movie was shot in 1965 in the Lodenice railroad station. The strikingly fresh and original *Closely Watched Trains* was an international triumph and endures as a cherished film classic.

The year is 1944. The young Milos Hrma (Vaclav Neckar) is proud to begin work as a trainee at the railroad station. The middle-aged stationmaster (Vladimir Valenta) fulminates against the philandering train dispatcher Hubicka (Josef Somr), but the shy youth envies the latter's way with women. Councillor Zednicek (Vlastimil Brodsky), who supervises the country's railroads for the Nazi occupiers, drives up and cautions the staff to be specially careful of priority trains carrying ammunition headed to the front. Masha (Jitka Bendova), a train guard, invites her boyfriend Milos to spend the night with her at the photographic studio of her lusty uncle (Ferdinand Kruta). Milos, elated, is soon devastated when he cannot perform sexually. He rents a hotel room and cuts his wrists in the bathtub. Fortunately, he is caught in time. Meanwhile, during a night shift, Hubicka playfully rub-

Just as Masha (Jitka Bendova) leans over to kiss an expectant Milos, a mischievous Hubicka blows the whistle for the train to start.

100

ber-stamps the derriere of the amused telegraphist Zdenicka (Jitka Zelenohorska). Later, her mother notices the markings and is outraged. In the psychiatric clinic, a sympathetic Dr. Brabec (Jiri Menzel) tells Milos his problem is premature ejaculation. Zdenicka's mother complains to the authorities and demands that Hubicka be jailed. The psychiatrist encourages his forlorn charge to gain sexual proficiency with an older woman. Hubicka, a partisan, learns that an ammunition train is due to pass the next day and that he'll be supplied with sufficient detonation. Since the guerrillas destroyed a train the night before, the Germans seize poor Milos as hostage briefly. The train dispatcher takes the lad into his confidence and explains the sabotage plan. That night Victoria Freie (Nada Urbankova) appears with a bundle of explosives. At Hubicka's prompting she generously helps Milos lose his troublesome virginity. The next day he's calm and feels assured of his manhood. Seven minutes before the appointed train is to go by, Zednicek, his aides, Zdenicka, and her irate mother turn up to hold an official disciplinary committee meeting concerning Hubicka. In the midst of the hearing the brave Milos steps in and removes the deadly package. From the signal arm atop a gantry, he drops the detonation onto the passing train, is shot by a guard, and falls on a canvas-topped railcar. There is a tremendous explosion behind the hill. In the vehement wind Masha comes upon Milos's cap.

Milos is a thoroughly endearing youth for whom sexual ability is the norm by which he can accept himself as a man. Sexual dysfunction induces an attempt at self-destruction, while sexual success spurs him to act courageously albeit fatally. Delightful is the plump stationmaster, fondling his pigeons, paying deference to the anachronistic trappings of monarchy via the countess, dreaming of promotion to inspector in spite of the scandals of Hubicka's "immorality" and Milos's try at suicide, lusting after young and unobtainable ladies then hiding under the facade of self-righteous indignation. He is outlandish and very funny. The ordinary German soldiers are not stereotyped. When a group stare with libidinous longing at a train of smiling nurses, who invite them in, Menzel stresses a humanity common to all. The acting is subtle, unstrained, and completely natural. Vaclav Neckar plays the difficult role of Milos with total conviction. Jitka Bendova is charming as his pretty girlfriend.

Menzel's direction shows masterly control in handling such disparate elements as the comic and

Train dispatcher Hubicka (Josef Somr) *(left)* ponders what to make of the fledgling trainee Milos. We discover subsequently that the womanizing man is a resistance fighter.

the tragic. The many fine details come from a close observation of life. At the photographer's studio while the randy uncle has a client push out her bust for the shot, a mother watching this covers her small daughter's eyes. In an unforgettable sequence, Milos, held captive briefly on a train, stares out the window to glimpse a beloved world he is in danger of leaving. Poignantly, from the trainee's point of view, accompanied by Jiri Sust's lovely music, we see countryside scenes, houses, fields, a small river, trees in bloom. . . . The consequences of Zdenicka with her rubber-stamped buttock are both hilarious and calamitous (when one considers that Milos volunteers to replace a cornered Hubicka, who was supposed to drop the explosives.) Her straitlaced mother, head wrapped in a babushka, catches sight of the strange designs on her sleeping daughter's thigh and rushes over to get her spectacles. At the local police station she lifts up the "violated" Zdenicka's skirt; an officer kneels down and puts on his glasses to get a better look. Sent to the regional magistrate, the mother intrudes upon a trial and again demonstrates the evidence to three happy judges, who refer her to the railway authorities. Exasperated, she pulls up her daughter's dress in an appeal to the shocked prisoner, a man being tried for strangling a woman!

The rich humor is intercut with unbearable suspense when she arrives with Zednicek at the railroad station for the ill-timed inquiry. What a brilliant juxtaposition of comedy and tragedy!

The black humor of the film is traditional in Czechoslovakia. Milos Forman explained, "To laugh at their own tragedy has been in this century the only way for such a little nation, placed in such a dangerous spot in Europe, to survive." Menzel said characteristically, "Let us show we're brave by laughing at life. And in that laughter let us not look for cynicism but rather reconciliation." He was the only Czechoslovak director mentioned in this book to stay during the"normalization" (i.e., repression) that followed August 1968. His subsequent *Larks on a String* (1969) was banned and he retreated to the theater for a while. *Closely Watched Trains*, which Czechoslovak director Evald Schorm called "an expression of love for human beings," has lost none of its exhilarating, special qualities and remains Menzel's masterpiece thus far.

HONORS

Oscar for Best Foreign Language Film (1967)

27
LA GUERRE EST FINIE

FRANCE/SWEDEN / 1966

SOFRACIMA (PARIS)/EUROPA-FILM (STOCKHOLM)

CREDITS

Director: Alain Resnais; *Assistant directors:* Jean Léon, Florence Malraux; *Producers:* Catherine Winter, Giselle Rebillon; *Screenwriter:* Jorge Semprun; *Cinematographer:* Sacha Vierny (black and white); *Music:* Giovanni Fusco; *Editor:* Eric Pluet; *Art director:* Jacques Saulnier; *Running time:* 121 minutes; *16mm rental source and videocassette:* New Yorker.

CAST

Diego Mora: Yves Montand; *Marianne:* Ingrid Thulin; *Nadine Sallanches:* Geneviève Bujold; *The Chief:* Jean Dasté; *Inspector:* Michel Piccoli; *Ramon:* Jean Bouise; *Ramon's Wife:* Yvette Etiévant; *Roberto:* Paul

Dedicated revolutionary Diego Mora (Yves Montand) has a warm reunion with Ramon (Jean Bouise), his fellow worker in the cause, as Ramon's wife (Yvette Etiévant) looks on.

Crauchet; *Manolo:* Jacques Rispal; *Carmen:* Françoise Bertin; *Antoine:* Roland Monod; *Juan:* Jean-François Rémi; *Tramp:* R. J. Chauffar; *Sarlat:* Bernard Fresson; *Narrator:* Jorge Semprun.

In 1964, Alain Resnais contacted novelist Jorge Semprun to ask him to prepare a screenplay on a political subject. "I have been enticed," the director said, "by the description of a milieu one has rarely seen on the screen and which seems to me to play a big role in the evolution of the world. If one percent of men transform the world, one should be comfortable now and then to make a film about them." Semprun decided on Spain as a theme and eventually focused on the situation of an aging revolutionary, steadfast in his efforts to overthrow the apparently interminable Franco regime, which stretched back to the defeat of the Loyalists in 1939. The time in the film would be the present and the stress would be on characterization, not on a plot of derring-do. Semprun wished to criticize the romantic, false notions of the "myth of Spain," including the myopic view of those in exile, and to insist that the only way to effect a change in Spain was a realistic approach, as it existed then. "This film is intentionally provocative," the writer said. "It should stimulate a reflection, perhaps ire, bitterness, but it is necessary for those who leave it to have had a thought there." The project, Resnais's fourth feature, became *La Guerre Est Finie* (*The War Is Over*), released here in its original French

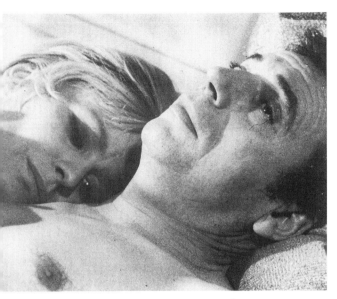

An intimate moment between Diego and Marianne (Ingrid Thulin), who loves him.

When Diego learns that the seedy character (R. J. Chauffar) to whom he just gave a pack of cigarettes is an informer for the police, he takes it back, displaying his unwavering probity.

title. Shooting took place between August and November 1965 in Stockholm and Paris. The film was intended to represent France at Cannes, but the Spanish government, coping with riots in Madrid, pressured the host nation to exclude it. Nonetheless, a group of Spanish film critics awarded the movie, shown out of competition, the newly created Prix Luis Buñuel. Alain Resnais had another controversial—and successful—film. Internationally praised, *La Guerre Est Finie* is beautifully written, acted, and directed and deserves to be better known today.

Diego Mora (Yves Montand) is a forty-year-old Spaniard living in France who has devoted his life to being a professional revolutionary. The action is compressed within a four-day period, April 18–21, 1965. The film opens as Diego, learning that several of his comrades have been rounded up and that the Spanish government is ready to unmask their organization and arrest one of the leaders, interrupts his lengthy stay in Spain to return to France to warn his chief. At the border his car is stopped and a call is put through to Paris to verify that Diego is the Sallanches on the passport. He is concerned about the fate of Juan (Jean-François Rémi), apparently still in Spain, who is the probable figure to be exposed. He visits his revolutionist friend Ramon (Jean Bouise) and then calls on his "daughter," Nadine Sallanches (Geneviève Bujold), whose earlier telephone lie got him past the border police. She finds Diego attractive and they

make love. Later he returns home to Marianne (Ingrid Thulin), his long-term lover. The next day Diego meets his chief (Jean Dasté) and is criticized for leaving Spain suddenly and having lost "all political perspective." A general strike in that country is promoted, but Diego doesn't agree that conditions are opportune for it. He is told to remain in Paris and reflect on his impulsive behavior. Diego encounters Nadine's young radical friends and disagrees with their advocacy of terrorist activity in Spain. News comes of Ramon's unexpected death from a heart attack, and Diego is ordered to replace him and leave for Spain to save Juan. Nadine finds out that it is Diego, not Juan, who is known as an important leader to the Spanish authorities, who plan to apprehend him when he enters. Marianne is subsequently enlisted to fly to Barcelona to leave a warning that her lover and Juan should come back to France immediately by different routes. The film ends with her at the airport, the outcome left in doubt.

La Guerre Est Finie penetratingly dramatizes the state of crisis that is engulfing the middle-aged Diego. There is the inevitable doubt as to the efficacy of decades of sacrifice, the weariness from constant trips to Spain, the official rhetoric from his superiors, which he challenges—in brief, the pain and ennui of exile. The omniscient voice of the narrator (Jorge Semprun) objectifies and distances Diego's complex predicament and adds dimension and depth to his plight. Besides his professional difficulties, he is being urged by Marianne into settling into a life of domestic stability that includes a child she dreams of having with him. Diego finally affirms a commitment to her. It is the death of Ramon that brings the crisis to a conclusion by reinspiring Diego, who, filled with his late friend's spirit, will go back to the country he now loves passionately anew. Yves Montand's strong screen presence makes the character of Diego come to life. Montand will play the role of a fervent liberal several times again, notably in *Z* (1969), screenplay also by Semprun. Ingrid Thulin, with her mature beauty, is captivating as Marianne.

Resnais's direction is elegant and controlled. An innovative aspect—demonstrating his fascination with the power of imagination—is his novel and extensive use of the future conditional tense, "anticipatory shots" or the "flash-forward," to illustrate what Diego considers *might* take place. Thus, en route to the Sallanches apartment he tries to envisage what the daughter will look like, and we have four quick shots of various young ladies. Similarly, there are several shots of Juan, who haunts the revolutionist. "The imaginary scenes," Semprun wrote, "are always treated in an absolutely realistic manner because a man like that does not imagine the future in the form of a dream, but in the form of a terrific realism." Striking is the closing scene at the airport in which a superimposed shot of Diego gracefully dissolves into one of Marianne, suggesting their indissoluble union. The film is superbly photographed by Sacha Vierny. Although officially "the war is over," the conflict must continue for the vision of justice and freedom should not be stifled. *La Guerre Est Finie* is still a vital and pertinent film, while Yves Montand was the quintessential screen image of the politically engagé man with his quiet, impressive strength and towering integrity.

HONORS

International Film Critics' Prize, Cannes Film
  Festival (1966)
L'Étoile de Cristal for Grand Prix and to Yves
  Montand for Best Actor (1966)
Prix Méliès (1966)
Prix Louis Delluc (1966)
Best Foreign Film, New York Film Critics Award
  (1967)
Nominated for an Oscar for Best Story and
  Screenplay—Written Directly for the Screen (1967)

28
THE BATTLE OF ALGIERS

La Battaglia di Algeri

ITALY/ALGERIA / 1966

Igor Film (Rome)/Casbah Films (Algiers)

CREDITS

Director: Gillo Pontecorvo; *Assistant directors:* Fernando Morandi, Moussa Haddad; *Producers:* Antonio Musu, Yacef Saadi; *Screenwriters:* Franco Solinas, Gillo Pontecorvo; *Cinematographer:* Marcello Gatti (black and white); *Music:* Ennio Morricone, Gillo Pontecorvo; *Editors:* Mario Serandrei, Mario Morra; *Art director:* Sergio Canevari; *Running time:* 120 minutes; *16mm rental source:* Films Inc., *Videocassette:* Axon.

CAST

Ali la Pointe: Brahim Haggiag; *Colonel Mathieu:* Jean Martin; *Saari Kader:* Yacef Saadi; *Fathia:* Samia Kerbash; *The Captain:* Ugo Paletti; *Hassiba Ben Bouali:*

"Habitual offender" Ali la Pointe (Brahim Haggiag) is caught by police in the European quarter of Algiers. The year is 1954.

In the Casbah, young revolutionist Little Omar (Mohamed Ben Kassen) reads the N.L.F.'s first order to the newly recruited though illiterate Ali la Pointe. The year is 1956.

On his initial assignment—a test of his loyalty—Ali la Pointe, finding no bullets in his revolver, resorts to kicking the French policeman.

Fawzia El-Kader; *Little Omar:* Mohamed Ben Kassen; *Captain Dubois:* Tommaso Neri.

In 1964, Italian director Gillo Pontecorvo (1919–) was approached to make a film on the Algerian struggle for independence (1954–62). The director pointed out, "For me . . . the most touching, fascinating, and illuminating moment of the Algerian War . . . was the birth, development, and crumbling of the N.L.F. [National Liberation Front*] organization in Algiers, in effect, the battle of Algiers." Two years of intensive preparation followed, which included gathering eyewitness accounts from former French paratroopers along with revolutionary partisans, documents, and photographs. The shooting in Algeria took more than five months. Pontecorvo went to the streets of Algiers to cast his film, looking for faces to give verisimilitude to his project. Thus Brahim Hag-

*An English rendering of F.L.N. as it's known in French

giag, discovered in the marketplace, was given the role of Ali la Pointe because he bore a resemblance to the celebrated rebel leader. Yacef Saadi as the insurrectionary strategist Saari Kader played himself since he was military commander for the autonomous zone of Algiers during the conflict. The French paratroopers were cast from tourists. The only professional actor was Jean Martin portraying Colonel Mathieu, a composite of several French officers, selected as the director said because he was "physically imposing."

Pontecorvo commented on this, his third and most famous feature: "My subject is the sadness and laceration that the birth of a nation means in our time." A far remove from Julien Duvivier's famous, romantic *Pépé-Le-Moko* (1937), the acclaimed *The Battle of Algiers* was stunningly realistic and had the immediacy and force of a bombshell. Fearing reprisals, the French banned it for five years. In America members of the Black Panther Party were required to see it, a visual textbook for planned urban guerrilla warfare. *The Battle of*

The year is 1960. Three years after the N.L.F. had been exterminated, the people, shouting, "Long live Algeria!" rise up against their colonial oppressors.

Algiers is a brilliant reconstruction of a turbulent period and its impact has not diminished. This classic helped popularize political films.

The plot transpires over nine years. Throughout, actual dates—even a precise time—are mentioned to add specificity. The action begins in Algiers in the early morning of October 7, 1957. After torture by French paratroopers under the command of Colonel Mathieu (Jean Martin), an Arab reveals the hiding place of the head of the almost vanquished N.L.F. The troops or "paras" dash to the Casbah, surround the apartment in which Ali la Pointe (Brahim Haggiag) is concealed, and threaten to blow up the building if he doesn't surrender. The scene dissolves as the young chief recollects the steps that led to this crisis. November 1954: Ali is arrested on some undisclosed charge; a narrator reviews his criminal history, which encompasses theft and pimping. While in prison he is proselytized into the N.L.F. After release, he meets a member, Omar (Mohamed Ben Kassen), a mere boy, who reads the initial instructions to the unlettered man. Ali is to shoot a certain policeman in the back with a gun provided by a female partisan—actually this is a trial to determine if he can be trusted. When the time comes, since the gun proves to be empty, he knocks down the officer. Ali is introduced to Saari Kader (Yacef Saadi), who is organizing the uprising. Before striking out against the French, the N.L.F. cleans up the Casbah of drug abusers, alcoholics, etc. In June 1956 they commence their sporadic attacks on French policemen; the authorities soon seal off the Casbah and search the residents entering the European section. In retaliation for the mounting violence, a commissioner detonates the tenement of an arrested man in the Arab quarter. Thereupon three Algerian women pass as Frenchwomen and carry explosives in their bags that are set off with devastating effect at a cafeteria, a dance bar, and an airport terminal. On January 10, 1957, Colonel Mathieu arrives with his paratroopers to restore order and explains the pyramidlike structure of the N.L.F. to his men. Since the Algerian problem has been placed on the U.N. agenda, the rebels declare an eight-day general strike to show the world their popular support. While the city is paralyzed, the soldiers hunt for the ringleaders inside the Casbah. The colonel justifies his utilization of torture to gain results. Kader surrenders. The flashback over, Ali and his group remain silent. The house is demolished, the N.L.F. destroyed. Yet, unaccountably in December 1960 there is a spontaneous uprising as thousands of Algerians demonstrate to demand their freedom. Independence finally comes on July 5, 1962.

With his rugged features and alluring eyes Brahim Haggiag is convincing as Ali la Pointe; Jean Martin projects an intelligent, militaristic presence as Colonel Mathieu. However, it is the Algerian people themselves who are highlighted. With their handmade flags, the defiant women dancing and chanting, the angry Arabs insurge in 1960. The film is a homage to their spirit thirsting for liberty. *The Battle of Algiers* has an authentic, compelling, documentarylike quality that, to quote the director, "looked as though it had literally been 'stolen' from reality." The use of a telephoto lens for long shots, sweeping pan shots, vigorous zoom shots, a fluid hand-held camera for scenes in the Casbah to catch the players' movements, and dynamic editing helped Pontecorvo create a sense of urgency. The director and writer Franco Solinas avoided the temptation of making the Algerians appear heroically noble or the French as evil incarnate. While the screenwriters' sympathies are obviously with the Arabs, they do not flinch from showing that *both* sides resorted to terrorism. Ennio Morricone's religious, soulful music accompanies both the terrifying aftermath of the explosives from the three Arab women as well as the French destruction of the Casbah dwelling and subsequent torture of suspects as if to underscore the appalling sins of man against his brothers. The employment of an artful, grainy photography in black and white was of vital importance to produce a newsreel effect. So persuasive was cinematographer Marcello Gatti's expert achievement that a disclaimer was inserted at the outset: "This dramatic reenactment of the Battle of Algiers contains NOT ONE FOOT of newsreel or documentary film." The director stated, "We desired to make an objective, fair-minded film, one that is not a trial of a people or of a nation, but is only a heartfelt act of accusation against colonization, violence, and war." In creating a riveting film celebrating a people's unstoppable fight for self-determination, Pontecorvo in *The Battle of Algiers* has made a stirring work as timely as it is memorable.

HONORS

Best Film, Venice Film Festival (1966)
Nominated for three Oscars: Best Foreign Language Film (1966), Best Director, and Best Story and Screenplay—Written Directly for the Screen (1968)
The United Nations Award,* British Academy Award (1971)

29
THE HUNT

La Caza

SPAIN / 1966

Elias Querejeta Producciónes Cinematográficas

CREDITS

Director: Carlos Suara; *Assistant director:* José Luis Ruiz Marcos; *Producer:* Elias Querejeta; *Screenwriters:* Angelino Fons, Carlos Saura; *Cinematographer:* Luis Cuadrado (black and white, Panoramico); *Music:* Luis De Pablo; *Editor:* Pablo Gonzales Del Amo; *Running time:* 93 minutes; *16mm rental source:* Kit Parker; *Videocassette:* International Film Forum.

CAST

José: Ismael Merlo; *Paco:* Alfredo Mayo; *Luis:* José Maria Prada; *Enrique:* Emilio Gutiérrez Caba; *Juan:* Fernando Sanchez Polack; *Carmen:* Violeta Garcia.

*"The United Nations Award has been given to that film which best embodies one or more of the principles of the U.N. Charter"—British Academy of Film and Television Arts. Henceforth referred to as the U.N. Award.

A sick and troubled José (Ismael Merlo) prepares for the rabbit hunt in an area where he formerly killed Loyalists during the Spanish Civil War.

Luis (José Maria Prada) *(right)*, holding the German Luger of Enrique (Emilio Gutiérrez Caba) *(left)*, recalls its use in the Civil War while Paco (Alfredo Mayo), the youth's brother-in-law, watches.

In the 1950s under the stifling control of the Franco government, the Spanish cinema was moribund. Films were censored on sexual and religious grounds as well as for political reasons—mention of the Civil War (1936–39) was especially taboo. Gradually, several Spanish directors emerged to reproach the declining Falangist establishment—the privileged classes who battened under the dictatorial regime—albeit via cautious allusions. Prominent among them was Carlos Saura (1932–   ), who later said, "While Franco was alive I felt obliged to make films that were a criticism of the repressive mechanism of Francoism. Franco was like a wall, a barrier beyond which it was impossible to advance." The director spoke of a modus operandi throughout that period: "It was necessary to work indirectly, in symbol and metaphor, very slowly and carefully." A brilliant result of such a process was *The Hunt*, his third feature. This seemingly innocuous account of how a mere rabbit shoot turned into a human slaughter—the three victims, it should be mentioned, were Nationalist veterans—escaped the watchful eye of the censor. Even the locale was provocative. The film was shot near Aranjuez, a region south of Madrid that was the scene of terrible carnage

during the fascist revolt. "For me, the subject of *The Hunt* is a little civil war," Saura said. "Above all I have wished to show the process of disintegration of those who have waged the Spanish war, their degradation." The exciting and engrossing film, a caustic character analysis with the force of a thriller, helped to make the director one of the leading figures of the new Spanish cinema and gained him an international reputation.

The entire action of *The Hunt* unfolds within one day. Don José (Ismael Merlo), a middle-aged man faced with an expensive separation from his wife whom he's left for a younger woman and plagued with ill health, invites his old friend Paco (Alfredo Mayo) to join him for a day of hunting rabbits on his land. He has secret hopes of securing a much-needed loan from Paco. Joining the pair at a bar is Luis (José Maria Prada), an unhappy person who drinks; he works for José and is much belittled by his boss. The three are veterans of the Spanish Civil War in which they fought on the side of Franco. Enrique (Emilio Gutiérrez Caba), Paco's young brother-in-law, accompanies them. They drive in the youth's jeep to the hot, barren hills where the rabbits thrive. Luis informs Enrique that Loyalists hid in the remote caves on the site in the war; the three men took part in shooting them when they eventually came out. They load up and start firing; many rabbits are felled. The farmhand Juan (Fernando Sanchez Polack) prepares lunch

A bored Enrique starts a fire while Luis is in a bitterly reflective mood.

109

Luis lies dead after he and José exchange fatal shots—the cataclysmic climax to this disturbing film.

and tries unsuccessfully to borrow money from Don José for his ailing mother. Luis and Enrique motor into town to fetch bread. José surmises that the opportunistic Paco married the youth's sister for her money. Paco refuses to lend José any money and offends his dignity mightily by offering him a job. Later, an inebriated Luis interrupts his companions' siesta with his target practice on a mannequin. José slaps him angrily. The oppressive heat exacerbates the smoldering tensions among the three former soldiers. Juan brings some ferrets to use in the afternoon chase. While one of them is pursuing a rabbit from his tunnel, Paco deliberately and maliciously shoots the animal, which annoys an unwell José. Luis rejects his employer's attempt at apology, goes over to the tent where Paco is shading himself, and asks for work. The wealthy man is agreeable and, when Luis leaves to assist Enrique in hunting rabbits, mentions in a loud voice for José to hear that he'll soon have a good position for him. Luis drives the jeep to flush out rabbits while Enrique stalks nearby. An incensed José loads his rifle and aims it at Paco, but hesitates. A rabbit darts forth; Enrique, then Paco, start shooting at him. Suddenly José fires at Paco point-blank; hit in the head, he tumbles into the river. An enraged Luis accelerates the vehicle to run over his enemy. José shoots him in the face and he falls out of the jeep. Still alive, Luis gets his gun and manages to deliver some lethal rounds at the fleeing man, then collapses. The film ends with a shocked Enrique in a freeze-frame, uncomprehending the vicious bloodbath he has just witnessed.

With the assistance of an occasional interior monologue from each of the four leads, *The Hunt* becomes a finely developed character study. José, suffering significantly from "an old wound," recognizes that his life is a failure and is consumed with envy over Paco's material success. Rapacious, self-serving, and ruthlessly aggressive, Paco is even more obnoxious. Although many years earlier José gave him his start in business, he treats his friend's request for desperately needed money contemptuously. Though weak, a heavy drinker, and painfully aware of the bankruptcy of his existence, Luis is the sole moral voice of the veterans. He ponders whether they have a symbolic myxomatosis—an infectious and crippling rabbit disease—and is given to uttering apocalyptic pronouncements. The three men are sadistic, hostile, and suspicious; the violence that is so facilely expressed by killing rabbits can quickly be directed at each other. Enrique, who rebuked as cruel Paco's casual defense of the doctrine of survival of the fittest, is the sole survivor, representing hope for the younger generation if they disavow the destructive values of their parents. All these roles are excellently cast and are acted with thorough conviction. Jockeying between revealing close-ups of the characters and long shots of the arid, treeless hills, Saura directs in an impressively taut and suspenseful fashion. What could have been impossibly melodramatic turns out to be natural and inevitable. Luis Cuadrado's skillful photography captures the scorching heat that helps to make the catastrophe seem unavoidable. The martial drum roll of Luis De Pablo creates an ominous mood.

The employment of a rabbit hunt immediately calls to mind Renoir's *The Rules of the Game* (1939). Whereas in that classic French film the shooting sequence is brief and the aristocrats are depicted as frivolous though generally appealing, Saura's entire film is concerned with the chase, and the Civil War veterans—and, by extension, their generation—are mercilessly and savagely indicted. In a cave José shows a disgusted Paco a skeleton remaining bolt upright, emblematic of the verity that the casualties from that fraternal tragedy are not buried but persist to vex the victors. *The Hunt* is a harsh, brutal work whose fierce impact and perturbing thoughts linger in the memory.

HONORS

Silver Bear for Best Director, Berlin International
  Film Festival (1966)

30
PERSONA

SWEDEN / 1966

SVENSK FILMINDUSTRI

CREDITS

Director and screenwriter: Ingmar Bergman; *Assistant director:* Lenn Hjortzberg; *Producer:* Lars-Owe Carlberg; *Cinematographer:* Sven Nykvist (black and white); *Music:* Lars Johan Werle and excerpts from Bach's Violin Concerto in E Major; *Editor:* Ulla Ryghe; *Art director:* Bibi Lindstrom; *Running time:* 84 minutes; *16mm rental source:* Corinth; *Videocassette:* Facets.

CAST

Alma: Bibi Andersson; *Elisabet Vogler:* Liv Ullmann; *The Doctor:* Margaretha Krook; *Mr. Vogler:* Gunnar Bjornstrand; *The Boy:* Jorgen Lindstrom.

Like his trilogy, Ingmar Bergman referred to *Persona* as a "chamber" film; in this new work metaphysical speculation would be replaced with probing psychological analysis. A friend had shown the director slides of Bibi Andersson and her friend, the young Norwegian actress Liv Ullmann. He was struck, he said, at how "devilishly alike" they seemed, and the resemblance stuck with him. He later said, "I thought it would be wonderful to write something about two people who lose their identities in each other. . . . Suddenly I got the idea of them sitting comparing hands. And that was the first image." Bergman envisaged no one but Bibi Andersson and Liv Ullmann for the lead roles and filmed *Persona*, some of whose working titles were *Sonata for Two Women* and *Kinematografi*, in Stockholm and Faro, that island where he would build a retreat, between mid-July and mid-September 1965.

Persona is a richly implicative title indicating the actor's mask worn in classical drama or, in plural form, the characters in a play or novel. More significant to the director's purposes is the desig-

nation of *persona* advanced by Carl G. Jung to typify the necessary mask an individual assumes "in contrast to his inner character, with intent to serve as a protection, a defense, a deception, or an attempt to adapt to the world around him," as the great psychiatrist wrote. While most features create an instant illusion that what we are watching is actually taking place, Bergman in *Persona* deliberately introduces some distancing effects to make us aware of the undeniable artifice of the film medium and to elicit a reflective response rather

Caught in a moment of paralyzing anguish during a performance of *Electra*, actress Elisabet Volger (Liv Ullmann) finds herself unable to speak. An apt illustration of Ingmar Bergman's remark that "The cinematography of the human face has brought to us the most fantastic thing that we can see in art. That is, the human face in movement. . . . No other art had the chance to do that, and did it."

During an apparent dream sequence Elisabet *(right)* and Alma (Bibi Andersson) discern how much they look alike. Sven Nykvist's grainy shot contributes to a dreamlike effect.

Elisabet concludes her letter to her doctor, which an approaching Alma will read with destructive consequences.

Alma pleads with a taciturn and fearful Elisabet to cease her unnerving silence. Notice Alma's theatrical appearance and posture; gradually she is submerging herself into the actress's identity.

than emotional involvement. In spite of an enigmatic prologue and a bewildering commingling of dreams and reality in the lives of the two women—a "difficult" film as Bergman acknowledged—*Persona* is nevertheless an original, fascinating, and provocative motion picture experience.

The film begins with a montage of cryptic images with themes developed associationally, not logically. After quick shots of a whirring projector and reels of film, a sequence of disturbing scenes follows, including a crawling spider, a close-up of a man's hand with a spike being pounded into it, and corpses in a mortuary. A telephone's ringing awakens a boy (Jorgen Lindstrom) sleeping on a slab. He rises, stares at the camera, and covers it with his hand. In a reverse shot we see him moving his hand on a foggy wall to reveal the screen-size face of Bibi Andersson; it is as if the youth were conjuring the narrative that ensues. In a hospital Nurse Alma (Bibi Andersson), a vibrant young woman, is assigned to care for Elisabet (Liv Ullmann), who, three months ago, stopped speaking briefly during a performance of *Electra* and hasn't uttered a word since the following day; the actress is otherwise healthy. Alma instinctively feels she won't be able to cope with her mentally, but the doctor (Margaretha Krook) restores her confidence. In her room Elisabet watches the television news in horror as a Vietnamese Buddhist monk sets himself on fire as a remonstrance. When the nurse reads aloud a letter from the actress's concerned husband, Elisabet tears up the enclosed photo of her son. The physician suggests the patient would make better progress if she would stay with Alma in the doctor's summer place. The doctor conjectures that feelings of dishonesty and self-disgust may have forced the actress to decide not to talk. She respects this and thinks Elisabet will drop the role when she's played it to the end. In the physician's vacation home Alma rattles on about her first affair and, after some drinks, mentions an orgy she participated in with two boys that led to a guilt-inducing abortion. She tells the actress, "We're quite alike," and adds, "I could change myself into you if I tried hard." Later in a possible dream sequence Elisabet enters Alma's bedroom and embraces her; the succeeding day the actress shakes her head when the nurse inquires about the visit. While mailing Elisabet's letter to the doctor, Alma notices it wasn't sealed and is shocked and hurt to read that the rejuvenated actress has been studying her. The next day the spiteful nurse leaves a piece of glass for Elisabet to walk on. At this point the

movie catches fire and we see a blank screen. After a recapitulation of shots used in the prelude, the story resumes. A restless Alma implores the actress to speak and soon works herself into a fury. She strikes Elisabet, who hits her back harder. The nurse begs her forgiveness. In a surrealistic sequence Mr. Vogler (Gunnar Bjornstrand) arrives and converses with Alma as if she were his wife while Elisabet observes them. Soon, having absorbed her identity, Alma projects an account of the actress's loveless marriage and unwanted son while Elisabet reacts in pain. During what seems to be a dream the nurse cuts her arm; the actress sucks the wound like a vampire. Alma starts slapping her violently. Awake, the nurse sees Elisabet pack. Alone, Alma closes up the house and boards a bus. The boy traces his hand against the screen; the film runs off the spool.

Why does Elisabet decline to speak? Has she realized that her craft is quite pointless in a world of brutality and self-immolation? Bergman insists that her silence is not neurotic: "It's a strong person's form of protest." Why is Alma so weak and vulnerable that she lets herself merge into Elisabet? At first she learns to smoke like the actress, then by degrees plunges into a dangerous identity crisis. Throughout the film the viewer ponders what lies beneath Elisabet's silent facade and the nurse's ministering mask. What really constitutes their "inner character"? Because of the self-reflective nature of *Persona*, along with the intermingling of dream and reality, the director was more successful at evoking the interchanging personalities than if he had attempted to develop this concept via realism. The inability of Elisabet to love her husband and son is a recognizable theme in Bergman's films. The acting is brilliant. The scenes in which Bibi Andersson screams in schizophrenic torment are quite powerful; Liv Ullmann as the mute Elisabet makes her beautiful, expressive face register many emotions. Shifting between penetrating close-ups and long shots, Bergman's direction is taut and compelling. A striking, brief shot follows Alma's intuitive dissection of Elisabet's marriage. The left half of a close-up of the nurse combines with the right half of that of the actress to visually indicate an identity. Sven Nykvist's photography captures the strange realism of our dreams; Lars Johan Werle's atonal score complements the action. *Persona* is open to interpretation, from its initial ciné-poem, through its confusing narrative, to its ambiguous ending. Some critics have described the picture as a study of the double. However one ultimately conceives the movie, *Persona* remains a daring, challenging, imaginative film—a work of pure cinema.

31
THE WILD CHILD

L'Enfant Sauvage

FRANCE / 1970

LES FILMS DU CARROSSE/LES PRODUCTIONS ARTISTES ASSOCIÉS

CREDITS

Director: François Truffaut; *Assistant director:* Suzanne Schiffman; *Producer:* Marcel Berbert; *Screenwriters:* François Truffaut, Jean Gruault, based on *The Memorandum and Report on Victor de l'Aveyron* by Jean Itard (1806); *Cinematographer:* Nestor Almendros (black and white); *Music:* Antonio Vivaldi; *Editor:* Agnès Guillemot; *Art director:* Jean Mandaroux; *Running time:* 84 minutes; *16mm rental source and videocassette:* MGM/UA.

CAST

Victor of Aveyron: Jean-Pierre Cargol; *Dr. Jean Itard:* François Truffaut; *Mme. Guérin:* Françoise Seigner; *Dr. Philippe Pinel:* Jean Dasté; *Rémy:* Paul Villé; *Attendant:* Pierre Fabre; *Lémeri:* Claude Miller; *Mme. Lémeri:* Annie Miller.

For his ninth feature, *The Wild Child*, François Truffaut chose a subject that had intrigued him since 1966 when he had come upon an account of the remarkable, factual story of a person known as Victor of Aveyron. Near the end of the eighteenth century a "wild" boy about eleven or twelve who moved like an animal—erect but at times on all fours—was detected and caught in a forest in southern France. It was thought that he had been living in isolation from human contact for approximately seven or eight years. He was naked and hirsute. His scarred body evinced battles with animals and he had subsisted on nuts and roots. Unable to speak, he could only grunt. A deep,

healed wound was found on his trachea; someone had apparently stabbed him in the throat when he was three or four years old—had he been younger he couldn't have managed to survive—and abandoned him to die in the woods.

This report of his background is a supposition for the truth was never uncovered. Doctors at the National Institute for Deaf-Mutes presumed that he was critically retarded, but Dr. Jean Itard, who felt that the boy could be helped under his personal tutelage, interceded and he was spared institutionalization. The plight of a child victimized by the loss of that most basic of needs, language, attracted Truffaut. Together with his coadaptor Jean Gruault, they envisioned Dr. Itard's scientific reports as a diary, which they then dramatized. The director's periodic narration relating the child's development adds a reflective dimension. Jean-Pierre Cargol, a Gypsy boy, was noticed in Montpellier and selected to play the title role. Fearing an actor might try to dominate the film, Truffaut decided to play Dr. Itard himself. The picture, dedicated to Jean-Pierre Léaud, was shot in Auvergne and Paris from July to September 1969. "I simply wanted to make a film," the director said, "in praise of communication between people." *The Wild*

Portrait of "The Wild Child of Aveyron" (Jean-Pierre Cargol) resting on a limb of a tree in the forest before his capture.

At the National Institute for Deaf-Mutes, Dr. Pinel (Jean Dasté) *(right)* examines the "savage" boy, while holding him is his future benefactor, Dr. Itard (François Truffaut).

Child, an intimate and touching work, is one of Truffaut's most effective and memorable films.

The year is 1798. A peasant woman collecting woodland mushrooms is frightened by the sight of a nude, wild boy (Jean-Pierre Cargol) and runs away. Soon men with dogs track him down. Dr. Jean Itard (François Truffaut), researching deafness, becomes interested in the newspaper articles on him and wishes to explore the mental processes of a youth deprived of learning. "The Wild Child of Aveyron" is brought to the National Institute for Deaf-Mutes in Paris where Dr. Pinel (Jean Dasté) examines the bewildered lad and, judging him abnormal, wants him confined at Bicêtre, a mental asylum. However, Dr. Itard regards him as educable and seeks permission to have him placed under his care. At the doctor's home the boy encounters a maternal housekeeper, Mme. Guérin (Françoise Seigner), and such novel activities as bathing, walking upright, wearing shoes, etc. Wandering in the countryside delights him, as does a visit to the doctor's friend, Lémeri (Claude Miller), where he is treated to milk. Since he responds to the sound of *O*, the physician names him Victor. Itard subjects the boy to an intensive pedagogical program in an effort to have him speak. Feeling helpless and pressured, Victor sporadically explodes with rage.

After a disorderly lesson, the boy is put into a dark closet and cries. Progress is measured by minor triumphs, such as Victor's practical invention of a chalk holder, along with failures. To test his understanding of fairness, Itard orders Victor to the closet, an undeserved punishment. The boy refuses to go and bites Itard's hand; nonetheless, the doctor is gratified to see evidence of "the full stature of a moral being." Later Victor runs way but, realizing he has lost his ability to live in the wilderness, returns reluctantly to the home of the worried physician. "You're no longer a wild boy," Itard states. "You're an extraordinary youth, a youth of great promise." The film ends as Victor climbs the stairs to his room.

Deracinated from his sylvan environment and "civilized," but at the same time incapable of mastering language and functioning in society, the unfortunate Victor, with his disturbing seizures, is in limbo. He is depicted realistically and not sentimentalized as a variant of the "noble savage." Dr. Itard, heir to the French Revolution's belief in the perfectibility of man, has a challenge with Victor. Far from smug, he has moments of doubt concerning the efficaciousness of his self-imposed task. Jean-Pierre Cargol plays Victor with an appealing naturalness; François Truffaut brings earnestness

At the Lémeri house, Dr. Itard demonstrates to the much-transformed feral youth how to turn the key to open the cupboard where his desired milk is stored.

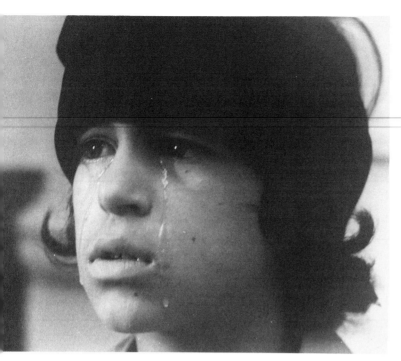

Discouraged and confused by Dr. Itard's severe tutorial regimen, Victor starts crying.

and authority to his portrayal of Dr. Itard. And in his meticulous direction he replaces the exuberance of *Jules and Jim* with restraint and a documentary style, unelaborate yet forcefully precise and immediate. To stress the remoteness of the period the director utilizes such silent-screen techniques as the iris transition in addition to Vivaldi's music. Nestor Almendros contributed notable cinematography.

The film has many haunting scenes. In one, Itard, carrying a candle, enters Victor's room at night and finds him missing. Through the window he sees the boy in his nightshirt on the grass staring in awe at the full moon, then rocking back and forth and pacing about on all fours. What joy, what vital communion, has he been wrenched from? The movie details the first year of Victor's stay with Dr. Itard. However, in actuality, the "great promise" that the doctor announced at the picture's end must be qualified, for in the remaining five years with him Victor never acquired speech and subsequently lived a sedate life under the care of Mme. Guérin until his death at forty. While some critics have faulted those who snatched Victor away from an idealized existence "close to nature," Truffaut's position is not ambiguous but decidedly in rapport with Itard's mission. The director emphasized that the boy's life in the

wild was "wretched," coping with animal attacks, merciless winters, etc. "My message," Trauffaut said, "is simply this: man is nothing without other men." While it was impossible for Itard to accomplish the sort of wondrous breakthrough similar to the one in which a young, blind, and deaf Helen Keller discovered the miracle of language, his achievement with Victor was nevertheless solid and substantial. The director said, "We inherit what is natural, but culture can come only through education. Hence the importance of this education and the beauty of this theme." *The Wild Child* is an unusual, deeply moving, and superb film that has acquired the status of a classic.

HONORS

Prix Méliès (1970)

32
THE CONFORMIST

Il Conformista

ITALY/FRANCE/WEST GERMANY/1970

MARS FILM PRODUZIONE (ROME)/MARIANNE PRODUCTIONS (PARIS)/MARAN FILM (MUNICH)

CREDITS

Director and screenwriter: Bernardo Bertolucci, based on the novel by Alberto Moravia (1951); *Assistant director:* Aldo Lado; *Producer:* Maurizio Lodi-Fé; *Cinematographer:* Vittorio Storaro (Technicolor); *Music:* Georges Delerue; *Editor:* Franco Arcalli; *Art director:* Ferdinando Scarfiotti; *Running time:* 108 minutes; *16mm rental source:* Films Inc., *Videocassette:* Paramount (dubbed).

CAST

Marcello Clerici: Jean-Louis Trintignant; *Giulia:* Stefania Sandrelli; *Anna:* Dominique Sanda; *Lino:* Pierre Clementi; *Manganiello:* Gastone Moschin; *Quadri:* Enzo Tarascio; *Italo:* José Quaglio; *Marcello's Mother:* Milly; *Marcello's Father:* Giuseppe Addobbati; *Giulia's Mother:* Yvonne Sanson; *Colonel:* Fosco Giachetti; *Marcello as a Boy:* Pasquale Fortunato.

116

For his fifth feature Italian director Bernardo Bertolucci (1940–) chose to adapt Alberto Moravia's *The Conformist*, a realistic novel set in Mussolini's Italy in which Marcello, the troubled young protagonist bearing the onus of the murder of a male seducer at puberty, marries and embraces Fascism in a vain undertaking to find redemption amidst "normality." In lieu of the author's linear plot development and omniscient narrator, the director narrowed an account that unfolded between 1920 and 1943 essentially to one bodeful autumn day and shifted the point of view to Marcello, who recalls previous events in random, vivid, intermittent flashbacks that constitute the bulk of the film. Bertolucci discarded Moravia's stress on a Fate so implacable that when Marcello and his family flee from a bombarded Rome, their car is strafed by an Allied aircraft that appears like the intervention of an angry, death-demanding god. "Here I substituted," the director said, "Marcello's unconscious—a psychoanalytic explanation, that is—for the presence of Destiny in the book." Bertolucci makes his principal—a psychologically complicated though fascinating personage—less predestined and more responsible for his behavior. Besides skillfully dramatizing a heavily analytical story, the director had the inspiration to invent the sinister and sightless Fascist, Italo, who reinforces the movie's central metaphor of blindness, which pertains not only to the delusions of

Marcello (Jean-Louis Trintignant) calls on his late-sleeping mother (Milly) whose dissolute lifestyle, which includes a Japanese chauffeur-lover and morphine, he finds repugnant.

Marcello but also to his self-deceived country. Intermingling a probing character study with a powerful political thriller, Bertolucci created a sensation with *The Conformist* that launched his international career. Visually arresting, beautifully directed and acted, this film has not lost its ability to astonish.

In a Paris dance hall Anna (Dominique Sanda) *(left)* leads Giulia (Stefania Sandrelli) in a seductive and scandalizing tango.

117

On the evening of Mussolini's capitulation, Marcello *(far left)*, walking with his blind companion, Italo (José Quaglio), is caught off guard when he sees Lino (Pierre Clementi), whom he believed he murdered twenty-six years ago, against a wall propositioning a youth.

The film opens on October 15, 1938, in Paris. Marcello Clerici (Jean-Louis Trintignant), combining a honeymoon with Giulia (Stefania Sandrelli) and a Fascist mission, receives a telephone call from agent Manganiello (Gastone Moschin). Contrary to expectation, Anna (Dominique Sanda), whom Marcello is infatuated with, left for Savoy with her husband, Quadri (Enzo Tarascio), who is leftist, anti-Fascist, and marked for death. Marcello races there with Manganiello in an effort to save her life. Obsessive memories haunt him during the lengthy trip: In a radio studio we meet Italo (José Quaglio), Marcello's blind mentor, who broadcasts for the Fascists. There the colonel (Fosco Giachetti) discusses Clerici's desire to join the Fascist party and his offer to help entrap Quadri, his university professor of philosophy, now an exile in France. Marcello visits his decadent, drug-addicted mother (Milly), and they go to see his father (Giuseppe Addobbati), confined to a mental institution where he inscribes "murder and melancholy" repeatedly on paper. A confession before the wedding to please his fiancée triggers in Marcello a crucial recollection: When he was thirteen, a chauffeur named Lino (Pierre Clementi) took him (Pasquale Fortunato) to his room in a mansion. During an attempted molesta-

tion the boy fired a revolver at him and ran off. . . . Marcello is commissioned to gain Quadri's confidence and then aid in his execution. In Paris he and his bride visit the teacher and his young wife, Anna, who is amorously drawn to Giulia. Quadri is convinced that his former student can be disabused from Fascism. Marcello finds Anna passionately exciting; she fears he'll harm them. The quartet dine. Anna dances with Giulia; Clerici slips the Savoy address to the ever-shadowing Manganiello. Since she feels his wife cannot stand her, Anna tells Marcello she's going with her husband to their home in Savoy tomorrow; to have her stay he lies and says Giulia finds her captivating. . . . Approaching their country house, Quadri is tricked into leaving his car to assist a blocked automobile in front; assassins come from the woods and stab him. Anna panics and runs to the vehicle behind hers. Inside, the cowardly Clerici sits impassively. Gunmen follow the frightened woman and shoot her in the forest. Epilogue: July 25, 1943. Mussolini has abdicated. Marcello leaves his wife at night to meet Italo. At the Colosseum he is startled to recognize Lino, alive and making advances to a male prostitute. Releasing decades of pent-up guilt, he screams at him the date in 1917 when he was positive that he killed him as well as

118

the date of the Quadri manslaughter. "Murderer!" he screeches at the fleeing man, projecting onto him his own tortured conscience. Hysterical, Marcello turns on his friend and denounces him as a Fascist. In the rear the streetwalker prepares for bed in the famous ruin and watches Marcello. The disburdened man sits and in a closing close-up turns his head and stares protractedly at what was for so long forbidden.

In the complex matrix of Marcello's mind Fascism becomes an irresistible lure that can satisfy, he considers, his needed sense of belonging, his craving for a stable existence far removed from his mother's debasement and his father's insanity. Since that system legitimizes murder, he's willing—in his curious logic—to compensate for the slaying of Lino, which traumatized him, by committing a second murder ("Blood washes away blood"), a voluntary homicide, the price he rationalizes society demands from him for acceptance in the "secure" Fascist order. Insofar as it is homophobic, too, he thinks he can suppress his

sexual leanings via a conventional marriage. Mussolini's fall wrecks all his underpinnings, forcing him to confront his repressed desires. We can understand why Giulia, an unwilling mistress of her father's lawyer and who has a poor self-image, would marry such a man. With his stiff walk and taciturn, furtive expression, which magnetizes many frequent close-ups, Jean-Louis Trintignant is brilliant as the confused Marcello. The ravishing Dominique Sanda is riveting as Anna, especially when, thumbs in her slacks, smoking a cigarette *à la française*, she swaggers in tomboyishly, sultrily, to invite the Clericis to dinner. One recalls the androgynous allure of Marlene Dietrich.

Bertolucci's direction is remarkably fluid, taut, and most impressive. He evokes the subjective, hallucinatory remembrances of Marcello—the massive asylum that constrains his father; the sterile, cavernous Fascist ministry that dwarfs the solitary figure; and the chaos of an overthrown dictatorship that finally liberates his libido—with such an intensity as to move beyond realism to an almost

Bedding down for the night in the Colosseum, the male prostitute feels assured of his pending conquest of Marcello, who has yet to notice him.

operatic level. A dreamlike, surreal atmosphere is poetically created. Fascism is depicted as a form of pandemic gigantism. Vittorio Storaro's outstanding cinematography and striking chiaroscuro lighting effects, Georges Delerue's moody score (one of his finest), and Franco Arcalli's superb editing contribute to the film's stunning impact. The costumes, cars, decor, authentically capture the feel of the period. *The Conformist* is a major achievement and one of the director's most memorable works.

HONORS

British Film Institute Award (1970)
Nominated for an Oscar for Best Screenplay (adaptation) (1971)

A solicitous Micol (Dominique Sanda) kisses her sickly brother Alberto (Helmut Berger) good-night.

33

THE GARDEN OF THE FINZI-CONTINIS

Il Giardino dei Finzi-Contini

ITALY/WEST GERMANY / 1970

DOCUMENTO FILM (ROME)/CCC FILMKUNST (WEST BERLIN)

CREDITS

Director: Vittorio De Sica; *Assistant director:* Luisa Alessandri; *Producers:* Gianni Hecht Lucari, Arthur Cohn; *Screenwriters:* Ugo Pirro, Vittorio Bonicelli, from the novel of Giorgio Bassani (1962); *Cinematographer:* Ennio Guarnieri (Eastmancolor); *Music:* Manuel De Sica; *Editor:* Adriana Novelli; *Art director:* Giancarlo Bartolini Salimbeni; *Running time:* 103 minutes; *Videocassette:* RCA/Columbia.

CAST

Giorgio: Lino Capolicchio; *Micol:* Dominique Sanda; *Alberto:* Helmut Berger; *Malnate:* Fabio Testi; *Giorgio's Father:* Romolo Valli; *Micol's Father:* Camillo Angelini-Rota; *Micol's Mother:* Katina Viglietti; *Micol's Grandmother:* Inna Alexeiff; *Ernesto:* Raffaele Curi.

Veteran director Vittorio De Sica was drawn to Giorgio Bassani's acclaimed, semiautobiographical novel, *The Garden of the Finzi-Continis,* set at the time the Fascists began oppressing the Jews. Giorgio, a young, middle-class Jew in Ferrara, narrates his attraction to the formidable Finzi-Continis, coreligionists but aristocratic and aloof. "That period was the blackest page in the history of mankind," De Sica said. "Yet, today in Italy there are many Fascists—young people who do not believe what it was like then. And, unfortunately, there are many old people who have forgotten. That is why I felt I must make *The Garden of the Finzi-Continis*—as an act of atonement and as a warning." The screenwriters focused on the years 1938–43 when the recently passed "Racial Laws" trigger the dramatic conflict, with several brief flashbacks to re-create earlier scenes between the hero and Micol Finzi-Contini, who wakens romantic stirrings in the boy. Surprisingly, for in no way did the director betray the novel, Bassani, who collaborated on the screenplay, renounced the film and requested his name be removed from the credits. Lino Capolicchio played Giorgio, while the French Dominique Sanda and the Austrian

Helmut Berger portrayed the overrefined, possibly incestuous, siblings of the rich and doomed Finzi-Continis. The film was a personal triumph for the master of Italian neorealism, restoring De Sica's great reputation, which had faded considerably due to the spate of commercial films he had been forced to make to survive. *The Garden of the Finzi-Continis* is a haunting, elegiac film and deserves to be remembered.

The movie opens in 1938 when the new Racial Laws, which disallow, among other things, Jewish membership in sport clubs, spur Micol (Dominique Sanda) and her brother Alberto (Helmut Berger) Finzi-Contini to terminate their long-held isolation from the community and make available their tennis court to other ostracized Jews as well as gentiles. Among the former is the student Giorgio, (Lino Capolicchio), who has admired the affluent young lady since childhood; among the latter is Alberto's college friend Malnate (Fabio Testi), a dedicated Communist. Giorgio, strongly opposed to Mussolini's rule, disagrees with his merchant father (Romolo Valli), a party member himself, who believes the Fascists can be accommodated. When Micol realizes Giorgio's affection for her, she retreats to Venice. Soon he is no longer permitted to use the public library, and Signor Finzi-Contini (Camillo Angelini-Rota) consents to let him do his research at his estate. Barred entrance to college, Ernesto (Raffaele Curi), Giorgio's younger brother, departs to attend a French university. Giorgio sees Micol again but she rebuffs his advances, insisting she only cares for his friendship and nothing more. She tells him not to telephone or come back. Bringing money to Ernesto in Grenoble, Giorgio hears a firsthand account of the Nazi concentration camps. Unable to break his ties, he goes back to Ferrara where he befriends Malnate. A lovesick Giorgio dares to visit his unapproachable inamorata again, but she disheartens him by analyzing why they could never become lovers. Italy declares war; Malnate is called up (Jews are not allowed in the armed forces). One night a brooding Giorgio notices his friend's bicycle parked against a wall outside the Finzi-Contini grounds. He climbs over and observes a naked, defiant Micol and a resting Malnate alongside her in a cottage. Giorgio's father tries to console him. The delicate Alberto dies and is buried during an air raid; Malnate is killed in Russia. Then in September of 1943, with Mussolini overthrown, the invading Germans with Fascist support begin the roundup of the Jews. Two official cars arrive to

Running from the downpour, Micol and Giorgio (Lino Capolicchio) dash into the coach house where the wealthy young lady will discourage his ardor.

Herded into a familiar classroom and soon to be deported to Germany, Micol comforts her tired grandmother (Inna Alexeiff).

121

arrest the Finzi-Continis. Taken to a school, Micol meets Giorgio's apprehended father and learns that the son managed to escape with his family.

The gentle Giorgio's love for Micol is inevitably thwarted. She sees him as too similar to excite her and expresses her desires in violent imagery: "Lovers have to overwhelm one another, tear each other to pieces." In Bassani's words she welcomes "a cruel, ferocious relationship" and would logically gravitate to the earthier Malnate. The effete Alberto, lacking a zest for life, suggests along with his sister a decadent underside to this memorialization of the cultivated Finzi-Continis. Remote in their splendid villa, hermetically sealed from the ominous, impinging reality surrounding them, they are supremely—and myopically—confident that, with their excellent breeding and intelligence, they shall indubitably prevail, that a few select bribes to the odious Fascists will suffice to maintain their cherished status quo of blissful solitude. Lino Capolicchio perfectly embodies the sensitive Giorgio. Beautiful but glacial, Dominique Sanda makes Micol mysterious yet enticing. Helmut Berger is effective as the languorous Alberto, and Romolo Valli is excellent as Giorgio's father. While he quarrels constantly with his son, he nonetheless projects a genuine love and concern for him.

Under De Sica's adroit direction the period comes to life. The use of soft focus and vibrant color enhances the marvelous garden of the Finzi-Continis and provides a visual representation of Bassani's description of it as "a paradise from which he's been banished" when Micol expelled Giorgio from the estate. The director skillfully creates suspense—the harassing telephone calls during a Passover gathering—as one restriction against the Jews follows another, leading to the shocking climax. Avoiding sentimentality and bathos, De Sica's tenderness and regard for the men and women he depicted is evident. "When I make a picture," he said, "I love all the characters, their vices and their defects. My work is human work. There is always an excuse, even for the criminal. Humanity is a very deep mystery."

The ending is powerful. With grace and dignity the surviving Finzi-Continis descend the stairs to their despicable captors and pass their servants grouped together. Then through the rear window of the car we see their magnificent house recede in a long shot. Later, after Micol's meeting with Giorgio's father, the film ends in an unforgettable montage. To the accompaniment of a Hebrew lament the camera pans over the towers of a misty Ferrara, followed by long shots of the streets, then the celebrated tennis court and garden of the Finzi-Continis, evoking a feeling of irretrievable loss. The poignancy of an unrequited first love is muffled by the unspeakable fate of a people singled out for destruction. Melancholic and deeply moving, *The Garden of the Finzi-Continis* has not lost its ability to fascinate and disturb.

HONORS

Golden Bear for Best Film, Berlin Film Festival (1971)
Oscar for Best Foreign Language Film; nominated in addition for Writing (adaptation) (1971)
U.N. Award, British Academy Award (1972)

34
TWO ENGLISH GIRLS
Les Deux Anglaises et le Continent

FRANCE / 1971

LES FILMS DU CARROSSE/CINÉTEL

CREDITS

Director: François Truffaut; *Assistant director:* Suzanne Schiffman; *Producer:* Marcel Berbert; *Screenwriters:* François Truffaut, Jean Gruault, based on the novel by Henri-Pierre Roché (1956); *Cinematographer:* Nestor Almendros (Eastmancolor); *Music:* Georges Delerue; *Editors:* Yann Dedet, Martine Barraqué; *Art director:* Michel de Broin; *Running time:* 132 minutes; *16mm rental source:* Janus; *Videocassette:* CBS/Fox.

CAST

Claude Roc: Jean-Pierre Léaud; *Anne:* Kika Markham; *Muriel:* Stacey Tendeter; *Mrs. Brown:* Sylvia Marriott; *Mme. Roc:* Marie Mansart; *Diurka:* Philippe Léotard; *Mr. Flint:* Mark Peterson; *Lawyer:* Georges Delerue; *Art dealer:* Marcel Berbert; *Narrator:* François Truffaut.

It was inevitable that François Truffaut would be drawn to Henri-Pierre Roché's second novel, another autobiographical variation of a love triangle.

At a museum in Paris, Anne (Kika Markham) shows a photo of her sister, Muriel, taken when she was ten, to Claude (Jean-Pierre Léaud) and tells him to come and see them in Wales.

Playing a game near their home in Wales: Claude wheels both Anne and her sister, Muriel (Stacey Tendeter) *(right)*. When he stops, they "freeze" into statues. His role as a shaper in their lives is implied visually.

Whereas the author's earlier narrative, *Jules and Jim*, tells the story of two close friends who love the same woman for many years, *Two English Girls* is an account of two sisters, Anne and Muriel, who love the same man for a long time. Truffaut, in collaboration with Jean Gruault, had problems preparing an effective screenplay. In *Jules and Jim* conflict was inherent in the fact that the three characters lived together, but *Two English Girls* is, in the director's words, "a story of separation" whose introspective, literary personages rarely meet but communicate chiefly via letters and diaries. The action covers the years 1899–1927, which the scenarists curtailed to approximately 1900–1922. To strengthen the film's tragic nature they appropriated certain aspects from the Brontë sisters lives; thus Anne dies early of turberculosis like Emily Brontë (although in the book she marries and bears a son), while Muriel, like Charlotte Brontë, goes to Brussels to teach English. To provide a distancing effect to encourage the audience to weigh the proceedings and not simply relate to them emotionally, they added a narrator (who is the director).

Truffaut went to London to find a pair of unknown actresses who could speak French. Jean-Pierre Léaud was given the role of Claude Roc (Roché), "Le Continent" as the English girls call him. The director shot the film, his eleventh feature, from April to July 1971 in Normandy, Paris, Vivarais, and Jura. "I wanted to show an aspect of

love," Truffaut said, "that is never shown. . . . To make a film where there is sweat, fever, vomiting—all the physical things that correspond to the things that explode in one's head." He stated succinctly, "I tried to make not a film of physical love but a physical film about love." Before the release of *Two English Girls* Truffaut declared that "behind the plot . . . we propose, through images, to sing the praises of life." However, the film took a drubbing from the critics and the director was persuaded by his distributors to cut fourteen min-

On a Swiss island Anne is now ready to make love for the first time with Claude.

utes. This proved in vain to save the film. Always regretting the amputation, he attempted to reconstruct the uncut version with editor Martine Barraqué soon before his untimely death in 1984, despite the fact that the original negative had been destroyed and there were other technical problems. Truffaut succeeded and one can see how those missing segments enhance and heighten his vision. In *Two English Girls* we behold Rodin's impressive statue of Balzac, initially rejected yet subsequently hailed as a masterwork; so, too, with this exquisite film, derided at its debut, yet later discerned to be among Truffaut's most lyrical achievements.

Visiting Paris, Anne Brown (Kika Markham) befriends Claude Roc (Jean-Pierre Léaud). Thinking he would be ideal for her younger sister, Muriel (Stacey Tendeter), she invites him to Wales. There he discovers the puritanical Muriel, who suffers from weak eyesight. When his relationship with her deepens, Mrs. Brown (Sylvia Marriott), cautious of her daughter's reputation, asks Claude to move in with a neighbor, Mr. Flint (Mark Peterson). The Frenchman proposes to her by letter but Murial rejects him. Thinking her son is being manipulated into marriage, the possessive Mme. Roc (Marie Mansart) comes over, and the duo are forced to accept these terms: They will abstain from seeing or writing to each other for a year; then

After many years Muriel is able to give herself to Claude while they stay at a Calais hotel.

if they wish to marry, they may. Muriel's love intensifies during his absence, while Claude, now an art critic installed in his own Parisian apartment, has many women friends. After six months he writes to terminate their engagement. Muriel is devastated. Later Claude encounters Anne, currently a sculptress with a studio in Paris. With Muriel no longer an obstacle, she agrees to vacation with him on a Swiss isle where they become lovers. Focusing on her career, she will permit him to have other women; however, Claude is uncomfortably obliged to reciprocate when she takes up with the publisher Diurka (Philippe Léotard). Muriel mails Claude an intimate diary revealing her compulsory masturbatory habits since childhood. Afterward, when Claude sees her again, her unexpected passionate response disconcerts him, arousing buried feelings. Before the pair holiday together, Anne feels the need to disclose her and Claude's affair to Muriel; she reacts by throwing up. Muriel writes a farewell letter to Claude stressing that she considers Anne his real wife. Thereupon it is his turn to suffer. Subsequently, he urges Diurka to pursue Anne, whom the publisher still loves. But he finds his beloved dying of consumption in Wales. Later Claude learns of Muriel's arrival in Calais and they finally consummate their love. However, she declines his marriage offer, aware of their basic irreconcilable differences. Fifteen years pass. Muriel has wedded and has a daughter. A solitary Claude in the Rodin museum hears English schoolgirls. Could one be Muriel's? The film ends as he observes how old he looks.

The vibrant Anne, open to experience, "lives in harmony with life" as the palmist declares. Opposite is the guilt-ridden, inhibited Muriel hopelessly enamored of the self-centered Claude. They fail to become a couple, Truffaut said, "because Muriel has too absolute a conception of love while Claude's is purely relative." Kika Markham, Stacey Tendeter, and Jean-Pierre Léaud strikingly incarnate Roché's characters. As a reserved dilettante, Léaud is distinguished in a part far removed from his familiar role as Antoine Doinel, the director's alter ego. It is evident from every carefully framed shot that Truffaut reveres the novel. His inspired direction supported by Almendros's ravishing cinematography and Delerue's haunting score creates memorable scenes such as a radiant picnic with Claude and the sisters atop a cliff, and two dazzling superimpositions, first of Mme. Roc, then later of Muriel reciting her message of adieu to Claude, both against a glowing countryside.

During the Swiss idyll, a long, graceful tracking shot moving left on the water catches glimpses through the trees of Anne carrying a ladder to the cabin where Claude is repairing the roof, then continuing on her way. In the epilogue as the lonely Claude passes *The Kiss* of Rodin, we poignantly feel how he has missed out on the ecstasy sculptured in marble. "With this film," the director said, "I had wanted to squeeze love like a lemon." A picture of rare and delicate sensibility, *Two English Girls* will never be as popular as the ebullient *Jules and Jim* because of its pervasive melancholy. Yet this elegant movie is possibly Truffaut's most visually beautiful film and justifiably merits recognition as a poetic classic.

35
THE DECAMERON

Il Decamerone

ITALY/FRANCE/WEST
GERMANY/1971

PEA (Produzioni Europee Associate) (Rome)/Les Productions Artistes Associés (Paris)/Artemis Film (West Berlin)

CREDITS

Director and screenwriter: Pier Paolo Pasolini, based on Giovanni Boccaccio's *The Decameron; Assistant directors:* Umberto Angelucci, Sergio Citti; *Producer:* Alberto Grimaldi; *Cinematographer:* Tonino Delli Colli (Technicolor); *Music:* Pier Paolo Pasolini, Enni Morricone; *Editors:* Nino Baragli, Tatiana Morigi; *Art director:* Dante Ferretti; *Running time:* 111 minutes; *16mm rental source:* MGM/UA; *Videocassette:* Water Bearer.

CAST

Ciappelletto: Franco Citti; *Andreuccio:* Ninetto Davoli; *Giotto:* Pier Paolo Pasolini; *Peronella:* Angela Luce; *Caterina:* Elizabetta Davoli; *Ricciardo:* Francisco Gavazzi; *The Madonna:* Silvana Mangano.

The Decameron is the first and finest of Pasolini's "Trilogy of Life," which also includes *The Canterbury Tales* (1972) and *The Arabian Nights* (1974).

A hilarious touch: Andreuccio (Ninetto Davoli) *(center)* and the two thieves who recruited him pause to genuflect in front of the altar before robbing the tomb of the recently deceased archbishop.

While Mother Superior is joyfully ringing the bells, a bevy of delighted nuns fondle Masetto, the "rooster" in the convent, permitted to remain because of the "miraculous" cure of his "muteness."

From the hundred tales that Giovanni Boccaccio wrote between 1348 and 1353, the director selected eight of the bawdiest to emphasize his view of the libidinous, violent character of the period. With Giotto's paintings as a model for costumes, Pasolini aspired to a genuine re-creation of the fourteenth century. Instead of the structure used by the author in which ten upper-class young people flee a plague-ridden Florence to the suburbs and recount stories to pass the time, the director substituted two figures, the scoundrel Ciappelletto in the first part and Giotto in the second, around whom the tales are casually framed. Whereas Boccaccio screened his indelicacies with euphemistic phrasing suitable for his genteel storytellers, Pasolini is explicit and riotously candid. We are plunged into a raw, earthy world that is not cushioned by the writer's moralizing and exhortations. Since Florence was too modernized to serve as a location, the director focused on a far less industrialized Naples and subsequently changed the settings of several narratives. Aside from such actors as Franco Citti and Ninetto Davoli, the large cast was nonprofessional. The film was shot mainly in Naples (the Ciappelletto episode in Bolzano) from September to November 1970. It proved an enormous success. *The Decameron* is a dynamic, lusty, high-spirited film—a far cry from Hugo Fregonese's bland and innocuous earlier treatment of Boccaccio, *Decameron Nights*

(1953)—and richly deserves to be recognized as a classic.

The film opens mysteriously as Ciappelletto (Franco Citti) bludgeons someone to death, then disposes of the corpse. *Andreuccio:* Coming to Naples to buy horses and showing off his wealth, Andreuccio (Ninetto Davoli) is lured into the home of a pretty woman who claims she's his illegitimate sister. The trusting lad is invited to stay the night. As he steps on the deliberately sawn floorboards of the privy, he lands in a deep pile of ordure. The door is bolted and the "sister" grabs his gold. The reeking youth scrambles down and confronts a locked entrance and angry neighbors. Two grave robbers enlist him to despoil the riches of the newly buried archbishop in the church. Forced inside the sepulcher, Andreuccio pockets the prelate's ruby ring, then insists he can't find it. The skeptical men below shut the massive lid on the frightened man. However, the sacristan arrives to plunder with two henchmen. When the cover is raised, Andreuccio bites the custodian's leg. All three flee in panic; the now ungullible lad prances off with his jewel. *Masetto:* A young man, Masetto, feigns aphasia to enter a nunnery to satisfy his randy appetite. Mother Superior, thinking him harmless, retains him as their gardener. Two sisters use the compliant fellow to resolve their curiosity about sex. Espied by the other nuns, Masetto finds his "services" duly taxed, and when Mother Superior demands her share, the exhausted man protests, "I've got nine women on my hands and now you!" She gets up shouting, "A miracle! You can stay!" *Peronella:* The unexpected return of her husband forces Peronella (Angela Luce) to hide her lover in a huge vat. But the spouse has brought a buyer for the container! The quick-thinking wife rejoins that she's already found someone inspecting it at present who'll pay a larger price, whereupon the swain pops up complaining of the encrusted interior.

While the duped mate goes inside to scrape it, the couple resume lovemaking. *Ciappelletto:* Notorious blasphemer, murderer, bugger, etc., Ciap-

Working on the fresco is the renowned painter Giotto (Pier Paolo Pasolini) who, like the director, came to Naples to create a work of art and drew inspiration from the local inhabitants.

pelletto is sent north to collect outstanding debts from two brothers. There he contracts a fatal illness. The men are in a quandary: they can't throw him out; yet if he should confess, they'd be implicated in his misdeeds. The dying rogue tells them not to worry and requests the holiest priest, to whom he prevaricates, concocting an amusing record of an impossibly flawless existence. When he dies, the cleric calls him a "blessed Saint!" *The Anecdote of Giotto:* In a downpour Master Giotto (Pier Paolo Pasolini), en route to Naples to paint a fresco, and a comrade stop to borrow humble, dry clothes from a peasant and laugh that no one would detect the most famous painter of the age in such attire. *Ricciardo and Caterina:* A young pair, Ricciardo (Francisco Gavazzi) and Caterina (Elizabetta Davoli), ache to be alone together. He tells her to sleep outdoors on her roof and he'll climb up. They share a blissful evening. When her father discovers them in the morning, he simulates out-

After being caught sleeping together *au naturel* by the girl's father, a happy Caterina (Elizabetta Davoli) and Ricciardo (Francisco Gavazzi) consent to marry on the spot.

127

rage and demands the boy wed Caterina. They comply elatedly. The shrewd parent saved his daughter's honor and gained a wealthy son-in-law! *Lisabetta:* A youthful merchant notices the worker Lorenzo leaving the bedroom of his sister Lisabetta. Later he and two brothers take him to the woods and slay him. In a dream the victim appears to the heartsick girl and tells her where he was killed. Lisabetta reaches the site, decapitates Lorenzo, and puts his head in an herb pot. *Dom Gianni:* Relegated to the barn, the old Dom Gianni, a guest at the tiny house of Pietro and his attractive wife, Gemmata, tells them not to be concerned for his comfort for he knows the charm of changing his mare into a woman. The credulous twosome realize the economic possibilities if this could be done to *her* and beseech the friar for his secret. Cautioning the husband to be silent and stressing that the hardest part is to get the tail to stick, Dom Gianni has a naked Gemmata bend over and is all set to penetrate her when a furious Pietro shouts, "I won't have a tail there!" thus ruining the "conjuration." *Tingoccio and Meuccio:* While the stocky youth Tingoccio is wearing himself out sleeping with his sister-in-law, his skinny companion Meuccio, fearful of damnation, abstains from sex. They vow that the first one to die will return and inform the other what the afterlife is like. The enervated Tingoccio expires and soon appears to his friend. No, he's not in hell but in purgatory. "What's the punishment for sins of the flesh?" Meuccio inquires. When the ghost shrugs and says no one cares about such matters there, an invigorated Meuccio, yelling, "It's not a sin!" runs off and jumps on his girlfriend. The film ends with Giotto regarding his unfinished fresco.

The Decameron employs a fascinating array of faces. "I steal from them," Pasolini said, "I use their reality." The director displays a strong narrative gift with no slowing down of the pace and sparkle. "In *The Decameron*," he said, "I have sought to represent sex as liberty, not as a problem, not as a tragedy, but simply with all the freedom of the natural." Bursting with energy and joie de vivre, Pasolini's splendid medieval canvas, enhanced by Tonino Delli Colli's superb photography, is a major accomplishment.

HONORS

Silver Bear for Best Director, Berlin Film Festival (1971)

In the early morning Karin (Ingrid Thulin) *(left)* arrives to learn how her sick sister is faring. With her is the attentive maid Anna (Kari Sylwan) *(center)* and sister Maria (Liv Ullmann), who had spent the night near the terminally ill Agnes.

36
CRIES AND WHISPERS

Viskningar och Rop

SWEDEN / 1972

CINEMATOGRAPH/SVENSK FILMINSTITUTET

CREDITS

Director, screenwriter, and producer: Ingmar Bergman; *Assistant director:* Arne Carlsson; *Cinematographer:*

Sven Nykvist (Eastmancolor); *Music:* Chopin: Mazurka in A Minor (Opus 17, No. 4) and Bach: "Sarabande" from Suite No. 5 in E Minor; *Editor:* Siv Lundgren; *Art director:* Marik Vos; *Running time:* 90 minutes; *16mm rental source:* Films Inc., *Videocassette:* Warner (dubbed).

CAST

Agnes: Harriet Andersson; *Karin:* Ingrid Thulin; *Maria/ The Mother:* Liv Ullmann; *Anna:* Kari Sylwan; *The Doctor:* Erland Josephson; *The Pastor:* Anders Ek; *Joakim:* Henning Moritzen; *Fredrik:* Georg Arlin.

After *Persona*, Ingmar Bergman made a series of films that did not meet with either critical or commercial success. However, *Cries and Whispers*, written as he states in his autobiography, *The Magic Lantern*, "during a long attack of melancholy," reconfirmed his venerated, international reputation as a director of genius; in America, in particular, it was showered with honors and proved a popular film. Viewers of the director's work will recognize here the Bergmanesque characteristics through which he creates his private, claustrophobic world: incommunicability; isolated characters tortured with anxiety, the loss of faith, and an inability to love; the ubiquitous presence of death—in brief the desiccated, barren landscape of the soul. This time his universe, set in turn-of-the-century Sweden, is enhanced by varying dark hues of red for the decor of the eighteenth-century manor house where the story is placed and bright blood-red for many of the film's startling dissolves. The director explained the predominance of that color: "Ever since my childhood I have pictured the inside of the soul as a moist

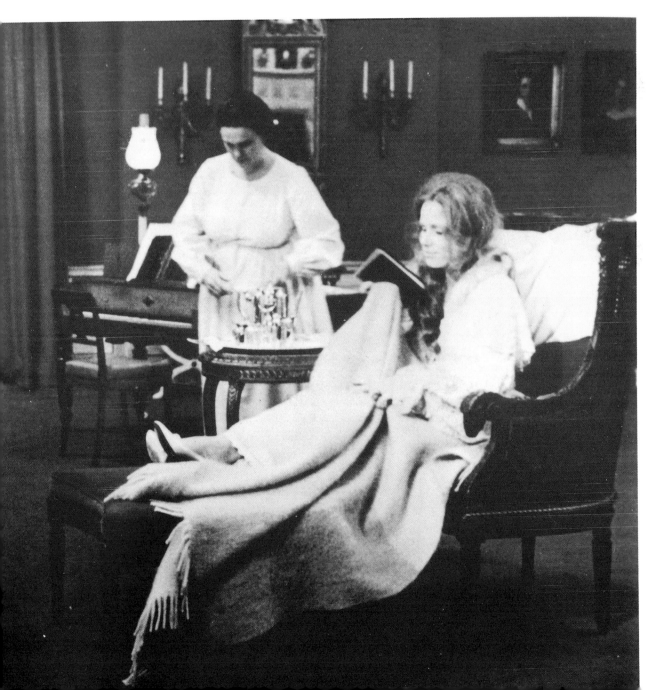

Her terrible pain abating temporarily, Agnes (Harriet Andersson) stares at a rose, which triggers a poignant reminiscence of her late mother.

The director derived the title of the film from a Swedish music critic who alluded to Mozart's music as "whispers and cries" (the terms are reversed in English). Bergman told reporters the narrative's origins lay in a vision he had of "a large red room with three women in white who were talking, who whispered together." This image persisted stubbornly for months until "suddenly it came out," he said, "that they were watching another woman who was dying in the next room." Shooting occurred between September and October 1971 at the Taxinge-Nasby estate in Mariefred, near Stockholm. With *Cries and Whispers*, Bergman produced a visually stunning as well as a dramatically shattering masterpiece.

Unlike *Persona*, the story line is clear and accessible. In her ancestral home Agnes (Harriet Andersson), only in her thirties, lies dying of cancer of the uterus attended by her older sister, Karin (Ingrid Thulin), her younger sister, Maria (Liv Ullmann), and her devoted maid, Anna (Kari Sylwan). Later, when her dreadful pain subsides for a spell, the afflicted woman recalls a childhood memory of her unreciprocated, jealous love for her beautiful but cold mother (Liv Ullmann). The doctor (Erland Josephson) examines Agnes. It won't be long, he tells Karin. Maria, with whom he's had a sporadic affair, calls to him. He kisses her passionately, then leaves. There is a flashback to a scene from

membrane in shades of red." With the assistance of the distinguished cinematographer Sven Nykvist, Bergman's disquieting movie seems as if a brooding Edvard Munch painting suddenly came to life.

Forcing his desultory lover Maria to look into a mirror, the doctor (Erland Josephson) mercilessly details the character flaws revealed in her face.

their former relationship. Treating Anna's little daughter and staying over in the empty house because of inclement weather, the physician points out signs of moral failings in Maria's visage. The next day her diplomat husband Joakim (Henning Moritzen), aware of her infidelity, stabs himself with a sharp letter opener.... The servant awakens the sisters; Agnes, in convulsions, has difficulty breathing. Soon, feeling better, she is washed and cared for by Maria and Karin. But shortly, screaming, "Can anyone help me?" the wretched soul expires. A minister (Anders Ek) prays for her and praises her faith. There is another flashback, this time concerning the unhappy Karin and her unloving, elder husband Fredrik (Georg Arlin). Repeating "It's nothing but lies," she presses a piece of a wineglass broken at dinner into her vagina, then in the bedroom smears blood from the wound across her face as she smiles at her hateful spouse.... A mourning Maria implores the icily reserved Karin to become friendly again. Only after the tormented woman spews forth her contempt for Maria and releases a piercing wail do the sisters have an emotional reconciliation. Anna dreams that Agnes first summons Karin, who declines to stay with her, and then Maria, who flees hysterically when the dead woman clasps her head to hers. Finally there in the bed is the maternal Anna with Agnes slumped beneath her in the manner of a pietà.... After the funeral, the family formally thanks the soon-to-be-discharged Anna. Karin wishes to hold her fresh rapport with Maria, but the younger sister is now standoffish and distant. Alone, Anna reads a passage from Agnes's diary. An autumn scene is depicted. The invalid, health improved, strolls with her two sisters and her constant servant. She is happy, Agnes narrates, and we overhear in the concluding close-up on the radiant woman, "I feel a great gratitude to my life, which gives me so much."

With minimal exposition and dialogue, Ingmar Bergman creates another impressive gallery of memorable characters. We see the hapless Agnes, who in spite of harrowing suffering does not bewail her lot and can still regard her life as a blessing. There is the troubled Karin trapped in a loveless marriage, full of rage against her fate and contemplating suicide. There is the spoiled and selfish Maria, callow and self-indulgent. In contrast there is the simple Anna whose dedication and care for Agnes are unstinting. The bitterness and shallowness represented by Karin and Maria respectively are counterbalanced by the faith and affirmation of life by Agnes and the selfless love of

Maria (right) attempts to get closer to her aloof sister, Karin.

Anna. Harriet Andersson as the doomed Agnes is extraordinary; her painful death agony is almost unbearable, certainly indelible. The incredibly versatile Ingrid Thulin brings the desolate and splenetic Karin to vivid life. The breathtakingly beautiful Liv Ullmann with her red hair and blue eyes makes the unsympathetic Maria captivating. Kari Sylwan lends strong support as the faithful Anna.

Bergman directs this intimate, poetic film with marvelous economy and brilliant inspiration. Relentless close-ups expose his characters to our probing gaze. The periodic, loud ticking of clocks; the muffled cries and the chorus of whispers throughout the close-ups on the main personages before each arresting, sanguineous dissolve create a chilling expressionistic and aural symphony. One sequence among many, which is superb, is that in which a hostile Karin is ultimately moved by Maria's entreaties for friendship. They embrace, caress each other, and speak volubly; all we hear, however, is a cello performing Bach's elegant "Sarabande"—how often has Bergman employed this composer to signify spiritual communication! In addition, his writing is beautiful, especially the reverend's invocation to the deceased Agnes: "Pray for us who are left here on the dark, dirty earth under an empty and cruel Heaven.... Ask Him for a meaning to our lives." The film's grim mood is made more acute by Sven Nykvist's acclaimed cinematography. The exquisite *Cries and Whispers* has a powerful, emotional impact. It is the work of a master and may be the influential director's greatest achievement. The highest tribute that I can think of is to say that Ingmar Bergman is the Strindberg of the cinema.

Best Picture; Liv Ullmann, Best Actress; Best
Direction; Best Screenplay Writing—New York
Film Critics Awards (1972)
Oscar to Sven Nykvist for Best Cinematography;
nominated in addition for Best Picture, Direction,
Story and Screenplay (original material) (1973)

37

UNCLE VANYA

Dyadya Vanya

USSR / 1972

MOSFILM STUDIOS

CREDITS

Director and screenwriter: Andrei Konchalovsky, based
on Anton Chekhov's play (1899); *Cinematographers:*
Georgy Rerberg, Yevgeny Guslinsky (in sepia and Sovcolor); *Music:* Alfred Shnitke; *Art director:* Nikolai
Dvigubsky; *Running time:* 110 minutes; *16mm rental
source:* Corinth.

CAST

Ivan Petrovich Voynitsky (Uncle Vanya): Innokenti
Smoktunovsky; *Dr. Astrov:* Sergei Bondarchuk; *Sere-
bryskov:* Vladimir Zeldin; *Sonya:* Irina Kupchenko;
Yelena Andreyevna: Irina Miroschnichenko; *Mother:*
Irina Anismova-Wolf; *Telyegin:* Nikolai Pastukhov.

With its use of the revelatory close-up, its ability
both to explore characterization and to evoke intimate moods, one might well imagine that the
cinema is an ideal medium in which to capture the
delicate beauty of Anton Chekhov's exquisite
plays. But there have been so many unsuccessful
ventures, among them Sidney Lumet's *The Sea
Gull* (1968) and Laurence Olivier's *Three Sisters*
(1970), that one could derive the mistaken notion
that the dramas of the great Russian playwright
cannot be filmed. Yet the superb screen adaptation
of *Uncle Vanya* by Russian director Andrei Konchalovsky (1937–   ) proves that with skillful
direction and brilliant acting Chekhov's plays can
indeed be most effectively cinematic. In fact, this
film is quite possibly the best movie treatment of
the Russian master's dramas ever made. Unfortunately, it is little known here. *Uncle Vanya* was
the fourth feature of Konchalovsky, who previously called himself Mikhalkov-Konchalovsky to
differentiate himself from his father, the poet and
writer Sergei Mikhalkov (Konchalovsky being his
mother's surname). However, when his younger
brother Nikita became an actor and director, Konchalovsky dropped the first part of his hyphenated
name. Since the 1980s he has made movies in
America and England—the fascinating *Runaway
Train* (1985), etc.

Chekhov referred to *Uncle Vanya,* a reworking
of an earlier, failed drama called *The Wood Demon*
(1889), as "Scenes From Country Life." Familiar
themes abound: the abrasion of the spirit amid the
daily minutiae, the terrible ennui of Russian provincial life, and the exhaustion of youthful ideals.
Here he would contrast the selfish "takers" of the
world, Serebryskov and his attractive wife, with
the generous, self-sacrificing "givers," Dr. Astrov
and Sonya and her "Uncle Vanya" Voynitsky. It is
a drama of courage and hope in the midst of
disillusionment and displays the writer's remarkable understanding of life and profound compassion. To make this subtle play—a work of understatement in which atmosphere is elevated over
plot—into a forceful and gripping film, Konchalovsky cast two of the USSR's greatest actors,
Innokenti Smoktunovsky in the title role and
Sergei Bondarchuk as Dr. Astrov, made judicious
cuts in the text, trimmed speeches, spread the
action among the rooms, while remaining faithful
to its beloved author, and produced a powerful and
deeply moving film.

The plot follows the play closely. The middle-
aged Serebryskov (Vladimir Zeldin), a completely
shallow and self-absorbed writer, has installed
himself for several months on the estate of his late
wife. With him is his young, beautiful, and bored
second wife, Yelena (Irina Miroschnichenko).
They would prefer to live in town, but it is cheaper
here in the country. With increasing exasperation,
Voynitsky, (Innokenti Smoktunovsky), the forty-
seven-year-old brother of the author's first wife,
bemoans all the years of sacrifice he has made to
help the "great" Serebryskov, whose lucubrations
now seem to him worthless, and harbors love for
the man's indolent wife. His younger friend, Dr.
Astrov (Sergei Bondarchuk), is an overworked physician with a passion for reforestation. (Chekhov's
views on the environment are amazingly contemporary). He, too, is smitten with Yelena. Complet-

On a cloudy afternoon tensions mount on the veranda. Staring at Dr. Astrov (Sergei Bondarchuk) is the youthful Sonya (Irina Kupchenko), who loves him unrequitedly. Standing is Telyegin (Nikolai Pastukhov), former owner of the estate; to the right is Uncle Vanya's mother (Irina Anismova-Wolf).

ing the quintet of central characters is Serebryskov's daughter, Sonya (Irina Kupchenko), from his first marriage, a plain young woman with a pure soul who has adored Dr. Astrov silently for several years. Voynitsky is her adored Uncle Vanya. Although Yelena is in a loveless union, she discourages Voynitsky's ardor and finds the atmosphere of the house hostile and nerve-racking. On a stormy evening Sonya is discouraged to learn from an intoxicated Astrov that he finds himself incapable of loving anyone; with Serebryskov's wife it is merely desire. Alone with her stepdaughter, Yelena speaks of the disenchantment in her marriage and of her abiding discontent. September arrives. The wife volunteers to sound out Astrov concerning his feelings for the unhappy Sonya. The doctor admits that a relationship with her might have been a possibility—that is, until the author's wife came along. He kisses Yelena passionately at the very moment Voynitsky appears with roses for her. Embarrassed, frightened of her feelings, she announces that she and her husband will leave that day. Serebryskov calls a family council and callously states his plans to sell the estate. Voynitsky objects that he is to be evicted from a place he's slaved for, reminds him that he'd be robbing his daughter of her patrimony, calls him a fraud who has destroyed his life, and storms off. The writer follows to placate him. A shot is heard. Serebryskov enters the drawing room aghast, while Voynitsky returns and takes another wild shot at him. That evening Astrov—fearing his friend may commit suicide—asks for the mor-

Later that evening Dr. Astrov admits to being drunk and growing vulgar to his embittered friend, Voynitsky (Innokenti Smoktunovsky) (right).

phine Voynitsky stole from his bag. The couple leave, then Astrov. Sonya expresses her faith to her disheartened uncle and her renewed dedication to work. The camera backs far away during her exalted speech: "We shall rest! We shall rest!"

Having a late-night snack with the radiant Sonya, Dr. Astrov criticizes the members of the household in particular and the dreary rural life in general.

After failing in his attempts to shoot Serebryskov, Voynitsky straightens up the drawing room while close by is a disconsolate Yelena (Irina Miroschnichenko).

Konchalovsky captures all the nuances of these fascinating, introspective characters: The terrifying recognition of Uncle Vanya that he has wasted his life in self-denial for his pretentious brother-in-law; the complicated Astrov, struggling to keep his ideals alive beneath a cynical facade; brave little Sonya, whose religious fervor triumphs over blighted hopes; the unfulfilled Yelena, too preoccupied with her own misery to do anything that would give significance to her existence; the vain, self-centered Serebryskov with an inflated view of his importance—interestingly the only major character in the movie who does not undergo some sort of change save for the realization that he's no longer welcome in his brother-in-law's residence. Seething with rage at the parasitical author and bewailing the ruins of his life, Innokenti Smoktunovsky gives an extraordinary, unforgettable performance. He is absolutely chilling when he crouches near a seated Serebryskov and in a low, impassioned voice starts lashing out at his former idol. The gifted Sergei Bondarchuk permits us to peer into the very soul of Dr. Astrov, while the lovely Irina Kupchenko beautifully projects the spiritual nature of Sonya.

Konchalovsky's exemplary direction is fluid, unobtrusive, and controlled. Especially memorable are his wonderful close-ups as revelation follows upon revelation. Georgy Rerberg and Yevgeny Guslinsky's impressive cinematography alternates a portion of the film shot in sepia with another shot in Sovcolor. Since Dr. Astrov's distressing photographs of sick children, dead bodies of the poor, and hospitals are always shown in sepia, may we consider that the intermittent colored sequences are a chromatic device equivalent to those passages in the play that presage a brighter, happier future? There is very little music with the result that the pattering of rain or an occasional train whistle serves to deepen the mood. Maxim Gorki found the original stage production "incomparable." Konchalovsky's sensitive yet vigorous screen version is unmatched as well, a model Chekhov adaptation and a film justly deserving to be regarded as a classic.

38
AGUIRRE, THE WRAST OF GOD

Aguirre, der Zorn Gottes

WEST GERMANY / 1972

WERNER HERZOG FILMPRODUKTION
(MUNICH)/HESSISCHER RUNDFUNK (FRANKFORT)

A portrait of the ruthless Don Lope de Aguirre (Klaus Kinski), the self-styled "Wrath of God."

CREDITS

Director, producer, and screenwriter: Werner Herzog; *Assistant director:* Gustavo Cerff Arbulu; *Cinematographer:* Thomas Mauch (Eastmancolor); *Music:* Popul Vuh; *Editor:* Beate Mainka-Jellinghaus; *Running time:* 93 minutes; *16mm rental source and videocassette:* New Yorker.

CAST

Don Lope de Aguirre: Klaus Kinski; *Inez:* Helena Rojo; *Br. Gaspar de Carvajal:* Del Negro; *Don Pedro de Ursua:* Ruy Guerra; *Don Fernando de Guzman:* Peter Berling; *Flores:* Cecilia Rivera; *Perucho:* Daniel Ades; *Okello:* Edward Roland; *Gonzalo Pizarro:* Alejandro Repullés.

While leafing through a young adult's book about discoverers in 1971, German director Werner Herzog (1942–   ) came upon an account of a minor

A rebellious Aguirre listens with mounting resentment to the commander's order to end the expedition and return to Pizarro's group.

conquistador, Don Lope de Aguirre (c. 1508–61), infamous for his treachery and vindictiveness, and, fascinated, Herzog knew he had the subject for his third feature. In the resulting *Aguirre, the Wrath of God* he incorporated the nobleman's expedition of 1560 in quest of the legendary city of gold, El Dorado, in the Amazon basin with another voyage, undertaken without him but recorded by a Dominican friar nearly twenty years before. Herzog had no intention of limiting herself to historical veracity—in actuality Aguirre survived the trip only to be assassinated by his troops later on—but wished to capture a dramatic, psychologically accurate portrait of an obsessed man, an archetype of a megalomaniacal leader. Following the film's structure of diary entries narrated by the monk, Brother Gaspar, we witness Aguirre's gradual rebellion and usurpation of power as the overweeningly ambitious man goads his famished but greedy soldiers ever farther along the hazardous river in futile pursuit of the illusory El Dorado. Aguirre, like all the protagonists in the director's films, far exceeds the boundaries of conventional behavior and thus provides Herzog with an ideal subject with whom to explore the human condition. "People under extreme pressure give you much more insight about what we are, about our very innermost being," the director said. With the exceptional Klaus Kinski in the title role, the film was shot between January and February 1972 in isolated regions of Peru under the most perilous of conditions. Filled with exotic images, enhanced by a stirring plot with outstanding acting and directing, *Aguirre, the Wrath of God* was critically acclaimed as well as popular. A rich and poetic meditation upon history, it has deservedly achieved the status of a classic.

The film opens as the Spanish expedition led by Gonzalo Pizarro (Alejandro Repullés) cautiously descends the steep Andes to the Urubamba Valley below. The leader, confronted with difficult terrain and diminishing rations, commands three floats to be built and selects forty soldiers under the authority of Don Pedro de Ursua (Ruy Guerra) to forage for food and to monitor for both belligerent Indians and El Dorado, which should be close by. Among the chosen crew are the crippled deputy, Don Lope de Aguirre (Klaus Kinski), his young daughter Flores (Cecilia Rivera), Ursua's mistress Inez (Helena Rojo), and the recording friar, Brother Gaspar (Del Negro). On January 4, 1561, they set out. Soon, however, one of the rafts is trapped in a whirlpool. When a detail manages to reach it, they

discover all have been killed with arrows. To thwart Ursua's plan to give the men Christian burial, Aguirre has his loyal aide Perucho (Daniel Ades) discharge a cannon, which blows the raft up. Overnight, rising waters bear off the remaining floats. Without consulting the commander, Aguirre orders a new, larger raft to be constructed. Ursua announces they are to march back to Pizarro since the current is too strong. "I don't turn back," Aguirre retorts and tries to foment the soldiers to revolt by citing Cortés, who refused to retreat and went on to overpower Mexico, thereby gaining untold wealth. The commander demands the insurgent be put in chains, but is wounded. Assuming control and intimidating the rest, Aguirre appoints his vain puppet, Don Fernando de Guzman (Peter Berling), as emperor and concocts an edict severing themselves from the Spanish crown. Wanting the commander murdered, Aguirre pressures the ruler to stage a mock trial in which Ursua is condemned. Guzman nonetheless exercises clemency, infuriating Aguirre. They sail off and come upon a village of cannibals. The emperor is callously gluttonous as the men starve. He commands their skittish horse to be thrown overboard, which would have been food for a week; shortly the emperor's discovered strangled. Perucho takes Ursua ashore and hangs him. Later, as the soldiers skirmish with the natives, Inez resignedly walks off into the jungle. Overhearing a man planning an escape, Aguirre orders his trusty assistant to behead him, then issues ferocious decrees against desertion and appropriation of more food than one's allotment. "I am the Wrath of God," he asserts. As the float advances, one by one the soldiers are hit by unseen shafts. Morale is low, hunger prevalent. The enervated men hallucinate. Finally after Flores is fatally pierced, Aguirre is alone, by now a delusional paranoid. As marmosets swarm over the raft, he projects grandiose plans of seizing Trinidad, then Mexico, and of marrying his daughter to "found the purest dynasty the earth has ever seen."

Although Aguirre is depicted as brutal, cynical, and merciless, he is not caricatured as a monster and displays such humanizing traits as his devotion to his child. Shrewd enough to realize that the inducement of incalculable gold will motivate his mercenary men to follow him, he himself is unaware that the power and fame he thirsts for are as chimerical as the mythical El Dorado. The director skillfully distances us from Aguirre, forcing us to reflect upon this disturbing figure. With his rugged

Aware that Aguirre intends to murder her lover, Inez (Helena Rojo) cautions, "God will punish you for it!"

Holding Flores (Cecilia Rivera), his slain daughter, a crazed Aguirre is now the sole survivor on the ill-fated raft.

features and dynamic screen presence, the late Klaus Kinski as Aguirre gave a galvanic performance in what was to be his best-known film.* Herzog's direction is masterly as he provides us, scene after scene, with remarkable and unusual images: The opening, a truly breathtaking, zooming extreme long shot of Pizarro's army snaking down the vast mountain accompanied by unworldly choral music, succeeded by close shots of a caravan of Spaniards, slaves, llamas, etc., caught with a hand-held camera to highlight the clumsiness of their passage. Lengthy shots of treacherous rapids which are mesmeric. The deadly silence while the soldiers fearfully await the next victim of a blow-dart. The bloodcurdling moment when the Indians' clamor is translated by the guide as "They shout that meat is floating by." And the unforgettable closing sequence as the camera encircles the mad Aguirre embarked on a course to become the conqueror of New Spain, while hordes of monkeys sweep across the desolate float twitting the solitary lunatic. The 360-degree movements emphasize the meaninglessness of the protagonist's folly. Credit Thomas Mauch's striking cinematography and Popul Vuh's eerie, synthesized score.

Aguirre, the Wrath of God is on one level both a critique of colonialism and Catholicism as the predatory Spaniards prepare to rape and enslave a continent under the pretext of forcibly bringing Christianity to the heathen. It is also a microcosm of our century, when a tyrant such as Hitler could lead his people to destruction. An exciting, suspenseful, and visually impressive adventure film, it is, besides, a provocative contemplation upon man's pursuit of delusive dreams. Intense and unforgettable, this film has not lost its capacity to startle and enthrall.

HONORS

L'Étoile de Cristal for Prix International (1975)
Prix Moussinac (1975)

---

*It is unfortunate that due to a falling-out with the director, his voice was subsequently dubbed by someone else.

39

DAY FOR NIGHT

La Nuit Américaine

FRANCE/ITALY / 1973

LES FILMS DU CARROSSE/P.E.C.F. (PRODUCTIONS ET ÉDITIONS CINÉMATOGRAPHIQUE FRANÇAISE) (PARIS)/P.I.C. (PRODUZIONE INTERNAZIONALE CINEMATOGRAFICA) (ROME)

CREDITS

Director: François Truffaut; *Assistant directors:* Suzanne Schiffman, Jean-François Stévenin; *Producer:* Marcel Berbert; *Screenwriters:* François Truffaut, Jean-Louis Richard, Suzanne Schiffman; *Cinematographer:* Pierre-William Glenn (Eastmancolor, Spherical Panavision); *Music:* Georges Delerue; *Editors:* Yann Dedet, Martine Barraqué; *Art director:* Damien Lanfranchi; *Running time:* 115 minutes; *16mm rental source:* Swank (dubbed); *Videocassette:* Warner (dubbed).

CAST

Ferrand: François Truffaut; *Julie Baker/Pamela:* Jacqueline Bisset; *Alexandre:* Jean-Pierre Aumont; *Séverine:* Valentina Cortese; *Alphonse:* Jean-Pierre Léaud; *Joëlle:* Nathalie Baye; *Bertrand:* Jean Champion; *Stacey:* Alexandra Stewart; *Bernard:* Bernard Menez; *Liliane:* Dani; *Dr. Nelson:* David Markham; *Odile:* Niki Arrighi.

For a number of years François Truffaut contemplated a movie whose subject was the actual making of a film. He took notes on incidents that occurred during his various projects and collected anecdotes about other directors. Then, editing *Two English Girls* at the Victorine Studios near Nice, he daily walked by the dilapidated remains of a set of a Parisian square used when Bryan Forbes shot *The Madwoman of Chaillot* (1969) and began to see its possibilities for a film of his own. Everything jelled for the director: "I decided to construct, using as its starting point a film in progress, a *fictional* story which would, at the same time, furnish a maximum of *factual* information." *Meet Pamela*, the melodrama being filmed, is ostensibly mediocre and uncomplicated—although no one connected with it patronizes it—to keep the film-within-the-film from upstaging the far more engrossing lives of the cast and the staff. Unlike *8½*, which dealt with a director's preproduction difficulties, *Day for Night* would treat the intricate process of shooting a film beginning when the camera starts to roll on the first day and ending on the last, a sort of a "filmed journal of a shooting," Truffaut said, dramatizing "all the various troubles that can plague a movie production." Thus in the narrative of the filmmaking we have the harried director, played by Truffaut himself, coping with the pressures of a tight schedule, temperamental performers, an actor's death, etc., while interspersed throughout, in documentary fashion, is a series of elegant montage sequences depicting the filming of various scenes. When Americans do films about moviemaking, we generally portray vicious characters in power ploys, backstabbing, etc.—as Robert Aldrich's *The Big Knife* (1955) from Clifford Odets's play—but refreshingly different is Truffaut's tone, which implies that in spite of its hectic aspects filmmaking is a joyous occasion, a "privileged period," as he said, when artists come together as a loving family to create a film.

Day-for-night (or *la nuit américaine* in French) is a technical term originating in the making of westerns in which an effect of evening is achieved by use of a dark filter inserted over the camera lens in daylight. Jacqueline Bisset, Jean-Pierre Aumont, and Valentina Cortese headed an international cast. *Day for Night*, Truffaut's thirteenth feature, was shot between late September and December 1972 at the Victorine Studios and in the Riviera. This appealing and vibrant motion picture was showered with awards and has become *the* classic movie about filmmaking.

The plot centers around the struggles director Ferrand (François Truffaut) has in filming in seven weeks this story of *Meet Pamela*: When Pamela, played by Julie Baker (Jacqueline Bisset), an English bride, is introduced to her French in-laws, she falls in love with her father-in-law, played by Alexandre (Jean-Pierre Aumont), and runs off with him to Paris. Her outraged husband, played by Alphonse (Jean-Pierre Léaud), ignores the pleas of his mother, played by Séverine (Valentina Cortese), to forget them and fires on his father in the streets of Paris. (Pamela was killed when her car careened off a highway).

Day for Night opens on the first day of the shooting. A mistrustful Alphonse is involved in a stormy relationship with apprentice script girl Liliane (Dani). A tippling Séverine botches a scene with Alexandre; we learn from Joëlle (Nathalie

Baye), the script girl, that the distraught actress has a son with terminal leukemia. Julie Baker, the film's star, arrives; Ferrand trusts that she has recovered sufficiently from her nervous breakdown. When the coquettish Liliane elopes with an English stuntman, Alphonse petulantly barricades himself in his room. Julie tries to dissuade him from deserting the film and concludes by sleeping with him. The next day Alphonse, enmeshed in his latest romantic illusion, calls Dr. Nelson (David Markham), Julie's husband, and insists, "Set her free!" The physician telephones his wife. Overwrought, the actress shuts herself in her room. The appearance of her sympathetic husband calms her. Shooting resumes, interrupted by Bertrand the producer (Jean Champion), who announces the sudden and tragic death of Alexandre in an auto accident. The insurance people force Ferrand to wind up the film in five days in order to be indemnified. The director hits upon the idea of having Alphonse shoot a stand-in resembling Alexandre in the back from a distance. *Meet Pamela* completed, cast and crew bid farewell to each other and disperse.

The reserved and solitary Ferrand with his hearing aid quietly commands the chaotic, high-tension enterprise of filmmaking, which he thrives on. Since Truffaut acknowledged, "I am being myself behind and in front of the camera," we can say that Ferrand affords us a glimpse of the working habits of this renowned and popular director. The beautiful Jacqueline Bisset makes the insecure Julie believable. Jean-Pierre Aumont endows Alexandre with magnetic charm. Valentina Cortese is unforgettable as the flamboyant Séverine—hilarious, vulnerable, and touching. Jean-Pierre

Ferrand (François Truffaut) *(right)* coaches Alphonse how to hold the revolver for the forthcoming scene in which he's to kill his father.

Léaud is engaging as the callow Alphonse. The five portraying the actors as well as the five playing technicians are all treated with equal importance, without judgment.

Whether employing a hand-held camera accompanying Ferrand as he encounters various crew members—suggesting the pressing work of picture-making—or shooting *Meet Pamela* in a more traditional mode, Truffaut's direction is always precise and exemplary. Georges Delerue's classical score lends polish to the film. As would be expected with this director, *Day for Night* is prodigal with allusions to cinema—the group, for instance, passes Rue Jean Vigo en route to a shoot—making it a feast for film buffs. Although some trade secrets are revealed—for example how technical tricks of rain and snow are faked—Truffaut does not demystify the magical medium of film, but instead succeeds in glorifying it, albeit recognizing the tragic undercurrents that accompany any human endeavor. At the conclusion of the filming, Bernard (Bernard Menez), the prop man, addresses a TV interviewer with the stock but sincere phrase, "We hope the public will have as much fun watching this movie as we all had making it!" We certainly did, and for the fresh and brilliant *Day for Night* in addition to the rest of his wonderful oeuvre, we may gratefully say to the late director, "Merci!"

HONORS

Prix Méliès (1973)
Best Picture; Best Director; Valentina Cortese, Best Supporting Actress; New York Film Critics Awards (1973)
Best Film; Best Director; Valentina Cortese, Best Supporting Actress; British Academy Awards (1973)
Oscar for Best Foreign Language Film (1973); nominated in addition for Best Director, Valentina Cortese for Supporting Actress, and Original Screenplay (1974)

40

THE SPIRIT OF THE BEEHIVE

El Espíritu de la Colmena

SPAIN / 1973

Elias Querejeta Producciónes Cinematográficas

CREDITS

Director: Victor Erice; *Producer:* Elias Querejeta; *Screenwriters:* Angel Fernandez Santos, Victor Erice; *Cinematographer:* Luis Cuadrado (Eastmancolor); *Music:* Luis De Pablo; *Editor:* Pablo G. Del Amo; *Art director:* Adolfo Cofina; *Running time:* 98 minutes; *16mm rental source:* Janus; *Videocassette:* Connoisseur.

CAST

Fernando: Fernando Feran Gomez; *Teresa:* Teresa Gimpera; *Ana:* Ana Torrent; *Isabel:* Isabel Telleria; *Milagros:* Lali Soldevila; *Doctor:* Miguel Picazo; *Fugitive:* Juan Margallo.

The Spirit of the Beehive was the extraordinary first feature of the talented Spanish director Victor Erice (1940–   ). He was initially commissioned to make a horror film, an adaptation of *Frankenstein*, but the project was considered too expensive to undertake. Stimulated by the scene of the monster's meeting with the little girl—immortalized by Boris Karloff in the James Whale classic, *Frankenstein* (1931)—the screenwriters began to conceive an imaginative movie in which a seven- or eight-year-old (indelibly portrayed by Ana Torrent) would become fascinated with the creation of Dr. Frankenstein, with potentially harmful re-

Father (Fernando Feran Gomez) points out the difference between edible and poisonous mushrooms to his daughters, Isabel (Isabel Telleria) *(left)* and Ana (Ana Torrent). This scene represents in addition a symbolic introduction to good and evil.

writes a letter to her lover not knowing if he still lives. An enthralled Ana watches the movie with her sister. Later at bedtime she insists Isabel tell her why the monster killed the little girl. The prevaricative sister tells the gullible Ana that she wasn't killed, that he's still alive, too. She's seen him and knows where he lives. He's really a spirit whom you can talk to if you're his friend. Just close your eyes and say, "It's me, Ana." After school Isabel points out a stable near a well in a distant field as "his" house. A solitary Ana returns and finds a huge man's footprint in the mud. Afterward a fugitive Loyalist soldier (Juan Margallo) jumps from a train. Injuring his leg, he limps to the stable to hide out. Ana comes upon him and offers the hungry man an apple. Soon she reappears with her father's watch, jacket, and food. However at night he's cornered and shot. Fernando is brought in by

sults. The director wished essentially to show the way in which a small child perceived reality. No longer a genre film, with its slight plot subordinated to mood and characterization, *The Spirit of the Beehive* "is rather a work," Erice emphasized, "which has a fundamentally lyrical, musical structure and whose images lie deep in the very heart of a mythical experience." It was shot in Hoyuelos (Segovia) and Parla (Madrid). The picture received awards at various festivals, marked the debut of a director of significance, and gave him an international reputation (being especially popular in Japan). Ironically, due to the vagaries of the Spanish film industry, the movie caused him to be labeled a specialized director and prevented him from being offered other assignments—ten years passed before he could make a second feature. *The Spirit of the Beehive* is original and unforgettable cinema and ranks among the greatest films produced in Spain.

The film is set in a remote Catilian village in 1940. During the recent Civil War, Fernando (Fernando Feran Gomez) retreated to a farmhouse there with his wife, Teresa (Teresa Gimpera), and two daughters, Isabel (Isabel Telleria), around ten, and the younger Ana (Ana Torrent). He devotes much time to beekeeping. The movie opens as a truck arrives in the square, bringing a dubbed *Frankenstein* to the excited children; chairs are quickly set up in the town hall. At home Teresa

A confused Ana kneels at the place where sister Isabel was playing dead, then disappeared.

In the stall, Ana ties the shoes of the injured "monster" (Juan Margallo) she's befriended.

may commingle. (Even in her anatomy class, the teacher personifies a dummy as "Don José.") Although a gentleman in the introduction to *Frankenstein* cautions the audience not to take the film very seriously, little Ana is oblivious to his advice. What does the monster represent for the small child? What is she yearning for through him? Fortunately, Erice does not disclose this secret and it remains open for us to ruminate on. Possessing big, expressive eyes, Ana Torrent makes the impressionable Ana totally convincing in a mesmerizing, highly acclaimed performance.

Victor Erice's direction is brilliantly controlled. Employing little dialogue with scant exposition—which engages the spectator in deciphering the film—the director's style may be described as elliptical, both in the sense of being economical as well as cryptic. In a wonderful scene with the

the police to identify the man's body, laid out pointedly beneath the screen in the town hall. He shakes his head, then receives his timepiece and clothing. At home at the table he opens his chiming watch and notices Ana's surprised reaction. The child subsequently races to the shed and sees the man's bloodstains on the straw. The father reveals himself and orders her to come to him, but Ana dashes off. A search party starts looking for the girl. Meanwhile a meditative, resigned Teresa puts a letter she received into the flames (did it concern her lover?) Alone in the woods by a river, Ana has a vision of Frankenstein's monster approaching her as in the film, then faints. The girl is found the next morning. The worried mother tells the doctor (Miguel Picazo) that Ana hardly sleeps, doesn't eat or respond to anyone. He replies that she's had a terrible shock but it will pass. Ana wakes up at night, heads to the terrace, and there whispers Isabel's words to summon the monster, "It's me, Ana."

Fernando is an introverted man, obsessed with his bees. Like Maurice Maeterlinck in *The Life of the Bees*, which he frequently quotes, he ponders "the spirit of the hive" and its implications regarding the human condition. He spends insomniac evenings writing his reflections in a journal. With Ana we enter the private, mysterious world of a child where actuality, fantasy, and hallucination

Late at night Ana invokes the spirit of the "monster." The senary pattern on the doors and windows in this and other rooms produces an intentional apiary effect.

stable in long shot, Ana scurries away from aiding her friend in the afternoon. We cut to evening, the same shot. Suddenly, breaking the silence, we witness a brief outburst of gunfire like distant fireworks, then a quiet fade-out—a scene worthy of Robert Bresson. Erice pays meticulous attention to detail and with the assistance of noted cinematographer Luis Cuadrado provides us with breathtaking long shots, such as those of the farmhouse and the school, which the lively pupils enter from various approaches. We sense the devastating effect of the war obliquely in a village filled with the elderly and children; the only young men we glimpse are soldiers passing through on a train. Avoiding the pitfalls of depicting the little girls either in a sentimental fashion or as miniature adults spouting "cute" remarks, Erice joins the handful of directors such as Jean Vigo and François Truffaut who can skillfully evoke childhood in a natural manner, who unobtrusively observe their irrepressible subjects during this magical period.

Clearly, with recurring shots of the apiary—there's one indoors also—in a house whose windows, suffused with amber light, have a provocative, hexagonal latticework, the beehive is an all-embracing, though ambiguous, symbol with implications that are psychological, political, and philosophical. To limit an interpretation to one meaning, one discovers, is to deprive the film of its rich, manifold connotations. Repeated viewings augment the density of this work. With *The Spirit of the Beehive* Erice charts our interior world and produces a splendid, haunting masterpiece, an outstanding model of poetic cinema.

41
LACOMBE, LUCIEN

FRANCE/ITALY/
WEST GERMANY / 1974

N.E.F. (Nouvelles Éditions de Films)/U.P.F. (Paris)/Vides Films (Rome)/Hallelujah Films (Munich)

CREDITS

Director and producer: Louis Malle; *Screenwriters:* Louis Malle, Patrick Modiano; *Cinematographer:* Toni-

Near one of the ubiquitous pictures of Marshal Pétain—here in a nursing home—Lucien (Pierre Blaise) aims his slingshot at a bird outside the window—the first demonstration of his propensity for savagery.

Lucien comes to invite France (Aurore Clément) to a party at the Hotel Grotto. Displaying his usual disdain for the suitor is her father, Albert Horn (Holger Lowenadler).

no Delli Colli (Eastmancolor); *Music:* Django Reinhardt and the Quintet from the Hot-Club of France; *Editor:* Suzanne Baron; *Art director:* Ghislain Uhry; *Running time:* 141 minutes; *16mm rental source:* Films Inc.

CAST

Lucien: Pierre Blaise; *France:* Aurore Clément; *Albert Horn:* Holger Lowenadler; *Grandmother:* Therese Giehse; *Jean-Bernard:* Stéphane Bouy; *Betty Beaulieu:* Loumi Iacobesco; *Faure:* René Bouloc; *Aubert:* Pierre Decazes; *Tonin:* Jean Rougerie; *Marie:* Cecile Ricard; *Mme. Lacombe:* Gilberte Rivet; *Peyssac:* Jean Bousquet.

A German noncommissioned officer and Lucien arrive in town to collect hostages in reprisal for the Maquis attack on the hotel.

Controversial French director Louis Malle (1932–   ) had another provocative film with *Lacombe, Lucien,* his ninth feature. Here he would pass over the traditional presentation of the heroes of the Resistance and focus instead upon the role of the French collaborators during the German Occupation, concentrating on—but without judging—a young peasant teenager with very aggressive leanings and showing how he could easily be manipulated into becoming an instrument of the Vichy government. In *Lacombe, Lucien* the youth's name is presented in reverse order, suggesting more than a formal custom, rather a case study or a disturbing statistic to contemplate. Malle said, "I am trying to say that Lucien could be any of us, given the right set of circumstances." The director depicts the quislings in a realistic manner: "I have shown them to be mediocre people," he said, "not devils but bureaucrats. It is important to understand they are not monsters, just normal people that torture and kill others."

Originally Malle considered making a film about the *Halcónes* ("Hawks") of Mexico, adolescent boys with police records from the slums whom an extreme right-wing group recruited for training and then sent to play havoc with student demonstrators. Since permission to shoot it there would hardly be granted, he thought of Algerian fifth columnists before perceiving that a similar situation existed in his own country throughout World War II. After an exhaustive search, the director made the fortuitous discovery of Pierre Blaise, "the real version of someone I had made up," he said. The film was shot in Lugagnac, a village in the feral region of Lot. Assailed by both the left and the right, *Lacombe, Lucien* was nevertheless a critically applauded and popular movie. A superbly crafted film, it still vexes audiences with upsetting issues.

The film opens in June 1944 in a minor prefecture in southwestern France. Lucien (Pierre Blaise), a sturdy youth of seventeen, is employed at a nursing home in an unnamed town. He bicycles to his village, Souleillac, to see his mother (Gilberte Rivet); his father is a POW. Bored with his position, Lucien attempts to join the underground, but Peyssac (Jean Bousquet), schoolteacher and Resistance member, rejects him for his age and for not being seriously motivated. En route to his job, the lad has a flat tire. Arriving after curfew, he is captivated by the brightly lit Hotel Grotto, where a party is in progress. A sentinel pushes him inside where a group of collaborators are gathered; the place is used as a police station by the Vichy French. They act friendly and ply him with drinks and questions until he blurts out Peyssac's name as a maquis. The naive and apolitical adolescent, indifferent to the fact of the Allied landing in Normandy, agrees to work for these adjuncts to the Gestapo. Among them are the ex-racer Aubert (Pierre Decazes), who teaches Lucien how to fire a Luger, and the corrupt aristocrat Jean-Bernard (Stéphane Bouy), who treats him to suits made by Albert Horn (Holger Lowenadler), formerly of Paris—a Jewish tailor in hiding locally.

Lucien meets the man's daughter, France (Aurore Clément), whom he's attracted to. He returns with champagne and tries unsuccessfully to ingratiate himself with her father.

Later, in spite of Horn's disapproval, Lucien takes France to the hotel where there's a celebration for the departing Jean-Bernard and his girlfriend, the starlet Betty Beaulieu (Loumi Iacobesco). The jealous servant Marie (Cecile Ricard), who was sleeping with the hireling, hurls anti-Semitic insults at France, who flees upstairs. Lucien consoles her; they make love. The quislings come upon the bodies of the ambushed Jean-Bernard and his lover. Lucien sleeps at the Horns; with mounting anger the father calls France a whore. Then, despite the danger, he heads to the hotel to confront the boy, but the vicious turncoat Faure (René Bouloc) recognizes Horn and takes him into custody. Some Resistance men raid the Grotto. In retaliation, a German officer and Lucien start rounding up hostages, beginning with the Horns. There the young man pockets a watch that he had given the tailor; the NCO orders him to hand it over. Leaving, Lucien suddenly fires upon the German, retrieves his timepiece, and with France and her grandmother (Theresa Giehse)

strikes out impulsively for Spain. Their car breaks down. The trio find refuge in an abandoned house in the woods and share a pastoral interlude. We're informed by words superimposed over his face that Lucien was taken captive on October 12, 1944, tried by a military court, sentenced to death, and executed.

With their cars, guns, fine clothes, and money, the collaborators seduce Lucien into joining them, arousing his longing for adventure, glamour, and power. Instinctively cruel, hot-tempered, lacking in ideals and pity, Lucien remains not only an enigmatic figure—unreflective and inarticulate—but a disquieting one as well. The delicate France, prevented from going to the conservatory to study the piano, has absorbed the deadly self-hatred preached by the Jew-despising Nazis. In her complex relationship with Lucien there is, besides physical attraction, an element of self-abasement. Boyishly handsome, Pierre Blaise perfectly incarnates Lucien. (Unfortunately he died in a car accident on August 31, 1975, twenty-four years old.) Aurore Clément is impressive as the unhappy France, and the Swedish actor Holger Lowenadler

During their sojourn in the country, touching the bird Lucien has just felled, France might seem to be reflecting on her peculiar affair with the young man with such brutal tendencies.

145

lends authenticity to the part of Horn. Louis Malle's direction is sensitive and assured. He carefully evokes a feeling of the quotidian life under the Occupation, such as the tiresome, daily chore of the Vichy police wading through two hundred denunciatory letters. He skillfully brings his characters to memorable life and utilizes convincing detail such as Mme. Lacombe's receiving a death threat from the maquis for her son, a miniature black coffin embellished with a swastika and the name *Lucien*. The conclusion is most appropriate. Sparing us the shock of the youth's violent death, Malle prefers to show us final scenes in the country with Lucien as a free man and an able provider. This adds a feeling of dignity and a sense of peace to his last days and is most fitting. Tonino Delli Colli's photography is outstanding.

Lacombe, Lucien has not dated. "It could happen now," Malle said. "I wanted to show the mechanism by which people become fascists for no reason." How apt to preface the film with George Santayana's immortal caution: "Those who do not remember the past are condemned to relive it." Unsentimental, striking, forceful, *Lacombe, Lucien* is a major work.

HONORS

Prix Méliès (1974)
Best Film and the U.N. Award, British Academy
  Awards (1974)
Nominated for an Oscar for Best Foreign Language
  Film (1974)

42
THE MYSTERY OF KASPAR HAUSER

Jeder für Sich und Gott gegen Alle

WEST GERMANY / 1974

WERNER HERZOG FILMPRODUKTION (MUNICH)/ZDF (ZWEITES DEUTSCHES FERNSEHEN) (MAINZ)

CREDITS

Director, producer, and screenwriter: Werner Herzog;
Assistant director: Benedikt Kuby; *Cinematographer:*
Jörg Schmidt-Reitwein (Eastmancolor); *Music:* Pachelbel, Orlando Di Lasso, Albinoni, and Mozart; *Editor:* Beate Mainka-Jellinghaus; *Art director:* Henning von Gierke; *Running time:* 110 minutes; *Videocassette:* RCA/Columbia.

CAST

Kaspar Hauser: Bruno S.; *Daumer:* Walter Ladengast; *Käthe:* Brigitte Mira; *Unknown Man:* Hans Musäus; *Circus Manager:* Willy Semmelrogge; *Lord Stanhope:* Michael Kroecher; *Cavalry Captain:* Henry van Lyck; *Pastor Führmann:* Enno Patalas; *Hiltel:* Volker Prechtel; *Frau Hiltel:* Gloria Doer; *Court Clerk:* Clemens Scheitz; *Professor of Logic:* Alfred Edel.

For Werner Herzog a famous nineteenth-century German cause célèbre became an ideal subject for his highly praised fourth feature, *The Mystery of Kaspar Hauser*, known alternatively in the U.S. in film and video as *Every Man for Himself and God Against All*, the translation from the bitter German title. Kaspar had stunned Nuremberg when he was discovered—a bewildered seventeen-year-old, inarticulate, unkempt, bruised, and scarcely able to walk—in the town square on a Sunday morning in 1828. After he learned to speak, he disclosed that he had been kept chained in a dark cellar all his life and had neither contact with a fellow human being nor a conception of the world outdoors. Food was brought while he slept. There was much speculation concerning his origin. Was he perhaps an heir of the Baden dynasty? Then, after several unsuccessful attempts on his life, in 1833 an unascertained assailant fatally stabbed him. The puzzle of Kaspar Hauser's identity has never been solved, and his brief existence has intrigued poets and writers ever since. "After Kaspar is exposed and pushed into a petit-bourgeois, nineteenth-century Biedermeier world," the director said, "the story of a passion unfolds, a slow deadening of what was spontaneously human in him." In Truffaut's *The Wild Child* there was a painstaking effort to bring to his outcast hero the benefits of education and culture, which, in Herzog's eyes, do nothing but shackle Kasper, the "natural" man.

In Bruno S., a factory worker, the director found his ideal leading man, whose pitifully deprived life mirrors that of Kaspar. Born illegitimate to a Berlin prostitute who beat him, he was put away with retarded children at the age of three. Later frequent escapes meant incarceration in stricter correctional institutions until he was finally released as "cured" after twenty-three years. "I think Bruno

The confined Kaspar Hauser (Bruno S.) plays with his toy horse in the cellar.

understood that this was also to be a film *about* him," Herzog said. The picture was shot in Dinkelsbühl between May and July of 1974. Splendidly written, directed and photographed, this poetic and provocative film is quintessential Herzog.

We first encounter the passive Kaspar Hauser (Bruno S.) in a cellar where he squats playing contentedly, indifferent to the chains around his waist secured to the ground. An unknown man (Hans Musäus) enters and attempts to teach him the rudiments of writing. Before leaving, he drubs the youth's arm. Then, as Kaspar sleeps, he returns, dresses him, and shoulders him away. In the countryside the gruff man forces a staggering Kaspar to walk for the very first time. By daybreak they arrive in the town square of N. Commanding the young man—who holds himself erect extending a letter for a cavalry captain—to wait for him, he steals off. Kaspar is bewildered by the sight of a cow and the curious people who stare at him. Led, eventually, to the officer's home, he is relegated to the stable. When the captain (Henry van Lyck) comes back, he reads aloud the stranger's message while the court clerk (Clemens Scheitz) dutifully records it in his ledger. Anonymous and replete with misspellings to disguise authorship, it purports to be written by an overburdened laborer who explains that the lad was imposed on him in 1812, that he was reared in isolation and is desirous of serving his king faithfully. Kaspar is able to scrawl his name and is taken into custody without

protest. Hiltel (Volker Prechtel), the amicable prison guardian, helps him sit up straight at the table; his boy coaches him on basic words. Kaspar arouses enormous interest; to offset the cost of his care he is soon exhibited at the fair by the circus manager (Willy Semmelrogge) as "The Riddle of the European Continent." A paternal Daumer (Walter Ladengast) brings him to his home where Käthe (Brigitte Mira), his sympathetic housekeeper, looks after him. A foppish English nobleman, Lord Stanhope (Michael Kroecher), considers adopting him but at an elegant reception realizes that the uncomfortable lad is boorish. Afterward, when Kaspar is in the outhouse, the unknown man suddenly reappears and brutally cudgels him over the head. Subsequently, after recuperating, one day Kaspar totters into the garden having been knifed in the chest. His autopsy reveals anomalous brain hemispheres, which satisfies the registering clerk, who smugly asserts, "Finally we have got an explanation for this strange man."

After the ordeal of his internment, Kaspar confronts an arrogant society bent on ensnaring his mind as thoroughly as did those bonds that cramped his body. "You must have faith," a rabid minister screams at the uncomprehending lad. "The tenets of a faith transcend mortal doubt!" Fleeing a church service, Kaspar describes the warbling of the congregation to Daumer as "awful howling, and when the singing stops, the pastor starts to howl." The youth is examined by a pedan-

Kaspar Hauser rests during his initial venture into the outside world. Behind him is the baffling unknown man (Hans Musäus).

tic professor to determine if he thinks "logically," but his unorthodox response is dismissed as not properly "deductive." His dignity is affronted whether on display for inquisitive spectators or an ostentatious English aristocrat. Throughout Kaspar's lengthy stay, the gentle Daumer tries patiently to acclimatize his unhappy ward to a universe that he feels hostile and inhospitable. "It seems to me that my coming into the world was a terrible fall," he announces. Despite Daumer's considerate treatment, Kaspar declares, "The people are like wolves to me!" and elsewhere that life in the cellar was "better than outside." Bruno S. makes the difficult title role entirely credible and convincing.

Herzog directs with consummate skill. Especially impressive is his tone of compassion for his ill-fated hero. A powerful scene shows Kaspar holding Frau Hiltel's baby and, sensing his immeasurable loss, saying poignantly to the woman, tears streaming down his face, "Mother, I am far away from everything." *The Mystery of Kaspar Hauser* is an extraordinary parable of the human condition, harrowingly depicted as abysmal alienation. Ingmar Bergman stated, "If I had to name the ten most important films of my life, *The Mystery*

In the town square of N., an astounded Kaspar Hauser stands, patiently holding a letter.

of *Kaspar Hauser* would be one of them. I found the film incredible and wise and beautiful." Herzog wrote, "At the end, after Kaspar has been murdered, he is desperately examined for some deformity; that the deformities, in fact, lie within bourgeois society itself, which wanted to drill him according to its own norms, is invisible to them all." The tragic protagonist aptly symbolizes man's life, fraught with suffering and enigma. Schmidt-Reitwein's photography provides haunting images. Intimate, disturbing, and memorable, Herzog's masterwork induces one to alter Melville's concluding ejaculation in "Bartleby, the Scrivener": "Ah, Kaspar! Ah, humanity!"

HONORS

Special Jury Prize and International Critics Award, Cannes Film Festival (1975)

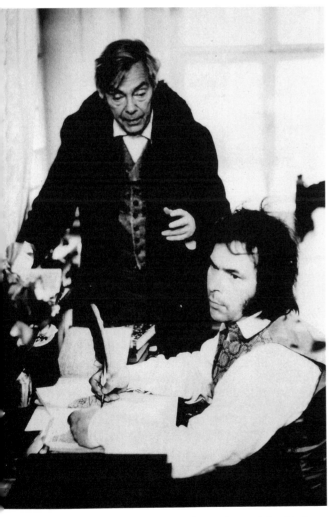

At the residence of Daumer (Walter Ladengast), his kind protector, Kaspar writes his autobiography.

43
SEVEN BEAUTIES

Pasqualino Settebellezze

ITALY / 1976

MEDUSA DISTRIBUZIONE PRODUCTION

CREDITS

Director and screenwriter: Lina Wertmuller; *Producers:* Lina Wertmuller, Giancarlo Giannini, Arrigo Colombo; *Cinematographer:* Tonino Delli Colli (Technicolor); *Music:* Enzo Iannacci; *Editor:* Franco Fraticelli; *Art director:* Enrico Job; *Running time:* 116 minutes; *Videocassette:* RCA/Columbia (dubbed).

CAST

Pasqualino Frafuso: Giancarlo Giannini; *Pedro:* Fernando Rey; *Commandant:* Shirley Stoler; *Concettina:* Elena Fiore; *Don Raffaele:* Enzo Vitale; *Francesco:* Piero Di Orio; *Mother:* Ermelinda De Felice; *Totonno:* Mario Conti; *Lawyer:* Lucio Amelio; *Socialist:* Roberto Herlitzka; *Doctor:* Doriglia Palmi.

When Italian director Lina Wertmuller (1928–) was working on *The Seduction of Mimi* (1972), she encountered an extra who told her his life story—which she found harrowing—consisting of crime in Naples; confinement to an insane asylum; a discharge to fight during World War II; a stay in a concentration camp where he was compelled to have sex with a female officer; and a return to Italy where he sired fifteen children. This embodiment of a primitive survival instinct "seemed . . . very much of our times," the director said, "this deadly side of a life force that has no illumination, no intelligence, no civic sense." The cinematic result of this fortuitous meeting was the celebrated black comedy *Seven Beauties*, Wertmuller's sixth feature, starring her favorite leading man, Giancarlo Giannini. The film was shot in Naples and in Tivoli, near Rome, where an abandoned paper factory was converted to a forced-labor camp. Vastly popular in

The outrageous Concettina (Elena Fiore) *(left)*, one of the "seven beauties," in her unsuccessful bid at becoming a vaudevillian star.

His "honor" endangered, Pasqualino (Giancarlo Giannini) forces his sister Concettina to look at herself in the mirror and concede that she's making a spectacle of herself.

America, the film was controversial as well, stemming to a degree from its apparent distortions of actual concentration-camp experience—Miss Wertmuller, working in farce, was under no obligation to be dutifully realistic—but in large measure due to a misunderstanding of her tone toward the antihero Pasqualino, who would do anything to stay alive. He is repugnant to her—commenting on his options, she said, "Pasqualino has chosen death, in fact"—and she goads us to laugh at, not with, this impossible figure with his machismo, Fascist sympathies, and destructive self-centeredness. A most imaginative commingling of tragedy and comedy, skillfully written and directed and delightfully performed, *Seven Beauties* has not lost its vitality and has become a contemporary classic.

The film begins as a brief black-and-white documentary, with newsreels of Hitler and Mussolini, then various shots of bombings accompanied by a sardonic commentary, then singles out a man jumping off a train under attack. The film turns to color. The fugitive is Pasqualino, (Giancarlo Giannini), an Italian soldier bolting to avoid the Russian front. He meets another deserter, Francesco (Piero Di Orio). Wandering through Germany, they come upon Jews being machine-gunned and flee.While his friend feels guilty for not trying to rescue them, Pasqualino has no qualms. Francesco regrets his senseless killings for Il Duce; his comrade announces that he committed homicide for a woman. . . . There's a flashback to a shabby Naples music hall where Concettina (Elena Fiore) battles a hostile audience. Backstage, her angry brother, Pasqualino, the sole male with a mother (Ermelinda De Felice) and six other homely sisters to "protect," finds her act vulgar and commands her to get her agent-boyfriend, Totonno (Mario Conti), to marry her in one month or else he'll kill him. "Seven Beauties," as the philandering Pasqualino is called, pays a call on Don Raffaele (Enzo Vitale), a Mafia leader, and learns that Totonno has installed his sister in a brothel. There he berates Concettina and, confronting Totonno, insists that the pimp marry her, but the heavyset man knocks him out. At night the vengeful Pasqualino enters his enemy's room. Wanting a fair duel, he tells the startled man to get his gun, but suddenly his goes off unexpectedly and fatally.

Back in Germany after robbing food, Pasqualino and Francesco are apprehended and sent to a concentration camp run by a cruel commandant (Shirley Stoler). There they come upon Pedro (Fernando Rey), the failed anarchist. Terrified of dying, Pas-

qualino recalls his mother's advice that no matter how bad a woman is, if you can just reach her heart . . . and, relying on his unaccountable appeal to women, eyes the odious official. Pedro depicts a nightmarish future in which overpopulatio will result in a cutthroat competition for food. . . . Back in Naples, Don Raffaele tells Pasqualino that he bungled the murder; ineligible for a plea of self-defense—after all Totonno had no gun—Pasqualino must dispose of him "imaginatively." Fortifying himself with alcohol, he eviscerates the corpse and, after hauling three weighty suitcases stuffed with the remains to the station and shipping them to several destinations, telephones the Don to proudly inform him that the "provolone" was sent off. The police seize him. . . . Back in the camp "Seven Beauties" starts warbling feebly in a wild essay to woo the ogress and for his pains is made to stand in the compound with his hands behind his head. He recalls his trial. . . . His exasperated lawyer (Lucio Amelio) tries to convince him that the only way "The Monster of Naples" can avoid the death penalty is to plead insanity. Compromising his honor, he agrees reluctantly and is given thirteen years. En route to his institution he meets an idealistic Socialist (Roberto Herlitzka) sentenced to twenty-eight years. Pasqualino is caught raping a tethered woman and is

Tracked by a blind man with his hungry, barking dog, Pasqualino lumbers along with his three heavy valises of "provolone."

A desperate Pasqualino readies himself to copulate with the impassive commandant (Shirley Stoler).

beaten. To prevent imminent madness he readily accepts the offer of a commiserative doctor (Doriglia Palmi) to alter his classification to allow him to volunteer in the army. . . . Summoned by the commandant, Pasqualino feigns ardor for her. She puts a bowl of food on the floor to invigorate him, then orders him to couple with her—or else "It's kaput!" With enormous strain he succeeds. "Your thirst for life disgusts me," she says. She makes him foreman of his barracks and demands six victims or else all will be exterminated. Francesco urges him to say no to these undignified terms. Sickened with his existence, Pedro defiantly dives into a pool of excrement. When Francesco protests the Germans' barbarity, an officer requires the collaborating *Kapo* to shoot his companion. . . . We cut to a liberated Naples. Pasqualino wants to marry and have many children for self-preservation in a kill-or-be-killed future. "You're alive!" his mother exclaims. "Yes, I'm alive," he replies, staring in a mirror at a hollow shell.

Oozing with self-love and peacock pride, Pasqualino is a hilarious caricature of the Italian male supremacist. Unperceptive, amoral, he learns nothing from his ordeal; if anything, his selfishness has intensified with his vehement wish to overbreed. We are not in a moral vacuum, however. "The positive symbols of the film," the director said, "are the anarchist, the Socialist, the ones who choose liberty even if it represents dy-

ing." With his pomaded hair, dapper appearance, and rooster strut, Giancarlo Giannini is simply splendid as Pasqualino. The American actress Shirley Stoler is effective as the icy commandant. Lina Wertmuller's direction is controlled and pointed. With her hand-held camera and use of frequent close-ups, she manages to keep the film intimate, although operating on an epic scale. An inferno-resembling concentration camp dominated by an ashen blue is strikingly captured by Tonino Delli Colli's photography. Enzo Iannacci contributed a lively score. *Seven Beauties* remains a brilliant and provocative dark comedy concerning our aberrant century.

HONORS

Nominated for four Oscars: Best Actor, Giancarlo Giannini; Director; Original Screenplay; and Foreign Language Film (1976)

44
THE INNOCENT

L'Innocente

ITALY/FRANCE / 1976

Rizzoli Film (Rome)/Les Films Jacques Leitienne/Francoriz Production (Paris)/Société Imp. Ex. Ci (Nice)

CREDITS

Director: Luchino Visconti; *Assistant directors:* Albino Cocco, Giorgio Treves; *Producer:* Giovanni Bertolucci; *Screenwriters:* Suso Cecchi D'Amico, Enrico Medioli, Luchino Visconti, from the novel by Gabrielle D'Annunzio (1892); *Cinematographer:* Pasqualino De Santis (Technicolor, Technovision); *Music:* Franco Mannino and selections from Chopin, Mozart, Lizst, and Gluck; *Editor:* Ruggero Mastroianni; *Art director:* Mario Garbuglia; *Running time:* 128 minutes; *16mm rental source:* Films Inc.; *Videocassette:* Vestron.

CAST

Tullio Hermil: Giancarlo Giannini; *Giuliana Hermil:* Laura Antonelli; *Teresa Raffo:* Jennifer O'Neill; *Tullio's Mother:* Rina Morelli; *Count Stefano Egano:* Massimo

Girotti; *Federico Hermil:* Didier Haudepin; *Filippo D'Arborio:* Marc Porel; *Princess Di Fundi:* Marie Dubois; *Mrs. Elviretta:* Roberta Paladini; *The Prince:* Claude Mann.

In 1975, Luchino Visconti, handicapped from a severe stroke he had suffered a while before in addition to a recent fall that fractured his right leg, started what was to be his final film, an adaptation of a novel by Gabrielle D'Annunzio known in English as *The Intruder.* Like Sacha Guitry, he was forced to helm his last movie from a wheelchair; the stoic director joked that he would direct his next film from a stretcher, "but I shall never give up," he said. Though Visconti was working in excruciating pain, no evidence of it appears in the lavish and graceful result, called, like the novel, *The Innocent.* The film was shot in Rome and Tuscany between September 1975 and January 1976, and sadly, on March 17, 1976, the great director died before the editing was completed. Thanks to Visconti's irrepressible willpower, we were left another elegant and impressive film.

The screenwriters made some significant changes in D'Annunzio's study of the destructive force of jealousy. The novel opens on the anniversary of an infanticide. The murderer, the overbearing aristocrat Tullio Hermil, though bothered with guilt, feels no tribunal on earth is competent to judge him. The film ends more appropriately with his suicide. D'Annunzio depicts Giuliana, his wife, as fragile and saintly—unlike the film—and presumably dead before Tullio begins his feverish retrospection. His mistress Teresa is mentioned but not developed. The scenarists omitted his two daughters, tightened the plot, which is now developed chronologically, and stressed more dramatic conflict than in the novel to produce a stronger movie. When Alain Delon and Romy Schneider were not available to play the unhappy couple, Visconti cast instead Giancarlo Giannini and the voluptuous Laura Antonelli, whom he believed bore a resemblance to the great actress Eleonora Duse, the novelist's lover, and possessed, he said, "a figure that D'Annunzio would have been mad about." Thanks to the personal intervention of Giannini, the distributors restored twenty minutes of footage cut from the print intended to be shown in America. *The Innocent,* the highest-grossing foreign film when it was shown here in 1979, is a beautiful picture and deserves to be remembered.

The setting is Rome in the 1890s. At a social gathering the freethinking and philandering Tullio Hermil (Giancarlo Giannini), accompanied by his wife, Giuliana (Laura Antonelli), notices his impetuous mistress, Countess Teresa Raffo (Jennifer O'Neill), who, seized with jealousy, gives him an ultimatum: leave with her or she'll never see him again. The husband quickly joins the countess. The totally self-centered Tullio has ceased marital relations with Giuliana, regarding her as a sister and expecting her to be brave and stalwart while he runs off at Teresa's bidding for an extended stay in Florence. He is obsessed with the manipulative countess, but has no desire to marry her. The deserted and lonely Giuliana meets Filippo D'Arborio (Marc Porel), a romantic novelist and friend of Tullio's younger brother, Federico (Didier Haudepin). Soon Tullio complains to his wife that his mistress is making a fool of him. A soignée Giuliana tells her husband she's off to an "auction"; he doesn't find her when he arrives there later but encounters Teresa, who bitchily suggests, after they reconcile, that perhaps his wife has a lover. Tullio gradually becomes aware that D'Arborio is his rival. Rather than go to Paris with Teresa, Tullio heads to the Villa Badiola, the estate of his mother (Rina Morelli), where his wife has retreated. Jealousy sparks a reawakened passion for Giuliana. However, his newfound contentment is threatened when he learns that she is pregnant. Since the affair is over, Tullio is willing to overlook her "moment of weakness," but she must consent to an abortion. Due to Catholic scruples she refuses; the atheistic husband thinks it a greater sin to give his name to a bastard, a lifelong punishment to him. Wanting to duel D'Arborio, he discovers the young man passed away from a tropical disease contracted in Africa. Giuliana has a boy, and to placate her husband pretends to ignore him. Unable to contain his hatred any longer, Tullio places the infant by an icy window while the household is at midnight mass on Christmas Eve. After the baby dies, the wife confronts Tullio with the murder. She hates him, she hisses; the man she will always love will be the child's father. Tullio visits Teresa. For the first time you feel defeated, she observes; she calls him a monster and says she doesn't love him any longer. His haughty self-esteem hurt, Tullio fires a revolver into his heart, while a nervous countess flees from the villa.

Tullio, a totally arrogant and egocentric patrician, is far removed from the sympathetic and

153

The Countess Raffo (Jennifer O'Neill *(right)* apologizes to the Princes Di Fundi (Marie Dubois) *(seated left)* for having to leave her soirée, while Signora Hermil (Laura Antonelli) *(center)* stares at her rival.

Tullio Hermil (Giancarlo Giannini) resumes his affair with his mistress, Teresa Raffo.

noble Don Fabrizio whom Visconti brought to screen life earlier in *The Leopard.* Convinced of his "superior" nature, which is accountable to no one, Tullio is self-indulgent, cruel, and decadent. Even his suicide is prompted not from a belated recognition of guilt and a subsequent need to punish himself, but from a wounded pride that can no longer allow him to live in a world that he cannot control. "Belief in supermen," Visconti said concisely, "has been killed by extermination camps." Handsome Giancarlo Giannini accomplishes the difficult task of arousing our interest in the repellent Tullio. We never see D'Arborio's affair with Giuliana; we can only imagine it through Giannini's successful projection of an overwhelming jealousy so intense that it leads to murder. Laura Antonelli gives a fine performance as his wife, demonstrating that she is much more than a sex symbol. Jennifer O'Neill is glamorous as the self-absorbed mistress.

A perfectionist, Visconti directs this riveting drama with complete assurance and authority.

Jealousy triggers a renewed passion in Tullio for his wife (Laura Antonelli).

A tormented Tullio picks up his wife's love child to place him by the freezing open window.

The Innocent was shot in actual villas, such as the Palazzo Colonna where Tullio and Giuliana attend a concert. The film is a sumptuous visual treat with its magnificent costumes, villas, and decor—one even marvels at the luxurious wallpaper! Franco Mannino contributed an achingly tender love theme. Significant use is made of the Gluck aria "*Che farò senza Euridice?*" ("What Shall I Do Without Euridice?"), which underscores Giuliana's love for D'Arborio and prefigures Tullio's eventual loss of his wife. There is a cogent scene without dialogue where—after dueling with Tullio in a gymnasium—D'Arborio showers. The camera tilts upward from his feet—the point of view of the outraged husband, who glares in jaundiced animosity at his competitor. We watch in fascination as the pernicious canker of jealousy eats away at Tullio and drives him to an unspeakable act. With The Innocent, Visconti, a true master, concluded his brilliant screen career with a gripping and exquisite film.

45
KINGS OF THE ROAD

Im Lauf der Zeit

WEST GERMANY / 1976

WIM WENDERS PRODUKTION

CREDITS

Director, producer, and screenwriter: Wim Wenders; *Assistant director:* Martin Henning; *Cinematographer:* Robbie Müller (black and white); *Music:* Axel Linstädt, Improved Sound Ltd.; *Editor:* Peter Przygodda; *Art directors:* Heidi Lüdi, Bernd Hirskorn; *Running time:* 176 minutes; *Videocassette:* Pacific Arts.

CAST

Bruno Winter: Rüdiger Vogler; *Robert Lander:* Hanns Zischler; *Pauline:* Lisa Kreuzer; *Robert's Father:* Rudolf Schündler; *Man Who Lost His Wife:* Marquard Bohm; *Theater Owner:* Franziska Stömmer; *Boy:* Patrick Kreuzer.

The inspiration for *Kings of the Road*, the remarkable sixth feature of German director Wim Wenders (1945–   ), came when he found himself stalled behind two trucks on the autobahn. Finally passing them, Wenders was struck by the apparent insouciance of the teamsters and thought to make a film about truck drivers. Everything coalesced when he linked the subject with the plight of German provincial movie theaters. Reacting against the previous constraints of adhering precisely to a completed script, the director wanted his next film to be open-ended, "which could give me," he said, "the freedom to invent the story during the shooting of the film." The resulting picture concerns Bruno, an itinerant movie-projector repairman in his thirties who lives in his truck and cocoons himself from emotional commitment, and Robert, about the same age, whom Bruno picks up, who evaluates linguistic research on children's formative reading and writing habits. Having just separated from his wife in Genoa, in his perturbed state he is willing to drift along with the serviceman.

Pauline (Lisa Kreuzer) meets Bruno (Rüdiger Vogler) at an amusement park. When he ignites his cigarette from her lit Hitler-head candle that she has just won, he will quip, "Light from the Führer."

This film concludes Wender's "road movie" trilogy, preceded by *Alice in the Cities* (1974) and *Wrong Move* (1975), all three of which star Rüdiger Vogler. While ostensibly influenced by the American western and the "buddy movie" whose personages "hit the road" in a car or on their motorcycles, *Kings of the Road* differs markedly in that its emphasis is on characterization along with mood and theme, not violence-studded action, and that its protagonists are embarked upon a quest for self-discovery, not an escape from their problems. With the director writing the next day's scenes in the evening, *Kings of the Road* was filmed between July 1 and October 31, 1975, in chiefly economically depressed regions, from Lüneberg to Hof along the frontier of East Germany. Beautifully directed, acted, and photographed as well as vital and engrossing on several levels, *Kings of the Road* is a haunting and hypnotic film, the work of a poet. However, due partially to its length of almost three hours, its almost plotless narrative, and its poor initial reception here, it is a neglected film in the United States—although it has great potential to achieve a "cult" status—and remains

An animated Bruno and Robert (Hanns Zischler) *(right)* prepare to break loose from the treadmill of the former's job and set out for the Rhine.

Arms widespread in imitation of a wayside figure of Christ, Robert says significantly (in English), "Double-crossed for the very last time, but now I'm, I'm finally free."

to be discovered.

In a prologue Bruno (Rüdiger Vogler) is furbishing a motion-picture projector, learning from the old owner how impossible it is to make a living from his cinema today. The film proper opens with shots of an agitated Robert (Hanns Zischler) tearing along the highway and towns in his Volkswagen intercut with shots of Bruno waking up in his truck parked near the Elbe River. As he shaves, he watches the amusing spectacle of Robert driving headlong into the water. The man manages to open the top of the sinking vehicle and, grabbing his luggage, swim to shore. While the strange character whom he nicknames Kamikaze naps, Bruno drives to a village to repair a projector. Periodically at stops Robert dials his wife's number, then hangs up. He finds out that Bruno has been living this solitary existence for two years, something inconceivable to him. The men feel awkward and are generally taciturn. At an abandoned basalt mine they encounter a distressed man (Marquard Bohm) whose wife killed herself

the day before by smashing their car into a tree. Robert leaves a note informing Bruno he's off to visit his father in Ostheim. Confronting his father (Rudolf Schündler), who publishes a local newspaper, Robert is unable to express his long pent-up hostility, in particular for the man's treatment of Robert's late mother, and finally resorts to printing a special edition with the headline "How to Respect a Woman." Throughout this sequence there is crosscutting to Bruno, who befriends Pauline (Lisa Kreuzer) at a midway, then later sees her in the evening when she's a ticket seller at a movie theater. They spend the night together there, but each is locked in solitude, which precludes intimacy. Bruno rejoins Robert in his hometown. Resuming their journey, Robert persuades his companion to take a holiday; together in a borrowed motorcycle with sidecar they head to Bruno's childhood home on an island in the Rhine. After inspecting his deserted house, the anguished man weeps. Soon he resumes his schedule. One night they find themselves at a disused U.S. Army patrol hut on the border of East Germany. Roused by whiskey and the buildup of sexual tension between them, they start quarreling. Bruno calls Robert a coward who's afraid of himself; Robert retorts that Bruno has so isolated himself in the "bunker" of his truck that he's "as good as dead!" They brawl briefly, then a vulnerable Bruno, lying down, confesses to his longing for a woman yet fear of involvement. Robert counters. "It's no life at all not being able to imagine any change or want it." In the morning Robert departs, leaving a message: "Everything must change. So long. R." At a train station he trades his sunglasses and valise for the journal of a little boy (Patrick Kreuzer) to examine the child's magical discovery of language. That night Bruno, after performing maintenance on a projector and hearing the proprietress (Franziska Stömmer) inveigh against the debasement of current cinema—but who keeps her theater ready just in case there's a revival of quality films—reflects a moment in his truck, then begins shredding his route.

Kings of the Road is an account of two men in crisis. Beneath the bulwark of his defense mechanism, Bruno—whose father was killed in the war—is a lonely, unfulfilled man whose desire for love is in conflict with a strong need to be alone. Robert is another complicated person, more aware than Bruno of his dependency upon a woman yet cognizant of the unfeasibility of preserving his individuality in a marriage. Their contact with the husband whose wife committed suicide underscores the pain of the loss of women in their lives. Each touches base with his past, which enables both to grow. When they take refuge in the barren military post, it is a symbolical dead end. Afterward Robert entrains, eager to resume his project with children, although it is not specified if he plans to reunite with his wife, and Bruno realizes that his occupation is a cul-de-sac. "One sees their shortcomings, their emotional insecurity," Wenders said, "and how they try to hide it. . . . The story of the absence of women is at the same time the story of yearning for them." The director observed elsewhere, "To travel is for me an entirely phenomenological movement," one that has the

In a carefree moment while driving along, Robert and Bruno play and sing along to Heinz's "Just Like Eddy."

capacity to alter an individual. "Through the voyage," he continued, "my characters are taken out of their routine; to be sure one does not know exactly in what sense they are going to transform themselves, but one knows that they never will return to the point of departure. They are now capable of seeing their situation with a new look."

Underplaying the role of Bruno, Rüdiger Vogler is completely natural and convincing. Hanns Zischler is effective as Robert. Wenders displays elegance and authority in his direction. His style is distinguished by graceful transitions, such as the slow dissolve and the wipe. In the course of one week, employing sparse dialogue and relying essentially on exceptional visual imagery, he brings his personages to memorable life. The pacing is deliberately leisurely, inviting the viewers to contemplate and share vicariously the characters' lives. The lustrous black-and-white photography of Robbie Müller and the affecting music of Axel Linstädt reinforce the soulful and desolate atmosphere of the movie.

Kings of the Road is a richly thematic film. On one tier it is an honest depiction of the postwar generation of Germans searching for an identity. Rejecting the Nazi epoch of their parents, they succumb to the seductive artifacts of the occupiers. (Bruno constantly plays 45-rpm pop singles; we recognize a Texaco gas station, Coca-Cola sign, hula hoop, etc.) In the most quoted line from the picture Robert declares laughing, "The Yanks have colonized our subconscious." On a philosophical plane there are echoes of contemporary feelings of anomie, alienation, and existentialism.

In a shot that calls to mind John Ford's westerns, a black-eyed Robert—no longer wishing to roam with Bruno—approaches a railway station.

After performing an improvised bit of clowning backstage for an audience of tots, Bruno and Robert notice an implicative rope shaped like a hangman's noose swinging between them. The movie can also be seen as an elegy to the dying German film industry in which the surviving, remote theaters are run without profit by elderly people; staffed with inept and indifferent technicians; and sometimes reduced to a sex parlor (in Pauline's cinema Bruno catches the projectionist masturbating to a pornographic strip). This motif reaches its apogee in the concluding speech by the proprietress, sitting indicatively beneath a picture of Fritz Lang, who attacks exploitation in today's films: "I won't be forced to show films where people stagger out stunned and rigid with stupidity that kills any joy of life inside them." An extraordinary achievement, *Kings of the Road* is a rewarding and unforgettable film and, for me, Wenders's masterpiece thus far.

HONORS

International Critics Award (shared), Cannes Film Festival (1976)

46
A SPECIAL DAY

Una Giornata Particolare

ITALY/CANADA / 1977

COMPAGNIA CINEMATOGRAFICA CHAMPION (ROME)/CANAFOX FILMS INC. (MONTREAL)

CREDITS

Director: Ettore Scola; *Assistant directors:* Silvio Ferri, Claude Fournier; *Producer:* Carlo Ponti; *Screenwriters:* Ruggero Maccari, Ettore Scola, with the collaboration of Maurizio Costanzo; *Cinematographer:* Pasqualino De Santis (Technicolor); *Music:* Armando Trovaioli; *Editor:* Raimondo Crociani; *Art director:* Luciano Ricceri; *Running time:* 106 minutes; *Videocassette:* RCA/Columbia (dubbed).

CAST

Antonietta: Sophia Loren; *Gabriele:* Marcello Mastroianni; *Emanuele:* John Vernon; *Concierge:* Françoise

With the assistance of Gabriele (Marcello Mastroianni), Antonietta (Sophia Loren) has recaptured Rosamunda, her mynah bird.

Berd; *Romana:* Patrizia Basso; *Arnaldo:* Tiziano De Persio; *Fabio:* Maurizio De Paolantonio; *Littorio:* Antonio Garibaldi; *Umberto:* Vittorio Guerrieri; *Maria Luisa:* Alessandra Mussolini.

Italian director Ettore Scola (1931–   ), known chiefly for his comedies, wished to make a serious film dealing with the contemporary problems of the conditions of women and of homosexuals, which he felt had numerous aspects in common. The concept crystallized when he decided to place his story in the Fascist epoch "because precisely then," he said, "the intolerance and the repression were more direct, more violent, more exemplary." Women—voteless—were totally submissive to the male will; their exclusive duty was to procreate for Mussolini's expanding army. And in their strident machismo, the Italian leaders refused to accept even the idea of homosexuality; it simply didn't exist, and if one were discovered to be "different," one was immediately suspected of being a menacing dissident, subject to forced removal to Carbonia, Sardinia. The resulting film, *A*

Special Day, would not be a didactic tract, but a compelling drama of the brief, inspiriting relationship between two marginal, ordinary people: an oppressed housewife with six children and a gay man preparing for banishment who nonetheless support the dictatorship. The plot—observing the classical unities of time, place, and action—would be set in Rome on May 6, 1938, when Hitler was given an exuberant reception when he came to sign the Rome-Berlin Axis accord with Il Duce, an event witnessed by the director, who remembers marching as a child of six before Der Führer. Scola did painstaking research; the grating rhetoric of the radio broadcast that we hear intermittently and loudly throughout the film contains the exact words heard then. To make his two-character study work, the director needed strong support and cast the reigning stars of the Italian cinema, Sophia Loren and Marcello Mastroianni, in parts that ran counter to their prevailing images. Thus the glamorous Loren changes into a wearied, frumpish housewife, while Mastroianni sheds his ladies' man persona to transform into a persecuted invert. Extraordinarily acted, skillfully written and directed, brimming with relevant thought, *A Special Day*, which brought Scola an international reputation, becomes indeed a special occasion.

The film opens with an extended sepia newsreel of Hitler's arrival in Rome where he is given a wildly enthusiastic welcome. The next day, we're informed, he will review an imposing parade of Italy's military might at the Forum. . . . Early the following morning in a large, U-shaped middle-class apartment building before six A.M., Antonietta (Sophia Loren) is already ironing uniforms for her family. Mechanically she wakes up her six children and her husband, Emanuele (John Vernon). Leaving the bathroom, he dries his hands on her drab dress, then criticizes her appearance. She sends them off and remains behind to do the staggering housework; the tenement quickly empties. While she is readying fresh birdseed, her pet mynah, Rosamunda, escapes and flies across the way to a ledge outside the apartment occupied by a brooding Gabriele (Marcello Mastroianni). Facing exile, he is staring at a revolver contemplating suicide. She races over; he lures Rosamunda inside. Grateful for the interruption, he encourages her to stay, to dance the rumba with him, anything to ward off the loneliness of this particular day, but she has to go. The Fascist-loving concierge (Françoise Berd) sits in the courtyard and blasts her radio, which reports the pageant with hyperbole.

Soon a restless Gabriele is at Antonietta's door insisting she take a copy of *The Three Musketeers*, which she had admired, and requesting coffee. He states he's a temporarily retired radio announcer and learns her husband is in the Ministry. Flipping through her carefully mounted photo album of Mussolini, Gabriele reads, "A man is not a man if he is not husband, father, soldier," and, "Genius is strictly masculine." She cannot fault that. The prying doorkeeper stops by and cautions her that her guest was fired for being antifascist. Antonietta criticizes her "subversive" acquaintance. On the roof to collect her laundry, he breaks her tirade by making her laugh. Sexually aroused, she protectively accuses the innocent man of trying to se-

After a misunderstanding that leads to wrangling, Antonietta flees with her wash from a roiled Gabriele.

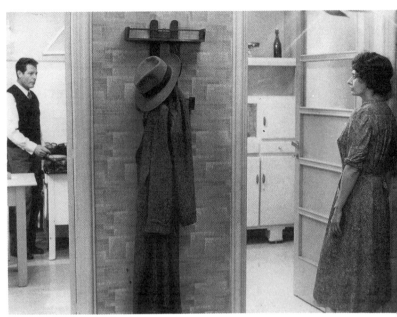

Antonietta returns to ask Gabriele to forgive her for her behavior on the roof.

ducer her; softening, folding sheets together, she entreats him to leave, all the while holding his hands and kissing him. Gabriele awkwardly backs off and explains the real reason for his dismissal, his "tendency toward depravity." Rejected, hurt, she slaps him hard. Angrily he begins to maul her, parodying the lustful encounter he imagines she was anticipating. She rushes to her apartment, but shortly after visits him to apologize. Sharing lunch, he pours out his troubles with the authorities because of his sexual orientation. She can empathize with him for she has known humiliation and starts confessing her woes with a domineering, philandering husband. They reach out to comfort each other; the affection takes a physical

turn. Antonietta has no regrets; Gabriele replies that while he's capable of making love to a woman—and it was beautiful with her—he's still the same. Noticing children returning, she leaves after they have a final kiss. Later, the husband boasts of the famous day and complains about the cold supper. She ignores his order to come to bed and starts reading Dumas. Gabriele packs a suitcase and sets forth with two officials supervising his deportation. Antonietta watches him depart, then heads to her quiet bedroom.

Both Antonietta and Grabiele partake in a parallel victimization, each evinced in a carefully balanced, subtle manner. They internalize the negative attitudes of their society, from the subordinate status of women to the shame-inflicting macho values that view homosexuality as a contaminant. Ashamed of her ignorance and treated with contempt by her husband, Antonietta responds to Gabriele, who reawakens her buried sense of femininity. And Gabriele has found a needed, compassionate friend. In spite of the radio's ghastly bluster ("Benito Mussolini is second only to God") and strident marches that threaten to muffle two isolated voices struggling for expression, the couple manage to make it a special day by

163

Gabrielle smokes after his distressing disclosure, which Antonietta finds very moving.

loving and consoling each other. Possessing riveting screen presences, Sophia Loren and Marcello Mastroianni give remarkable performances. Totally convincing and deeply affecting, they act together splendidly. Scola's direction is fluid and controlled, evoking a sense of the daily life with telling detail. Avoiding melodrama and sentimentality, he develops the action and fascinating characterization with the utmost simplicity, naturalness, and restraint. We are not merely watching an authentic, historical re-creation, but a timely, provocative film as long as there are exploitation of women and homophobia in our world. *A Special Day* endures as a poignant and memorable achievement.

HONORS

Special Jury Prize, Cannes (1977)
César for Best Foreign Film, Académie des Arts et Techniques du Cinéma* (1977)
Nominated for two Oscars: Best Actor, Marcello Mastroianni, and Best Foreign Language Film (1977)

47

EMPIRE OF PASSION

Ai no Borei

JAPAN/FRANCE / 1978

OSHIMA PRODUCTIONS (TOKYO)/ARGOS FILMS (PARIS)

CREDITS

Director and screenwriter: Nagisa Oshima, after a story by Itoko Nakamura; *Producers:* Nagisa Oshima, Anatole Dauman; *Cinematographer:* Yoshio Miyajima (Eastmancolor); *Music:* Toru Takemitsu; *Editor:* Keiichu Uraoka; *Art director:* Jusho Toda; *Running time:* 108 minutes; *16mm rental source:* Kit Parker; *Videocassette:* Fox/Lorber.*

CAST

Seki: Kazuko Yoshiyuki; *Toyoji:* Tatsuya Fuji; *Gisaburo:* Takahiro Tamura; *Inspector Hotta:* Takuzo Kawatani; *Mother of Landowner:* Akiko Koyama; *Toichiro:* Taiji Tonoyama; *Odame:* Sumie Sasaki; *Grocer:* Eizo Kitamura; *Oshin:* Masami Hasegawa; *Landowner:* Kenzo Kawarazaki; *Denzo:* Takaaki Sugiura.

Nagisa Oshima (1932–) is one of the most important and prolific directors to emerge in postwar Japan. He can be seen as an antipode to Yasujiro Ozu, whose films affirm the very traditional national values that Oshima criticizes and repudiates. Many of his movies, like those of Godard, who influenced him strongly, are didactic and tendentiously political. In ensuing years he revealed that he was "profoundly attracted" by the themes of "sex and crime" and produced, he said, a "kind of diptych": the controversial *In the Realm of the Senses* (1976), a naturalistic, explicit depiction of an all-consuming carnal desire, and *Empire of Passion*, a poetical, restrained rendering of an adulterous relationship in the Meiji period that leads to a husband's murder and subsequent return as a ghost. In both instances the director's tone was sympathetic toward his sexually obsessed, self-destructive characters. Coming upon Nakamura's

*The videotape has been retitled *In the Realm of Passion*.

After another unnerving appearance of her slaughtered husband, Seki (Kazuko Yoshiyuki) attempts suicide by setting her house on fire.

tale, based on an actual homicide in 1896, Oshima said he was "touched by the life of the starved couple and by the story of the phantom"; he was fascinated that "in this somber period in Japan's history, love existed." The resultant *Empire of Passion*, his twenty-first feature, is a film of remarkable beauty and deserves to be better known in this country.

The story, which commingles elements of the supernatural with realistic events, begins in 1895 in a small village in Japan. Gisaburo (Takahiro Tamura), an elderly man who pulls a jinrikisha, lives meagerly with his wife, Seki (Kazuko Yoshiyuki), a woman in her forties, their girl, and a little boy. Toyoji (Tatsuya Fuji), a young veteran regarded as a wastrel by the villagers, is attracted to Seki despite her age and marital status. Flirtation grows more ardent; the sexually neglected woman and the ex-soldier are soon lovers. Toyoji becomes increasingly jealous and insists that they

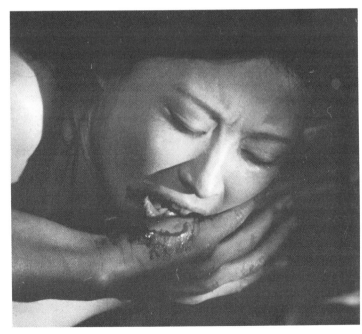

In a state of hysteria, thinking of Gisaburo's body decomposing in a well, Seki bites the hand of her lover, Toyoji (Tatsuya Fuji), when he endeavors to calm her.

After making love, Seki and Toyoji decide to remove
Gisaburo from the cistern and bury him.

must kill Gisaburo. "I can't live without you," he
declares. She offers feeble resistance. Consequently, on a frigid winter's evening, Seki makes
repeated trips to the grocer (Eizo Kitamura) to
replenish the sake that her husband is blissfully
drinking. When he collapses on the floor, she
admits Toyoji and together each pulls on a piece of
rope strung about Gisaburo's neck and they strangle him. They drag the corpse through the snowy
forest and throw him into a well. In autumn Toyoji
compulsively dumps leaves down the pit, which
arouses the curiosity of a young landowner (Kenzo
Kawarazaki). Seki maintains that Gisaburo left
abruptly for Tokyo. Three years pass and the villagers gossip. On the Night of All Souls a sleeping
Seki hears her name called and is horrified to see
by the fire her greenish-faced husband raising his
empty cup to her. She wakes up the proprietor to
obtain sake, rushes to the cistern, and pours liber-
ally from the bottle. In the morning her lover finds
her asleep nearby. Even neighbors witness Gisaburo's manifestations and presently Inspector Hotta

(Takuzo Kawatani) shows up and intimidates Seki
with his questioning. An alarmed Toyoji tells her
they must not be seen together. After another visit
by the specter, the distraught wife sets her home
ablaze. The lover tries to rescue the guilt-driven
woman, who wants to die and set Toyoji free, and
manages to break down the door. When the local
residents and Hotta arrive to put out the flames,
they see the embracing couple outside. All she
wishes is to live with her man for three days.
Toyoji notices the landholder peering into the well
and, suspicious, slays him. Hotta spies on the pair
from her attic. Afterward, they head to the pit in a
frantic attempt to inter the body, and there, incredibly, Seki loses her eyesight. At home, blind, she
makes love to her devoted Toyoji, who will not
leave her. At dawn Hotta and his men intrude and
string the couple from an oak tree; after repeated
beatings both confess their evildoing. When Gisaburo's remains are exhumed, he enigmatically
possesses Seki's eyes. A lady narrator informs us
that the pair had been condemned to death.

166

Under Oshima's carefully controlled direction Seki and Toyoji are not portrayed as monsters—rather, compassionately, as people caught up in a devouring, unconditional love that ends in death. Manslaughter aside, their rapport is unselfish to the extent that each is willing to assume complete responsibility for the malefaction to spare the other. "It is to those beings, like Seki and Toyoji," Oshima said, "to those who live and die without being able to comprehend their destiny, whom I identify with. It is those that I feel closest to." While wraiths are traditionally represented in Japanese films as malignant—Mizoguchi's *Ugetsu* (1953) and Kobayashi's *Kwaidan* (1965) are two examples best known to Western audiences—Gisaburo is seen as gentle and, aside from seizing Seki's eyes, one not bent on vengeance. The director refers to him as a "phantom of love." Although the treatment of Hotta verges on slapstick, it is in keeping with Oshima's delineation of the police as figures of ridicule. Kazuko Yoshiyuki, Tatsuya Fuji, and Takahiro Tamura play their tragic roles with total conviction.

In *Empire of Passion* Oshima not only creates an authentic atmosphere of a remote village, but skillfully evokes an unsettling sense of anxiety with the apparitions of the throttled husband. One sequence is especially noteworthy. Without any of the standard transitional clues, Oshima plunges us into a disturbing, disorienting dream. On a misty, deserted road Seki, leaving the grocer's with sake, encounters the dead Gisaburo, who offers her a ride in his ricksha. Nervously she declines, yet he follows. The mist becomes impenetrable fog, covering the ground thoroughly, and she enters the carriage with trepidation. A lantern provides a dim gleam. After proceeding a short distance she realizes they are not on the right road; he tells her he forgot the way, then veers in another direction in eerie slow motion. Seki doesn't recognize where they are. There is a magnificent shot of the wheels gyrating in a lavender light. Panicking, she cries out, "Is that really you? Show me your face!" In a close-up he turns to her. She pours sake over his head, which changes into a mannequin while the drink transforms into blood. Then she awakens in

Inside the pit Toyoji and Seki start sinking suddenly in the mud and leaves.

her home. Truly breathtaking is this illumination of an oneiric landscape! All the shots in the movie are brilliantly composed; Miyajima's exquisite cinematography has a rich, pictorial quality. While some critics have read an Oedipal construction into the young Toyoji's involvement with the older Seki, the director has specified that "each is free to interpret my films as he understands it." *Empire of Passion* can simply be seen as a powerful narrative that is both visually stunning and unforgettable.

HONORS

Best Director, Cannes Film Festival (1978)

48
ANGI VERA

HUNGARY / 1979

HUNGAROFILM

CREDITS

Director and screenwriter: Pal Gabor, from the novel by Endre Veszi; *Assistant director:* Dezso Koza; *Cinematographer:* Lajos Koltai; *Music:* Gyorgy Selmeczi; *Editor:* Eva Karmento; *Art director:* Andras Gyorky; *Running time:* 96 minutes; *16mm rental source and videocassette:* New Yorker.

CAST

Vera Angi: Veronika Papp; *Anna Trajan:* Erzsi Pasztor; *Maria Muskat:* Eva Szabo; *Istvan Andre:* Tamas Dunai; *Comrade Sas:* Laszlo Halasz; *Josef Neubauer:* Laszlo Horvath.

Angi Vera gave Hungarian director Pal Gabor (1932–87) his international reputation and remains his most successful and best-known work. The movie is set in 1948, the year Hungarian Communists with Soviet support began to seize power. "I didn't want to deal with politics per se," Gabor said, "but with what politics did to people." He would focus on a simple but intelligent young woman, Vera Angi (the names are traditionally reversed in Hungarian), orphaned during World War II. Displaying potential for leadership, she is singled out for indoctrination to prepare for a career within the Communist Party. It was the treacherous time of Stalin, of the infamous "cult of personality," and our misguided protagonist is forced to choose between fealty to the Party and her normal stirrings toward affection. "Vera Angi's destiny, her tragic betrayal of herself and her love," Gabor said, "provides an illustration of the fact that it is possible to manipulate society only if there are individuals who are willing instruments that may be manipulated." The director pointed out that "the theme is the responsibility of the individual." That such a powerful indictment of a totalitarian regime in the making was permitted to be made in the first place and then released to the

Vera Angi (Veronika Papp) *(left)* at the Marxist training school with her friend Maria (Eva Szabo).

West is a mystery unless the censors possibly misunderstood Gabor's critical point of view toward the heroine. Be that as it may, *Angi Vera* is a tightly controlled, beautifully acted film with a powerful impact. A low-keyed, honest, and altogether remarkable work.

The picture opens at a staff meeting in a hospital. After an address with the usual clichés about "the building of socialism," the speaker dutifully asks for questions. Breaking the silence, Vera Angi (Veronika Papp), an eighteen-year-old assistant nurse, bravely stands up and stammers complaints about unsanitary conditions and routine corruption. "Where is this new world?" she tearfully concludes. Far from being reprimanded for insolence, she attracts the attention of a party official

During the social evening Vera turns from her companions Maria *(center)* and Anna (Erzsi Pasztor) *(right)* to smile at her teacher, whom she is enamored of.

Balancing a plastic ball between their foreheads, Vera dances with Istvan (Tamas Dunai). Humor and yearning are effectively captured in this noteworthy scene.

After the crucible of her recent schooling, the dedicated Communist Vera heads to her new vocation with the veteran Anna.

who, recognizing her natural aptitude, sends her to a provincial reeducation camp for an intensified three-month program devoted to Communist ideology. Poor, lacking any formal education, she's grateful for the opportunity. There, in a dormitory she befriends the earthy Maria (Eva Szabo) and the older, puritanical-seeming Anna Trajan (Erzsi Pasztor). Vera's teacher is the young Istvan (Tamas Dunai), who awakens her romantic inclinations. When the miner Josef (Laszlo Horvath), who, longing for his family, went AWOL, is castigated before the group by Comrade Sas (Laszlo Halasz), Vera volunteers to help him with his studies. All applaud. Anna asks her, "How did you know that was the right thing to do?" At night, in an unguarded moment, the mature woman recounts her tragic affair during the war with a married man and starts weeping. Upset at Maria's sensual account, which follows, Anna changes rooms the next day and informs on the randy young lady. Vera perceives Anna's formidable aspect when, canvassing together, they encounter a man who participated in a strike whom Comrade Trajan will denounce, with the youth's compliance, after first indulging themselves in liqueur and sweets at a café. During a party for the students Vera and Istvan dance

tenderly. Later, after sending his wife and daughter to Budapest for a vacation, the instructor meets Vera in a café and both declare their love for each other. That evening, she goes to his room where they blissfully make love. Sneaking back in the morning, she is noticed by Anna. Attempting a second rendezvous, Vera is intimidated by Maria—possibly feeling envy. An arrogant, important official arrives for a day "of criticism and self-criticism" and discloses the shortcomings of each student (obtained undoubtedly from tattle). Vera is praised as hardworking and accommodating, but faulted for being undereducated and too sensitive. Is there anything she wishes to add? Confused and frightened that Anna will inform on her, she shockingly blurts out that she went to her teacher's room one night: "I feel so ashamed." Anna tells her to shut up. Istvan states, "All this is inhuman," and admits publicly that they love each other. Vera emphatically denies this and claims she merely lost her head. A new instructor replaces Istvan. Afterward Maria drags a hysterical Vera—clad only in a nightshirt in the freezing cold, screaming, "I want to die"—inside from the terrace and slaps her. During the graduation ceremony Sas commends a listless Vera for her perseverance in choosing correctly when she had to decide between "illusory emotions and the truth." She faints. Anna reveals that Vera's to work with her as a journalist—a privileged position. As the pair are driven to Budapest, Vera looks out her window and sees a bicycling Maria, who was not as well favored. As Vera stares behind her, there is a slow dissolve.

It is not difficult to understand that the deprived and vulnerable Vera who craves acceptance and recognition—"Never in my life have so many paid such attention to me," she proclaims to her questioner—would permit the Communist Party to become her surrogate family and would be impressed with the words of a functionary early in the film: "The Party will take care of your life from now on." That she should put as a priority the political system while denying her genuine instincts is entirely credible and, ironically, the means of both her advancement as well as her destruction as a human being—even stalwart Communists Anna and Maria know that love is more important than the Party. Her attempt at suicide and subsequent apathy indicate the toll taken on her spirit. At the end she is well on her way to evolving into a soulless machine. The lovely and poignant Veronika Papp arrests our attention as Vera; Erszi Pasztor lends strong support as Anna.

Utilizing brief, darkly lit scenes and many close-ups, Pal Gabor compels us to live Vera Angi's life in a restrained and intimate way without relying on melodrama. Her startling confession on the day of evaluation is brilliantly directed. His choice of details—at the celebration each comrade is allowed *one* bottle of beer!—helps to evoke a realistic microcosm of Eastern Europe. We can see that 1948, glibly referred to as "the milestone in Hungarian history," was in reality a millstone. Gabor commented that the film deals "with the faults of our fathers"; it is also, he asserts, a "warning": "Today will be tomorrow's history. So we must be very careful what we do." Besides retaining its undiminished pleasure as a cinematic treat, *Angi Vera* will, I think, be useful in political science courses for its subtle, accurate depiction of the workings of Communist bureaucracy. A neglected film, a fascinating character study, *Angi Vera* awaits rediscovery as a very significant achievement.

HONORS

Shared International Critics Prize, Cannes Film Festival (1979)

49
CONFIDENCE

Bizalom

HUNGARY / 1979

Mafilm/Objektiv Film Studio (Budapest)

CREDITS

Director and screenwriter: Istvan Szabo, from a story by Erika Szanto and Istvan Szabo; *Cinematographer:* Lajos Koltai (Eastmancolor); *Music:* a song of Tibor Polgar; *Editor:* Zsuzsa Csakany; *Art director:* Jozsef Romvary; *Running time:* 117 minutes; *16mm rental source and videocassette:* New Yorker.

CAST

Kata: Ildiko Bansagi; *Janos Biro:* Peter Andorai; *Pali:* Zoltan Bezeredi; *Old Woman:* Oszkarne Gombik; *Old Man:* Karoly Csaki; *Bozsi:* Ildiko Kishonti; *Kata's Husband:* Lajos Balazsovits; *Hoffmann:* Tamas Dunai; *Dr. Czako:* Laszlo Littmann; *Janos's Wife:* Judit Halasz.

Though Hungarian director Istvan Szabo (1938–) was a child during World War II, the experience was so momentous that that period dominates most of his films, supplying him, as he said, with "my particular idiom." In *Confidence*, his seventh feature, the wartime setting was exploited to achieve a work of extraordinary intensity and power. The time is autumn 1943; the locale is Ujpest, slightly north of Budapest. In a single day a politically naive woman's life will be turned upside down when she learns that her physician husband is a clandestine member of the resistance and has gone into hiding to avoid arrest by the fascist government. With a forged ID she is hastily sent to pose as the "wife" of a political activist living in concealment, who is highly wary of her. The focus of the movie is on their developing, ambivalent relationship in a climate of fear and suspicion, which leads nonetheless to a poignant yet problematical love. "You've got to have an atmosphere of trust," Szabo said, "in order to be able to live a life fit for human beings. . . . To be

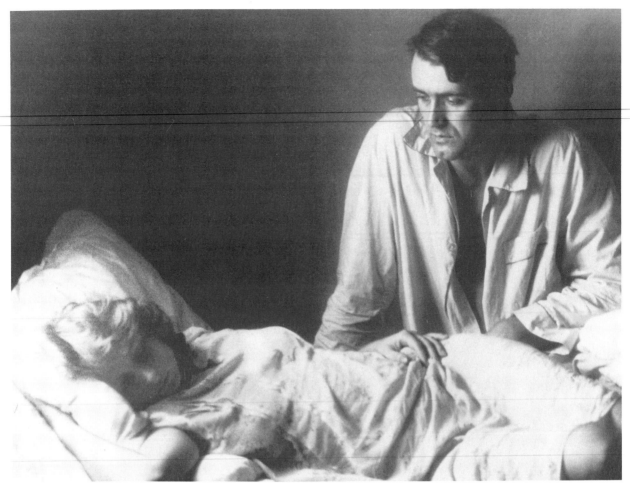

While Kata (Ildiko Bansagi) sleeps on his pallet, Janos (Peter Andorai) broods on his complex affiliation with his "wife."

able to demonstrate . . . the more sinister paths of mistrust, I needed a period in which confidence is a question of life and death." In his film the director skillfully emphasizes psychological analysis of character rather than the inherent melodrama of the situation and creates a taut, beautifully acted, thrilling film. Eclipsed by the international success of his subsequent pictures, *Confidence* is an overlooked masterpiece.

The film opens inside a sparsely attended theater. Leaving, Kata (Ildiko Bansagi) is quickly met by a stranger who startles her by cautioning that she can't go home—it's being searched—and that her spouse (Lajos Balazsovits) had to disappear. Having no place to sleep, she is told to go to St. Ferenc's Hospital in an hour and see Dr. Czako (Laszlo Littmann). There, given an alias, "Mrs. Janos Biro," she surrenders her identification papers and is sent to meet her "husband," who rents a room in the home of an elderly couple outside of town. An uneasy Janos (Peter Andorai), irked that this woman was foisted upon him, greets her unfeelingly. (We never learn his real name.) He warns her she can't go out without his permission. The confused Kata is understandably concerned about the fate of the doctor and their small daughter, who's sojourning with her mother in the country. Later Janos criticizes her for commenting on their child's long hair over dinner with the owners: "Little details can lead to great danger." Kata finds him overbearing, intimidating, and cannot relax. He wakes her up at night with a bright lamp, barraging her with questions to test her. Before long she sneaks off to the hospital to obtain news of her spouse, but sees the military patrolling the entrance. An angry Janos, who followed her, grabs her. Pali (Zoltan Bezeredi), a partisan disguised as a soldier, calls on his friend and deems Kata attractive. In a café, Bozsi (Ildiko Kishonti) entreats her former schoolmate for asylum, but Kata doesn't recognize the terrified Jewish woman and ignores her pleas. Afterward, Janos maintains that they mustn't take risks and Kata releases her pent-up hostilities at him. A late night police search in the neighborhood aggravates the strain on them. Drawn to each other, though Janos has qualms about involvement, they finally make love. Next day Kata calls him a coward, afraid to share intimacy, and declares she's in love with him. In town Janos runs into Hoffmann (Tamas Dunai), a college companion now a German officer, and improvises a false address. Janos receives a letter from his wife (Judit Halasz)—she addresses the camera and speaks of her devotion, anguish, and longing. He surreptitiously telephones her from the street and discloses that he misses her. With Pali a go-between, Kata visits her husband in the city. He makes her stay the night; we see she's reluctant to sleep with him. Finding himself jealous of her husband, even of Pali's attention, Janos tries unsuccessfully to dampen their ardor. At Christmas the Russian Army begins their attack. Kata, in love with Janos, feels somehow as though a holiday were soon ending. The Germans are retreating. A

An intimate moment between Kata and Janos.

173

jubilant Janos informs Kata, in line for water, that his colleagues have come for him. Interrogated by the officials, Kata cannot verify her identity. At the house she is reunited with her spouse but thinks of someone else. Meanwhile Janos hurries through the crowd, lined up for questioning, shouting, "Mrs. Janos Biro! Where are you?"

Overprotected, coming from the comfortable middle class, Kata is completely unprepared for the perilous existence she is suddenly forced to endure with a cold, distrustful man. Her husband had deliberately kept her ignorant of his underground activities, fearing she would crack under pressure from the police. Nervous about him and her little girl, she must not let herself get hysterical. The cautious Janos is one well-acquainted with treachery—a decade earlier his mistress had denounced him to the Nazis. "The only strength is not to trust," he asserts after Kata challenges him with, "How could anyone betray you? Is anyone in your confidence?" Janos sees himself as a mere second-class revolutionary, lacking the needed quality of bravery. Missing his wife, edgy, suspicious of everyone in these troubled times, he even wonders if Kata is a Gestapo agent. Together they must pass as a normal married couple while coping with unrelenting stress and turmoil. At times each ponders, "Am I going mad?" We can sympathize with Janos's subsequent statement, "Man was not born to live at the limit of his moral capacity." To complicate matters, they fall deeply in love with each other with the accompanying mutual guilt, waffling over a commitment on his part, and jealousy—to punish her after Kata spent the evening with her spouse, Janos remains out all night when she returns. The acting is subtle, abetted by the use of occasional interior monologues to expose their apprehensions and conflicts. Ildiko Bansagi and Peter Andorai bring the pair to life with total conviction.

From the beginning scene in the movie house of newsreels to calm people's horror of aerial bom-

Janos instructs Kata how to operate a gun, knowledge that might save his life in the difficult days ahead.

50

STALKER

Kata and Janos quietly and tenderly celebrate the New Year, 1944, as they wait for the terrible war to end.

CREDITS

Director and art director: Andrei Tarkovsky; *Producer:* Alexandra Demidova; *Screenwriters:* Arkady and Boris Strugatsky, based on their novella *Roadside Picnic* (1973); *Cinematographer:* Alexander Knyazhinsky (color); *Music:* Eduard Artemyev; *Editor:* Ludmila Feyganova; *Running time:* 161 minutes; *16mm rental source:* New Yorker; *Videocassette:* Fox/Lorber.

CAST

Stalker: Alexander Kaidanovsky; *Writer:* Anatoli Solonitsin; *Scientist:* Nikolai Grinko; *Stalker's Wife:* Alissa Freindlich.

bardment, Szabo plunges us into an almost unbearable world of anxiety and suspense. Shunning the anodyne of music—save that which is played in the credits and the popular song the couple dance to—keeping their room lit very dimly and employing many medium and close shots of the actors, the director evokes a claustrophobic ambience—the season always seems wintry and bleak—and never slackens the tension. In *Confidence* Szabo has produced an intimate, engrossingly cinematic film of the highest order.

HONORS

Silver Bear for Best Director, Berlin Film Festival (1980)
Nominated for an Oscar for Best Foreign Film (1980)

Andrei Tarkovsky (1932–86) was the most brilliant Russian filmmaker of his generation and one of the most troublesome for the authorities. As an Orthodox Christian, the few films he was allowed to make are imbued with religious fervor and do not conform to the prescribed atheistic and "realistic" tenets geared for a mass audience. Abroad he was a showcase director, gaining prestige for the USSR with films that won prizes at Cannes; yet in his native land they were shelved or had very limited distribution, while he was forced to waste precious creative years in the long, frustrating wait between assignments. By the time of *Stalker*, his fifth feature, the higher echelons went so far as to undercut its chances of receiving recognition by begrudgingly showing it in Cannes as a "surprise," not as a competing film. His next two pictures were shot in Italy and Sweden; the expatriate director died in Paris at the age of fifty-four.

In the Strugatsky novella on which *Stalker* is very loosely based, the setting is Canada, which Tarkovsky changed to a desolate, unspecified country—clearly, nonetheless, the Soviet Union, seen as a dismal, overindustrialized and polluted police state. A mysterious Zone is close by, an alluring wasteland with tricky force fields that the officials are frightened of and have sealed off,

forbidding anyone to enter. People speculate whether a meteorite had fallen there or if it was the site of an extraterrestrial visitation by a spaceship thirty years ago whose occupants had lunched and left an assortment of perilous debris. A "stalker" shepherds an occasional inquisitive few to the locale at the heart of which lies the Room, where, it is alleged, one's secret wishes are realized. The director and the screenwriters retained some basic elements of the story; jettisoned the science fiction trappings; condensed an eleven-year narrative to one day; changed the tough-guy smuggling protagonist to one with dimensions of a Dostoevskian character; and made the film more of a metaphys-

ical quest. "Only one kind of journey is possible: the one we undertake to our inside world," Tarkovsky said. "Wherever you get to," he continued, "you are still seeking your own soul." *Stalker* was made in Estonia. When the original negative was damaged in processing at the laboratory, the director painstakingly reshot the entire picture. With their unhurried pace, with their pictorial qualities frequently more emphasized than their dramatic aspects, and with their demands for intense viewer concentration, Tarkovsky's films may be said to be an acquired taste. *Stalker*, though little known here, is perhaps the most accessible of his later pictures. Masterfully directed, richly significant

By the tunnel archway the Scientist (Nikolai Grinko) *(center)* wants to go back to pick up his knapsack over the objection of the Stalker. The seated figure is the Writer (Anatoli Solonitsin). This still provides some idea of Tarkovsky's carefully framed shots.

The Stalker (Alexander Kaidanovsky) returns to the Zone. Oddly, the flowers have lost their scent in this curious spot.

After quitting the passageway, the Writer *(left)* and the Stalker come upon a waterfall and notice that the Scientist is missing.

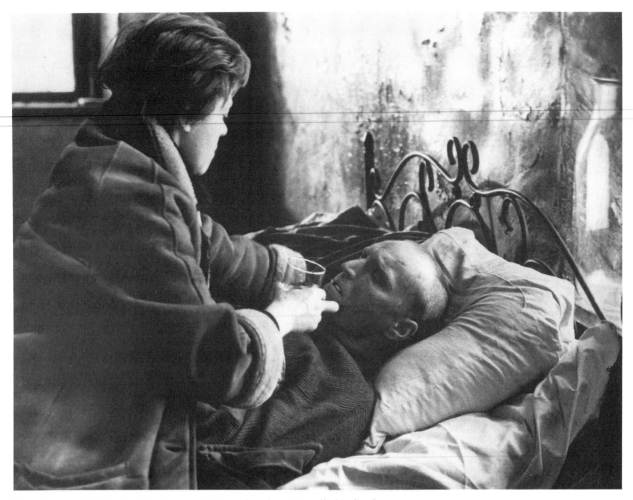

The exhausted Stalker is offered water by his wife (Alissa Freindlich) after he comes home from his trek.

and universal in its theme, *Stalker* is a remarkable, powerful work—with a great potential to be a cult movie—and awaits discovery.

The film opens in the early morning as the man known only by his profession, the Stalker (Alexander Kaidanovsky), rises from bed in his hovel and prepares for his forthcoming hazardous trip. His wife (Alissa Freindlich) wakens and argues with him not to go since he'll be sent to jail again if caught. He departs leaving her deeply upset and meets his group, whom he'll take to the Zone for a meager fee: a cynical, tippling man called the Writer (Anatoli Solonitsin) and a reserved, older man referred to as the Scientist or Professor (Nikolai Grinko). When the police open the enormous fence to permit a train to pass through, the party follows swiftly in their Land Rover, narrowly avoiding the bullets fired by the guards. In a ruined railroad yard they mount a handcar and move to the prohibited area, a grassy field with broken telephone poles. The Stalker feels at home here and treats the place reverentially. From the Scientist we learn that exposure to this strange terrain resulted in the Stalker's daughter (called Monkey) being born deformed. Since the guide claims that the dangers in the region are constantly shifting, they proceed slowly and in a circuitous manner to evade "traps." Impatient with this roundabout approach, the Writer starts heading directly to the Room, but a voice orders him to stop. The other men deny shouting it; the Scientist suggests the Writer said it himself. After the Writer and the Stalker traverse a tunnel, they unaccountably come upon the Scientist, who went back for his rucksack. The men go by ignited, glowing rocks and rest on a mossy tract. Subsequently, a reluctant Writer leads the way through a lengthy underground route. When the frightened man produces a gun, an angry Stalker demands that he drop it. The Writer veers off to a sand-filled room, named the meatgrinder, and compulsively delivers a lengthy monologue on the futility of his existence. They advance to the threshold of the Room where the Scientist removes a bomb that he has been carrying. He thinks to destroy the chamber to prevent some future tyrant from entering and having his evil dreams fulfilled. The Stalker fights him but is overpowered when the Writer turns against him, too. However, the Scientist dismantles the explosive, but neither he nor the Writer dare go inside. The antechamber becomes golden; luminous water descends by the entrance. . . . At home a wearied Stalker complains of the lack of faith in the intellectuals he escorted. Addressing the camera, his steadfast wife expresses her love for the "eternal jailbird" she's married to. The last scene shows their sensitive child at a table displaying a telekinetic ability to move glasses and jars.

With his shaven head, the Stalker, wearing dirty old clothes that suggest those of a political prisoner in a gulag, is an archetype of the Holy Fool, resembling the Christlike Prince Myshkin in Dostoevsky's *The Idiot*—another aborted Tarkovsky film project. Plunged into despair prior to a strong, renewed belief, he is an anguished man, yet one with a vocation. "In this period of destruction of faith," Tarkovsky said, "that which matters to the Stalker is to illuminate a spark, a conviction in the heart of the men." Both the tormented Writer, who considers his life a void, and the Scientist, locked into a totally rationalistic frame of mind, aware of their shortcomings, cannot penetrate the Room. The director said, "They had summoned the strength to look into themselves—and had been horrified; but in the end they lack the spiritual courage to believe in themselves." Alexander Kaidanovsky and Anatoli Solonitsin give extraordinary performances. Tarkovsky's direction is deliberate, allowing mood and characterization to dominate the tight plot. With a painterly eye, he produces visually stunning scenes. Color is used beautifully: after we see the Stalker's foul world depicted in grimy sepia tones, a sudden effulgence of light floods the screen as we enter the Zone. Interpretations of *Stalker* abound, from a dystopian look at the Communist state to an ecological warning. It is, fundamentally, a spiritual analysis of contemporary man. An hypnotic film, yielding more and more on each viewing, *Stalker* is a striking and poetic masterpiece.

51
NOSFERATU THE VAMPYRE

Nosferatu—Phantom der Nacht

WEST GERMANY/FRANCE / 1979

Werner Herzog Filmproduktion (Munich)/Gaumont S.A. (Paris)/ZDF (Zweites Deutsches Fernsehen) (Mainz)

CREDITS

Director, producer, and screenwriter: Werner Herzog, based on the novel *Dracula* by Bram Stoker (1897) and F. W. Murnau's film *Nosferatu, a Symphony of Horror* (1922); *Assistant directors:* Remmelt Remmelts, Mirko Tichacek; *Cinematographer:* Jörg Schmidt-Reitwein (Eastmancolor); *Music:* Popul Vuh/Florian Fricke, Wagner, Gounod, the Gordela Vocal Ensemble; *Editor:* Beate Mainka-Jellinghaus; *Art director:* Henning von Gierke; *Running time:* 106 minutes; *16mm rental source:* Films Inc.; *Videocassette:* Festival Films.

CAST

Count Dracula: Klaus Kinski; *Lucy Harker:* Isabelle Adjani; *Jonathan Harker:* Bruno Ganz; *Renfield:* Roland Topor; *Dr. Van Helsing:* Walter Ladengast; *Captain:* Jacques Dufilho; *Schrader:* Carsten Bodinus; *Mina:* Martje Grohmann.

The enduring myth of Transylvania's infamous Count Dracula, the subject of Bram Stoker's macabre late-Victorian novel, has proven to be an enormously popular staple both on the stage and in the film medium. Whether played as a straight horror movie, from a campy perspective, or awash in special effects as Coppola's 1992 treatment, all versions took liberties with the original material, which is structured essentially as diary entries and placed in the present-day world of its author. The great German director F. W. Murnau made the first screen adaptation of it which appeared in 1922 as *Nosferatu, A Symphony of Horror*. (*Nosferatu* is the Rumanian word for "undead," by which a vampire was designated.) In an attempt—unsuccessful as it turned out—to skirt copyright restrictions, the names were altered, the chief locale was changed from London to Bremen, the setting was

179

tifully acted, directed, and photographed, this distinguished and elegantly stylized film remains haunting and sinister.

Jonathan Harker (Bruno Ganz) is dispatched by his deranged boss Renfield (Roland Topor) to remote Transylvania where a certain Count Dracula wants to purchase a ruinous house in their city of Wismar. Jonathan leaves despite the apprehensions of his devoted, psychic wife, Lucy (Isabelle Adjani). At a hostelry he terrifies the local Gypsies when he mentions his client's dreaded name; before he retires, the innkeeper's wife throws holy water on him, places a crucifix around his neck, and gives him a book on vampires. Since the coachman refuses to take him farther, Jonathan sets out on foot to the Count's castle. He meets a mysterious driver who delivers him in a hearselike carriage to Dracula's gloomy estate near midnight. The welcome by the cadaverous Count Dracula (Klaus Kinski) is polite yet menacing. When a nervous Jonathan cuts his thumb at dinner, the thirsting host seizes it and starts sucking the wound. In the morning the traveler notices slight puncture marks on his throat. At night, glimpsing Jonathan's cameo of his alluring wife, Dracula decides to purchase the house instantly. Next day

Lucy (Isabelle Adjani), fearing that her husband, Jonathan (Bruno Ganz), will be endangered, pleads with him not to go to Transylvania.

moved back to the 1840s, and a new climax was introduced in which the heroine unselfishly immolates herself to save her townspeole from the threat of pestilence. Murnau created an influential, expressionistic masterpiece. When director Werner Herzog decided to make *Nosferatu the Vampyre,* he wished to pay homage to him. Disingenuously he refrained from referring to it, his seventh feature, as a remake, although the plot follows closely that of its silent predecessor and many shots duplicate those of the original. The ending, however, is bleaker than Murnau's for it is not ascertained if the sacrifice of Lucy, actually spares the town from the epidemic, while her husband, Jonathan, transformed into a vampire, sets forth to perpetuate the curse of Count Dracula—reinforcing the Antichrist motif of the Stoker book. Herzog assembled an exceptional cast including Klaus Kinski, Isabelle Adjani, and Bruno Ganz. *Nosferatu the Vampyre* was shot between May and July of 1978 in eastern Czechoslovakia (to simulate Transylvania), in the Dutch city of Delft (to represent Wismar), Bavaria, and Mexico. Beau-

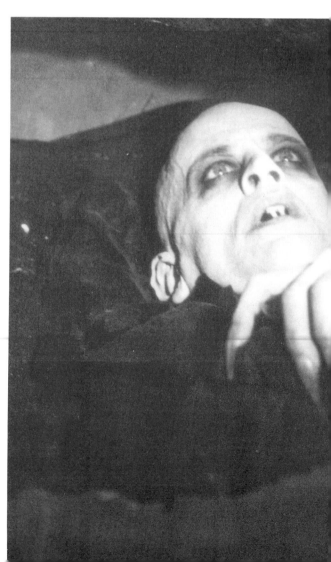

In the daytime, searching for his gruesome host, Jonathan descends to a crypt and discovers Count Dracula (Klaus Kinski) resting in a casket.

from his window, Jonathan, appalled, sees the Count loading a wagon with coffins, then departing. The imprisoned man contrives to escape. A schooner with an ominous cargo sails from Varna. Although ill, Jonathan rides back hurriedly. Aboard ship, a distressed captain (Jacques Dufilho) records the deaths and disappearances of his crew on this accursed voyage. When the vessel, teeming with rats, the captain dead, appears in Wismar, the officials dread plague. A feverish Jonathan is brought home. The town is in the grip of the contagion. Lucy reads in her husband's book that the *nosferatu*'s victims become phantoms of the night; that a consecrated Host will bar a vampire's passage; and should such a fiend stay with a woman pure of heart, the first light of day shall destroy him. She recognizes that the Count is responsible for the plague, but no one will heed her, not even trusted Dr. Van Helsing (Walter Ladengast). When her sister-in-law Mina (Martje Grohmann) is killed, Lucy resolves to act. Hemming in her mutating husband by spreading crumpled Host around his chair, she lies in bed and fearfully awaits the arrival of Dracula. After the Count's repletion, to detain him the valiant woman pulls him down onto her throat for more.

A cock crows. Dracula expires following agonized convulsions. Lucy, smiling, dies. Van Helsing enters and orders a hammer and a stake to drive through the Count's heart. Jonathan demands the arrest of the doctor for murder, commands a maid to clean up the "dust" before him, and rips off his crucifix. Now a vampire, he rides away into the night.

In a noteworthy innovation Herzog succeeds in eliciting a certain degree of sympathy for the tortured Count Dracula, languishing for the peace of death and love. "To be unable to grow old is terrible," Dracula tells Jonathan; to Lucy he remarks, "The absence of love is the most abject pain." The director said, "I wanted to show his loneliness and his melancholy." With his bald

A noble Lucy offers her throat to the satanic Count Dracula.

pate; repulsive, elongated ears; haggard face; cold, sunken eyes; bloodred lips; pronounced fangs; and long, curling talons, Klaus Kinski masterly projects an abysmal desolation and dominates the film with his frightening presence. Herzog called the actor, who died in 1991, a "genius" with "an intensified sensibility," the "only real authentic demon of contemporary cinema." The lovely Isabelle Adjani is outstanding, especially in the climatic scene in which her expressive features convey both terror and sensual arousal during Dracula's obscene repast. Bruno Ganz is persua-

181

Jonathan, metamorphosed into a vampire, orders a horse to commence his diabolical mission.

52

THE MARRIAGE OF MARIA BRAUN

Die Ehe der Maria Braun

WEST GERMANY / 1979

ALBATROS FILMPRODUKTION/TRIO FILM (MUNICH)/
WDR (WESTDEUTSCHER RUNDFUNK) (COLOGNE)

CREDITS

Director: Rainer Werner Fassbinder: *Assistant director:* Rolf Bührmann; *Producer:* Michael Fengler; *Screenwriters:* Peter Märthesheimer, Pea Fröhlich, Rainer Werner Fassbinder; *Cinematographer:* Michael Ballhaus (color); *Music:* Peer Raben; *Editors:* Juliane Lorenz, Franz Walsch (Rainer Werner Fassbinder); *Art director:* Norbert Scherer; *Running time:* 120 minutes; *16mm rental source and videocassette:* New Yorker.

CAST

Maria Braun: Hanna Schygulla; *Hermann Braun:* Klaus Löwitsch; *Karl Oswald:* Ivan Desny; *Willi:* Gottfried John; *Mother:* Gisela Uhlen; *Betti:* Elisabeth Trissenaar; *Hans:* Günter Lamprecht; *Senkenberg:* Hark Bohm; *Bill:* George Byrd; *Black Market Dealer:* Rainer Werner Fassbinder; *Grandpa Berger:* Anton Schirsner; *Mme. Devoald:* Christine Hopf de Loup.

When the shooting plans for his mammoth production of *Berlin Alexanderplatz* were delayed in January of 1978, prolific German director Rainer Werner Fassbinder (1945–82) decided to dash off another film in the interim. Ever the sharp and severe critic of his contemporary society, Fassbinder in the ensuing *The Marriage of Maria Braun* would relate an account of a young wife separated from her husband by the war whom circumstances soon force to become an enterprising professional, while waiting a decade to be reunited with him. Since her story mirrors the postwar period in West Germany when women temporarily took an active role to help rebuild a devastated country only to be replaced by men, who returned to power by the mid-1950s, Maria Braun is meant to be a metaphor for her nation, triumphant after its spectacular "economic miracle" but enmeshed in an ethos of materialism that in Fassbinder's view is markedly

sive, both as solicitous husband and neophyte vampire. Herzog's direction is tight and well-controlled as he skillfully evokes our subconscious fears and anxieties concerning death and our perverse attraction toward evil, producing scene after chilling scene: The camera is stationary in early-morning Wismar while to the eerie strains of Popul Vuh's impressive score the foreboding ship coasts slowly into port, gradually revealing the captain slumped over the wheel. A high-angle shot discloses a grave processional of two parallel columns of white coffins being borne by black-dressed pallbearers into the town square. The concluding scene shows Jonathan, now an evil Messiah, galloping across drifting sands—an alarming epilogue counterpoised with Gounod's "Sanctus" from his *Messe Solennelle*. Schmidt-Reitwein's photography is striking. In *Nosferatu the Vampyre* Herzog has imaginatively captured a nightmare world and made a remarkable addition to the great horror films of all time.

HONORS

Best Art Direction, Berlin Film Festival (1979)

dubious. Using the format of a melodrama, the director purposely distances us from emotional involvement with Maria's plight and instead forces us to appraise the values of the character. "I try to illustrate," Fassbinder said, "that we have been led astray by our upbringing and by the society we live in." Romy Schneider was slated to play the protagonist, but after a falling-out with the director was superseded by Hanna Schygulla. Typical of Fassbinder's rapid work habits, *The Marriage of Maria Braun* was filmed in only thirty-five days, between January and March of 1978, in Coburg and West Berlin. It proved both a critical and commercial success in Germany and here. Skillfully directed, superlatively acted—as original as it is provocative—the movie became the best-known film of the most celebrated German director of his generation.

The film opens in a registrar's office in an unspecified German town during World War II. An Allied aerial bombardment briefly interrupts the civil marriage ceremony of Maria (Hanna Schygulla) and Hermann Braun (Klaus Löwitsch), a soldier. We next see her after the war in a bomb-damaged apartment with her mother (Gisela Uhlen) and grandfather (Anton Schirsner). Steadfast in her conviction that her POW husband is still alive, she keeps vigil at the railway station with a sign inquiring as to his whereabouts. There a GI makes an improper remark to her and, to compensate, gives her cigarettes, which the ambitious Maria swaps afterward for her mother's brooch, which she then exchanges in the black market for an attractive dress. She is determined to be a hostess at a bar for the occupation forces. Her mother says, "I just hope it doesn't do your soul any harm." There Maria meets Bill (George Byrd), a bulky black American serviceman who fancies her. Willi (Gottfried John), husband of Betti (Elisabeth Trissenaar), Maria's best friend, comes home and reports that Hermann is dead. Bill and Maria become lovers; presently she's pregnant. Hermann appears as the couple get ready to make love; in the subsequent confusion Maria hits Bill over the head

A portrait of Maria Braun (Hanna Schygulla) as a prosperous businesswoman who personifies West Germany in the years following World War II.

Karl Oswald (Ivan Desny) is
contemplative after a telephone call
from Maria, the woman he loves.

keeper, alter his will. A proud Hermann rejects Maria's gift of a checkbook. When he's finally released, she finds his note—not him—at the prison. He's left—perhaps for Canada—and will come back "when I've become a man." Maria, disappointed, plunges into work and purchases a country house. Her mother mentions with disapproval how much her daughter's changed. Oswald's death comes as a blow to Maria. On July 4, 1954, the date of a major soccer game between Germany and Hungary which is broadcast via radio in her home, an affluent Hermann turns up unexpectedly. Maria ignites her cigarette from a burner on the stove and blows out the flame while neglecting to turn off the gas. Senkenberg and

with a bottle, accidently killing him. During the court of inquiry the husband suddenly assumes responsibility for the man's death. Visiting him in jail, Maria states, "Our life will start again when we're together again." The inexperienced woman is resolved to find profitable employment. After her miscarriage in the country, an aggressive Maria, heading home, opts for the train's first-class compartment and encounters Karl Oswald (Ivan Desny), wealthy owner of a textile factory. Impressed with her command of English when she scolds a foulmouthed GI, he offers her a position as personal advisor. She encourages the firm to get involved with a seemingly risky venture with an American industrialist. Maria and Oswald begin a liaison. She compartmentalizes her private life from her career; Hermann detects a growing coldness about her. Oswald sees the husband secretly and, consequently, aware that he has but a few years left and genuinely in love with Maria, has Senkenberg (Hark Bohm), his conservative book-

184

Mme. Devoald (Christine Hopf de Loup) stop by and disclose Oswald's will. Half of his estate is to go to Maria, the other half to Hermann as per their contract drawn up in his penitentiary back in 1951. She is dumbfounded to learn that her husband had consented to allow Oswald to spend his remaining years with her in return for monetary recompense. Alone together, an unmindful Maria enters the kitchen to light another cigarette. There is a fatal blast, following which we hear the jubilant announcement that "Germany is World Champion!"

Maria's union with Hermann was restricted by the war to "half a day and a whole night." It is the illusion of her future bliss with a now idealized husband that motivates an uneducated Maria to transform herself into a calculating, shrewdly capable businesswoman. She adopts masculine, commercial imperatives—while exploiting her sexual attributes—and becomes increasingly competitive and avaricious. Through her various compromises and in her unswerving pursuit of financial gain, there is a gradual atrophy of her feelings; she grows toughened, dissatisfied, and cynical. "It's a bad time for emotions," Maria observes to Hermann in jail. In the end with the startling revelation of her husband's perfidious agreement with Oswald, everything she sacrificed for now seems empty and meaningless. Maria has traded cigarettes, jewelry, sex, in her steady rise, but

A gathering to celebrate Mother's birthday *(left to right):* Hans (Günter Lamprecht), Mother (Gisela Uhlen), Willi (Gottfried John), Grandpa Berger (Anton Schirsner), Maria, and Betti (Elisabeth Trissenaar).

185

discovers that she herself has been bartered between the two men. Her "absurd" death is a fitting resolution. The director replaced the screenplay's initial climax in which a disillusioned Maria drives over an embankment with Hermann with the ambiguous explosion in her home that leads us to question if it was unconsciously induced. Scenarist Märthesheimer commented, "Fassbinder was always of the opinion that seemingly inadvertent things signified more about people's true motivations than their superficial, conscious actions." Maria is not meant to be regarded as a feminist since she goes along with, rather than challenges, the rules laid down by men and is surprised to hear Willi aver that women should be treated equally. In his relationship with his wife Hermann displays traditional male values. Accordingly, he pleads guilty to protect Maria, feels he must be the provider, and cannot permit himself to be dependent upon her, only reentering her life when he's well-off and able to assert dominance over her. His accord with Oswald is indicative of his callous use of her. Hanna Schygulla is a memorable Maria. With her strong screen presence she is sensual and totally convincing as she exhibits the full range of her enormous talent. Her brilliant performance was the highlight of her career thus far. Klaus Löwitsch and Ivan Desny lend effective support.

The Marriage of Maria Braun is grounded in reality with authentic fashions and hairstyles, yet it is deliberately stylized to accomplish an "alienation effect," arousing intriguing reflection instead of the affections. Fassbinder's direction is graceful, fluid, and masterly. Early in the movie at the depot with Maria and her handmade sign, a

hand-held camera darts among the crowd as if seeking Hermann; later with her husband's unanticipated arrival at her new home, the camera pursues the heroine in circular movements conveying her indecision and distracted state. There is an adroit use of sound. The prevalent radio not only supplies significant background information about historical events but is also a source of irony—insinuating political duplicity (Chancellor Adenauer's reversing his position on rearmament). The recurrent pneumatic drill we overhear in the background connotes the country's economic resurrection. The film is cleverly framed by photographs and detonations, with a picture of Hitler at the outset and in the conclusion the successive chancellors from Adenauer to Schmidt, implying a resumption of authoritarian figures (with the omission of Willy Brandt, whom the director re-

spected as a reform leader). West Germany, whom Maria embodies, has survived the catastrophe of the war and is rich and mighty—a "World Champion"—but at what cost? Fassbinder asks. A dense, fascinating film, an absorbing drama and engrossing allegory, *The Marriage of Maria Braun* is acknowledged as a masterpiece and has achieved the status of a classic.

HONORS

Silver Bears to Hanna Schygulla for Best Actress and to the technical crew, Berlin Film Festival (1979)

A forlorn Maria, alone in her villa, resorts to drink after Oswald's death.

Maria Braun prepares to recommence her married life with Hermann, who reappeared after being away for ten years.

187

53

BERLIN ALEXANDERPLATZ

WEST GERMANY/ITALY / 1980

Bavaria Atelier GmbH (Munich)/
RAI-TV (Radio Audizioni Italiana) (Italy)
for WDR (Westdeutscher Rundfunk) (Cologne)

CREDITS

Director and screenwriter: Rainer Werner Fassbinder, based on the novel of Alfred Döblin (1929); *Assistant director:* Renate Leiffer; *Producer:* Peter Märthesheimer; *Cinematographer:* Xaver Schwarzenberger (color); *Music:* Peer Raben; *Editors:* Juliane Lorenz, Franz Walsch (Rainer Werner Fassbinder); *Art directors:* Helmut Gassner, Werner Achmann; *Running time:* 921 minutes; *Videocassette:* MGM/UA.

CAST

Franz Biberkopf: Günter Lamprecht; *Eva:* Hanna Schygulla; *Reinhold:* Gottfried John; *Mieze:* Barbara Sukowa; *Lina:* Elisabeth Trissenaar; *Frau Bast:* Brigitte Mira; *Pums:* Ivan Desny; *Meck:* Franz Buchrieser; *Max:* Claus Holm; *Ida:* Barbara Valentin; *Lüders:* Hark Bohm; *Cilly:* Annemarie Düringer; *Herbert:* Roger Fritz; *Bruno:* Volker Spengler; *Widow:* Angela Schmid; *Nachum:* Peter Kollek; *Trude:* Irm Hermann; *Franze:* Helen Vita; *Konrad:* Raoul Gimenez; *Frau Pums:* Lieselotte Eder*; *Manager of Flophouse:* Christiane Maybach.

In June 1979, after various setbacks, Rainer Werner Fassbinder was finally able to commence shooting his gigantic undertaking of Alfred Döblin's celebrated novel *Berlin Alexanderplatz,* which had been filmed previously by Piel Jutzi (1931). The protagonist of the long, experimental, and sprawling narrative that is set in Berlin's underworld between 1927 and 1929 is Franz Biberkopf, a burly, apolitical worker with violent tendencies who is released from prison at the book's outset after serving four years for the killing of his mistress Ida, which was treated as man-

*The mother of Rainer Werner Fassbinder. She appeared in several of her son's films, sometimes under the name Lilo Pempeit.

slaughter. Although he vows to live a decent life, personal weaknesses and destructive companionship inevasibly lead to an unsavory existence. Moral regeneration comes at the end, but only following terrible suffering and a bout of insanity. Influenced by Joyce's *Ulysses,* Döblin's novel employs internal monologue along with an omniscient narrator, is encyclopedic and topographical. *Berlin Alexanderplatz* becomes a monumental collage, an extraordinary vivid and trenchant time capsule. In tracing the laborious "pilgrim's progress" of his hero, the author captures his epoch precisely.

The sway of *Berlin Alexanderplatz* on Fassbinder was both acute and profound. An early reading at a troubled age of fourteen fascinated him as soon as Franz encounters the perverse Reinhold. The youth envisioned their bonding as undeclared homoeroticism and confessed that the work "helped me to admit my tormenting fear, which almost crippled me, the fear of acknowledging my homosexual desires." Five years later when he reread it, he realized, "I had . . . unconsciously made Döblin's fantasy my own life." Not only did the novel aid him to live, he affirms, but it also served as an artistic model to emulate in which melodramatic material is handled skillfully and social outcasts are depicted with gravity and compassion. Further, it was a paradigm of his great theme—which he utilized frequently—in which a pressing longing for love inevitably leads to frustration and betrayal. So thoroughly did he identify with Döblin's character that the name Franz appears in his numerous films; moreover, Franz Biberkopf is the personage the director himself plays both in *Gods of the Plague* (1970) and, more significantly, *Fox and His Friends* (1975) in which, as a hapless gay man, he is victimized and driven to suicide by a perfidious lover. Although Fassbinder had long hoped to make a movie of *Berlin Alexanderplatz,* it was thanks to television producers, who had the resources to provide the huge budget, $6.5 million, that he could fulfill his aspiration. A projected six-part television series was soon stretched out by him to fourteen episodes. The work was conceived as an "amphibian film," suitable for both TV broadcast and theatrical release. Coeditor Juliane Lorenz attests, "For Rainer it was always a movie in fourteen parts."

Fassbinder streamlined an unwieldy, diffusive novel into a tightly compressed story that focused on the protagonist and not his milieu, thereby making the film more dramatic and urgent. He deliberately constricted the writer's epic dimension of a palpitating Berlin to the murky, claustrophobic realm of Franz Biberkopf's rented rooms and pub. A delightful interpolation is the rendering of the landlady, Frau Bast, as an inveterate busybody, portrayed by the wonderful Brigitte Mira. While the director dropped the stream of consciousness, he retained and was himself the intermittent, all-knowing narrator whose sober, judgmental reflections on Biberkopf act as a distancing device. And while Fassbinder adhered to Döblin's story line more or less steadfastly, in the protracted epilogue he took the initiative to record Franz's transformation in a highly unorthodox, debatable, and even exasperating manner. A major point of departure was the director's interpretation of the affiliation between Franz and Reinhold as unperceived homoeroticism. Albeit in the vast novel Döblin makes but two oblique and undeveloped references—one, that in addition to Mieze Franz loves Reinhold best "but he doesn't dare say it," and, another, about his "curious devotion" to him—Fassbinder maintained, "It is an erotic but not a sexual relationship."

Günter Lamprecht had the role of his career as Franz Biberkopf, for which he was obliged to gain considerable weight. Hanna Schygulla was cast as Eva, while Barbara Sukowa made her impressive screen debut as Mieze. Working rapidly, with amazing energy, the director filmed his beloved book between June 1979 and April 1980 with locations in West Berlin and, chiefly, Munich.

Lina (Elisabeth Trissenaar) is about to start her affair with Franz (Günter Lamprecht) *(left)*, who is talking with his friend Meck (Franz Buchrieser) at Max's tavern.

Berlin Alexanderplatz was screened at the Venice Film Festival in 1980, then shortly afterward shown on German television. Fassbinder died in 1982. Here the film had a limited theatrical release in 1983, then a TV transmission—both of which drew superlatives from the critics. Owing to its colossal length, *Berlin Alexanderplatz* is a much neglected movie, though available on videocassettes. An emotionally and intellectually riveting experience, it is a powerful classic to be rediscovered and honored.

The following is of necessity a much abridged synopsis: A nervous Franz Biberkopf (Günter Lamprecht) is discharged from Tegel Prison; Nachum (Peter Kollek), a sympathetic Orthodox Jew, assists the temporarily disoriented stranger. The narrator recounts the death of Ida (Barbara Valentin), who was about to leave Franz for another man. Biberkopf meets his chum Meck (Franz Buchrieser), then over drinks at a bar run by Max (Claus Holm) notices the Polish Lina (Elisabeth Trissenaar). In her room after lovemaking Franz swears to stay honest and law-abiding. He attempts unsuccessfully to sell tie clips on the street. Eva (Hanna Schygulla), a high-class harlot who was his mistress before Ida and still loves him, dashes out of her car and hands him a large bill. Lina's widowed "Uncle" Lüders (Hark Bohm) suggests they team as door-to-door shoelace sales-

Searching for her missing Franz, a frantic Lina, accompanied by Meck, learns about her lover's odd behavior from Max, the bartender.

While the manager of the flophouse (Christiane Maybach) watches, a surly Franz threatens the devious Lüders (Hark Bohm).

A portrait of Eva (Hanna Schygulla), Franz's longtime friend, at whose elegant apartment he recovers his strength after his accident.

men. Peddling alone, Franz chances upon a lovely widow (Angela Schmid) and they make love. Subsequently he tactlessly brags of his remunerative conquest; the slimy widower drops in on her to extort money. When Biberkopf pays a return call, she shuts the door in his face. He disappears. Lina and Meck learn from Max that the day before, after a boy delivered the widow's letter, Franz's face turned green; he acted strange and left. Meck orders Lüders to find him. In a flophouse he discovers the embittered man; Franz leaves before Lina and Meck arrive. At a shabby boardinghouse, a miserable Franz goes on a drinking spree that results in delirium tremens. Eva appears but he insists that he has to get out of this situation by himself, which he eventually does.

At Max's, Meck introduces Franz to Pums (Ivan Desny), head of a gang of thieves. Biberkopf is curious about the man's associate, the brooding, stuttering Reinhold (Gottfried John). During their next meeting, Reinhold complains about his current mistress, Franze (Helen Vita), and asks Franz to take her off his hands. He obliges. Soon the neurotic Reinhold is eager to pass along Cilly (Annemarie Düringer). To humor him Biberkopf deliberately picks a quarrel with Franze. Subsequently, Reinhold is restless to dispose of Trude (Irm Hermann), but Franz refuses, telling him to control himself. Biberkopf calls on Pums to relay a

Cilly (Annemarie Düringer), together again with Reinhold (Gottfried John), announces she got a job as a performer in a cabaret.

Franz has a reunion with Mieze (Barbara Sukowa) following a misunderstanding.

After a long while, a mutilated Franz calls on an apprehensive Reinhold.

message: Bruno (Volker Spengler) was arrested that morning in a street fight. Pums offers Franz a lucrative "delivery" job that evening, which turns out to be lookout man while the crew burglarizes a house. Franz, alarmed, tries to flee but an angry Reinhold drags him back. In the rear of a departing car a ruffled Reinhold, loathing a now smiling, smug Franz, suddenly flings him out of the tailgate before an approaching automobile. At Max's, Reinhold reports Biberkopf's death and reconciles with a drunken Cilly. His right arm crushed by the car and amputated, a dejected Franz recuperates at Eva's apartment. She and her swindler lover, Herbert (Roger Fritz), aim to press Pums for indemnification, but a resigned Franz seeks no vengeance. They provide their downcast friend with a pretty young woman. Overjoyed, Franz dubs her Mieze (Barbara Sukowa); they share an idyllic vacation in Freienwalde. However, reading an impassioned love letter sent to her, Franz, dreading desertion, rushes to Eva. After investigating, she relates that Mieze has secretly resumed streetwalking to support the man she adores. Eva effects a reconciliation.

Summoning up courage, Biberkopf visits a tense Reinhold, who thinks he's come to blackmail him. All thoughts of reform gone, Franz joins Pum's group; they rob a warehouse. Having boasted of Mieze's devotion, Franz hides Reinhold in his bed to witness it. Unfortunately, when the woman enters, she reveals she's enamored of her patron's nephew. Outraged, Franz starts beating her, although she protests she loves him. Reinhold intervenes. Mieze pardons her repentant lover. When Biberkopf brings her to Max's, Reinhold considers taking Mieze away from him and charges Meck to drive her to Freienwalde. An unsuspecting Mieze is disappointed to find Reinhold there. The couple go for a walk. He tries to seduce her, but feels incensed and rejected when he recognizes that she prefers Franz. Cruelly, he divulges the truth of Biberkopf's accident. When she calls him a murderer and starts screaming, he strangles her. Franz is distraught at Mieze's absence. Conscience-stricken, Meck leads the police to the site where he helped Reinhold bury her. Eva brings a newspaper with a sensational account of Mieze's death to Franz, who derives consolation from the fact that at least she didn't leave him.

Epilogue: In a prolonged dream an agonized

Biberkopf encounters again people he's known. The police seize a now demented Franz. To avoid arrest for murder, Reinhold cleverly lets himself be captured, using the alias of a Polish pickpocket. In jail he becomes enamored of his cellmate Konrad (Raoul Gimenez) and discloses the homicide. When Konrad gets out, he turns Reinhold in for the reward. Biberkopf, in a catatonic stupor, is confined in the Buch Insane Asylum. While his doctors ponder electric shock therapy, he has hallucinatory dreams underscoring his self-disgust, fears, and traumas. Found guilty of unpremeditated murder, Reinhold is sentenced to ten years. Franz finds employment as an assistant porter at a factory. He has had to pay a high price for the knowledge he learned of the world.

By turns happy-go-lucky and despondent, the robust worker Franz Biberkopf is a universally recognizable Everyman—proud, stubborn, sensual, and unreflective. Only at the end of his ordeal does he resist the temptation of blaming fate for his difficulties and instead accept personal responsibility for his actions. Cold, malevolent, deadly, and remorseless, the demonic Reinhold is referred to as the Reaper, a personification of death. He is represented in imagery both reptilian—in a nightmare Franz is bitten by a snake that metamorphoses into Reinhold—and porcine—Cilly and Mieze each call him a swine. In his pattern of initial fierce attraction to a woman succeeded by revulsion, he is clearly displaying psychotic behavior. A notorious betrayer, Reinhold is himself ultimately betrayed when he becomes infatuated with Konrad, reinforcing Fassbinder's obsession with perfidy. Dominating this extended film with his formidable screen presence and giving a truly great performance that demonstrates a multifaceted range is Günter Lamprecht as the beleaguered, bearlike Franz Biberkopf. Gottfried John, with his glacial eyes and disturbing stutter, indelibly incarnates the tortured Reinhold, projecting a mesmeric image of evil. A major discovery is Barbara Sukowa, who plays the tragic Mieze; possessing a fragile beauty, she makes the sweet, childlike character immensely appealing and poignant. Hanna Schygulla as the loyal Eva and Elisabeth Trissenaar as the intuitive Lina are superb, along with the rest of the director's "stock company."

Fassbinder masterly transformed Döblin's sweeping, massive symphony into intimate chamber music. Seldom have viewers had the opportunity to study characters developed to such an extent and with such an intensity as here. Except for much of the epilogue, Fassbinder's direction is tightly controlled, unostentatious, and compelling with remarkably few longueurs. A striking innovation is the recurring scene of Ida's killing, each time shot from a different angle, triggered when Franz is anxious or racked with guilt. In the anticlimactic and often bizarre concluding segment the film is at its weakest, with Fassbinder failing to produce a viable, cinematic equivalent to an institutionalized Franz's struggle to come to terms with his past. In its place Fassbinder invents tedious, self-indulgent, elongated dream sequences marred by such excesses as vertiginous 360-degree camera movements and Biberkopf's "crucifixion." This phantasmagoria amounts to "frigid fireworks," to cite Virginia Woolf, but since

Pums (Ivan Desny) *(left)*, his wife (Lieselotte Eder), and Reinhold notice Franz entering Max's with the lovely Mieze.

it lasts less than two hours out of a gargantuan film of nearly fifteen and a half hours, it does not impair the overwhelming impact of the picture. *Berlin Alexanderplatz* is indeed a prodigious achievement. Who can forget the shocking scene of Reinhold hurling Franz out of the car or the sinister sequence in which Reinhold leads Mieze in a dance of death while evening mist softly swells through the deserted woods? Credit Xaver Schwarzenberger's cinematography in which—with subdued color and dim, expressionistic lighting—he creates deep facial shadows enhancing the gloomy mood of a "dark night of the soul"; and Peer Raben's haunting and melancholic score.

Whereas Döblin concluded his novel showing

Franz Biberkopf not as destiny's tragic victim but as a man with a spiritual potential to survive, one who will "keep sunshine" in his heart, Fassbinder seems to pay lip service to his hero's redemption in order to be faithful to the book, but both underemphasizes it and presents it without much conviction. The ominous Nazi marching music that is blended into the final sequence serves to undercut Franz's reformation and suggests that he will fall prey to the impending catastrophe. Undoubtedly, the director's idiosyncratic adaptation was the result of his seeing the film as *his* "autobiography." *Berlin Alexanderplatz* is Fassbinder's summa in which all his major preoccupations find their deepest and most personal expression. A brilliant, hypnotic film, it is, in my opinion, the director's masterpiece.

54
GERMANY PALE MOTHER

Deutschland Bleiche Mutter

WEST GERMANY / 1980

HELMA SANDERS FILMPRODUKTION/LITERARISCHES COLLOQUIUM (WEST BERLIN)/WDR (WESTDEUTSCHER RUNDFUNK) (COLOGNE)

CREDITS

Director and screenwriter: Helma Sanders-Brahms; *Assistant director:* Christa Ritter; *Producers:* Ursula Ludwig, Volker Canaris; *Cinematographer:* Jürgen Jürges (color); *Music:* Jürgen Knieper; *Editors:* Elfi Tillack, Uta Periginelli; *Art director:* Götz Heymann; *Running time:* 145 minutes; *16mm rental source:* New Yorker.

CAST

Lene: Eva Mattes; *Hans:* Ernst Jacobi; *Hanne:* Elisabeth Stepanek; *Lydia:* Angelika Thomas; *Ulrich:* Rainer Friedrichsen; *Aunt Ihmchen:* Gisela Stein; *Uncle Bertrand:* Fritz Lichtenhahn; *Anna:* Anna Sanders.

From Bertolt Brecht's caustic poem "Germany" (1933) in which that country, personified as a

Lene (Eva Mattes) attends a party with her husband-to-be.

allegoric way her forlorn nation. The director said, "The mother is the image of the German people, and the greatest strength of the people is its ability to survive, to carry on." The extraordinary Eva Mattes was cast in the vital role of the mother. Brilliantly directed and acted, *Germany Pale Mother* is a poignant and unforgettable cinematic experience. Though it won prizes at various international film festivals, it failed to find an audience when it appeared in America in 1984. An overlooked movie, it waits to be discovered and acclaimed.

The film opens with Hans (Ernst Jacobi) and his Nazi friend Ulrich (Rainer Friedrichsen) rowing. When a dog attacks the unflinching Lene (Eva Mattes), they are much impressed with her courage. Hans dates her, but Ulrich ignores her sister, Hanne (Elisabeth Stepanek), who is in love with him, and courts instead Lydia (Angelika Thomas). While Lene is consoling a rejected Hanne, screams from the latter's Jewish schoolmate Rachel bring them to the open window. They witness the woman being abused by a crowd, but Lene shuts the window and draws the curtains. Hans brings Lene, his new bride, to their home. Soon, since he

mother, is indicted for complicity in the crimes of her sons—an early attack on the Nazi regime—German director Helma Sanders-Brahms (1940–   ) chose the title for her powerful feature *Germany Pale Mother* and included it in the movie's preface. "It is an extremely autobiographical film in the sense that I described my own situation as a child in wartime Germany," the director said. The picture would focus on the unhappy life of her mother from the late 1930s through the next difficult decade ending with Konrad Adenauer as chancellor and be accompanied by an intermittent commentary by the daughter, now an unmarried adult. Everyone in the Third Reich, it is implied, was responsible and partook of the guilt—her soldier father, her housewife mother, and the countless average people who were to suffer enormously. Sanders-Brahms stated that during this terrible chronicle her countrymen "destroyed themselves . . . in spite of the fact that they survived the war. I wanted to show that there is no innocence in a war, and that there is no escape from it." While the mother is depicted in realistic, at times harrowing, terms, she is also, like the Brecht poem, meant to represent in an

196

is not a Nazi Party member, he is among the first to be called up. In Poland the sensitive soldier finds war repellent. On a pass he perceives that his wife is indisposed to lovemaking and angrily accuses her of sleeping with Ulrich, which she denies. Reconciled, she declares she wishes a child from him. Hans is sent to France. During an air raid Lene, after painful labor, has a baby girl. Later at Christmas, following another bombardment, she returns from the shelter to find her home demolished. With the infant Anna (Anna Sanders) she heads on foot to Berlin to stay at the home of an obnoxious, rich relative, Uncle Bertrand (Fritz Lichtenhahn), who is retreating to the country. There Lene has a joyless, awkward reunion with Hans, given a short leave. He sees she's changed, stronger and more resourceful. Heeding his advice to escape the capital, mother and daughter set out for the provinces.

Hitler's suicide ends the ghastly war. Plodding through the wintry forests, Lene relates the portentious fairy tale "The Robber Bridegroom" by the Brothers Grimm to the girl. Two American soldiers rape a stoical Lene while Anna watches. She endures the deprivation of postwar Berlin and

Carrying her baby daughter, Anna (Anna Sanders), Lene hikes to Berlin.

encounters Hanne. Hans comes back to his loveless marriage. Time passes; Lene feels increasing discontent and emptiness. Her face becomes swollen, palsied, and painful. All her teeth must be extracted to halt a spreading paralysis. She gets moodier and more withdrawn. In a confrontation with her husband, Lene screams, "Love is what I need. You've ruined everything for me." She blurts out, "I don't want to live anymore"; Hans storms off. Lene enters the bathroom, blows out the pilot light in the heater, shoves her pursuing daughter out of the room, and awaits asphyxiation. The distressed child bangs on the door pleading for her mother. She finally emerges and strokes Anna's head. The narrator remarks, "Sometimes I think she's still behind the door and never comes out to me. And I must grow up alone."

Sanders-Brahms refrains from portraying Lene as a blameless victim. By being apolitical and

197

Following an air attack Lene surveys the wreckage of her home.

Fleeing an endangered capital, Lene and little Anna rest along a country path.

form a row, are blindfolded, fired upon, and fall down. Sanders-Brahms uses interesting subjective shots—the lovesick Hans sees his wife everywhere from the Polish peasant he shoots to a lady in a bistro in Normandy (both played by Mattes)—as well as authentic, colored newsreels—long overhead tracking shots of Berlin in ruins for example—which lend a haunting, documentary effect to the film. Jürgen Jürges contributed excellent cinematography.

The frightening, murderous bridegroom who becomes betrothed to the miller's beautiful daughter in the Grimm story, that Lene recites to her daughter, is a coded reference to Hitler. This point is reinforced via a juxtaposition of its narration with startling footage of a destroyed Berlin. While the bridegroom and his slaughterous band, Der Führer and his cohorts, are brought to justice and executed, it is significant that the authors do not reveal what happens to the heroine following her ordeal. If possibly she did not live "happily ever after," we definitely see the fate of Lene/Germany: lost, wretched, living on with her soul shattered. A harsh, uncompromising film, *Germany Pale Mother* is intimate, disturbing, and deserves to be remembered.

passive, which includes shutting out the cries for help from the Jewish student, she does nothing to prevent the ensuing nightmare. Lene is much afflicted and grows to be an independent woman, but as both a character and as an embodiment of Germany, we are left to ponder the triumph of her survival at the price of the death of the spirit. Eva Mattes gives an astonishing performance, especially in the childbirth sequence during an Allied bombing when shots of the shrieking woman are intercut with actual footage of planes dropping their devastating explosives. Hers is acting of the highest order. Through Sanders-Brahms's carefully controlled direction we live Lene's life vicariously and forcefully. The director creates superb images—a party scene opens with a low-angle shot of an enormous Nazi flag with flies swarming around it—and can be impressively economical—in a single, stationary long shot with the camera at a low angle on a dune, eight French partisans march Indian file to the top where they

55
MEPHISTO

HUNGARY/WEST GERMANY / 1981

Mafilm/Objectiv Film Studio (Budapest)/ Manfred Durniok Produktion (West Berlin)

CREDITS

Director: Istvan Szabo; *Screenwriters:* Peter Dobai, Istvan Szabo, after the novel of Klaus Mann (published in America 1977); *Cinematographer:* Lajos Koltai (Eastmancolor); *Music:* Zdenko Tamassy; *Editor:* Zsuzsa Csakany; *Art director:* Jozsef Romvary; *Running time:* 144 minutes; *Videocassette:* HBO (dubbed).

CAST

Hendrik Höfgen: Klaus Maria Brandauer; *Nicoletta von Niebuhr:* Ildiko Bansagi; *Barbara Bruckner:* Krystyna Janda; *The Prime Minister:* Rolf Hoppe; *Hans Miklas:* Gyorgy Cserhalmi; *Otto Ulrichs:* Peter Andorai; *Juli-*

198

ette: Karin Boyd; *Lotte Lindenthal:* Christine Harbort; *The Professor:* Martin Hellberg; *Dora Martin:* Ildiko Kishonti.

If one may liken director Istvan Szabo's earlier, intimate film *Confidence* to chamber music, then his *Mephisto*—with its spectacular setting of Nazi Germany and larger-than-life characters whose occasionally charged speeches are highly theatrical "arias"—may be considered operatic. This, his ninth feature, was based on the controversial novel written in 1936 by Klaus Mann, son of the great German writer Thomas Mann, concerning

"This is my answer—Shakespeare!" the politically imperceptive Höfgen yells at his wife, who is entreating her husband to take a stand against the Nazis on the morning after Hitler is elected chancellor.

Before his mistress, Juliette (Karin Boyd), Hendrik Höfgen (Klaus Maria Brandauer) announces his wedding plans.

the career of the famous stage actor Gustaf Gründgens (1899–1963), who, ambitious for success, chose to remain in Germany when Hitler came to power and, while not a Nazi Party member himself, lent a veneer of respectability to that notorious regime as director and star of Berlin's Prussian State Theater. Mann wrote the novel, he said, to "analyze the abject type of treacherous intellectual who prostitutes his talent for the sake of some tawdry fame and transitory wealth." The book, a venomous lampoon on the artist, is a roman à clef; thus the pilloried thespian becomes Hendrik Höfgen; his protector, Field Marshal Hermann Göring, transforms into the prime minister; and Erika Mann, the author's sister and the actor's first wife, changes into Barbara Bruckner. Aside from dropping characters, compressing the action, and substituting a brilliant finale for the routine ending, the screenwriters' main divergence from the book was in excluding the protagonist's masochistic proclivities—itself a stratagem for concealing Gründgens's homosexuality. "I wanted the audience to identify with the hero," Szabo said. "Could they make the same mistakes, could they submit

199

Hendrik Höfgen made up as Mephisto for a performance of Goethe's *Faust*, his most prestigious role.

to evil in the same way?" If he focused on the player's sexual conduct, viewers could easily, self-righteously distance themselves from him. "The evil of Nazism does not result from perversion and homosexuality," the director continues. "Fascism and anti-Semitism are ultimately a special kind of perversion: the perversion of the soul. . . . So you must get the 'normal' audience, so vulnerable to this soul-perversion, to identify with the character." Szabo trusts that our empathizing with Höfgen will produce, he says, a "catharic sense of shame" that will serve as "a vaccination against actually *being* like that." The distinguished Austrian theater actor Klaus Maria Brandauer was perfectly cast in the lead role. *Mephisto*, shot in both Hungarian and German versions, is the first of a thematically related trilogy, followed by *Colonel Redl* (1985) and *Hanussen* (1988), all featuring Brandauer. Stylish, superbly acted and directed, *Mephisto* is a remarkable, fascinating, and dynamic film.

The time is the late 1920s. The film opens in a Hamburg theater. While guest artist Dora Martin (Ildiko Kishonti) performs an operetta, player Hendrik Höfgen (Klaus Maria Brandauer) has a paroxysm of envy backstage. He fears he's just a provincial actor who'll never achieve fame. His lover is the mulatto Juliette (Karin Boyd), who teaches him dancing and understands his weak nature. At the theater he meets the new actress Nicoletta von Niebuhr (Ildiko Bansagi) whose girlfriend Barbara Bruckner (Krystyna Janda) he feels himself attracted to and marries. Höfgen is invited to act in Berlin, although for much lower wages, by the theater magnate, styled the Professor (Martin Helberg). Gradually his popularity grows. Dora, a Jew, informs him she's learning English and leaving Germany before it's too late. She perceives that he is opportunistic and will survive no matter what happens.

Höfgen installs Juliette in a Berlin apartment. Barbara, packing to quit the country when Hitler becomes chancellor, castigates her theater-oriented, politically myopic husband, then departs

At an exhibition of a sculptress, Höfgen *(at the microphone)* mouths the platitudes of Nazi theories on art. The towering male statue incarnates those values: a strong, gigantic warrior to stun the onlooker into submission.

for Paris. In Hungary, on location for a film, Höfgen is hesitant to return since he's been blacklisted for his flirtation with Communism, but receives a reassuring letter from a confidante: her new friend, the actress Lotte Lindenthal (Christine Harbort), verified his acceptability with her suitor, a prominent Nazi air force officer soon to be prime minister. Höfgen's indiscretions will be pardoned; the Reich has need of his talent. Back in Berlin, when he discovers himself excluded from an impending production of *Faust*, he implores Lotte, "I must play Mephisto!" At its premiere the corpulent prime minister (Rolf Hoppe) finds Höfgen's performance intriguing. Ingratiating himself with this cruel leader, Höfgen dares to request the release of his Communist colleague Otto (Peter Andorai). The celebrated thespian is expected to make speeches at various cultural events. The prime minister offers his Mephisto the management of the State Theater, but first he must divorce Barbara and cease his "racial crime"; Juliette is quickly deported to France. In Paris he sees Barbara, who's actively fighting the Nazis with her newspaper. She asks what does freedom mean to him: "Do you need it at all to live? Or do you only need to be successful and beloved?" Esconced in his Grunewald villa, he marries Nicoletta. Learning of Otto's rearrest, Höfgren visits the prime minister, who tells him angrily to stop meddling. Interceding with Lotte, he's informed of Otto's "suicide." Following his festive birthday tribute at the Opera House, the prime minister drives Höfgen to the Nuremberg Stadium, has him walk alone to its center, then sadistically beams blinding lights at him to make him aware of his subservient position. Feeling hurt, trapped, and uncomfortable, he murmurs, "What do they want of me? I'm only an actor."

Although Hendrik Höfgen as the wily Mephisto adroitly entices a wary Faust onstage, the roles are ironically reversed in reality with the careerist actor being tempted, then signing a pact with the demoniacal prime minister. The unreflecting player may utter Goethe's significant line "You're in the end just what you are," yet he constantly justifies his behavior and refuses to assume responsibility for his actions. Caught at the conclusion in the harsh "spotlight" that he fatefully compromised himself to attain, is he cognizant that he's a mere puppet to be manipulated by the tyrannical Nazis? Throwing a tantrum, bursting with ideas at a rehearsal, displaying diabolical cunning as Mephisto, Klaus Maria Brandauer gives a supercharged, indelible performance. Szabo's direction is firm, vigorously capturing the sordid period. He does not see *Mephisto* bounded exclusively in a definite epoch, but rather as timeless and universal: "It is a human story about a kind of character which exists all over—whether doctors, professors, journalists, or filmmakers—the person who wants to be the center of attention, who craves the spotlight, a gifted person with a sense of inferiority. . . . If you recognize and applaud them, they will do anything for you. . . . Gifted people can be dangerous because they can be seduced." In *Mephisto* the director has created an electrifying and elegant film, heightened by one of the great screen portrayals in recent memory.

HONORS

Best Screenplay and International Critics Prize, Cannes Film Festival (1981)
Oscar for Best Foreign Language Film (1981)

56
DAS BOOT

WEST GERMANY / 1981

BAVARIA ATELIER GMBH/RADIANT FILM (MUNICH)

CREDITS

Director and screenwriter: Wolfgang Petersen, based on the novel by Lothar-Günther Buchheim (1973); *Assistant director:* Georg Borgel; *Producer:* Günther Rohrbach; *Cinematographer:* Jost Vacano (color); *Music:* Klaus Doldinger; *Editor:* Hannes Nikel; *Art director:* Gotz Weidner; *Running time:* 150 minutes; *16mm rental source:* Films Inc.; *Videocassette:* RCA/Columbia (dubbed).*

CAST

The Captain: Jürgen Prochnow; *Lieutenant Werner:* Herbert Grönemeyer; *Chief Engineer:* Klaus Wennemann; *First Lieutenant / Number One:* Hubertus Bengsch; *Second Lieutenant:* Martin Semmelrogge; *Chief Quartermaster:* Bernd Tauber; *Johann:* Erwin Leder; *Ullmann:* Martin May; *Hinrich:* Heinz Hönig; *Captain Thomsen:* Otto Sander; *Captain of the* Weser: Günter Lamprecht; *Monique:* Rita Cadillac.

*Tape title is *The Boat.*

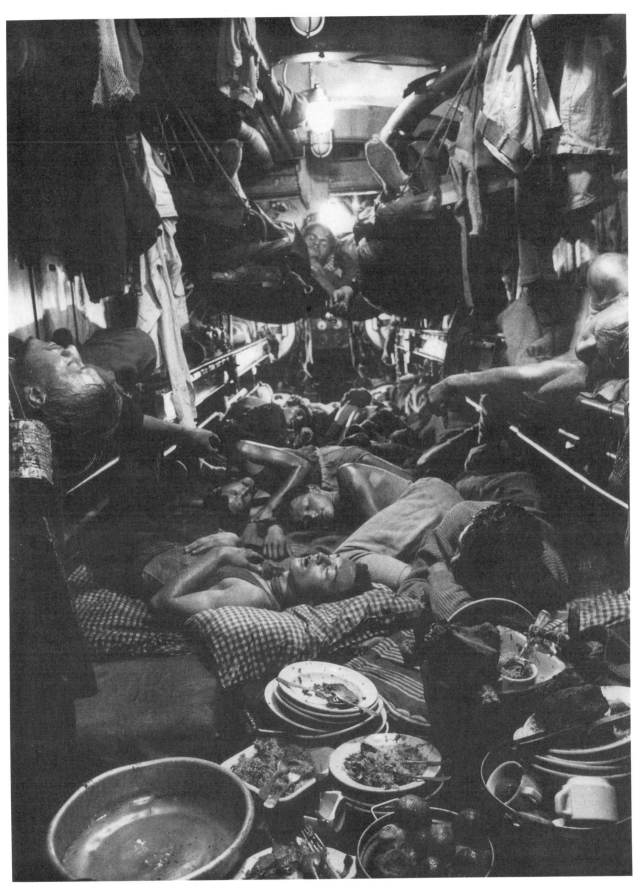

Next to the leavings of their dinner, the exhausted sailors sleep in a tumble.
A strong sense of the submarine's confined atmosphere is sharply caught.

The captain (Jürgen Prochnow) counts his triumphs as one ship after another in the convoy is hit with his boat's torpedoes.

When German director Wolfgang Petersen (1941–   ) came upon Lothar-Günther Buchheim's semiautobiographical novel *Das Boot* (or *The Boat* as the film adaptation is alternatively known here), which treated of the writer's experiences aboard U-boats in World War II, he was strongly impressed with its gripping, dramatic qualities. "I really felt that this story told what war is about," he said. The director, who never tasted battle, felt arise in him a challenge to re-create on film this cogent rendering of combat, "telling people," as he said, "that's war. That's what it was!" At one point *Das Boot* was to be a German-American coproduction, with Paul Newman as the captain, but the author objected to the cliché-ridden screenplays submitted for his approval. Ultimately, the Germans decided to produce it themselves, although at a budget of $13 million it became the most expensive movie shot in Germany up to then.

Jürgen Prochnow portrayed the captain. Enormous pains were taken to achieve an effect of versimilitude; thus the actual inside of a submarine made of metal, not wood, was constructed for the film, which was shot in sequence so that the cast would *live* the account. After its theatrical release, the uncut six-hour version was televised four years later in Germany. *Das Boot* is organized within an initiation framework in which a young war correspondent takes a submarine voyage in 1941—a time when the tide is turning against

German naval supremacy in the Atlantic—and learns that the ghastly reality of warfare is far removed from the delusory propaganda from Berlin. Petersen said, "If someone leaves the theater feeling that they've been on this boat for two and a half hours and knows how war feels, how horrible and claustrophobic it is, then I've done my job." An enormous triumph in Germany, the picture proved to be extremely popular in America also. Epic yet intimate, visually spectacular, with sparse dialogue and a shattering impact, *Das Boot* will undoubtedly remain the definitive film on submarine warfare.

At the outset an ominous caption strikes a pacifistic, elegiac note: "Forty thousand German sailors served on U-boats during World War II. Thirty thousand never returned." The film opens in autumn 1941 at the Bar Royal in the occupied French port of La Rochelle. The captain (Jürgen Prochnow) of *U-96*, referred to by the young sailors as *"Der Alte"* ("The Old Man") although he's only thirty, introduces Lieutenant Werner (Herbert Grönemeyer), a war reporter assigned to cover the trip, to his staff, most of whom are besotted and roistering to hide their fear. The inebriated veteran Captain Thomsen (Otto Sander) publicly makes sardonic remarks about Hitler's "great naval expertise." The following morning the boat embarks amidst cheering crowds and military music. The captain, aware of their heavy losses, bemoans government inefficiency, then to stir morale commands "It's a Long Way to Tipperary" to be played, the rousing British World War I tune that they have happily appropriated.

Following much tedium, on the forty-fifth day at sea a convoy is sighted, apparently without protective escort. The boat launches torpedoes successfully at several ships. Suddenly, however, an unnoticed destroyer starts dropping depth charges on them. The men realize the enemy is trying to detect them with ultrasonic equipment that they lack. In the ensuing chaos fires break out. Skillfully evading the warship, *U-96* encounters a second destroyer, and the captain orders the boat to sink to a perilous 230 meters, where pressure causes her gaskets to pop off and exploding charges jolt the threatened vessel. Submerged for six hours, *U-96* escapes her pursuers. A new mandate to head to La Spezia (Italy) countermands a yearned-for Christmas in France. The boat stops for food and supplies at Vigo (Spain), and the captain glowers at the disparity between the comfort of the German "merchant" ship, the SS *Weser*, which he visits, and the deprivations that his men

U-96 manages to return to La Rochelle. Saluting *(left to right)* are the chief engineer (Klaus Wennemann), the captain, and a now seasoned correspondent, Lieutenant Werner (Herbert Grönemeyer).

have to endure. Approaching Gibraltar, he bravely dissembles the dangers of the heavily defended strait and proceeds to drift with the current in the evening fog. Unexpectedly, a plane begins strafing the U-boat, which plummets to the sea bottom and lands on a sandbar. At 280 meters, with rivets bursting, the crew makes a superhuman effort to stay the leaks that are flooding the submarine. With the air supply diminishing and the men disheartened, the chief engineer (Klaus Wennemann) employs the ballast pump to force the water out, a gamble, for it's their sole chance to get the boat to rise. He brings it off; the engines surprisingly work again. *U-96* is forced to limp back to La Rochelle. Ironically, just as they arrive safely, an Allied squadron flies over wreaking havoc, bombing the U-boat and killing the captain.

Although the accent in *Das Boot* is on thrilling action, not characterization, we are provided with a variegated image of the captain as a stalwart, able leader, proud of his boat, cynical of the callous administration in the capital, albeit compassionate for—and inspirational to—his men. With his expressive blue eyes and virile presence, Jürgen Prochnow plays the captain with great conviction, a role that launched his international career. Wolfgang Petersen's fast-paced direction is tight and extraordinarily effective, not only in evoking the minutiae of daily living of volatile men—bored, anxious, homesick, in cramped quarters lacking

Lieutenant Werner looks on helplessly as the dying captain watches his cherished boat sink in the La Rochelle docks following an Allied attack.

privacy—but in capturing as well the frantic nightmare of the submarine in crisis, with nerve-racking charges detonating close by or her depth capacity exceeded, with resulting popping gaskets, gushing water, and shortage of oxygen. Attention to detail—one toilet for fifty men, the mildewed bread, the sweat and grime of the overworked sailors—heightens the film's realism. The use of a hand-held camera (mounted on a gyroscope to steady the picture) darting back and forth in the boat throughout violent clashes with the enemy increases the excitement. Many close-ups of the beleaguered crew keep it an intensely human drama. We must acknowledge Jost Vacano's distinguished photography, Klaus Doldinger's throbbing score, and the many talented technicians who helped make *Das Boot* remarkable. Demythologizing the aura of the "gray wolves," as the U-boats were called, and exposing the hell on earth that was the actuality of submarine warfare, the movie pays homage to the brave men who served, without espousing the cause for which they futilely offered their lives. Suspenseful and breathtaking, *Das Boot* brilliantly offers an audience an unforgettable, vicarious experience—which is almost unbearable at times—and ranks among the outstanding antiwar films of all time.

HONORS

Nominated for six Oscars: Direction; Screenplay Adaptation; Cinematography; Milan Bor, Trevor Pyke, and Mike Le-Mare for Sound; Editing; and Mike Le-Mare for Sound Effects Editing (1982)

57

CÉLESTE

WEST GERMANY / 1981

PELEMELE FILMPRODUKTIONS/BAYERISCHER RUNDFUNK (MUNICH)

CREDITS

Director and screenwriter: Percy Adlon, based on *Monsieur Proust* by Céleste Albaret (1973); *Producer:* Eleonore Adlon; *Cinematographer:* Jürgen Martin (color); *Music:* César Franck's String Quartet in D Major, performed by the Bartholdy Quartet; *Editor:* Clara Fabry;

A portrait of **Céleste** (Eva Mattes) waiting to see M. Proust regarding the position of housekeeper.

Art director: Hans Gailling; *Running time:* 107 minutes; *16mm rental source and videocassette:* New Yorker.

CAST

Céleste Albaret: Eva Mattes; *Marcel Proust:* Jürgen Arndt; *Odilon:* Norbert Wartha; *Robert Proust:* Wolf Euba.

German director Percy Adlon (1935–   ), after realizing a series of documentaries for television, made his auspicious feature film debut with the low-budget and highly praised *Céleste*, drawn from the memoirs of Céleste Albaret (1891–1984), the faithful housekeeper of the celebrated French writer Marcel Proust until his death in 1922. When she was eighty-two, she finally consented to be interviewed extensively by biographer Georges Belmont concerning the great author, whom she first ran errands for in 1912 before starting to manage his household two years later. Exemplary servant, nurse, and friend, Céleste had an unusual—even extraordinary—relationship with Proust, which forms the basis of the movie. For

After a shave by M. François, Marcel Proust (Jürgen Arndt), enjoying his footbath, looks forward to a rare reunion with the Countess Chevigné.

dramatic purposes the director focuses on the novelist's final years and restricts the action to his apartment in Paris at 102 Boulevard Haussmann with its legendary cork-lined bedroom where the writer wrote most of *Remembrance of Things Past*, although in point of fact he was forced to leave there in 1919 and subsequently resided at two other addresses.

Céleste is structured by means of association, not through chronology; thus Proust's returning from a rare evening out will trigger in the housemaid's mind memories of other excursions. The exceptionally versatile Eva Mattes portrayed Céleste, while theater actor Jürgen Arndt essayed the role of Proust. Though many pictures attempting to capture an author's life wind up with synthetic posturings or stilted veneration, *Céleste* is eminently convincing throughout and faithful to the spirit of the master novelist and his rapport with the sacrificing woman whom he admired enormously. Considering the slight plot, it is to Adlon's credit that this impeccably acted character study—an oblique look at a genius—remains con-

sistently engrossing. *Céleste*—which helped launch the director's international career—is an absolute gem of a movie and deserves to be better known.

The film begins by establishing the daily routine of the young housekeeper Céleste (Eva Mattes) patiently waiting in the kitchen in the late afternoon for her employer, M. Proust (Jürgen Arndt), to ring for his café au lait. She informs us that coffee and milk have been his sole nourishment for the last six months. He writes at night and through the early morning; she sleeps from eight A.M. till three P.M. Céleste recalls her husband, Odilon (Norbert Wartha), whose taxicab is always at the disposal of the writer, first bringing her to the apartment eight years ago in 1914. The persistent clangor of the alarm interrupts her reverie; she dashes inside his bedroom and hastily prepares an inhalant for the sickly man suffering an asthmatic attack. The resourceful Céleste, facing the chaotic disarray of Proust's copious additions to his manuscript, scattered on sheets of paper, pastes them together— thus assembling a "concertina." She chides him for neglecting his sleep, but he maintains that he must work continually on his novel. An animated Proust breaks his hermitic existence by arranging to call on the Countess Chevigné. Afterward he's exhausted, saddened at the changes in his once-beautiful friend. This awakens former homecomings, from a lively dinner with Jean Cocteau among others to a glum visit to a male brothel to

Coming back from a dinner party, M. Proust applauds heartily when Céleste repeats an anecdote regarding his friend, the Abbé Mugnier.

M. Proust escorts his cherished
housemaid Céleste into the salon to
hear a string quartet play Franck.

spy through a peephole on a masochist finding
release through a beating.

A day passes without Céleste's being summoned and the frantic servant discovers that the
writer was experimenting to apprehend what the
death experience is like. Winning the Prix
Goncourt in 1919 makes the ailing, private author
famous. At last he completes his magnum opus,
save for the ceaseless revisions. He hires musicians to perform a Franck piece in his home and
begs Céleste not to permit any injections that
might prolong his life. Later, weakened by the flu,
Proust spends every moment on the proof sheets
and rejects the exhortations of his physician
brother, Robert (Wolf Euba), to enter a clinic. "I'll
have no one but Céleste, she's the only one who
understands me," he insists. The wearied woman,
Odilon, and Robert attend Proust's death. Céleste
clips a lock of his hair for his brother, then another
for herself. Her unstinting, selfless labor is over;
she is contented with her contribution in aiding
her esteemed M. Proust finish his masterpiece.

Adlon carefully develops the complex relationship between Proust—hypersensitive, sophisticated, fastidious—and Céleste—simple, country
bred, genial—whom the novelist treats gently. She
is in awe of him and, instinctively sensing his
needs, acts both as his caring mother and adoring
child. The one area he perceives that she cannot
fathom is his homosexuality. In one scene Céleste
naively asks him why he never married since she
feels he would have been a kind husband and a
good father. Proust replies that he'd have to have a
wife who comprehends him: "And as I only know
one woman like that in the whole world, I could
only have married you." When he quickly adds
that she's much better suited to replace his
mother, we notice that she reacts as if rejected. Eva
Mattes completely submerges herself in the part of
Céleste and gives a subtle, flawless performance.
Jürgen Arndt persuades us that he is Marcel
Proust, the sensitive dandy who was a prodigy.

Adlon's direction is pure and irreproachable.
Confining himself chiefly to Proust's apartment,
he nonetheless produces a very cinematic film of
this most prolix of writers—even the scenes of
Céleste waiting with the clock ticking are most
dramatic. Many close and close-up shots accentu-
ate a feeling of intimacy. The director achieves a
documentary effect by permitting the considerate
housemaid to address the camera as if she were
being interviewed; by attending to such absorbing
minutiae of the eccentric author as his having his
mail disinfected; and by selecting the authentic
detail: When M. François, the barber, arrives, he
puts his hands to his forehead, then warms them
over the stove before touching Proust. Or, readying
for a jaunt, the novelist stuffs cotton plucked by
Céleste into his collar to prevent exposure to
drafts. Even his bed cluttered with crockery for
warming it and strewn with pages of notes adds to
the realism. There is a wonderful moment when
Proust, near death, tells Céleste, "I should've liked
to have written you a letter," and she answers in
her self-effacing manner, "You have better things
to do than that." Much shared affection is implied,
formal relations notwithstanding. Jürgen Martin's
dimly lit scenes capture the nocturnal world of
Marcel Proust; the exquisite Franck Quartet enhances the delicate mood. Like the music, the
movie may be described as chamber music. An
interior yet compelling film, an uncommon study
of mutual devotion, *Céleste* is a lovely work of art
that lets us quietly eavesdrop on the life of a genius
and his remarkable, consummate servant.

58
DANTON

FRANCE/POLAND / 1982

GAUMONT/T.F. 1 (TÉLÉVISION FRANÇAISE 1)
S.F.P.C.-T.M./LES FILMS DU LOSANGE
(PARIS)/PRODUCTION GROUP X (WARSAW)

CREDITS

Director: Andrzej Wajda; *Assistant directors:* Hugues de Laugardière, Krystyna Grochowicz; *Producer:* Margaret Ménégoz; *Screenwriter:* Jean-Claude Carrière, after the play *The Danton Affair* by Stanislawa Przybyszewska (1931), with the collaboration of Andrzej Wajda, Agnieszka Holland, Boleslaw Michalek, Jacek Gasiorowski; *Cinematographer:* Igor Luther (color); *Music:* Jean Prodromides; *Editor:* Halina Prugar-Ketling; *Art director:* Allan Starski; *Running time:* 136 minutes; *16mm rental source:* Swank; *Videocassette:* RCA/Columbia.

CAST

Georges Danton: Gérard Depardieu; *Maximilien Robespierre:* Wojciech Pszoniak; *Camille Desmoulins:* Patrice Chereau; *Lucile Desmoulins:* Angela Winkler; *Saint-Just:* Boguslaw Linda; *Eleonore Duplay:* Anne Alvaro; *Philippeaux:* Serge Merlin; *Legendre:* Bernard Maitre; *Fouquier-Tinville:* Roger Planchon; *Bourdon:* Andrzej Seweryn; *Westermann:* Jacques Villeret; *Billaud-Varenne:* Jerzy Trela; *Jacques-Louis David:* Franciszek Starowieyski; *Eleonore's Brother:* Angel Sedgwick.

Controversial Polish director Andrzej Wajda (1926–   ) had initially intended to film 40 percent of a drama of the French Revolution, *The Danton Affair*, in Poland where he had previously staged it, and 60 percent in France. Following the imposition of martial law in 1981, the director prudently left his country to shoot it entirely in Paris. Whereas playwright Przybyszewska was biased toward Robespierre, the screenwriters' sympathies favored Danton, although both figures are depicted as complex personalities and not reduced to simplistic villain/hero categorizing.

The time is spring 1794. Maximilien Robespierre, who heads the Committee of Public Safety, is in crisis. At war with almost all of Europe, confronting invasions, sundry uprisings, and food

A portrait of the revolutionary leader Georges Danton (Gérard Depardieu).

shortages that threaten to topple the fledgling Republic, the radial Jacobin leader feels he must accelerate his Draconian measures to prevent anarchy. Ironically Robespierre had earlier opposed the death penalty, but subsequently all perceived enemies are sent to the guillotine. Georges Danton, torchbearer of the left-wing Cordelier faction, returns to Paris from his country retreat in an effort to stem the bloody Terror, which, however, he was instrumental in inaugurating. The fateful clash between the two spokesmen is the film's central thrust. "What I'm interested in is the conflict of concepts," Wajda said. "Robespierre," he stressed, "believes in pushing the Revolution to its extreme limits. But Danton wants to stop the Revolution because he believes that each step is leading father away from its original ideals." Gérard Depardieu was perfectly cast as Danton; the talented Wojciech Pszoniak re-created his stage role of Robespierre. Confining itself to the tumultuous final days of the doomed Danton; emphasizing the thrilling collision of ideas, not mere spectacle; capturing, as the director said, "the atmosphere of revolution," Wajda's *Danton* is a powerful and provocative movie. More than a historical picture, this classic may be read not only as an allegory of contemporary Poland, but as a contemplation on the eternal questions of politics and revolution.

The film opens with Danton (Gérard Depardieu) approaching Paris in his carriage. After hearing a newspaper attack on the Committee of Public Safety's despotic behavior by Danton's friend, Camille Desmoulins (Patrice Chereau), an ill Robespierre (Wojciech Pszoniak) orders the Cordelier press closed down. At a heated meeting of the Revolutionary Tribunal, Saint-Just (Boguslaw Linda) and other members want Danton tried for subversion, but the Jacobin leader warns that a trial against the popular hero would reinforce the counterrevolution and compel him to rule by force, which he dreads: "Terror is merely despair." In the antechamber of the National Convention an anxious Westermann (Jacques Villeret) fails to enlist Danton's assistance in overthrowing the government. The Cordelier does not desire power and doesn't feel threatened. Desmoulins and additional colleagues urge him to act, but Danton suggests instead that they denounce one of Robespierre's feared secret police in the assembly that day. When his agent is accused, Robespierre arranges for a conciliatory reunion with his former ally. At the Café Rose a confident Danton greets the composed Jacobin, who invites him in vain to join the ruling ranks. Robespierre defends his use of violence to stifle opposition and objects to his rival's arrogance and opportunism. Danton mocks the Jacobin's unrealistic idealism and declares, "I'd rather be executed than be an executioner."

During a late-night Tribunal session Robespierre orders the immediate arrest of the Cordelier and his accomplices. Though forewarned, the cocky Danton doesn't flee but lets himself be taken into custody. News of his imprisonment convulses the Convention. Legendre (Bernard Maitre) introduces a motion that Danton be allowed to address it, but Robespierre indicts the Cordelier and adroitly manipulates the volatile group to retract the proposal. At the Luxembourg jail an assured Danton believes that with his oratory skill the jury trial will be the means of exposing and subverting the detested Committee. However, with reporters

A portrait of Danton's adversary, Maximilien Robespierre (Wojciech Pszoniak), the "Incorruptible."

barred, defense witnesses denied, and accusers absent, it is a rigged, political inquisition. Despite his rousing, impassioned speeches—"The people have only one dangerous enemy: the government!"—Danton is eventually muzzled after the "discovery" of trumped-up charges of a conspiracy and is sentenced to be executed. The Cordelier predicts—with uncanny accuracy—the collapse of the regime in three months. On April 5, Danton is guillotined. Saint-Just rushes into Robespierre's apartment with the good news that the Cordelier's death passed without incident and insists that the feverish Jacobin proclaim himself dictator now. Robespierre realizes agonizingly how far they have strayed from the democratic goals of the Revolution. This point is reinforced when his housekeeper (Anne Alvaro) ushers in her little brother (Angel Sedgwick) to recite by rote the "Declaration of the Rights of Man and the Citizen."

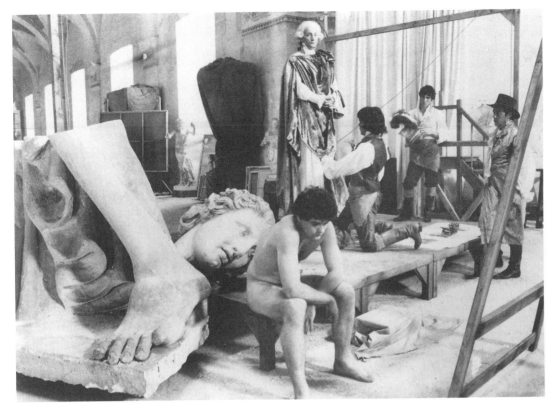

Robespierre poses for an official painting in the studio of Jacques-Louis David (Franciszek Starowieyski) *(in hat).*

Danton is represented as earthy, emotional, and self-serving. A humane character, his flaw is an overconfidence that blinds him to his vulnerable political position. Robespierre is portrayed as ascetic, intellectual, and inflexible. His Machiavellian quote, "When the Republic's at stake, we can do anything!" indicates his extremistic political philosophy. Gérard Depardieu is completely convincing and appealing as Danton and gives a bravura performance, particularly throughout the trial sequence during which his voice becomes increasingly hoarse as he perseveres with his stirring tirade against the repressive ruling clique. With his forceful screen presence Wojciech Pszoniak memorably incarnates Robespierre, making him a sinister, yet not totally unsympathetic, person.

Wajda's direction is tight. By restricting his shots to medium and close ones, he keeps his film intimate. The director concentrates on the pulsating drama of ideas while not neglecting the telling detail: After Danton's beheading the camera moves beneath the platform to catch his blood raining upon the fresh, absorbent hay and down the wooden beams. Jean Prodromides created a dissonant, ominous score. Contrary to some misconceptions, Wajda is not against the French Revolution, which he said "brought humanity the

Danton, about to be guillotined: "Show my head to the people; they do not see the like every day."

most beautiful ideals imaginable." Critics noticed a parallel to modern Poland, Danton representing Lech Walesa and the forces of Solidarity and Robespierre standing for the Communist Party chief, Gen. Wojciech Jaruzelski, or Stalin. The

211

director admits that the struggle of the Polish workers "is certainly evoked—but, of course, from a great distance." Beautifully acted and directed, full of stimulating lines—regarding a free press, Desmoulins remarks, "If Moscow had one, it would be free"—*Danton* succeeds in making the French Revolution a burning, timeless issue.

HONORS

Prix Louis Delluc (1982)
César for Best Director (1982)
Best Foreign Language Film, British Academy Award (1983)

59
L'ARGENT

FRANCE/SWITZERLAND / 1983

Marion's Films/FR 3 (France Régions 3) (France)/EOS Films, S.A. (Switzerland)

CREDITS

Director and screenwriter: Robert Bresson, based on Leo Tolstoy's *The Forged Coupon* (aka *The Forged Note*) (1911); *Producer:* Jean-Marc Henchoz; *Cinematographers:* Pasqualino De Santis, Emmanuel Machuel (color); *Music:* Bach's Chromatic Fantasy and Fugue; *Editor:* Jean-François Naudon; *Art director:* Pierre Guffroy; *Running time:* 90 minutes; *16mm rental source:* New Yorker.

CAST

Yvon: Christian Patey; *Older Woman:* Sylvie van den Elsen; *Her Father:* Michel Briguet; *Elise:* Caroline Lang; *Lucien:* Vincent Risterucci; *Female Photographer:* Béatrice Tabourin; *Male Photographer:* Didier Baussy; *Norbert:* Marc Ernest Fourneau; *His Father:* André Cler; *His Mother:* Claude Cler; *Martial:* Bruno Lapeyre; *Yvette:* Jeanne Aptekman.

Following *Le Diable Probablement (The Devil Probably)* (1977), it took six years before veteran French director Robert Bresson (1907–   ) could obtain sufficient funding to make his thirteenth feature, *L'Argent (Money)*, not to be confused with the similarly titled Émile Zola novel or Marcel

L'Herbier's modernized, cinematic version of it (1929). The source was Russian—not the works of Dostoevsky, whom he had adapted twice before—but this time Leo Tolstoy's final short novel, *The Forged Coupon*, published posthumously. The novella was a harrowing account of the mushrooming effects of evil, which include destroyed lives and many murders, after an initial mere act of forgery by two teenage boys. Yet at a certain point—as a pebble dropped into a pond creates wavelets until, reaching the farther shore, they reverse their course and ripple back to the point of origin—the spreading contamination yields to the triumphant power of an all-encompassing goodness.

Bresson condensed and simplified a convoluted, multicharacter story that took more than a decade to unfold; merged two personages into a single protagonist; made such apt alterations as changing Ivan Mironov, the downtrodden peasant who peddles firewood, into Yvon Targe, the laborer who delivers heating oil; and set his narrative in contemporary Paris. The major difference is that the director ends his film suddenly after Yvon's second rampage without pursuing Tolstoy's theme of redemption. *L'Argent* afforded Bresson the opportunity to excoriate materialism: "O money, visible god!" exclaims a prisoner, while the director further stressed, "It is an abominably false god." In his traditional manner, Bresson used nonprofessionals, whom he referred to as "models." *L'Argent* was widely hailed as one of the greatest films of a director who can rightly be considered a master. Through its brilliant, personal style it produces a riveting impact. *L'Argent* is a disturbing, austere, and most vital film.

The film opens as Norbert (Marc Ernest Fourneau), a pampered adolescent, requests in vain an advance on his allowance from his bourgeois father (André Cler). Anxious to pay off a debt, the youth motorcycles to his friend Martial (Bruno Lapeyre), who produces a five-hundred-franc bill that is counterfeit. They head to a photography shop and successfully pass it off to the attendant (Béatrice Tabourin). Later the manager (Didier Baussy) angrily detects the note as fraudulent and, when Yvon (Christian Patey)—the fuel-oil deliveryman—presents his bill, has his employee Lucien (Vincent Risterucci) fob it off on him along with two others recently acquired. In a restaurant Yvon is told that all three are fake; the police are summoned. Back in the store in front of an inspector, Lucien denies knowing the worker—to his

Trouble starts for Yvon (Christian Patey) when the waiter rejects his money as counterfeit and calls him a thief.

Carrying her daughter, Yvette (Jeanne Aptekman), Elise (Caroline Lang) leaves the courthouse after her husband's hearing.

consternation—and commits perjury during a court hearing. The judge cautions Yvon about accusing innocent people; afterward, the lying witness receives a bonus from his supervisor. Yvon is discharged from his job. Caught overcharging, Lucien is dismissed. The photography saleswoman recognizes Norbert and follows him to his school, but his mother (Claude Cler) bribes her not to make any bother.

An unemployed Yvon gets involved in an aborted bank robbery and is sentenced to three years. Lucien ransacks the photographers and embarks on a life of crime. Elise (Caroline Lang) informs her husband, Yvon, by letter that their daughter, Yvette (Jeanne Aptekman), has died of diphtheria; he is devastated. Lucien capriciously mails a large check to his former employers, whose circumstances are now straitened. Taunted by convicts at mealtime, Yvon tries to hurt them with a heavy strainer but is constrained and sent to solitary confinement. Awaiting him when he's freed from detention is another letter from Elise, who doesn't wish to see her husband again. Yvon attempts suicide. Lucien is incarcerated in Yvon's penal institution; he reveals to the now hardened prisoner his desire to atone for hurting him. After leaving the penitentiary, Yvon murders a hotelier, then befriends an older woman (Sylvie van den Elsen), who allows him to sleep in her garage. Her

Elise visits her repentant spouse Yvon in prison. She cannot bring herself to disclose that their child is dead.

A guard restrains an enraged Yvon from hitting some mocking inmates with a skimmer.

relates his sober tale with striking precision in ninety swift minutes. Marvelous economy is exhibited in the brevity of scenes and such brief tableaux as Lucien's thwarted jailbreak during which the camera remains solely on the door inside a dark cell while we hear darting footsteps and sirens and see through the crack below a corridor instantly illuminated. The director's use of sound effects is impressive, notably the skimmer's startling noise as it crashes on the ground after a guard forces Yvon to drop it, or the jolting slap that the old man administers to his daughter for harboring the conceivably dangerous stranger. Violence, typically, is suggested offscreen. Thus at the Hotel Moderne after Yvon's pent-up fury begins to be released through murder, all that we glimpse of the horror is a shot of his washing his ensanguined hands over a sink. And later, raising his ax over the woman—his last victim—we cut to a wall being splashed with her blood. Though many critics have viewed *L'Argent* as a bleak and totally pessimistic film, Yvon's ambiguous surrendering and Lucien's transformation are signs of hope, although Bresson obviously stops far short of Tolstoy's manifestation of spiritual victory. Indeed, he seems to represent, like a Jansenist, a world enmeshed in corruption where, he says, "a simple fake bill provokes a fantastic avalanche of Evil." *L'Argent* is a provocative masterpiece crowning an extraordinary career.

HONORS

Shared Grand Prix du Cinéma de Création, Cannes Film Festival (1983)

60
EL SUR

SPAIN/FRANCE / 1983

ELIAS QUEREJETA PRODUCCIÓNES CINEMATOGRÁFICAS (MADRID)/CHLOE PRODUCTIONS (PARIS)

CREDITS

Director and screenwriter: Victor Erice; *Assistant director:* John Healey; *Producer:* Elias Querejeta; *Cinematographer:* José Luis Alcaine (color); *Music:* Ravel's

father (Michel Briguet) orders her to tell him to go away. One night Yvon butchers the man, some relatives—even the kind lady—with an ax. In a café Yvon walks up to a policeman and confesses the slayings. Several officers escort the handcuffed man from the place.

Since Bresson minimizes exposition—eschewing facile psychological theorizing—we must look for clues in Yvon's earlier behavior to comprehend his subsequent shocking manslaughter. A fierce pride is a factor. When Elise proposes he speak to his senior who cashiered him, he replies ominously that he will not grovel. His capacity for destruction is displayed in the prison mess hall when he abruptly and ferociously loses his temper. With his little girl dead and his wife forsaking him, Yvon has become a toughened character. Bresson said, "Society abandons him. His carnage is like the explosion of his despair." Significantly, prior to his concluding lethal outburst, he stares quickly at toys in a shop window. With their frequently downcast eyes and neutral voices—the better to emphasize internal conflict—Christian Patey as Yvon and the other cast of amateurs are remarkably effective.

Bresson's direction is idiosyncratically elliptical and original. Concentrating on the essential, he

Initiating his daughter, Estrella (Sonsoles Aranguren), into the mysteries of the pendulum is Agustin (Omero Antonutti).

Quartet in F Major, Schubert's Quartet in C Major, Granados's *Spanish Dances*, and popular songs; *Editor:* Pablo G. Del Amo; *Art director:* Antonio Belizon; *Running time:* 94 minutes; *16mm rental source:* New Yorker.

CAST

Agustin: Omero Antonutti; *Estrella at Eight:* Sonsoles Aranguren; *Estrella at Fifteen:* Iciar Bollain; *Julia:* Lola Cardona; *Milagros:* Rafaela Aparicio; *Dona Rosario:* Germaine Montero; *Laura,* aka *Irene Rios:* Aurore Clément; *Irene Rios's Costar:* Francisco Merino; *Casilda:* Maria Caro.

Agustin, his wife, Julia (Lola Cardona), and young daughter, Estrella, bid farewell to his departing mother and Milagros, who came for the child's first Communion.

From the street Estrella silently observes her father composing a letter in a café to a long-lost love.

After *The Spirit of the Beehive* it took almost a decade before Victor Erice was able to direct his second feature, *El Sur (The South).* Set in the 1950s in northern Spain, the film focuses on the relationship of a young girl, Estrella, with her enigmatic father and her efforts to understand this unhappy man, alienated from his roots in the South. The director had envisaged a much longer film, about two and a half hours—the first part with a locale in the North, the second in the South—which would eventually be shown on television in three episodes following its theatrical release. In the second, unfilmed section, Estrella would discover the South and not only come to comprehend her cryptic parent but also learn her true identity. However, a change in television administration resulted in loss of interest and backing for the project as originally conceived, and pressure was put upon Erice to ready the completed first portion for showing at Cannes in 1983. Hopes to resume shooting

215

A teenage Estrella (Iciar Bollain) starts wiping off the message that a tiresome boyfriend chalked on her wall: a star (representing her forename in Spanish) and "I love you" ending with the lad's caricature.

Part Two were dashed. In spite of the fact that the director considers his film unfinished, *El Sur* was accepted as a self-contained work and critically acclaimed. Although his penchant is to select nonprofessionals, Erice cast Omero Antonutti as Agustin, the troubled father. He's an actor best known for his work in films for the Taviani brothers. *El Sur* was shot in Madrid, Ezcaray, Vitoria, Zamora, and in El Escorial. As in his earlier film, mood and characterization predominate over plot. The picture is structured in the main as an extended flashback, with the voice-over of a mature Estrella eliciting the memory of her beloved father. Subtly, in an incremental fashion, we piece together a portrait of a tragic figure. Generally overlooked when it appeared in this country, this compelling and beautifully executed film is one of the finest movies to come from Spain.

The film opens in the fall of 1957. While her worried mother (Lola Cardona) shouts for her missing husband, Agustin (Omero Antonutti), Estrella (Iciar Bollain), their fifteen-year-old daughter, ominously finds her father's pendulum in a container under her pillow. She senses he won't be coming back and cries. The flashback begins as the narrator depicts a scene she's imagined in which her medical-doctor father determines with his pendulum that his pregnant wife will have a girl. The physician finds employment in a hospital and rents a sequestered house. Estrella (Sonsoles Aranguren) is near eight and is fascinated by her withdrawn father, who spends much time in a locked attic. The mother, who lost her teaching position after the Civil War, educates the child at home. The daughter knows nothing regarding the doc-tor's past but feels protected and secure in his presence. Estrella is told that Agustin had quarreled bitterly with his father and will never return to the South. She fantasizes about that alluring region—actually Andalusia—and collects postcards from there.

On the eve of Estrella's first Communion Agustin's aristocratic mother (Germaine Montero) and friendly nursemaid Milagros (Rafaela Aparicio)—but not his father—arrive. We learn from the nanny that her missing grandparent had supported the Fascists, while the physician was a Loyalist who was subsequently imprisoned. During the religious ceremony the father makes a rare appearance in the church, delighting Estrella. The women depart, whetting the child's interest in their homeland. Around that time the girl happens upon an envelope in her father's desk with drawings and the name *Irene Rios* written on it repeatedly. Who is she? Estrella supposes a hidden secret in his past. A few months thereafter Estrella finds his motorcycle parked close to a movie theater showing a melodrama featuring Irene Rios (Aurore Clément). Inside Agustin is entranced watching his former lover on the screen and, afterward, impulsively writes to her in a café. The daughter listens to her parents arguing, presumably about this actress whom he wishes to see. Estrella realizes that she knows nothing about her father.

Agustin hears from Irene Rios, whom he knew as Laura. In a voice-over the woman recalls their painful separation eight years ago, begs him not to write again, and closes her letter with "I love you." He packs a suitcase, disappears without leaving a word, but remains indecisively at a hotel close to the train station. He comes back; Estrella questions his strange behavior but her mother dissembles. The sullen child retaliates by hiding underneath her bed. Overhead in the garret the solitary Agustin thumps his walking stick on the floor, which she recollects as his indicating his pain was greater than hers. . . . Estrella, now fifteen, has grown emotionally distant from her father, who now drinks heavily. One day unexpectedly he invites her to lunch; he would like her to cut her class and stay, but she leaves. Later we see his dead body slumped over a rifle outside the town. The flashback ends as Estrella puts the pendulum—disused since Agustin's aborted flight—into its case. Milagros sends an invitation and the young girl eagerly awaits her trip to the South.

Estranged from his family, religion, and country, Agustin is a lonely, discontented man. Significantly, the walled city where he works emphasizes his solitude, and the name of his residence, The Seagull, evokes Chekhov's play, whose confused protagonist likewise eventually shoots himself. Agustin's feelings for Laura are torturous and unresolved. There is resonance in her screen murderer's passionate statement, "We could have been so happy." Estrella is sensitive, intuitive, and private like her father. We may wonder, what will be her fate? Omero Antonutti assuredly captures the elusive qualities of Agustin. With enormous sympathy for all his characters, Erice directs in his careful, idiosyncratically elliptical manner—was the father impetuously heading to Laura after receiving her response?—which nonetheless involves us deeply in their lives. He frequently uses a slow fade-in and concludes his scene with a gradual fadeout, suggesting the process of retrospection. The exquisite chamber music of Ravel and Schubert enhances these poignant remembrances as do the melancholic strains of "Andalusia" by Granados. José Luis Alcaine's subdued photography contributes to the somber mood. Impressive is the climactic luncheon scene. By requesting that his daughter remain with him, we perceive that Agustin's attempting to reach out to her and to break the impasse of communication between them. She declines and, by the door, waves her hand. He returns her greeting in a long shot that underscores his isolation. This last image of her father will haunt and disturb Estrella. An intense and deeply moving film, *El Sur* is a neglected gem awaiting recognition.

61

SUGAR CANE ALLEY

Rue Cases-Nègres

MARTINIQUE/FRANCE / 1983

SU. MA. FA. (MARTINIQUE)/ORCA PRODUCTIONS/ NEF DIFFUSION (FRANCE)

CREDITS

Director and screenwriter: Euzhan Palcy, based on the novel by Joseph Zobel (1950); *Assistant director:* Fred Runel; *Producers:* Michel Loulergue, Alix Regis; *Cinematographer:* Dominique Chapuis (color); *Music:* Groupe Malavoi; *Editor:* Marie-Josèphe Yoyotte; *Art direction:* Hoang Thanh At; *Running time:* 103 minutes; *16mm rental source:* New Yorker; *Videocassette:* Cinematheque.

CAST

José Hassam: Garry Cadenat; *M'man Tine:* Darling Légitimus; *Medouze:* Douta Seck; *M. Saint-Louis:* Joby Bernabe; *The Boss:* Francisco Charles; *Leopold's Mother:* Marie-Jo Descas; *Mme. Saint-Louis:* Marie-Ange Farot; *M. Stephen Roc:* Henri Melon; *"Twelve Toes":* Eugene Monna; *Carmen:* Joel Palcy; *Leopold:* Laurent Saint-Cyr.

Medouze (Douta Seck) *(left)* presents riddles for his clever protégé José Hassam (Garry Cadenat) *(right)* to solve. Hatless is "Twelve Toes" (Eugene Mona).

At fourteen, director Euzhan Palcy (1955–   ) made the exciting discovery of Joseph Zobel's autobiographical novel, *La Rue Cases-Nègres* (published here in 1980 as *Black Shack Alley*), set in her native Martinique. Beginning shortly after World War I when the author was five, the story—told in the first person—recounted the sacrifices of his grandmother and then his mother for the boy's education—the sole means of his escaping the hopeless fate of poor blacks, which was cutting

Bringing her grandson José to register at the school in Fort-de-France is M'man Tine (Darling Légitimus).

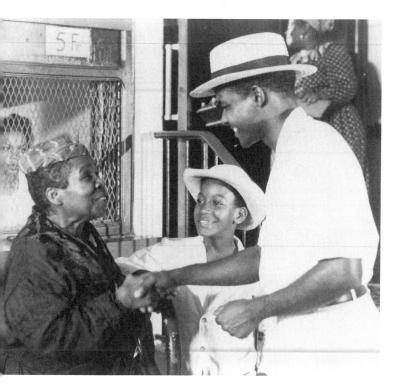

M'man Tine is delighted with the offer of Carmen (Joel Palcy) to permit José to sleep on the boat until they find accommodations in the capital.

sugarcane for the rich *békés* (white landowners). The book was as well a powerful indictment of colonialism. "The truth, the beauty, the violence, and the grandeur of this work astounded me," the director said. Four years later she prepared a scenario of it, one of several during the ten years it took the determined woman to bring *Sugar Cane Alley* to the screen. Ms. Palcy compressed the time frame of the novel, starting the movie in 1930 when her young protagonist, José, is eleven, and combined the dual roles of devoted grandmother and mother into the single, superb M'man Tine (a contraction of *Amantine*). The lad's infrequent offscreen commentary replaces the "I" narrator. Missing is the overt satire of religious instruction that inculcates submission of the oppressed to the oppressors. The heavy intrusion of social protest in the book—which at times seems far beyond the acumen of a little boy—is more subtlety conveyed in the film when José is a witness to various injustices. Actually in this, the director's affective first feature, the treatment of character is far more dimensional and developed than in the novel. Darling Légitimus and Douta Seck were the only professional actors; the rest were carefully selected when the picture was shot in Martinique. Rich in characterization, skillfully related, *Sugar Cane Alley* marks the noticeable debut of a fresh, remarkable talent who soon commenced an international career.

The film opens in Rivière Salée, Martinique, where the owners provide lowly shanties for the underpaid blacks who have the backbreaking task of cutting sugarcane and live in permanent economic dependency. It is August 1930. M'man Tine (Darling Légitimus) kisses her grandson José (Garry Cadenat) and heads to her arduous work in the fields. When kids break her treasured bowl, the boy gets punished. He sees Carmen (Joel Palcy), his womanizing friend whom he's teaching to write. At night the elderly Medouze (Douta Seck), a spiritual mentor for the orphaned child, describes the troubled plight of the blacks on the island: an uprising ended slavery, but not the financial bondage to the *békés*. He gives José a talisman that he carved. One day the mischievous, unsupervised children invade the garden of "Twelve Toes" (Eugene Mona) and, intoxicated on rum, manage to set fire to the place. For their pains they are recruited to help their parents, but M'man Tine refuses to allow José to join them: "I won't let you end up in the cane fields!" When school resumes, the teacher, M. Roc (Henri Melon), exhorts them to apply themselves; he becomes impressed with

José's intelligence and verbal abilities. The lad finds the missing Medouze dead in the cane fields. Learning that a supposed friend in town has been exploiting her grandson in return for lunch, M'man Tine moves near school so that she can cook for him. His mulatto chum Leopold (Laurent Saint-Cyr) is upset when his dying father—injured from a kick by a horse—refuses to legitimize his marriage and give him his aristocratic surname: "It's a white man's name." The boy runs away.

M. Roc escorts José to Fort-de-France where he takes a scholarship exam. He's successful, but it's only a quarter stipend as a day pupil. Undaunted by the enormous tuition balance, the grandmother relocates and turns to taking in laundry. At the new school an instructor accuses José of plagiarizing his outstanding essay; later he visits him in his car-crate home to apologize and arranges for the bright student to obtain a full scholarship and living expenses. The tired grandmother leaves by boat for home to have a new suit made for him. When she doesn't return, an anxious José goes back to Rivière Salée and finds her exhausted and ill. Leopold has been captured stealing a ledger whereby he'd hope to prove that the natives were being cheated. M'man Tine dies and José narrates, "Tomorrow I'll return to Fort-de-France, and I'll take my Black Shack Alley with me."

Outwardly tough, the pipe-smoking M'man Tine is caring, wise, and self-sacrificing for her young charge, knowing full well the meaning of the phrase that M. Roc has the pupils copy down on the first day of school: "Learning is the key that opens the second door to our freedom." A simple, pious, beautiful soul, she is an archetypal grandparent; when she passes away, we feel we've lost a friend. The impassioned Medouze transmits history orally to the youth and hones his political consciousness. José—a sensitive, healthy boy—benefits from the counsel and example of these two. Darling Légitimus is unforgettable as M'man Tine; Douta Seck lends authority to Medouze; and the photogenic Garry Cadenat is totally convincing as José.

Euzhan Palcy directs with control and grace. She avoids the pitfalls of sentimentalizing the children or else treating them as miniature adults; they act completely natural at all times. The director employs delightful humor and makes significant political revelations without being didactic. Two scenes linger in memory. In one, José in town, seeing M'man Tine ailing and resting on her bed, says through tears, "Someday I'll take care of you. We'll have a big house . . . with flowers, a hen, rabbits, pigs. . . . You won't have to go to the cane fields." She is deeply touched and smiles broadly—a lovely demonstration of the genuine love of each. In another scene, in Fort-de-France after realizing that she'll have to pay 87.50 francs tuition per trimester, M'man Tine is shocked and José disheartened. Suddenly she explodes: "They're wicked. A quarter scholarship. That's like giving nothing!" Turning in the courtyard, facing the school and raising her fist, with mounting anger she blurts out, "They don't know I'm a fighting woman! I won't give up that quarter scholarship! You'll attend their school!" A stirring display of her indomitable spirit. Palcy referred to learning in the period of the film as a "life buoy." In this well-acted, honest, and deeply moving human drama, the director has not only created a believable world but succeeded in expressing eternal truths with artistry and force.

HONORS

Darling Légitimus, Best Actress, and Silver Lion for
  First Work, Venice Film Fetival (1983)
César for Best First Film (1983)

62
HEIMAT

WEST GERMANY / 1984

EDGAR REITZ FILMPRODUKTION (MUNICH)/
WDR (WESTDEUTSCHER RUNDFUNK) (COLOGNE)/
SFB (SENDER FREIES BERLIN) (BERLIN)

CREDITS

Director and producer: Edgar Reitz; *Assistant directors:* Elke Vogt, Martin Höner; *Screenwriters:* Edgar Reitz, Peter Steinbach; *Cinematographer:* Gernot Roll (black and white, color); *Music:* Nikos Mamangakis; *Editor:* Heidi Handorf; *Art director:* Franz Bauer; *Running time:* 940 minutes; *Videocassette:* West Glen Communication.

CAST

Maria: Marita Breuer; *Paul as a Middle-aged Man:* Dieter Schaad; *Paul as a Young Man:* Michael Lesch; *Pauline as an Older Woman:* Eva Maria Bayerwaltes; *Pauline as a Young Woman:* Karin Kienzler; *Eduard:*

Rüdiger Weigang; *Lucie:* Karin Rasenack; *Katharina:* Gertrud Bredel; *Mathias:* Willi Burger; *Marie-Goot:* Eva-Maria Schneider; *Mäthes-Pat:* Wolfram Wagner; *Anton as an Older Man:* Mathias Kniesbeck; *Anton as a Young Man:* Markus Reiter; *Ernst as an Older Man:* Michael Kausch; *Ernst as a Young Man:* Roland Bongard; *Hermann as a Young Man:* Peter Harting; *Hermann as an Adolescent:* Jörg Richter; *Hermann as a Boy:* Frank Kleid; *Martha:* Sabine Wagner; *Wiegand:* Johannes Lobewein; *Frau Wiegand:* Gertrud Scherer; *Wilfried as a Young Man:* Hans-Jürgen Schatz; *Wilfried as a Child:* Markus Dillenburg; *Lotti as a Young Woman:* Gabriele Blum; *Lotti as a Child:* Andrea Koloschinski; *Glasisch:* Kurt Wagner; *Otto Wohlleben:* Jörge Hube; *Hans:* Alexander Scholz; *Klärchen:* Gudrun Landgrebe; *Robert Kröber:* Arno Lang; *Pieritz:* Johannes Metzdorf; *Apollonia:* Marlies Assmann; *Horst:* Andres Mertens; *Gabi:* Tanja Schlarb; *Robertchen:* Markus Schlarb.

Outraged by the distortions and stereotyping evinced in the American TV film *Holocaust* when it was broadcast in Germany in 1979, German director Edgar Reitz (1932–   ), protesting "the Americans have taken away our history," promptly set about beginning a long novel that would draw on his Hunsrück background and be an authentic and accurate alternative. A television producer friend suggested he prepare it as a script instead, in spite of the fact that the resulting film would far exceed a traditional length. The first fruits of this prodigious labor were a documentary, *Stories from the Hunsrück Villages,* made in 1981. Eventually, with backing from two leading Germany TV stations and his own life savings, Reitz began shooting his mammoth, two-thousand-page screenplay cowritten with Peter Steinbach, which came to be called *Heimat*—not to be confused with Carl Froelich's *Heimat,* a vehicle for Zarah Leander released in 1938, which it quotes from and parallels to an extent in theme and plot.

Rather than present the "Great German Events" in the manner of a didactic lecture, the director would focus on a particular Hunsrück village, the fictitious Schabbach, and three interconnecting families, a commingling of the Catholic and Protestant faiths, showing the way life was actually lived from the post–World War I period through far-reaching adjustments and catastrophe culminating in the early 1980s. History, thus, would be represented obliquely as it brought changes and challenges to the inhabitants, for the locality was preoccupied first and foremost with the daily problems of life and relegated to the periphery such

matters as politics, the Jewish problem, French POWs, etc. The work would not be a continuous narrative but would leap forward constantly to certain significant epochs and be developed episodically. A major unifying device is the introduction of technological inventions—the radio, the automobile, the telephone, highways, the "Simon Optical Works," etc.—which indicate the slow alteration of Schabbach from an agricultural to an industrial community. "My prime concern," Reitz said, "was not to transfer ideas but to recount concrete happenings, to stay, always, with the details of existence." He felt the traumatic repercussions after the collapse of the Reich inhibited his nation's recollections: "We have this enormous block that makes us fear the slightest connection with a past tormented by the weight of moral judgments." He hoped the film would be a means to help people release their suppressed remembrances and feelings and be a way "to generate communication." The director emphasized that *Heimat* "is an attempt of sorts to revive memories. . . . Our film takes place in those human gardens called villages. We are taking a close look. We try to avoid making judgments."

"I made *Heimat* as a film, not as a television serial," Reitz specified. Shot in 35mm, the truly epic movie—running fifteen hours and forty minutes, making it nineteen minutes longer than Fassbinder's lengthy *Berlin Alexanderplatz*—was shot chiefly in Woppenroth (Schabbach) and four other villages nestled among the Hunsrück Mountains in the Rhineland, with additional shooting elsewhere in Germany, from May 1981 to November 1982. The editing and lab work occupied another year and a half. Desiring fresh faces, the director selected little-known actors as well as townspeople to bring his vast cast to life. Some parts are played by different actors as the characters age whereas other roles, such as Maria, portrayed by Marita Breuer, are enacted by a sole performer. In all, Reitz spent over five years on his gargantuan project, which was his eighth feature film. *Heimat* was halved into approximately eight-hour sections for theatrical presentation on two successive days and divided into eleven parts for television transmission. The title is perfect: *Heimat* is a richly connotative word meaning "home" and "homeland" yet evoking an idealized, imagined world we impossibly long to return to. Regardless of its multitude of characters and time span of sixty-three years, *Heimat* remains a personal, even intimate, movie. This extraordinary picture had a limited exposure here and deserves to be better known; in Germany it has already achieved a legendary status.

The following is a much-condensed synopsis adhering to the more familiar television format: I. "The Call of Far Away Places" (1919–28). At the end of World War I, Paul Simon (Michael Lesch), a POW, walks from France to his home in Schabbach. He is incommunicative, absorbed in experimenting with the new marvel of radio, and not interested in pursuing the blacksmith trade of Mathias (Willi Burger), his father. He loves Apollonia (Marlies Assmann), an outsider whom the town scorns, but courts her halfheartedly. When she leaves for France, Paul marries Maria Wiegand (Marita Breuer), daughter of the mayor (Johannes Lobewein) and long in love with him. They have two sons, Anton and Ernst. Pauline (Karin Kienzler), Paul's younger sister, marries the jeweler Robert (Arno Lang) and lives with him in Simmern. One day the restless Paul disappears without saying a word. II. "The Center of the World" (1928–33). Eduard (Rüdiger Weigang), Paul's older brother, is sent to Berlin to cure his tuberculosis and there encounters and weds the ambitious Lucie (Karin Rasenack), who runs a brothel. The Nazis march and many anticipate a prosperous future. Mayor Wiegand is a staunch member; so is his cruel son Wilfried (Hans-Jürgen Schatz), who joins the SS. Katharina (Gertrud Bredel), the perceptive wife of Mathias, is suspicious of the Nazis, especially when her Communist nephew is imprisoned for "reeducation." III. "The Best Christmas Ever" (1935). Eduard is now mayor of nearby Rhaunen. Lucie tries to prod him in furthering his career, but the weak and unaspiring man is more interested in photography than in politics. They live in a sumptuous, newly built villa and entertain several prominent Nazi figures. IV. "The Highway" (1938). Otto Wohlleben (Jörg Hube), an engineer building a major highway near Schabbach, is billeted in Maria's house. Gradually the two lonely people fall in love. V. "Up and Away and Back" (1938–39). Unexpectedly, a letter arrives from Paul in America. He was successful, owns his own electrical equipment company in Detroit, and plans to sail to Germany in a year. Maria receives the news coldly; he has been dead to her for a long time. Otto is transferred. When Maria visits him, she learns that he's lost his position because his mother was Jewish. The perturbed woman terminates her affair with Otto and dutifully heads to Hamburg to see her husband.

However, since Paul lacks a certificate to prove that he's an Aryan, he's not allowed to disembark. World War II breaks out.

VI. "The Home Front" (1943). Martha (Sabine Wagner) marries by proxy Anton (Markus Reiter), assigned to a cinematographic crew in Russia. Otto has a tender reunion with Maria and is thrilled to lay eyes on their little boy, Hermann. Schabbach is bombed; Wilfried cooly mentions plans for a "final solution." VII. "Soldiers and Love" (1944). Otto is killed attempting to dismantle a bomb. The GIs come and requisition Eduard's villa. Mathias dies. VIII. "The Americans" (1945–47). A wealthy Paul (Dieter Schaad) shows up; Maria acts distant with him. Anton comes home after escaping from a Russian POW camp. Katharina expires; a disillusioned Paul departs. Anton tells Martha his dream of founding an optics manufacturing plant. IX. "Little Hermann" (1955–56). Germany experiences her economic miracle. With Paul's assistance, Anton (Mathias Kniesbeck) runs the flourishing Simon Optical Works. Ernst (Michael Kausch) has married into the comfortable family of a lumber merchant. Hermann (Jörg Richter), a sensitive teenager drawn to poetry and music, is the first in the family to attend secondary school. He becomes romantically involved with Klärchen (Gudrun Landgrebe), eleven years older. When she gets pregnant, she runs away and has an abortion. A possessive Maria finds a note from her to her son and, with Anton's support, takes action. After spending New Year's Eve together, Klärchen leaves Hermann with a letter she received from Maria and Anton threatening her with prison—for the illegal abortion and for corrupting a minor—should she see or write to the boy again. Devastated, Hermann grows estranged from his mother and will quit Schabbach for good when he's eighteen.

X. "The Proud Years" (1967–69). Anton is offered a large amount of money to sell his company. He finds his father in Baden-Baden, who advises him to accept the deal. Anton, however, declines the proposal and will persist in maintaining his standards of integrity and quality. Paul is more interested in encouraging Hermann (Peter Harting), now a serious composer of electronic music. When the son eventually drops in, bearded, with two girlfriends, Maria declares that she doesn't understand him. XI. "The Feast of the Living and the Dead" (1982). Maria, as old as the century, succumbs. Hermann tells a sick Paul that neither of them appreciated her while she was alive. An-

1923. The family has a Sunday picnic and, thanks to Paul's efforts, hears a broadcast from Vienna of Leo Slezak singing Schubert's "Lindenbaum." Seated *(left to right):* Glasisch (Kurt Wagner), Alois Wiegand (Johannes Lobewein), Paul (Michael Lesch), behind him Hans (Alexander Scholz), Maria (Marita Breuer), Eduard (Rüdiger Weigang), Katharina (Gertrud Bredel), Frau Wiegand (Gertrud Sherer), Wilfried (Markus Dillenburg), and Pauline (Karin Kienzler); standing behind Eduard *(left to right):* Mathias (Willi Burger), Marie-Goot (Eva-Maria Schneider), and Mäthes-Pat (Wolfram Wagner).

1933. Schabbach celebrates Hitler's birthday. Eduard (Rüdiger Weigang) poses with his new bride, Lucie (Karin Rasenack). The sign to the left reads, "Hitler is a Columbus." The memorial on the right is to the fallen in World War I. "Hitler rolls" are distributed in the rear center

1933. The maternal Frau Simon (Gertrud Bredel) brings her brother's granddaughter, Lotti (Andrea Koloschinski), back home after the girl's father was arrested for being a Communist.

ton needs a government subsidy to survive. In a spectral sequence, Maria greets her deceased relatives and friends, who watch the living enjoy a county fair. The film concludes with a contented Hermann, reconciled with Schabbach, performing and recording his oratorio celebrating his remarkable region.

Although there are many men in the cast, it is mainly the women who stand out, in particular the nurturing, self-abnegating Maria, who discovers in herself resources to endure much loneliness and suffering. Yet there is a rigid, puritanical streak in her that compels her to reject Otto and to act punitively and harshly with their son, Hermann, whom she unwillingly alienates during his troubled adolescence. There is Katharina, the splendid, archetypical grandmother with her bedrock character and beautiful soul who sees through the hollow promises of the fascists. The dreamy, unsettled Paul must obey his instincts to flee and not be symbolically trapped like the mar-

1938. After being captivated by watching Zarah Leander in *La Habañera*, Maria (Marita Breuer) *(left)* and her sister-in-law, Pauline (Eva Maria Bayerwaltes), inspect the latter's improvised coif imitating the famous Swedish actress.

1946. The irrepressible Lucie (Karin Rasenack)—hat adorned with an American flag!—with her son, Horst (Andreas Mertens), has a GI drive her to Schabbach to introduce herself to the recently returned Paul from America.

1955. Young Hermann (Jörg Richter) experiences the joys and sorrows of his first love with the elder Klärchen (Gudrun Landgrebe).

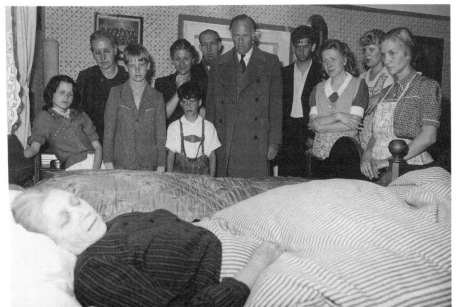

1947. Katharina (Gertrud Bredel), the beloved matriarch, passes away. Surrounding her *(left to right)* are Gabi (Tanja Schlarb) and Robertchen (Markus Schlarb) (Pauline's children), between them Marie-Goot (Eva-Maria Schneider), Pauline (Eva Maria Bayerwaltes), standing in front of her, Hermannchen (Frank Kleid), Eduard (Rüdiger Weigang), Paul (Dieter Schaad), Anton (Markus Reiter), Martha (Sabine Wagner), Lotti (Gabriele Blum), and Maria (Marita Breuer).

223

ten he caught. When he reappears, affluent, he feels out of place and cannot fit in. Anton calls his father a typical American, at home nowhere. To Reitz's credit, it is a sad moment when we have to leave these fascinating characters at the film's end since we have participated in their lives and have grown to know and love them—with the exception, of course, of such as the despicable Wilfried, who, unlike Eduard, has let Nazism destroy his humanity. The lovely and talented Marita Breuer is totally convincing at every stage in the long life of Maria; her performance is simply towering. Gertrud Bredel is wonderful as Katharina; Jörg Hube is memorable as Otto.

Reitz's direction is not flashy, but solid and controlled. When one considers that *Heimat* is the equivalent in length of eight feature films, the director manifestly demonstrates his superb strengths for narration and characterization as he skillfully depicts a nation in gradual transition. Through meticulous detail Reitz makes each epoch seem authentic and creates a sense of life as it was actually lived. There is an imaginative use of black and white shifting to color. When the young Paul comes back to his father's blacksmith shop following the close of World War I, the forge is momentarily seen in bright hues; when Ernst, a *Luftwaffe* pilot, drops a bouquet over Schabbach for his mother, the falling carnations burst into a breathtaking red. Gernot Roll's cinematography is exceptional.

Reitz avoids encapsulating Schabbach in sentimentality or rosy nostalgia. Far from rendering it as a pastoral paradise, he reveals its share of faults—its narrow-mindedness, complacency, xenophobia, and interolance that can persecute Apollonia or Klärchen, to say nothing of its contribution to the horrors of Nazism. Besides, the presence of pollution and the stress of contemporary life gainsay any idyllic representation of the village. For some, Schabbach is an area to escape from, like the young Paul and later Hermann; whereas for others like Katharina and Maria—even Anton—it is a *Heimat* where one's spirit may ripen. The sections re-creating the Reich are extremely powerful; "Little Hermann," with its intensive evocation of the flame of adolescent love and artistic yearning, makes a dynamic impression.

The force and intensity of the film tend to falter and slacken in the final two episodes, which fail to build to a strong climax. Perhaps the events depicted were too recent to permit a heightened, dramatic perspective that resonates. And while we may respect the screenwriters' endeavor to present in cogent imagery the transcendental concept of a demised Maria rejoining her family and companions who have passed on before her and continue to watch over those still alive, the result lacks the impact that would have made it truly poetic and astonishing on the order of that exquisite scene in Robert Benton's *Places in the Heart* (1984) in

224

which a communion ritual unites both the living and the dead. We need not quibble, for a tremendous pleasure and insight have been provided earlier. Although a youthful Paul has a vision of a slain comrade informing him, "In Heaven they speak Hunsrücker," the relevance of this spellbinding film is nonetheless universal. The director succeeded in generating a real village filled with believable people and evoking a sense of the irrevocable passage of time. With *Heimat* Edgar Reitz brought off a staggering feat and established himself as a masterful and lyrical recorder of the steps of his country in the twentieth century. A sequel, *Heimat II: Chronicle of a Generation,* running twenty-six hours, was released in 1992.

HONORS

International Film Critics Award, Venice Film Festival (1984)

63
RAN

JAPAN/FRANCE / 1985

HERALD ACE INC./NIPPON HERALD FILMS INC. (TOKYO)/GREENWICH FILM PRODUCTIONS (PARIS)

CREDITS

Director and editor: Akira Kurosawa; *Assistant director:* Fumiaki Okada; *Producers:* Masato Hara, Serge Silberman; *Screenwriters:* Akira Kurosawa, Hideo Oguni, Masato Ide; *Cinematographers:* Takao Saito, Masaharu Ueda, with the collaboration of Asakazu Nakai (color); *Music:* Toru Takemitsu; *Art directors:* Yoshiro Muraki, Shinobu Muraki; *Running time:* 160 minutes; *16mm rental source:* New Yorker; *Videocassette:* Foxvideo.

CAST

Hidetora Ichimonji: Tatsuya Nakadai; *Taro:* Akira Terao; *Jiro:* Jinpachi Nezu; *Saburo:* Daisuke Ryu; *Lady Kaede:* Mieko Harada; *Lady Sué:* Yoshiko Miyazaki; *Tango:* Masayuki Yui; *Ikoma:* Kazuo Kato; *Kyoami:* Peter; *Fujimaki:* Hitoshi Ueki; *Kurogane:* Hisashi Ikawa; *Tsurumaru:* Takeshi Nomura; *Ogura:* Norio Matsui; *Hatakeyama:* Takeshi Kato; *Ayabe:* Jun Tazaki.

Ran, the celebrated twenty-eighth feature of internationally renowned Japanese director Akira Kurosawa (1910–   ), had a long gestation. In 1976 after reading about Motonari Mori, an impressive lord from medieval Japan who was distinguished among other reasons for having three noteworthy sons, the director pondered what would have happened had they not been righteous and, commingling plot elements from Shakespeare's *King Lear,* fashioned an imaginative, fictive screenplay entitled *Ran.* Although "chaos" is its nearest English equivalent, Kurosawa pointed out that the term also signifies "rebellion." "In *Ran* I've tried to give Lear a history," the director said. "I try to make clear that his power must rest upon a lifetime of bloodthirsty savagery."

While there are many similarities to the play—Tango is a transposition of Kent, for example—there are some noticeable differences: Hidetora Ichimonji, the Lear figure, has three sons instead of daughters, for in the Sengoku Period (sixteenth century) in which the story takes place, Kurosawa avers that "to divide a realm among daughters would have been unthinkable." Unlike his counterpart, Hidetora does not partition his kingdom among his scions but rashly makes the eldest the sole ruler, thereby whetting the middle son's un-

Portrait of the Great Lord, Hidetora Ichimonji (Tatsuya Nakadai), shortly after abdicating power, which will result in his precipitous fall.

225

The malevolent, recently widowed Lady Kaede (Mieko Harada) menaces her brother-in-law, Jiro.

bridled ambition. The parallel subplot of Gloucester and his sons Edgar and Edmund was omitted. An important innovation is the vengeance-driven Lady Kaede, for the Great Lord had earlier butchered her father and brothers. It is more precise to refer to *Ran* as a variant on *King Lear*. A prior adaptation from Shakespeare was the director's esteemed *Throne of Blood* (1957) from *Macbeth*.

When producers shied away from the costly *Ran* project—deemed too pessimistic to be profitable— Kurosawa had to content himself with making hundreds of paintings and sketches of his envisioned film while despairing of ever realizing it. However, he was able to make *Kagemusha* (1980), a high-budget movie set in the Sengoku Period, which he regarded as a run-through for *Ran*. Though it was successful, the director had to wait several more years before a coproduction accord made financing the next feature possible. Costing $12 million, *Ran* became the most expensive Japanese picture up until then. Tatsuya Nakadai, long associated with Kurosawa's films, was cast in the demanding role of Hidetora. The film was shot between June 1984 and February 1985. Critically acclaimed, *Ran* proved a popular movie. An epic film with magnificent spectacle, beautiful direction, writing, acting, and photography, it is also a pungent meditation about the abuse of power. "The problems I like to deal with are *human*

problems, which are ageless," the director affirmed. An extraordinary achievement, *Ran* is a genuine cinematic masterpiece.

After a boar hunt the weary Great Lord, Hidetora Ichimonji (Tatsuya Nakadai), nearing seventy, stuns his guests by announcing the transfer of absolute rule to his eldest son, Taro (Akira Terao). Hidetora will keep thirty retainers; Jiro (Jinpachi Nezu), his second son, and Saburo (Daisuke Ryu), the youngest, will defend the Second and Third Castles respectively and will be subject to Taro. The honorable Saburo, fearing a power struggle, bluntly calls his father's action foolish and shortsighted. In a rage Hidetora expels him. When Tango (Masayuki Yui), the lord's staunch follower, defends him, he shares his fate. Lord Fujimaki (Hitoshi Ueki) catches up with the exiles and, impressed with Saburo's courageous stance, invites him to his dominion and to be his son-in-law; Tango will remain and attempt to serve the Great Lord. In the First Castle, Hidetora smarts at the arrogant assertiveness of Lady Kaede (Mieko Harada), Taro's dominating wife, and fells a soldier imperiling his servant-entertainer Kyoami (Peter) in a melee over possession of the Ichimonji standard. The ruling pair humiliate the Great Lord by forcing him to sign a formal pledge that he will submit to Taro's authority. Outraged, he storms off to the Second Castle.

Kurogane (Hisashi Ikawa) along with other confidants galvanize the second son's lust for power. Hearing Jiro refuse to admit his samurai, Hidetora departs bitterly. Tango, disguised as a hunter, comes upon him with his men in a field and reports that the warlord was officially banished. The wily aide Ikoma (Kazuo Kato), secretly in league with Taro, insists they head to the Third Castle. There, the Great Lord awakens to behold with shock Taro's and Jiro's armies beseiging it. His men are massacred. A victorious Taro is shot by Kurogane while entering the fortress. Now completely deranged, Hidetora staggers out of the bastion. Kyoami and Tango encounter him and stay by his side. In a lucid moment he recounts his sons perfidy and the anguished loss of his warriors. Alone together, Kaede catches Jiro off guard and, holding his sword over his throat, furiously demands to know her husband's murderer. Unconcerned about Taro's death, she's really worried about her future and, after seducing him, threatens to expose his villainy unless he kills his wife Sué (Yoshiko Miyazaki) and marries her. From the deserted remains of Azusa Castle, Tango espies Ikoma and the traitorous Ogura (Norio Matsui), outcasts by Jiro's decree, and before disposing of them learns that the Great Lord is to be murdered if he regains sanity. Since Hidetora dare not face his son, the devoted samurai decides to bring Saburo back to rescue his father. Sué, fleeing the wrath of Kaede, with her brother Tsurumaru (Takeshi Nomura), whom the Great Lord blinded in childhood, pause at Azusa to pay final respects to their dead.

Saburo and his troops enter Hachiman Field. Fujimaki trails with his legion. Against Kurogane's counsel, Jiro prepares for battle. With his battalion facing Saburo, he allows him to fetch their father, then withdraw. Lord Ayabe (Jun Tazaki) and his phalanx now flank Fujimaki. Sué leaves Tsurumaru to search for his flute and is soon beheaded. At Hachiman a messenger brings in Kyoami, who confesses he's lost Hidetora; Saburo sets forth to find him. Jiro orders gunners to pursue his brother, then attacks. Saburo reconciles with his father. Soon Jiro's soldiers are in rout. While returning, Saburo's a victim of a sniper and the Great Lord dies of a broken heart. Ayabe's forces vanquish the First Castle. Kaede glories in the destruction of the House of Ichimonji; Kurogane swiftly dispatches her. In Azusa the lone Tsurumaru lingers on in the darkness.

We witness the gradual character development in Hidetora as he is changed through painful suffering from being a ruthless despot to a guilt-ridden, vulnerable old man. "Forced to confront the consequences of his misdeeds, he is driven mad," the director said. "But only by confronting his evil head-on can he transcend it and begin to struggle again towards virtue." Displaying a vast range of emotions from bristling pride to doddering senility, Tatsuya Nakadai as the Great Lord is splendidly convincing and encompasses the tragic stature of the protagonist. Mieko Harada is memorable and spine-chilling as the ferocious—even reptilian—Lady Kaede. Kurosawa's direction is masterly. One of the most inventive and unforgettable battle scenes ever filmed is the onslaught upon the Third Castle boldly executed in dreamlike silence—the exclusive sound being that of Takemitsu's penetrating, somber score—with recurring shots in the midst of the carnage of gray, overcast skies. "I wished to indicate that this was seen from the point of view of heaven: heaven sees this incredible, bloody combat and becomes literally speechless," Kurosawa said. In short, pulsating, and skillfully edited scenes there is a blizzard of arrows and one after another of Hidetora's brave and pitifully outnumbered samurai is slain as the yellow bannerets of Taro's soldiers and the small red banners of Jiro's forces push ever forward into the blood-drenched donjon. Only with the startling impact of a bullet in Taro's back from Kurogane's rifle does the conflict burst audibly into the brutally realistic pandemonium of war. The effect of this exquisite sequence is truly breathtaking.

Though set in medieval Japan, Kurosawa's san-

In a temporary abatement of his insanity, Hidetora recognizes his daughter-in-law, Sué, atop the ruins of her father's Azusa Castle, and the wrongs he himself has perpetuated. Near him is the faithful Kyoami (Peter).

Having entered the domain to find his father peacefully, Lord Saburo (Daisuke Ryu) discovers his brother's troops confronting him before long. Alongside *(left)* is the loyal Hatakeyama (Takeshi Kato).

guinary tale of the misuse of power is universal in its application. Stimulating our reflective more than our emotional response, the director engages our examination of these frightful events. Tango's rebuke to Kyoami following the death of the Great Lord is particularly significant: "Do not blaspheme! It is the gods who weep. They see us killing each other over and over since time began. They can't save us from ourselves." And so are the haunting, concluding images of the solitary, abandoned Tsurumaru. Having accidentally dropped the scroll of the compassionate Buddha that his devout sister had given him to console him, the lost and blind youth gropes to the edge of an enormous cliff, then stands motionless and helpless in ever-receding extreme long shots. An apt symbol of contemporary man. The compelling and visually opulent *Ran* has joined the ranks of the great film classics of all time.

HONORS

Best Foreign Film, New York Critics Award (1985)
Oscar to Emi Wada for Best Costume Design; in addition, nominated for Direction, Cinematography, and Art Direction (1985)
Best Foreign Film, British Academy Award (1986)

64

BABETTE'S FEAST

Babettes Gaestebud

DENMARK / 1987

PANORAMA FILM INTERNATIONAL/NORDISK FILM/
DANISH FILM INSTITUTE

CREDITS

Director and screenplay: Gabriel Axel, based on the short story by Isak Dinesen published in *Anecdotes of Destiny* (1958); *Assistant director:* Tom Hedegaard; *Producers:* Just Betzer, Bo Christensen; *Cinematographer:* Henning Kristiansen (color); *Music:* Per Norgard; *Editor:* Finn Henriksen; *Art director:* Sven Wichmann; *Running time:* 102 minutes; *16mm rental source:* New Yorker; *Videocassette:* Orion.

CAST

Babette Hersant: Stéphane Audran; *Martine (middle-aged):* Birgitte Federspiel; *Martine (young):* Vibeke Hastrup; *Philippa (middle-aged):* Bodil Kjer; *Philippa (young):* Hanne Stensgard; *General Lowenhielm:* Jarl Kulle; *Lorens Lowenhielm (young lieutenant):* Gudmar Wivesson; *Achille Papin:* Jean-Philippe Lafont; *Swedish Lady:* Bibi Andersson; *Pastor:* Pouel Kern; *Fisherman:* Lars Lohmann.

It took fourteen years for Danish director Gabriel Axel (1928–   ) to bring to the screen his treatment of a remarkable short story called "Babette's Feast" by fellow Dane, Isak Dinesen (pseudonym of Karen Blixen), a project long deemed uncommercial by producers. The tale told of two spinster sisters shepherding the waning congregation founded by their late father, a Lutheran minister who exhorted a severe asceticism to his sect in a remote village in northern Norway. In 1871 a French woman, Babette Hersant, fleeing the bloody government reprisals against the Paris Commune, which had already claimed her husband and son, arrives seeking refuge. For fourteen years she's their unpaid housekeeper stoically

Achille Papin (Jean-Philippe Lafont) greets his future pupil Philippa (Hanne Stensgard) *(center)* while her sister, Martine (Vibeke Hastrup), looks on.

cooking their frugal fare until, with sudden lottery winnings, she reveals her culinary genius at an extraordinary dinner marking the centennial of the pastor's birth. "The feast is totally symbolical," says the director. A parable on art, the movie is also a meditation upon the conflicting paths of pleasure and self-denial.

Discovering that several prospective Norwegian settings were entirely too picturesque and therefore unsuitable for the drab community he envisioned for his film, Axel changed the locale to Jutland, where he built his lusterless hamlet. He made the sisters more middle-aged and emphasized a tone of tenderness toward the unworldly flock. The wonderful French actress Stéphane Audran was inspiredly cast as Babette; in addition were several Danish players, such as Birgitte Federspiel, familiar to us from their films with the great Carl Theodor Dreyer. Axel's feast for the mind as well as the senses proved a popular and much-lauded movie. *Babette's Feast* is a wise and distinguished work of art.

A lady narrates the film, which opens in a far-off locality. We learn that two aging sisters, Martine (Birgitte Federspiel) and Philippa (Bodil Kjer), are devoting their lives and small income caring for the dwindling members of an austere religious group established by their decreased father (Pouel Kern). Incongruously, they have a French maid, Babette (Stéphane Audran). By way of explanation, there's an extended flashback to the time when, as lovely young women, they attracted the eye of many youths, who were soon discouraged by their puritanical parent, setting little store by earthly love. Lorens Lowenhielm (Gudmar Wivesson), a debt-ridden lieutenant in the hussars, is banished to his aunt's house to reflect on his conduct. There he's smitten with the neighboring, angelic-looking Martine (Vibeke Hastrup) and through his relative gains entry to the clergyman's house. Frustrated by her seeming indifference, he departs and quickly decides to concentrate upon his career. Then Achille Papin (Jean-Philippe Lafont), a vacationing French opera singer, hears the enchanting voice of Philippa (Hanne Stensgard) in church and offers to train her. Fearful of the fame he promises and troubled by her emotional awakening to the teacher, she abruptly breaks off her lessons; the disheartened man returns home. Decades pass. One stormy night an exhausted Babette reaches the sisters' doorstep begging asylum. She bears a letter from her friend, M. Papin, who recommended the ladies to her. Informed of their straitened circumstances, the desperate woman volunteers to work without salary.

Holding her pick, a shrewd Babette (Stéphane Audran) successfully underbids the price stated by a local fisherman (Lars Lohmann).

Babette adds the finishing touches to the salad during her
unforgettable dinner.

Years later, in time present, the elderly parishioners become quarrelsome and open up old wounds among themselves. Babette unexpectedly obtains ten thousand francs from a lottery. She requests permission to prepare and pay for "a true French dinner" to celebrate the preacher's impending centenary. The sisters agree reluctantly, but as the date approaches and the strange cargo appears, dreading that they are abetting some sort of a "witches' Sabbath" from this Papist, they share their misgivings with their fold, who pledge not to pass any comment on the food but keep their thoughts on heavenly matters. The dinner is a triumph, not only for Babette and the visiting, sophisticated Lowenhielm (Jarl Kulle), now a general attending the ceremony with his aged aunt, but also for the brethren, who are reunited in harmony. Afterward Babette discloses to the sisters that she was previously head chef at the Café Anglais in Paris. No, she will not go back to France; no one waits for her there, and besides, she has spent everything on this meal. The sisters are astonished; Philippa embraces the splendid culinary artist.

Babette's extravagant gesture is only partially a way of showing her gratitude toward her benefactresses or, if you will, of challenging the rigid, life-denying values of the church members; it is mostly, following numerous arid years and finally having the means, a manner of expressing herself as an artist. When, at the end, the sisters commiserate with her that now she'll have to face a lifetime of poverty, Babette counters, "An artist is never poor." Though Achille Papin may look forward to hearing Philippa's voice in heaven ("There you will forever be the great artist God intended you to be"), Babette is the one who truly fulfills her destiny here through the medium of her art. It is the general who has a profound insight during the sublime repast when he comprehends that the claims of the spirit and those of the body need not be irreconcilable, that "mercy is infinite." With her marvelous screen presence and mature beauty, Stéphane Audran is an ideal Babette. Regarding the composition of the feast, she said, "I felt as though I was transcending the ingredients and performing a sacred act."

Axel's firm direction makes the Dinesen story compelling and seamless. One remembers the delicate scene of Achille Papin blissfully singing "La ci darem la mano" from Mozart's Don Giovanni with a hesitant Philippa tempted fleetingly to experience the raptures of love; the bizarre processional through the humble streets of exotic provisions for the meal, Babette in the lead with a crate of live quail, trailed by her young assistant shouldering a block of ice wrapped in a cloth, with two loaded carts behind him, one of which bears a live tortoise; and of course the climactic, saliva-inducing dinner enticingly delineated and authentically created by a chef from Copenhagen consisting, among other delicacies, of turtle soup, blinis with crème fraîche and caviar, quail stuffed with truffles and foie gras and baked in puff pastry, baba *au rhum*, to say nothing of vintage wines and champagne. We have here in truth an august banquet realized by Babette; eclipsing sybaritism, it is a genuine communion—significantly there are twelve at the table. The glorious dinner is a metaphor for the healing, restorative powers of art, which not only subtly reconcile the participants to life, but furthermore provide enormous satisfaction for the creator, who quotes Papin: "Throughout the world sounds one long cry from the heart of the artist. Give me the chance to do my very best." Mme. Audran said that the film "speaks of the communication prevented here by dogmatic religion. The meal prepared by Babette brings on communication among the people. It is a miracle; it involves the union of the spirit and matter. A

Later, Martine (Birgitte Federspiel) *(right)* thanks Babette for her wonderful meal as Philippa (Bodil Kjer) smiles her approval.

metaphysical tale." Henning Kristiansen's outstanding photography enhances the film's mood. A quietly overwhelming picture, the superb *Babette's Feast* is an exquisite gem, a cherished classic. Viva Babette!

HONORS

Oscar for Best Foreign Language Film (1987)
Best Foreign Film, British Academy Award (1988)

65

PELLE THE CONQUEROR

Pelle Erobreren

DENMARK/SWEDEN / 1987

PER HOLST FILMPRODUKTION (DENMARK)/SVENSK FILMINDUSTRI (SWEDEN)/DENMARK RADIO/DANISH FILM INSTITUTE/SWEDISH FILM INSTITUTE/THE GENERAL WORKERS UNION IN DENMARK/SID

CREDITS

Director and screenwriter: Bille August, based on the novel by Martin Andersen Nexo (1906); *Assistant director:* Tove Berg; *Producer:* Per Holst; *Cinematographer:* Jongen Persson (color); *Music:* Stefan Nilsson; *Editor:* Janus Billeskov Jansen; *Art director:* Anna Asp; *Running time:* 150 minutes; *16mm rental source:* Films Inc.; *Videocassette:* HBO.

CAST

Lasse Karlsson: Max von Sydow; *Pelle:* Pelle Hvenegaard; *Manager:* Erik Paaske; *Erik:* Bjorn Granath; *Mrs. Kongstrup:* Astrid Villaume; *Kongstrup:* Axel Strobye; *Rud:* Troels Asmussen; *Anna:* Kristina Tornqvist; *Mrs. Olsen:* Karen Wegener; *Miss Signe:* Sofie Grabol; *Karna:* Anne Lise Hirsch Bjerrum; *Niels:* Thure Lindhardt; *The Sow:* Lena Pia Bernhardsson; *Trainee:* Morten Jorgensen.

After film-adaptation rights to *Pelle the Conqueror*, the four-volume autobiographical novel by Martin Andersen Nexo (1869—1954), had returned to Denmark in 1983, Danish director Bille August (1948—   ) set to work creating a screenplay. Since this masterpiece spans many years, it was decided to focus on the first tome, *Childhood*, which relates the misfortunes of Lasse Karlsson, a poor, illiterate, aging Swedish widower, and his little boy, Pelle, who migrate to Bornholm, the easternmost island in Denmark, in the late 1870s with the dream of a better life. But the reality they confront is one of insufferable hardship and exploitation. "I see this mainly as an emotional story between a lonely father and his son," August said of his third feature. "It's also a story of how people survive in an extremely cruel world." The director stressed, "Despite Lasse's humiliation, he is able to give his son so much love, which has a healing effect. . . . The film deals with a problem that is still relevant: how immigrants and refugees are mistreated." While thousands of schoolboys were tested for the role of Pelle—which fell to Pelle Hvenegaard, whose mother had presciently named him after the protagonist of Andersen Nexo's tetralogy, which she had read during her pregnancy—the great international actor Max von Sydow was already cast in August's mind as Lasse when he started the scenario. Voted Best Danish Film of 1987, this extraordinary movie went on to triumph at Cannes and Hollywood. Expertly directed, marvelously acted, exquisitely photographed, the popular and memorable *Pelle the Conqueror* is a picture of universal and epic dimensions.

The film opens on a vessel heading to Bornholm. Lasse (Max von Sydow) assures his son, Pelle (Pelle Hvenegaard), of the comfortable life they'll soon find in Denmark. When they land, the man is quickly passed over because of his age. Later, a gruff manager (Erik Paaske) of Stone Farm hires the tippling father and child for trifling wages. Installed in a section of a barn, they assume the toilsome labor of cattlemen. The boy befriends Rud (Troels Asmussen), the natural son of the lecherous owner Kongstrup (Axel Strobye) and the Sow (Lena Pia Bernhardsson). Pelle is bullied by the trainee (Morten Jorgensen), who whips and mortifies him. Lasse promises to punish the arrogant youth, but to the son's disappointment cringes before him. Lasse admits that he commands no respect, yet adds encouragingly, "You're still young Pelle. You can conquer the world." The boy buys brandy surreptitiously for the unhappy, alcoholic Mrs. Kongstrup (Astrid Villaume). A fiercely independent Erik (Bjorn Granath), a Swedish farmhand constantly abused by the sadistic manager, instills in Pelle his longing to leave in two years: "I'm going out to conquer the world!"

Lasse (Max von Sydow) with his son, Pelle (Pelle Hvenegaard), freshly arrived in Denmark, encounters difficulty in obtaining work.

The lad exclaims, "Take me with you!"

Lasse asks Karna (Anne Lise Hirsch Bjerrum), a fellow worker, for her hand in marriage; however, she replies that he's too old. Rebelling against the manager's badgering, Erik threatens him with his scythe. In the ensuing altercation, the stone weight of the water pump falls and hits the Swede on the back of his head, leaving him permanently brain damaged. Pelle makes a friend of Mrs. Olsen (Karen Wegener), whose captain husband has been gone for a year. Lasse starts courting the favorably inclined woman. At the fair Kongstrup seduces Signe (Sofie Grabol), his wife's niece, who had been staying with them. When, pregnant, she abruptly and sobbingly departs, her embittered aunt castrates the libertine. Pelle is pummeled by his disapproving schoolmates for his father's liaison with the seeming widow. Learning that Captain Olsen came back, a disheartened Lasse tries to hang himself, then gets drunk. Mrs. Kongstrup offers the position of trainee to Pelle; a delighted Lasse thinks this might lead to foreman. The boy sees the manager drag an unwilling, mentally defective Erik away in a carriage. Possibly fearing a similar fate, his thirst for adventure mounting, Pelle insists they must leave the farm immediately. Frightened and exhausted, Lasse in tears informs his beloved son that he cannot leave with him. The couple bid farewell and the stalwart Pelle embarks alone on his life's journey.

Though Lasse—a loving father—is weak-willed, young Pelle has the strength and courage to go off on his own. In a wonderfully nuanced performance, expressing a vast range of feelings, Max

Giving him sensible advice about handling bullies, Lasse brings Pelle to school.

At the fair Lasse dances with Mrs. Olsen (Karen Wegener), whom he hopes to wed.

When a bellicose Sow makes another unwelcome appearance demanding money from Kongstrup for their illegitimate son, the mentally impaired Erik (Bjorn Granath) and Pelle hide underneath a carriage.

von Sydow incarnates the impoverished Lasse. The handsome Pelle Hvenegaard makes the hero convincing and appealing. August transferred the classic novel to the screen with great devotion and skill and demonstrated his enormous talent for rich characterization and compelling narration. Avoiding both sentimentality and nostalgia, the director emphasized, "We wanted to show the cruelty as well as the beauty." Although the political aspects are kept in the distance, we cannot fail to perceive the terrible plight of the farmworkers, their oppression and lack of justice. August realistically evokes the period down to the flies buzzing around the sleeping Pelle.

From his striking opening of the gradual approach of a steamer through the fog, followed by tableaux of ravishing beauty, Jongen Persson's photography is simply breathtaking. Stefan Nilsson contributed a haunting score. Shots of a graceful schooner, remote and dreamlike, which recur throughout the film, serve as a visual symbol of escape; following a beating by the angry boys for his father's affair, Pelle determinedly carves one on a post in the barn. His leave-taking is splendid. In a long shot Lasse and Pelle, carrying his bundle, pace through a snowy field before sunrise—two dark silhouettes against a white background. They pause. In a close shot the father says, "Next time we see each other maybe they'll be a proper home for you, Pelle." The lad says, "Tell Karna goodbye," and extends his hand to Lasse. When the man takes it, the boy states tersely, "Good-bye,

Papa, thank you." The parent leans over and kisses him. The son heads off. Lasse walks a few feet, turns, and waves. In a long shot accompanied by Nilsson's lovely music, we observe Pelle advancing, veering around, and waving to his father, who does the same. In another long shot the youth comes to the beach and hurries along to his destiny. Much of the emotion in this wrenching sequence the characters cannot express verbally. A poignant and deeply moving film, *Pelle the Conqueror* is a major achievement.

HONORS

Best Film, Cannes Film Festival (1988)
Oscar for Best Foreign Language Film; in addition
   Max von Sydow nominated for Best Actor (1988)

66
AU REVOIR LES ENFANTS

FRANCE/WEST GERMANY / 1987

N.E.F. (NOUVELLES ÉDITIONS DE FILMS)/M.K. 2 PRODUCTIONS (PARIS)/STELLA FILM/N.E.F. (MUNICH)

CREDITS

Director, producer, and screenwriter: Louis Malle; *Assistant director:* Yann Gilbert; *Cinematographer:* Renato Berta (color); *Music:* Schubert's *Moment Musical No. 2* and Saint-Saëns' *Introduction and Rondo Capriccioso; Editor:* Émmanuelle Castro; *Art director:* Willy Holt; *Running time:* 103 minutes; *16mm rental source:* Goldwyn; *Videocassette:* Orion.

CAST

Julien Quentin: Gapard Manesse; *Jean Bonnet:* Raphaël Fejtö; *Mme. Quentin:* Francine Racette; *François Quentin:* Stanislas Carré de Malberg; *Father Jean:* Philippe Morier-Genoud; *Father Michael:* François Berléand; *Joseph:* François Négret; *Muller:* Peter Fitz; *Négus/Lafarge:* Arnaud Henriet; *Moreau:* Luc Étienne; *Mlle. Davenne:* Irène Jacob; *Dupré:* Damien Salot.

In 1944, Louis Malle, age eleven, attended the Petit Collège d'Avon, a Carmelite boarding school near Fontainebleau, to avoid the dangers of Paris, con-

Portrait of the young Julien (Gaspard Manesse) in a chilly classroom, the central figure in the film and a surrogate for the director.

A German patrol brings the frightened lost pair, Jean (Raphaël Fejtö) *(left)* and Julien, back to their school after curfew.

Next to a table of Wehrmacht officers, Mme. Quentin (Francine Racette) treats her sons, Julien and François (Stanislas Carré de Malberg), and the guest, Jean (Raphaël Fejtö) *(right)*, to an elegant meal, with allowance for wartime restrictions.

stantly being bombarded during the war. A new pupil joined them, intelligent and mysterious, whom he befriended. On one unforgettable morning, the Gestapo appeared to arrest the child and several others. The future director was not aware at the time that the apprehended students, carefully protected by the priests, were Jewish. The event was shocking, "the most dramatic memory of my childhood," Malle wrote, leaving him with a feeling of being somehow responsible and inflicting a wound that would help make him an artist. He contemplated making a movie of this painful recollection for a long time, then felt the moment had arrived. *Au Revoir les Enfants*—also known here as *Goodbye, Children*—as the director's sixteenth feature was called, would focus on Julien, his young alter ego, and have for dramatic structure the boy's disquieting initiation, "my discovery of the real world—its violence, its disorders, its prejudices," Malle wrote. The director had no wish to make his picture meticulously autobiographical—the locale would not be his former school, the relationship between Julien and his enigmatic friend would be more interesting than it was in actuality, and the informer would be singled out to be the abused cookroom helper, since the identity of the proper culprit had never been determined. "I

reinvented the past in the pursuit of a haunting and timeless truth," Malle said. The film was shot between February and March of 1987 in Provins, a village southeast of Paris. Impeccably directed and showered with honors, *Au Revoir les Enfants* is a beautiful and intimate memoir.

Led away from the grounds by the German officer, Father Jean (Philippe Morier-Genoud) turns and bids an affecting farewell to the schoolchildren. Behind him are the unfortunate Jewish boys, Jean *(left)*, Dupré (Damien Salot) *(center)*, and Négus (Arnaud Henriet).

The film opens in January 1944. At a train station young Julien Quentin (Gaspard Manesse) is unhappy to leave his mother (Francine Racette) to return to his Carmelite boarding school with his older brother, François (Stanislas Carré de Malberg). Soon in his dormitory at the school of St. John of the Cross the headmaster, Father Jean (Philippe Morier-Genoud), introduces a new pupil, Jean Bonnet (Raphaël Fejtö), who occupies a vacant bed next to Julien's. The newcomer is not popular with the students and at first even annoys Julien, who gradually finds him intriguing. From his kitchen where he's a harassed menial, the crippled Joseph (François Négret) operates a black market. Julien clandestinely opens Bonnet's locker and comes upon an inscription in a book to a "Jean Kippelstein." The two boys get separated from their classmates while on a scout patrol in a forest and are brought back to St. John's later by German soldiers. The ensuing day in the infirmary Julien incenses Jean when he tells him what his real name is. That Sunday at mass Jean attempts to take Communion to show he's a Catholic, but Father Jean notices him in time and moves the host to Julien. Friendship builds between the two boys, heightened by their mutual love of literature.

Joseph's thievery is uncovered and he is fired. Presently Muller (Peter Fitz) of the Gestapo interrupts a class demanding Jean Kippelstein. Julien cannot resist turning around to look at his friend; that instant is not lost on the officer, who snares Jean. He orders the school closed. Father Jean is taken into custody for harboring Jews; his links with the Resistance are disclosed. While packing, Jean tells Julien not to worry since the Germans would have found him anyway. Julien is upset to discover that it was Joseph who had denounced them. Before being taken away with Jean, Négus (Arnaud Henriet), and Dupré (Damien Salot) by the Germans, Father Jean says to the entire class assembled in the yard, "Good-bye, children. I'll be seeing you." With Julien in a close-up, a voice-over of the director informs us of the deaths of the Jewish youths at Auschwitz, of Father Jean's at Mauthausen, and that he'll remember that January morning until the end of his life.

Through Julien's sensitive, sharp eyes we perceive his growing awareness of the baneful evil rampant in the adult world. Innocent yet haughty, his vague aspirations to be a missionary are dismissed by the acute headmaster. The secretive Jean is not portrayed as a noble martyr, but rather as a normal—though exceptionally bright—child who becomes a hapless victim. Gaspard Manesse as Julien and Raphaël Fejtö as Jean are natural, typifying "authentic children," which Malle said he wanted. With his distinguished voice and ascetic features, Philippe Morier-Genoud renders Father Jean spiritual, forceful, and memorable. Malle's direction is masterly, totally controlled and made all the more striking by a marked simplicity, permitting us to be privy to a poignant and tragic moment of history without melodrama or needless embellishment. He evokes in brief scenes a realistic, terrifying period consisting of bitter winter, air raids, adulterated food, bedwetting, loneliness, and fear. Showing their ceaseless bullying and violent behavior—as evinced by their battles on stilts to prove their manhood—the director neither sentimentalizes his striplings nor stereotypes the "villains"—a pious German soldier requests Father Jean to hear his confession. We can understand the desperate situation that led to Joseph's betrayal. Renato Berta's excellent cinematography emphasizes the bleak, snowy days of Malle's somber boyhood remembrance.

Among the many remarkable scenes is the richly textured sequence in which the refectory is rearranged into a temporary theater and Chaplin's *The Immigrant* (1917) is projected for an audience of faculty and students. Charlie's familiar antics are greeted with hilarity; during an uproarious bit, Father Jean and Joseph are united in hearty, communal laughter. And when the Statue of Liberty passes into view, first Négus and then Jean stare wistfully at that universal symbol of hope. The war is mercilessly forgotten for a few, shared minutes. The conclusion is quietly astounding, as Father Jean's parting phrase to the pupils in the courtyard is echoed variously by his brave, affectionate charges. Last to depart is Jean, casting a final glance at Julien, who waves his hand softly. While the camera is on a tearful Julien—with Schubert's exquisite music in the background—the director recounts the disposition of the captured quartet. *Au Revoir les Enfants* is a deeply moving, resplendent work. Louis Malle said, "This is the film I want to be remembered by."

The angel Cassiel (Otto Sander) *(right)* inspires the frail, old writer Homer (Curt Bois) to persevere in his work.

HONORS

Prix Méliès (1987)
Prix Louis Delluc (1987)
Golden Lion for Best Film, Venice Film Festival (1987)
Césars for Best Film, Director, Screenplay, Cinematography, Editing, Art Direction, and Jean-Claude Laureux for Sound (1987)
Nominated for an Oscar for Original Screenplay and Best Foreign Language Film (1987)
Best Director, British Academy Award (1988)

67
WINGS OF DESIRE

Der Himmel über Berlin

WEST GERMANY/FRANCE / 1987

ROAD MOVIES (BERLIN)/ARGOS FILMS (PARIS)/ WDR (WESTDEUTSCHER RUNDFUNK) (COLOGNE)

A smitten Damiel (Bruno Ganz) listens in to the troubled reflections of Marion (Solveig Dommartin), who is apprehensive about her approaching trapeze act on the night of a full moon.

CREDITS

Director: Wim Wenders; *Assistant director:* Claire Denis; *Producers:* Wim Wenders, Anatole Dauman; *Screenwriters:* Wim Wenders, Peter Handke; *Cinematographer:* Henri Alekan (black and white, Eastmancolor); *Music:* Jürgen Knieper; *Editor:* Peter Przygodda; *Art director:* Heidi Lüdi; *Running time:* 130 minutes;

16mm rental source: New Yorker; *Videocassette:* Orion.

CAST

Damiel: Bruno Ganz; *Marion:* Solveig Dommartin; *Cassiel:* Otto Sander; *Homer:* Curt Bois; *As Himself:* Peter Falk.

237

Following a lengthy and frustrating stay in this country, Wim Wenders came to realize that he would not succeed as an American filmmaker and returned to Europe. Caught up in the exciting rediscovery of Berlin; mulling over a need to make a love story; jogging in the Tiergarten and encountering the golden angel atop the Victory Column *(Siegessäule)*; in addition to reading the poetry—leavened with angels—of Rainer Maria Rilke, Wenders was suddenly inspired to make a film focusing on the former capital. *Wings of Desire*, his eleventh feature, would treat of angels, eternally hovering over Berlin, faithfully witnessing then recording the thoughts and activities of its inhabitants, and of one in particular, Damiel, who, after yearning to be exposed to life, falls in love with a trapeze artist and finally dares to become a human being.

The director is not concerned with metaphysics; the celestial beings are merely a device to make us recognize the miracle of existence. "I invented these angels," he said, "because I wondered how one could make a film about how beautiful it is to live every moment. How privileged people are that they can taste, feel the rain in their faces, drink coffee, touch somebody—whereas the poor angels cannot." The angels serve as a metaphor, Wenders said, "for history and the memory of it" as well as for the "angel inside ourselves, who might be the child that we used to be." *Wings of Desire* was, moreover, a challenge to capture the spirit of Berlin, then long divided into the Western and Eastern sectors by the infamous Wall of 1961. "History here is both physically and emotionally present," the director stressed. "No other city is to such an extent a symbol, a place of survival." Berlin, split, "well represents not only Germany, but also our civilization," he said. Wenders engaged the distinguished Austrian writer Peter Handke to write the heightened dialogue of the angels and Marion's speech at the end, along with the interlinking poem about childhood; cast both the gifted Bruno Ganz as Damiel and—in a charming coup—the ingratiating Peter Falk playing himself in an extended cameo appearance; and had master cinematographer Henri Alekan create some of his finest work. Dedicated "to all the former angels" but especially to Yasujiro Ozu, François Truffaut, and Andrzej Munk, *Wings of Desire* won acclaim and was an international commercial success. Captivatingly original, richly poetic, it is already a cult film and has attained the status of a classic.

The film open in Berlin with the angel Damiel, (Bruno Ganz), visible only to children, on the top of the ruins of the Kaiser Wilhelm Memorial Church overlooking the streets below. The subjective camera—his eyes—intercuts among several passersby whose snippets of internal monologue he overhears. On an airplane heading to the city to shoot a movie is actor Peter Falk. Later in a car Damiel listens to a report from his colleague, the angel Cassiel (Otto Sander), and voices his growing dissatisfaction with his incorporeal condition. Bored with eternity, with sharing human life in a vaguely vicarious manner, Damiel catalogs the earthly details he's longing to experience. In the State Library *(Staatsbibliothek)*—headquarters for the celestial beings—he runs across the venerable storyteller Homer (Curt Bois); in the subway he eavesdrops on the worried introspection of the passengers and is able to inspirit one.

Damiel visits a soon-to-be-disbanding circus and is intrigued with the lovely rehearsing aerialist, Marion (Solveig Dommartin). Hearing her muse on her need for a lover, he consoles her. Then to Cassiel he reveals his decision to opt for mortality. When Cassiel fails to avert a young man from suicide, he is anguished. Damiel watches Marion's final performance and afterward nears her dancing at a rock concert; she feels a sudden infusion of joy. Marion has a prescient dream of Damiel while he contemplates her asleep in her trailer. At an outdoor snack bar Falk intuits the immediacy of Damiel; in a warm manner he whets Damiel's desires for embodiment by describing various sensuous gratifications. Afterward at the Wall with Cassiel's assistance, an elated and anticipatory Damiel "dies"; he awakens subsequently, now a man, while a providential helicopter drops an olden breastplate on him. Enthusiastic, he walks along discovering color, weather, the taste of coffee, time, etc., and in an antique shop trades the armor for a jacket and hat. On the film set he meets Falk, who discloses he's a former angel, too, and that Damiel will have to find out about life by himself. He comes upon the deserted site of the circus, yet is certain he'll find Marion. That night at a bar she apprehends that Damiel is the beloved she's searching for and unveils her soul. They kiss. The next day a contented Damiel helps her practice on a rope. "I know now what no angel knows," he writes. A forlorn Cassiel catches Marion's "We have embarked!"

Damiel in his winter coat and Cassiel in his raincoat, both ponytailed, are gentle angels deeply compassionate toward the lot of mankind, but

Peter Falk *(right)* sensing the company of an angel (Bruno Ganz) but unable to see him, exclaims how wonderful it is to be a human being and to partake of life's simple pleasures.

frequently ineffectual in relieving individual suffering. In Wenders's view they are enclosed in an abstract universe and "know only the essence of things," not their reality. Though aware of the pain of human existence, Damiel asserts that he wants "to conquer a history for myself!" and incarnates. With his expressive face, distinctive voice, and outstanding presence, Bruno Ganz gives another remarkable and convincing performance. Otto Sander lends strong support. Solveig Dommartin, who developed skills in acrobatics to play Marion, is appealing and impressive. The immensely popular Peter Falk adds a keen touch of gritty actuality to the movie.

Considering that *Wings of Desire* has a mere thread of a plot, that it is a film essentially more lyrical than dramatic, Wenders's precarious experiment proved a surprise winner. Expertly directed, with graceful camera movements (in particular tracking and crane shots), the picture has a delicate commingling of the documentary—sporadic newsreels of the devastation wreaked upon Berlin in World War II—with the ethereal world of the angels. The director skirts the trap of sentimentality; Damiel is well versed in the sorrows of a humanity he's eager to participate in. Henri Alekan's photography is simply breathtaking, from

haunting and dreamlike black and white (signifying the angels' point of view) to bright color (denoting what humans behold). The film is a rare affirmation of life, both making the audience, see afresh their existence which usually takes it for granted, and celebrating the triumph of love and art—the indefatigable Homer refers to himself as mankind's "spiritual guide." Innovative and vigorous, *Wings of Desire* is an extraordinary achievement.

HONORS

Best Director, Cannes Film Festival (1987)
Prix Moussinac (1987)
Best Cinematography, New York Film Critics Award (1988)

68
STORY OF WOMEN

Une Affaire de Femmes

FRANCE / 1988

MK 2 Productions/Films A2/Films Du Camélia/ La Sept/Sofinergie

CREDITS

Director: Claude Chabrol; *Assistant directors:* Alain Wermus, Michel Dupuy; *Producer:* Marin Karmitz; *Screenwriters:* Colo Tavernier O'Hagan, Claude Chabrol, freely adapted from the book by Francis Szpiner (1986); *Cinematographer:* Jean Rabier (Eastmancolor); *Music:* Matthieu Chabrol; *Editor:* Monique Fardoulis; *Art director:* Françoise Benoit-Fresco; *Running time:* 110 minutes; *16mm rental source and videocassette:* New Yorker.

CAST

Marie Latour: Isabelle Huppert; *Paul:* François Cluzet; *Lulu/Lucie:* Marie Trintignant; *Lucien:* Nils Tavernier; *Mouche 2:* Lolita Chammah; *Mouche 1:* Aurore Gauvin; *Pierrot 1:* Guillaume Foutrier; *Pierrot 2:* Nicolas Foutrier; *Ginette:* Marie Bunel; *Fernande:* Evelyne Didi; *Loulou:* Dani; *Attorney Fillon:* Vincent Gauthier; *Rachel:* Myriam David; *Colonel Chabert:* Jacques Brunet.

Marie (Isabelle Huppert) *(left)* befriends Lucie (Marie Trintignant), a streetwalker professionally known as "Lulu."

In bed Marie imparts to her husband Paul (François Cluzet) what a fortune-teller revealed: she'll have plenty of money and there will be a lot of women in her life.

An emboldened Marie takes a lover, Lucien (Nils Tavernier).

Consistent with a pattern that characterizes his entire career and following a recent interval during which his reputation was floundering once more, prolific French director Claude Chabrol (1930–   ) in *Story of Women* made a triumphal return to his position as a major and prestigious filmmaker. In this controversial movie, based on a factual account by a French lawyer of a certain Marie-Louise Giraud who was executed by the Vichy government for performing abortions in the time of World War II, the screenwriters fictionalized her life, "fleshed it out with ambiguity and contradiction," Chabrol said. "I kept feeling that the woman behind the symbol—and she was a scapegoat for the Vichy government—was as interesting as the case itself." To that end, the scenarists attempted to reconstruct her complex psychological matrix.

Set in Dieppe, the Norman port in Occupied France, in 1941, *Story of Women* traces the fortunes of an indigent young woman designated as Marie Latour, saddled with two children and a partially disabled husband whom she doesn't love, who discovers that she has a talent for ending unwanted pregnancies and embarks upon a course—which includes pandering for whores—without considering the consequences, until it leads to her undoing. Depicting her neither as a monster nor as a martyr or even protofeminist, Chabrol wisely adopts an equivocal tone toward Marie, leaving the audience to ponder the moral issues involved. "As a man, I wouldn't presume to make a judgment," he said. The gifted Isabelle Huppert was cast as the protagonist and won honors for her astonishing portrayal. With its volatile subject matter of abortion and its shocking scene of a condemned Marie's embittered, scatological parody of the Hail Mary, one would expect that the film's debut in this country would have been an occasion for angry picket lines, demonstrations, and thunder from the pulpits—thus creating that type of scandal that lures hordes to the box office. That did not occur. Instead, while critically applauded, it remains a somewhat neglected—even overlooked—picture. Chabrol's provocative and brilliantly realized *Story of Women* awaits the attention it merits as a classic.

The films opens on a field. Marie (Isabelle Huppert) and her little boy, Pierrot (Guillaume Foutrier), and daughter, Mouche (Aurore Gauvin), are picking herbs for their frugal meal. Later Marie confides to her friend Rachel (Myriam David) her ambition to be a singer. Chancing upon her neighbor Ginette (Marie Bunel) trying to abort herself in a mustard sitz bath—her boyfriend is being sent to work in Germany and doesn't want the child—Marie offers to help her, although she is a novice at it. Marie is saddened to learn that Rachel was taken away; she wasn't aware that the woman is Jewish. Paul (François Cluzet), an enervated POW, comes back; Marie is cold and unresponsive to her husband. Ginette, grateful for the young mother's efficacious assistance, bestows a phonograph upon her benefactress. In a beauty parlor Marie strikes up a friendship with Lucie (Marie Trintignant), a prostitute. Calculating that her freshly recognized skill might be a way out of her grinding poverty, she tells Lucie to see her if she's ever "in trouble." Marie demands they move from their gloomy apartment. Referrals are sent to her, enabling the family to relocate again, this time to spacious quarters where an enterprising Marie, without consulting Paul, rents a room to Lucie for her clients.

The incapacitated husband is fired from his job; he is chafed at his wife's avowal that she doesn't love him and her disinclination to have sex with him. There is passionate, mutual attraction, however, between Marie and the conceited Lucien (Nils Tavernier), a regular of Lucie's and an opportunistic collaborationist with the Germans. They soon become lovers. Paul, feeling worthless and emasculated, busies himself doing cutouts from the newspaper. One of Marie's customers—an overburdened young mother of six who had botched an earlier essay at abortion—dies; her spouse commits suicide. The woman's sister-in-law pays a visit. She won't make trouble she promises, but informs a defensive Marie, who refuses to accept any blame, that babies have a soul: "I pity you." A second room is let to a colleague of Lucie's. Through Lucien's influence, Paul finds employment patrolling docks. Becoming more affluent, Marie hires a maid, Fernande (Evelyn Didi), and encourages her to have sex with her husband. Returning from work, Paul spies his wife asleep with Lucien, then, after deliberating and being thoroughly disgusted, starts clipping words that will form a letter denouncing her anonymously to the authorities.

Coming home from a singing lesson, Marie is met by two policemen. The bewildered woman is shortly ordered to appear before a Special Tribunal in Paris. Fillon (Vincent Gauthier), her lawyer, discloses that the government wishes to make her an example as a deterrent to others: "Anything that goes against morals is considered a crime against the state." The prosecutor, Colonel Chabert (Jacques Brunet), states chillingly that when a nation has gangrene, "we must chop off the gangrened limb." In the trial she is found guilty of performing twenty-three abortions and sentenced to be guillotined. On July 30, 1943 the hapless woman is decapitated.

Marie is a self-centered, increasingly greedy woman, callously inconsiderate of her small son starving for affection and her slighted husband. Politically naive regarding the German attitude toward Jews and her government's particular abhorrence of abortion, she grows aware during her incarceration that "it's easy to have clean hands if you're rich." The director said, "What fascinated me is her extraordinary instinct for survival. Completely misunderstood by her peers, she is only trying to avoid asphyxiation. In her universe, all is geared toward survival. The problem is *how* to survive. I wanted this film to be very pathetic, in the noble sense of the word. I would like people to understand the anguish of those who are terribly poor." Playing an unsympathetic character and riveting our interest in her, Isabelle Huppert as Marie gives a truly bravura performance. She is

Shivering with fear and cold, Marie awaits the guillotine.

completely real, natural, and quite simply outstanding.

Chabrol's direction displays remarkable control and a masterly mise-en-scène. Avoiding sentimentality as well as a lurid approach to a topic that could easily be sensationalized, the director treats his story dispassionately—with great delicacy and understatement. Thus little Pierrot coming back from school helps himself to a cookie and then peeps through the kitchen keyhole, which briefly shows his mother inserting a syringe between the raised legs of a woman. The use of the telling detail aids Chabrol in re-creating the period. When Marie lets the grocer know she'll pay with cash instead of coupons, the man obligingly uncovers some precious jam. An impressive sequence evincing the director's virtuoso artistry begins with a happy Marie walking to her initial music lesson at the same time as we hear a voice-over of Paul reciting his ominous, indicting missive to the superintendent of police. She enters the apartment building of her vocal coach; the camera pans to the left as she commences singing Chausson's exquisite *Poéme de l'Amour et de la Mer*, then rises slowly in a crane shot—as if underscoring her aspirations—to a high-angle shot revealing the teacher with her pupil through the window. We cut to inside the studio where a delighted Marie is told that she has a lovely voice and if she'll work hard, it will be beautiful. Returning home, at the very peak of exultation, she plays merrily with her children in the courtyard—then abruptly confronts the officers. Chabrol manages to generate excruciating suspense after Marie is taken into custody; we're shocked at the trial, startled at the clanking of her shackled feet, and devastated at her harrowing decollation. Jean Rabier's striking photography captures the town's gray, oppressive atmosphere.

While the self-righteous Colonel Chabert as a spokesman for the Vichy government can fulminate against abortion—it should be pointed out that not only were birth-control devices unavailable to the French throughout the Occupation but that Marshal Pétain imputed France's defeat to women for delivering "too few children!"—and speak rhetorically of his nation's "pressing need for moral restoration," that very same government was simultaneously and meticulously engaged in rounding up thousands of Jews and—demonstrating initiative—their children as well and deporting them to Germany. Chabrol excoriates the hypocrisy of the regime graphically. "Countries become extremely 'moral' when they feel themselves to be weak," he said significantly. Miss Huppert commented, "This story could not happen to a man. A woman fights with whatever means she has at her disposal, to free herself, even if these means are dangerous or illegal." Fascinating, disturbing, and challenging, *Story of Women* is an emotionally compelling experience and has been justifiably hailed as a masterpiece.

HONORS

Isabelle Huppert shared the Best Actress Prize, Venice Film Festival (1988)
César to Isabelle Huppert for Best Actress (1988)
Best Foreign Film, New York Critics Award (1989)

69
LARKS ON A STRING

Skrivanci na Niti

CZECHOSLOVAKIA / 1990

BARRANDOV FILM STUDIO (PRAGUE)

CREDITS

Director: Jiri Menzel; *Assistant director:* Josef Sandr; *Producer:* Karel Kochman; *Screenwriters:* Jiri Menzel, Bohumil Hrabal, based on a collection of the latter's short stories; *Cinematographer:* Jaromir Sofr (color); *Music:* Jiri Sust; *Editor:* Jirina Lukesova; *Art director:* Oldrich Bosak; *Running time:* 96 minutes; *16mm rental source:* IFEX; *Videocassette:* Fox/Lorber.

CAST

Pavel: Vaclav Neckar; *Party Official:* Rudolf Hrusinsky; *Jitka:* Jitka Zelenohorska; *The Dairyman:* Vladimir Ptacek; *The Professor:* Vlastimil Brodsky; *Andel:* Jaroslav Satoransky; *Lenka:* Nada Urbankova; *Kudla:* Ferdinand Kruta; *Tiny:* Frantisek Rehak; *The Prosecutor:* Leos Sucharipa; *Saxophonist:* Evzen Jegorov.

In Czechoslovakia during the reform leadership of Alexander Dubcek, the so-called Prague Spring, Jiri Menzel audaciously started filming in 1968 a delightful, subversive movie mocking Communism called *Larks on a String*. Unfortunately, with the Soviet intervention in August of that year the Prague Spring met with a fatal frost and the former, repressive dictatorship was restored. Although the director cut some of the more offensive scenes from this, his fourth feature, after he managed to complete it in the following year, the censors refused its release and instead banned it, and it languished for over twenty years.

Larks on a String, based on stories of Bohumil Hrabal, poked fun at the Communist authorities' futile attempt to "reeducate" the country's rebellious "bourgeois dissidents." It's miraculous that Menzel himself did not wind up being forced to do manual labor in an industrial junkyard like the characters in his picture. Only when the nation threw off the yoke of the Communist Party and the Soviet Union in late 1989 was the now legendary film disinterred. It premiered at the Berlin Film Festival where it won laurels. Considering the terrible sufferings that Communism wreaked upon Czechoslovakia, one would think that such a film would treat its subject in nightmarish terms. Yet surprisingly and refreshingly, Menzel's tone is not sardonic but one of light—even gentle—satire; the tweak on the nose replaces the expected bludgeoning. Menzel arouses in us "gay contempt" through which we laughingly dismiss the horrors of Communism as some sort of absurd aberration. "If you want to touch something deeply," the director said, "humor is the easiest way for the audience to accept it. It is the best way to get to the heart." Though *Larks on a String* lacks the powerful, tragic quality of *Closely Watched Trains*, his previous collaboration with Hrabal, nonetheless it is a charming, warm film—albeit with grave undertones—that is fresh and ever so meaningful for us today and awaits discovery.

The film is set in the early 1950s in the town of Kladno, west of Prague. Following a note that informs us that "in February 1948 the working class took power" and "the defeated classes were sent into industry to atone for its bourgeois origins," the movie opens with an aerial tracking shot of a vast junkyard. The scrap heap of old typewriters, aluminum pots—even broken crucifixes—etc., will be melted down to make new tractors, washing machines, and so forth. A zealous Party official (Rudolf Hrusinsky) oversees a motley group of "voluntary workers"—the place is in reality a forced-labor camp—which includes, among others, the old professor (Vlastimil Brod-

sky), actually a librarian who refused to shred "forbidden" books; a public prosecutor (Leos Sucharipa) who believes in the rights of the defendants; and a young Seventh-Day Adventist cook, Pavel (Vaclav Neckar), who's unwilling to work on Saturday for religious reasons. The Party official boasts that like scrap he'll make these bourgeois into a new people. Adjacent is a prison for women, who likewise toil in the junkyard, detained mainly for trying to "desert" their country. Pavel is fascinated by one of them, Jitka (Jitka Zelenohorska). When another dissenter, the dairyman (Vladimir Ptacek), mentions the impermissible word *strike*, the functionary calls him an "imperialist."

Andel (Jaroslav Satoransky), the female convicts' guard, marries a Gypsy whose behavior is inscrutable to him. The prosecutor constantly points out inequities in the system. Two men in trench coats arrive in a car and haul the dairyman off into custody. A sexually deprived Andel has his hands full discouraging the flirtations between the ladies and the men; nevertheless Pavel gets Jitka to agree to marry him. The professor talks back; he, too, is driven away. Through the intercession of the Party official, Pavel weds Jitka by proxy in a sterile Communist ceremony. In prison uniform she is led to a shed on the grounds where she will be permitted to be with him briefly. The joyful groom heading to his bride is intercepted by the functionary and sent to welcome a visiting dignitary. Impulsively, Pavel asks the elderly figure what happened to the coworkers who disappeared, then finally resumes his rush to Jitka, but he is grabbed by the familiar policemen and whisked away. She gets transferred to the coal mines so she can be near her husband. A happy Pavel, reunited with the professor, who's at peace with himself, and the dairyman prepare to work; although imprisoned their spirits remain unbroken—and free.

Perched atop a mound of debris, the professor, like an Olympian deity, peers down amusedly at the oddities of the new socialist state. The wise man quotes Meister Eckhart—a strong contrast to the vapid, ubiquitous slogans. Vlastimil Brodsky brings him to life memorably. Vaclav Neckar and Jitka Zelenohorska make Pavel and Jitka an engaging pair. Leisurely paced, Menzel's skillful direction catches the everyday lives of the "misfits" and their oppressors with a sharp eye for the telling detail. Thus when an astringent schoolteacher marches into the area with her singing wards and the children attempt to tie a red kerchief around the prosecutor's neck, he growls at them fiercely

Andel the guard (Jaroslav Satoransky) acts as intermediary between the showering men and the female prisoners waiting to enter next.

Pavel (Vaclav Neckar) and Jitka (Jitka Zelenohorska) are recruited to smile for a propaganda newsreel. Their emerging sincere love will be a repudiation of the bogus "ideal" couple "marching to socialism" in the poster above.

Resisting all efforts to be turned into "a new Communist people," *(left to right)* capitalist washtub maker "Tiny" (Frantisek Rehak), the prosecutor (Leos Sucharipa), the saxophonist (Evzen Jegorov), and Seventh-Day Adventist cook Pavel huddle around an open fire in the rain.

In front of a sign that reads "We're not afraid of work to surpass the new norms" is the besieged Party official (Rudolf Hrusinsky) coping with the outcasts of society.

to frighten them away. Jiri Sust contributed a fine romantic score. Two scenes are especially noteworthy. In one, it is evening in the women's bunkhouse and they undress for bed smilingly aware they're being observed from across the yard by the men, who peep through cracks in the wooden fence, staring in awe and longing. Second, that extraordinary, inspiriting closing scene as the elevator plunges down the mine shaft—with the skylight receding ever farther—the professor exclaiming, "I'm so happy. I have found myself," while Pavel grins knowing that his beloved is close by. Moving and unforgettable. The director's affection for his characters is genuine.

The film can be read as an allegory. The Kladno scrap heap is a microcosm of Communism, an economic failure—only 50 percent of the recycled metal is effective—and an ideological one also that does not convert the resisters to its philosophy. How strangely prescient is this film, anticipating by twenty years the collapse of Communism in Eastern Europe! Yet the director does not get lost in abstractions or polemics; we are in a real junkyard with very believable people. And he makes us snicker at the inversions of a "worker's paradise" in which laborers have no say, no personal freedom, and any "impertinence" results in incarceration. Menzel is brave as well as talented, and *Larks on a String* is a lovely paean to mankind's irrepressible spirit.

HONORS

Cowinner of the Golden Bear for Best Film, Berlin Film Festival (1990)

70
LOVERS

Amantes

SPAIN / 1991

PEDRO COSTA PRODUCCIÓNES CINEMATOGRAFICAS, S.A. WITH THE PARTICIPATION OF TVE (TELEVISION ESPAÑOLA), S.A.

CREDITS

Director: Vicente Aranda; *Producer:* Pedro Costa-Muste; *Screenwriters:* Carlos Perez Merinero, Alvaro

When Paco refuses to accept money for a fraudulent transaction, Luisa (Victoria Abril) exerts her wiles to persuade him to overcome his scruples.

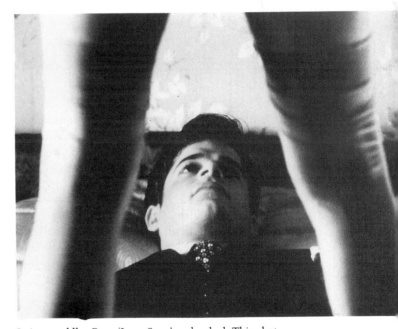

Luisa straddles Paco (Jorge Sanz) on her bed. This shot symbolizes her domination over the youth.

Del Amo, and Vicente Aranda; *Cinematographer:* Jose Luis Alcaine (color); *Music:* Jose Nieto; *Editor:* Teresa Font; *Art director:* Josep Rosell; *Running time:* 103 minutes; *16mm rental source:* New Yorker; *Videocassette:* Worldvision.

CAST

Luisa: Victoria Abril; *Paco:* Jorge Sanz; *Trini:* Maribel Verdu; *Major:* Enrique Cerro; *Major's Wife:* Mabel Escaño; *Trini's Mother:* Alicia Agut.

With *Lovers*, veteran Spanish director Vicente Aranda (1926–   ) once again created an important film set in Spain during the reign of dictator Franco in which the twin forces of the military and the Catholic Church were bulwarks for the oppressive and stifling regime. This, Aranda's sixteenth feature, was based on a celebrated murder case. Heading the distinguished cast is Victoria Abril who plays a seductress launching a torrid affair that culminates in tragedy. Jorge Sanz and Maribel Verdu complete the doomed trio. Aranda's strong, atmospheric evocation of a repressed society, heightened by the outstanding performances of his actors, not only garnered the film Goya Awards—Spain's equivalent to the Oscars—for Best Film and Best Director, but Abril was victorious at Berlin and Aranda received the Best Director award at the Chicago Film Festival (1991). Powerfully directed and acted, erotically charged with sex scenes that are as frank as they are dramatically necessary to establish motivation, *Lovers* is an intriguing and remarkable film.

In Madrid in the early 1950s Paco (Jorge Sanz) is about to be discharged from his military service. His girlfriend, Trini (Maribel Verdu), who works as a maid for the major (Enrique Cerro), shows him an advertisement for a room to let. The apartment owner is Luisa (Victoria Abril), an attractive widow who accepts him. A puritanical, deeply religious Trini rebuffs Paco's amorous advances, regarding sex as "filth." Paco attempts construction work unsuccessfully, and Luisa, that night, lifts his spirits by taking him to bed. He finds her erotic appeal overwhelming and begins ignoring Trini. Luisa has her unsuspecting lover act as witness at a swindle she and her cohorts perpetrate, and when Paco later balks at being involved in crime, she seduces him to sway him. A pouting Trini, feeling neglected, welcomes him coldly when he visits on Christmas Eve, yet offers him money she's thriftily saved to open a store. They run into Luisa on the street; the hapless fiancée senses the pair are lovers and storms off. Luisa's jealousy mounts. Taking the advice of the major's wife (Mabel Escaño), a determined Trini taxies to the apartment, waits for her rival to leave, then surprises Paco. Meanwhile, in a bar Luisa is ac-

Paco removes the dark glasses of Luisa and is disturbed to see that she's been beaten up.

cused by her underworld accomplices of holding back payment and is threatened with physical harm. A smug Trini waits on the stairwell for her to show up.

Trini and her fiancé visit her mother (Alicia Agut), hobbling on crutches. Trini discovers that the bored man she worships can think only of Luisa. Returning to Madrid, Paco is startled to see his lover with a bruised eye and suggests stealing the needed cash from Trini. He then gulls the maid into believing he wants to open a bar in Aranda de Duero with her and be rid of "that woman." Trini volunteers her life savings, secure in her triumph over Luisa. Paco has a crisis over fleecing Trini. Nonetheless, finding her napping, he removes the money from her pocketbook, which he hands to Luisa, telling her to go back to Madrid and settle her affairs; he cannot abandon Trini at this point. The thought of separation from him is unbearable to Luisa. "Kill her," she blurts out departing, and flings the pesetas onto the snow. Confronting a despondent Trini, Paco confesses that Luisa means everything to him and that this trip was just a hoax. In despair she heads to the bathroom and locks the door. Alarmed, Paco breaks the glass and approaches a suicidal Trini holding a razor to her throat. Vowing never to leave her, he pockets the blade. On a bench in a heavy downpour Trini realizes that Paco doesn't love her and begs him to kill her, freeing her from her torture. . . . Luisa and her lover have a tender reunion on the train platform. A legend imparts the denouement: The couple were arrested, tried, and condemned to death. Generalissimo Franco commuted their sentence to thirty years. One spent ten, another twelve, years in prison, but they never saw each other again. Luisa is dead now while a comfortable Paco lives in Zaragoza.

The characters in *Lovers* are fascinatingly complex. Luisa is not just a ruthless manipulator nor a sensual blue angel of illicit desire. When we watch her fall deeply in love with Paco to the extent that she is tormented with fierce jealousy toward Trini and wishes her dead, we comprehend that she is far beyond merely using him for selfish motives. Also, her shocking revelation to Paco after lovemaking that she had murdered her husband and gotten away with it lends a sense of mystery and allure to this sirenic femme fatale. Paco changes from a typical naive, provincial youth full of macho values (*he* will be the provider he declares when Trini first offers him her savings) to a man who not only robs but actually kills the woman who adores him. Trini, for all her obvious qualities of piety and modesty, soon displays an underside of ferocious jealousy and iron will as, casting aside her moral principles, she wages an all-out war to possess her beloved totally. We glimpse her predisposition to excessive behavior when we learn that her mother threw herself under a cart, crippling herself for life, because her husband was unfaithful. We may sympathize—to a degree—with these three troubled souls caught in the midst of violent passions they can no longer control, and since the director's tone is not judgmental, we are led to understand rather than condemn their behavior.

The sultry Victoria Abril is memorable as the sexy temptress initiating the willing Paco into the mysteries of erotic delight and erupting with vengeful fury when she fears losing him. Handsome Jorge Sanz is impressive, projecting an appealing masculinity beneath his boyish good looks. Maribel Verdu is excellent, especially in the poignant scene when she seeks death as a release from her agony. Were any of these three splendid actors not convincing, the film would fizzle instead of explode. Vicente Aranda directs this cautionary tale of sexual obsession with tight control. One noteworthy scene is the delicate handling of Trini's death. There is a long shot from behind of Paco and Trini huddled beneath a trench coat on a bench facing a church in a torrential rain. Next, a close shot of the back of her legs, which stiffen and rise from her shoes while drops of blood suddenly descend upon the snow. Then the blade drops. A distraught Paco hurries away in a long shot. An unforgettable treatment of *l'amour fou*, Spanish style, *Lovers* is first-rate filmmaking, one worthy of discovery.

HONORS

Silver Bear to Victoria Abril for Best Actress, Berlin Film Festival (1991)

After making love, Luisa and Paco scheme to obtain the savings of his girlfriend, Trini.

247

Pelle Hvenegaard and Max von Sydow in *Pelle the Conqueror*.

FILM RENTAL
INFORMATION
(16mm)

Eva Mattes, Jürgen Arndt, and the Bartholdy Quartet in *Céleste*.

CORINTH FILMS

34 Gansevoort Street
New York, NY 10014
(212) 463-0305

FILMS INCORPORATED

5547 N. Ravenswood Avenue
Chicago, IL 60640
(800) 323-4222

THE SAMUEL GOLDWYN COMPANY

10203 Santa Monica Boulevard
Los Angeles, CA 90067
(310) 552-2255

IFEX (INTERNATIONAL FILM EXCHANGE
    LTD.)

201 W. 52nd Street
New York, NY 10019
(212) 582-4318

IMAGES FILM ARCHIVE

2 Purdy Avenue
Rye, NY 10580
(914) 967-1203

JANUS FILMS

888 Seventh Avenue
New York, NY 10106
(212) 753-7100

MGM–UNITED ARTISTS
    ENTERTAINMENT

5890 W. Jefferson Boulevard
Culver City, CA 91230
(213) 838-2148

MUSEUM OF MODERN ART

11 W. 53rd Street
New York, NY 10019
(212) 708-9480

NEW YORKER FILMS

16 W. 61st Street
New York, NY 10023
(212) 247-6110

KIT PARKER FILMS

1245 Tenth Street
Monterey, CA 93940
(408) 649-5573

SWANK MOTION PICTURES

350 Vanderbilt Motor Parkway
Hauppauge, NY 11787
(800) 876-3344

Giancarlo Giannini in *Seven Beauties*.

VIDEOCASSETTE INFORMATION

AXON VIDEO

1900 Broadway
New York, NY 10023
(212) 787-8228

CBS/FOX VIDEO

1211 Avenue of the Americas
New York, NY 10036
(212) 819-3200

CINEMATHEQUE COLLECTION

Media Home Entertainment
510 W. Sixth Street, Suite 1032
Los Angeles, CA 90014
(213) 236-1336

CONNOISSEUR VIDEO COLLECTION

8436 W. Third Street
Los Angeles, CA 90048
(213) 653-8873

FACETS VIDEO

1517 W. Fullerton Avenue
Chicago, IL 60614
(312) 281-9075

FESTIVAL FILMS

2841 Irving Avenue
Minneapolis, MN 55408
(612) 870-4744

FOX/LORBER HOME VIDEO

419 Park Avenue South
New York, NY 10016
(212) 686-6777

FOXVIDEO

2121 Avenue of the Stars, 26th Fl.
Los Angeles, CA 90067
(213) 203-3900

HBO VIDEO

1100 Avenue of the Americas
New York, NY 10036
(212) 512-1000

HEN'S TOOTH VIDEO

1124 S. Soland, Suite E
Las Cruces, NM 88001
(505) 525-8233

HOLLYWOOD HOME THEATRE

1540 N. Highland Avenue
Hollywood, CA 90028
(213) 466-0121

MGM/UA PATHE HOME VIDEO

10000 W. Washington Boulevard
Culver City, CA 90232
(213) 280-6000

MPI HOME VIDEO

15825 Rob Roy Drive
Oak Forest, IL 60452
(312) 687-7881

NELSON ENTERTAINMENT

335 N. Maple Drive
Beverly Hills, CA 90210
(213) 285-6000

NEW WORLD VIDEO

1440 S. Sepulveda Boulevard
Los Angeles, CA 90025
(213) 444-8100

NEW YORK FILM ANNEX

163 Joralemon Street
Brooklyn, NY 11201
(718) 499-1621

NEW YORKER FILMS

16 W. 61st Street
New York, NY 10023
(212) 247-6110

ORION HOME VIDEO

1888 Century Park East
Los Angeles, CA 90067
(310) 282-0550

PACIFIC ARTS VIDEO

50 N. La Cienega Boulevard
Beverly Hills, CA 90211
(213) 657-2233

PARAMOUNT HOME VIDEO

5555 Melrose Avenue
Los Angeles, CA 90038
(213) 956-5000

RCA/COLUMBIA HOME VIDEO

3500 W. Olive Avenue
Burbank, CA 91505
(818) 953-7900

VESTRON VIDEO

1010 Washington Boulevard
Stamford, CT 06901
(203) 978-5400

VIDEO YESTERYEAR

P.O. Box C
Sandy Hook, CT 06482
(203) 426-2574

WARNER HOME VIDEO

4000 Warner Boulevard
Burbank, CA 91522
(818) 954-6000

WATER BEARER FILMS HOME VIDEO

205 West End Avenue
New York, NY 10023
(212) 580-8185

WEST GLEN COMMUNICATION

1430 Broadway
New York, NY 10018
(212) 921-2800

WHITE STAR VIDEO

121 Highway 36
W. Long Branch, NJ 07764
(908) 229-2343

WORLDVISION HOME VIDEO, INC.

1700 Broadway
New York, NY 10019
(212) 261-2900

SELECTED BIBLIOGRAPHY

GENERAL WORKS

Liehm, Antonin J. *Closely Watched Films: The Czechoslovak Experience.* International Arts and Sciences Press, Inc., 1974.

Richie, Donald. *Japanese Cinema.* Doubleday, 1971.

Sandford, John. *The New German Cinema.* Eyre Methuen Ltd., 1980.

Schwartz, Ronald. *The Great Spanish Films: 1950–1990.* Scarecrow Press, 1991.

Whyte, Alistair. *New Cinema in Eastern Europe.* Dutton, 1971.

Witcombe, R. T. *The New Italian Cinema: Studies in Dance and Despair.* Oxford University Press, 1982.

Zorkaia, Neia Markovna. *The Illustrated History of the Soviet Cinema.* Hippocrene Books, 1989.

SCRIPTS

Marion Boyars publishes Ingmar Bergman's *A Film Trilogy: Through a Glass Darkly, The Communicants [Winter Light], and The Silence,* as well as *Persona* and *Shame.*

Grove publishes *Last Year at Marienbad, La Guerre Est Finie, Day for Night,* and *Au Revoir les Enfants.*

Lorrimer publishes *Closely Watched Trains* and *Lacombe, Lucien.*

Rutgers University Press publishes *Breathless, 8½,* and *The Marriage of Maria Braun.*

Shambhala publishes *Ran* with the director's illustrations.

BOOKS BY AND ABOUT DIRECTORS

Bergman, Ingmar. *Bergman on Bergman.* Interviews with Ingmar Bergman by Stig Bjorkman, Torsten Manns, and Jonas Sima. Simon and Schuster, 1973.

————. *The Magic Lantern: An Autobiography.* Viking, 1988.

Buñuel, Luis. *My Last Sigh* (autobiography). Knopf, 1983.

Kurosawa, Akira. *Something Like an Autobiography.* Knopf, 1982.

Richie, Donald. *Ozu.* University of California Press, 1974.

Tarkovsky, Andrei. *Sculpting in Time: Reflections on the Cinema.* University of Texas Press, 1989.

Truffaut, François. *Truffaut by Truffaut.* Texts and documents compiled by Dominique Rabourdin. Harry N. Abrams, 1987.

————. *Correspondence 1945–1984.* The Noonday Press, 1989.

Klaus Kinski in *Nosferatu the Vampyre.*

Alexander Kaidanovsky in *Stalker.*

Sophia Loren in *A Special Day.*

ORDER NOW!
More Citadel Film Books

If you like this book, you'll love the other titles in the award-winning Citadel Film Series. From James Stewart to Moe Howard and The Three Stooges, Woody Allen to John Wayne, The Citadel Film Series is America's largest and oldest film book library.

With more than 150 titles--and more on the way!--Citadel Film Books make perfect gifts for a loved one, a friend, or best of all, yourself!

A complete listing of the Citadel Film Series appears below.
If you know what books you want, why not order now!
It's easy! Just call 1-800-447-BOOK and have your MasterCard or Visa ready.

STARS

Alan Ladd
Arnold Schwarzenegger
Barbra Streisand: First Decade
Barbra Streisand: Second
  Decade
Bela Lugosi
Bette Davis
Boris Karloff
The Bowery Boys
Buster Keaton
Carole Lombard
Cary Grant
Charles Bronson
Charlie Chaplin
Clark Gable
Clint Eastwood
Curly
Dustin Hoffman
Edward G. Robinson
Elizabeth Taylor
Elvis Presley
Errol Flynn
Frank Sinatra
Gary Cooper
Gene Kelly
Gina Lollobrigida
Gloria Swanson
Gregory Peck
Greta Garbo
Henry Fonda
Humphrey Bogart
Ingrid Bergman
Jack Lemmon
Jack Nicholson
James Cagney
James Dean: Behind the Scene
Jane Fonda
Jeanette MacDonald & Nelson
  Eddy
Joan Crawford
John Wayne Films
John Wayne Reference Book

John Wayne Scrapbook
Judy Garland
Katharine Hepburn
Kirk Douglas
Laurel & Hardy
Lauren Bacall
Laurence Olivier
Mae West
Marilyn Monroe
Marlene Dietrich
Marlon Brando
Marx Brothers
Moe Howard & the Three
  Stooges
Norma Shearer
Olivia de Havilland
Orson Welles
Paul Newman
Peter Lorre
Rita Hayworth
Robert De Niro
Robert Redford
Sean Connery
Sexbomb: Jayne Mansfield
Shirley MacLaine
Shirley Temple
The Sinatra Scrapbook
Spencer Tracy
Steve McQueen
Three Stooges Scrapbook
Warren Beatty
W.C. Fields
William Holden
William Powell
A Wonderful Life: James Stewart
DIRECTORS
Alfred Hitchcock
Cecil B. DeMille
Federico Fellini
Frank Capra
John Ford
John Huston
Woody Allen

GENRE

Bad Guys
Black Hollywood
Black Hollywood: From 1970 to
  Today
Classic Foreign Films: From
  1960 to Today
Classic Gangster Films
Classic Science Fiction Films
Classics of the Horror Film
Cult Horror Films
Divine Images: Jesus on Screen
Early Classics of Foreign Film
Films of Merchant Ivory
Great French Films
Great German Films
Great Romantic Films
Great Science Fiction Films
Harry Warren & the Hollywood
  Musical
Hispanic Hollywood: The Latins
  in Motion Pictures
The Hollywood Western
The Incredible World of 007
The Jewish Image in American
  Film
The Lavender Screen: The Gay
  and Lesbian Films
Martial Arts Movies
The Modern Horror Film
More Classics of the Horror Film
Movie Psychos & Madmen
Our Huckleberry Friend: Johnny
  Mercer
Second Feature: "B" Films
Sex in Films
They Sang! They Danced! They
  Romanced!: Hollywood
  Musicals
Thrillers
The West That Never Was
Words and Shadows: Literature
  on the Screen

DECADE

Classics of the Silent Screen
Films of the Twenties
Films of the Thirties
More Films of the 30's
Films of the Forties
Films of the Fifties
Lost Films of the 50's
Films of the Sixties
Films of the Seventies
Films of the Eighties
SPECIAL INTEREST
America on the Rerun
Bugsy (Illustrated screenplay)
Comic Support
Dick Tracy
Favorite Families of TV
Film Flubs
Film Flubs: The Sequel
First Films
Forgotten Films to Remember
"Frankly, My Dear"
Hollywood Cheesecake
Hollywood's Hollywood
Howard Hughes in Hollywood
More Character People
The Nightmare Never Ends:
  Freddy Krueger & "A Night-
  mare on Elm Street"
The "Northern Exposure" Book
The Official Andy Griffith Show
  Scrapbook
The 100 Best Films of the
  Century
The "Quantum Leap" Book
Rodgers & Hammerstein
Sex In the Movies
Sherlock Holmes
Son of Film Flubs
Those Glorious Glamour Years
Who Is That?: Familiar Faces and
  Forgotten Names
"You Ain't Heard Nothin' Yet!"

For a free full-color brochure describing the Citadel Film Series in depth, call 1-800-447-BOOK; or send your name and address to Citadel Film Books, Dept. 1442, 120 Enterprise Ave., Secaucus, NJ 07094.